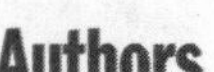

enVision® Mathematics

Common Core

Volume 2 Topics 8–16

Authors

Randall I. Charles
Professor Emeritus
Department of Mathematics
San Jose State University
San Jose, California

Jennifer Bay-Williams
Professor of Mathematics Education
College of Education and Human Development
University of Louisville
Louisville, Kentucky

Robert Q. Berry, III
Professor of Mathematics Education
Department of Curriculum, Instruction and Special Education
University of Virginia
Charlottesville, Virginia

Janet H. Caldwell
Professor Emerita
Department of Mathematics
Rowan University
Glassboro, New Jersey

Zachary Champagne
Assistant in Research
Florida Center for Research in Science, Technology, Engineering, and Mathematics (FCR-STEM)
Jacksonville, Florida

Juanita Copley
Professor Emerita
College of Education
University of Houston
Houston, Texas

Warren Crown
Professor Emeritus of Mathematics Education
Graduate School of Education
Rutgers University
New Brunswick, New Jersey

Francis (Skip) Fennell
Professor Emeritus of Education and Graduate and Professional Studies
McDaniel College
Westminster, Maryland

Karen Karp
Professor of Mathematics Education
School of Education
Johns Hopkins University
Baltimore, Maryland

Stuart J. Murphy
Visual Learning Specialist
Boston, Massachusetts

Jane F. Schielack
Professor Emerita
Department of Mathematics
Texas A&M University
College Station, Texas

Jennifer M. Suh
Associate Professor for Mathematics Education
George Mason University
Fairfax, Virginia

Jonathan A. Wray
Mathematics Supervisor
Howard County Public Schools
Ellicott City, Maryland

SAVVAS LEARNING COMPANY

Mathematicians

Roger Howe
Professor of Mathematics
Yale University
New Haven, Connecticut

Gary Lippman
Professor of Mathematics and Computer Science
California State University, East Bay
Hayward, California

ELL Consultants

Janice R. Corona
Independent Education Consultant
Dallas, Texas

Jim Cummins
Professor
The University of Toronto
Toronto, Canada

Reviewers

Katina Arnold
Teacher
Liberty Public School District
Kansas City, Missouri

Christy Bennett
Elementary Math and Science Specialist
DeSoto County Schools
Hernando, Mississippi

Shauna Bostick
Elementary Math Specialist
Lee County School District
Tupelo, Mississippi

Samantha Brant
Teacher
Platte County School District
Platte City, Missouri

Jamie Clark
Elementary Math Coach
Allegany County Public Schools
Cumberland, Maryland

Shauna Gardner
Math and Science Instructional Coach
DeSoto County Schools
Hernando, Mississippi

Kathy Graham
Educational Consultant
Twin Falls, Idaho

Andrea Hamilton
K-5 Math Specialist
Lake Forest School District
Felton, Delaware

Susan Hankins
Instructional Coach
Tupelo Public School District
Tupelo, Mississippi

Barb Jamison
Teacher
Excelsior Springs School District
Excelsior Springs, Missouri

Pam Jones
Elementary Math Coach
Lake Region School District
Bridgton, Maine

Sherri Kane
Secondary Mathematics Curriculum Specialist
Lee's Summit R7 School District
Lee's Summit, Missouri

Jessica Leonard
ESOL Teacher
Volusia County Schools
DeLand, Florida

Jill K. Milton
Elementary Math Coordinator
Norwood Public Schools
Norwood, Massachusetts

Jamie Pickett
Teacher
Platte County School District
Kansas City, Missouri

Mandy Schall
Math Coach
Allegany County Public Schools
Cumberland, Maryland

Marjorie Stevens
Math Consultant
Utica Community Schools
Shelby Township, Michigan

Shyree Stevenson
ELL Teacher
Penns Grove-Carneys Point Regional School District
Penns Grove, New Jersey

Kayla Stone
Teacher
Excelsior Springs School District
Excelsior Springs, Missouri

Sara Sultan
PD Academic Trainer, Math
Tucson Unified School District
Tucson, Arizona

Angela Waltrup
Elementary Math Content Specialist
Washington County Public Schools
Hagerstown, Maryland

Savvas Learning Company LLC, 15 East Midland Avenue, Paramus, NJ 07652

ISBN-13: 978-0-13-495477-6
ISBN-10: 0-13-495477-7
10 2022

Digital Resources

You'll be using these digital resources throughout the year!

Go to SavvasRealize.com

Interactive Student Edition

Access online or offline.

Visual Learning

Interact with visual learning animations.

Interactive Additional Practice Workbook

Access online or offline.

Activity

Solve a problem and share your thinking.

Videos

Watch Math Practices Animations, Another Look Videos, and clips to support 3-Act Math.

Practice Buddy

Do interactive practice online.

Math Tools

Explore math with digital tools.

Games

Play math games to help you learn.

Glossary

Read and listen in English and Spanish.

Assessment

Show what you've learned.

SAVVAS realize™ Everything you need for math anytime, anywhere

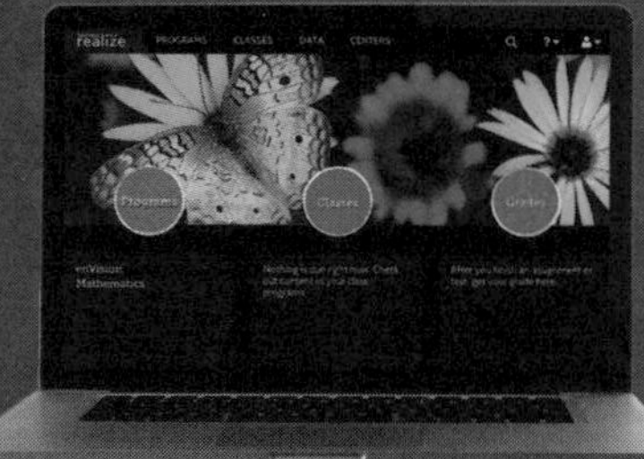

Hi, we're here to help you.
Let's have a great year!

Contents

Digital Resources at SavvasRealize.com

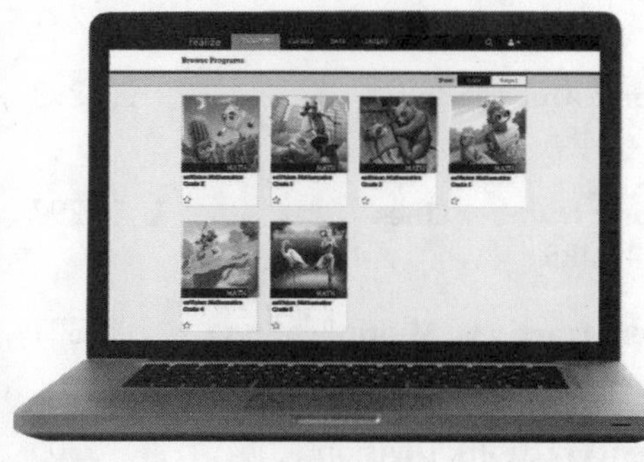

And remember your Interactive Student Edition is available at SavvasRealize.com!

TOPICS

This shows how fraction strips can be used to determine equivalent fractions.

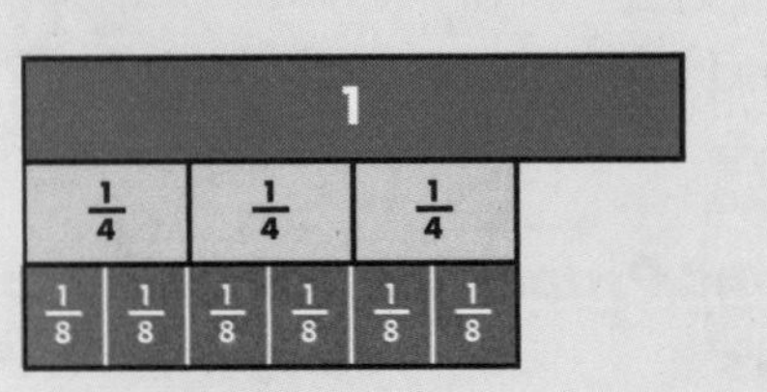
1
1/4
1/4
1/4
1/8
1/8
1/8
1/8
1/8
1/8

TOPIC 8 Extend Understanding of Fraction Equivalence and Ordering

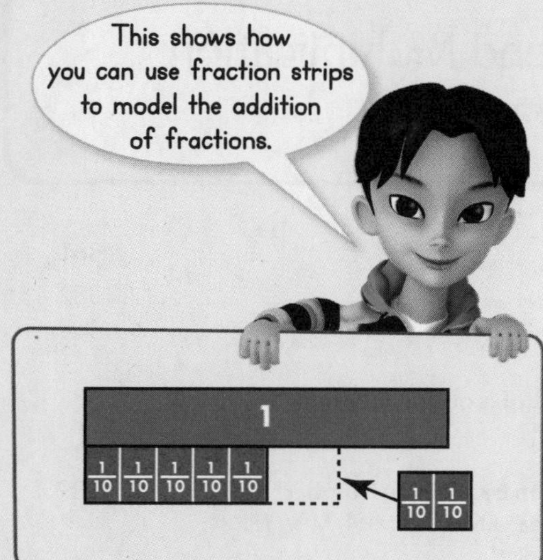

This shows how you can use fraction strips to model the addition of fractions.
1
1/10
1/10

TOPIC 9 Understand Addition and Subtraction of Fractions

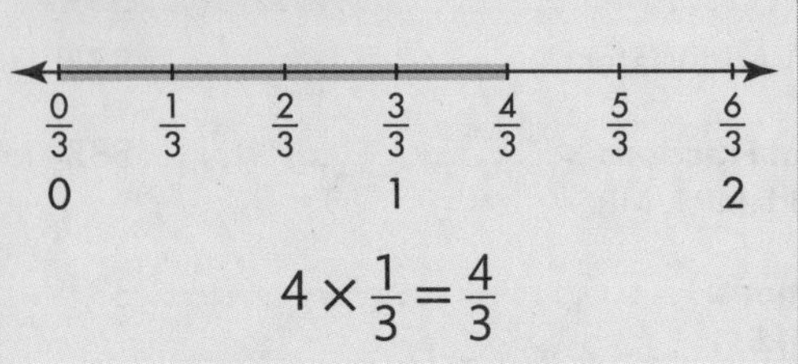

TOPIC 10 Extend Multiplication Concepts to Fractions

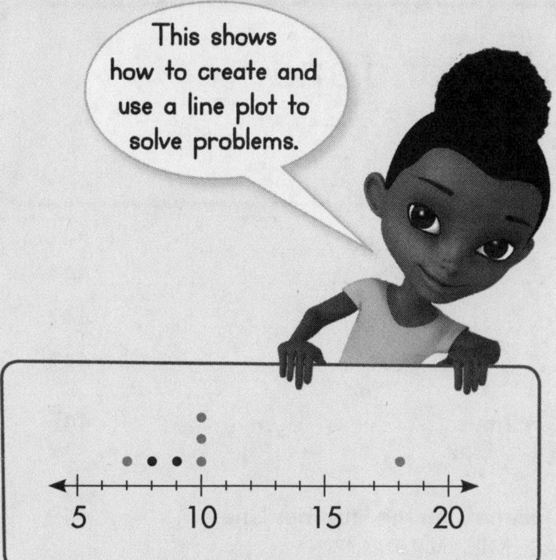

This shows how to create and use a line plot to solve problems.
5
10
15
20

TOPIC 11 Represent and Interpret Data on Line Plots

This shows how
to represent 1.64 or
$1\frac{64}{100}$ using grids.

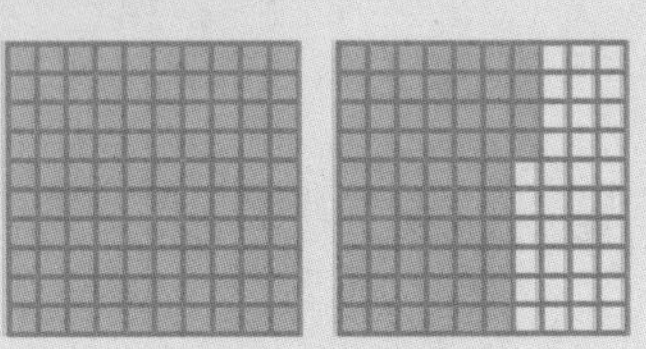

$1.64 = 1\frac{64}{100}$

TOPIC 12 Understand and Compare Decimals

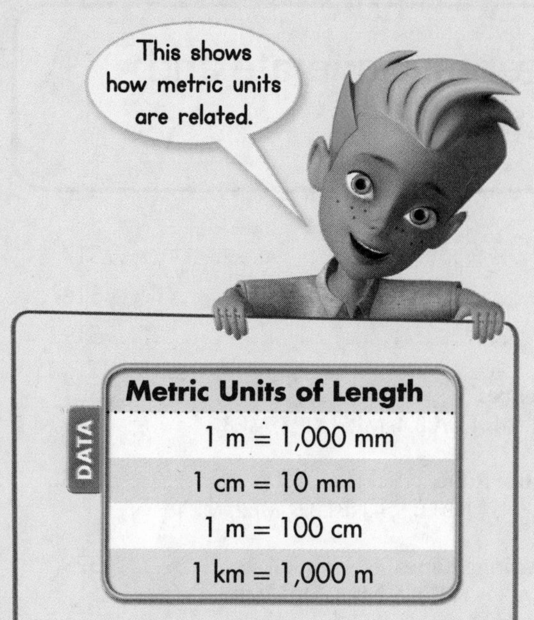
This shows how metric units are related.
DATA

Metric Units of Length
1 m = 1,000 mm
1 cm = 10 mm
1 m = 100 cm
1 km = 1,000 m

TOPIC 13 Measurement: Find Equivalence in Units of Measure

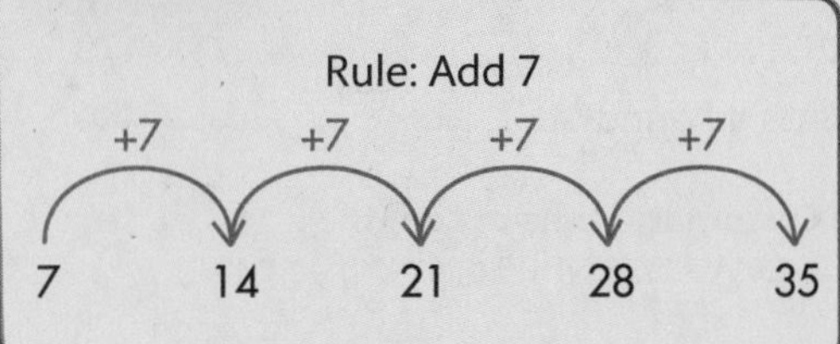

TOPIC 14 Algebra: Generate and Analyze Patterns

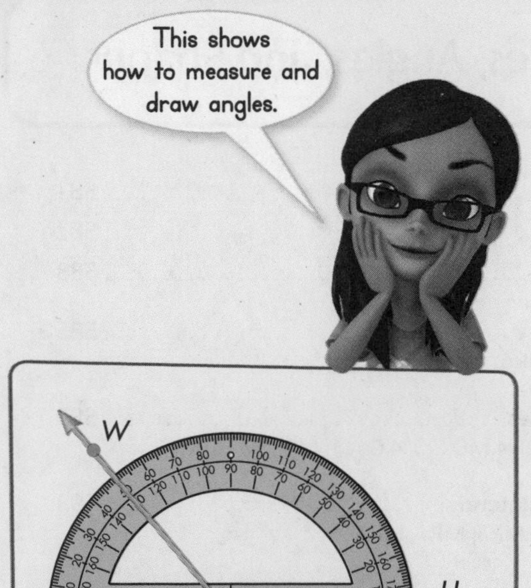

This shows how to measure and draw angles.
W
T
U

TOPIC 15 Geometric Measurement: Understand Concepts of Angles and Angle Measurement

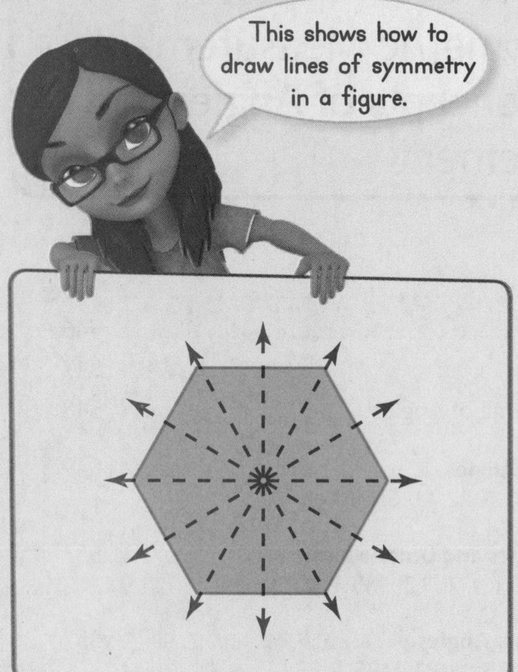

This shows how to draw lines of symmetry in a figure.

TOPIC 16 Lines, Angles, and Shapes

Grade 4 Common Core Standards

DOMAIN **4.OA**
OPERATIONS AND ALGEBRAIC THINKING

MAJOR CLUSTER **4.OA.A**
Use the four operations with whole numbers to solve problems.

4.OA.A.1 Interpret a multiplication equation as a comparison, e.g., interpret $35 = 5 \times 7$ as a statement that 35 is 5 times as many as 7 and 7 times as many as 5. Represent verbal statements of multiplicative comparisons as multiplication equations.

4.OA.A.2 Multiply or divide to solve word problems involving multiplicative comparison, e.g., by using drawings and equations with a symbol for the unknown number to represent the problem, distinguishing multiplicative comparison from additive comparison.

4.OA.A.3 Solve multistep word problems posed with whole numbers and having whole-number answers using the four operations, including problems in which remainders must be interpreted. Represent these problems using equations with a letter standing for the unknown quantity. Assess the reasonableness of answers using mental computation and estimation strategies including rounding.

SUPPORTING CLUSTER **4.OA.B**
Gain familiarity with factors and multiples.

4.OA.B.4 Find all factor pairs for a whole number in the range 1–100. Recognize that a whole number is a multiple of each of its factors. Determine whether a given whole number in the range 1–100 is a multiple of a given one-digit number. Determine whether a given whole number in the range 1–100 is prime or composite.

ADDITIONAL CLUSTER **4.OA.C**
Generate and analyze patterns.

4.OA.C.5 Generate a number or shape pattern that follows a given rule. Identify apparent features of the pattern that were not explicit in the rule itself.

Dear Families,

The standards on the following pages describe the math that students will learn this year. The greatest amount of time will be spent on standards in the major clusters.

Common Core Standards

DOMAIN **4.NBT**
NUMBER AND OPERATIONS IN BASE TEN

MAJOR CLUSTER **4.NBT.A**
Generalize place value understanding for multi-digit whole numbers.

4.NBT.A.1 Recognize that in a multi-digit whole number, a digit in one place represents ten times what it represents in the place to its right. *For example, recognize that $700 \div 70 = 10$ by applying concepts of place value and division.*

4.NBT.A.2 Read and write multi-digit whole numbers using base-ten numerals, number names, and expanded form. Compare two multi-digit numbers based on meanings of the digits in each place, using >, =, and < symbols to record the results of comparisons.

4.NBT.A.3 Use place value understanding to round multi-digit whole numbers to any place.

MAJOR CLUSTER **4.NBT.B**
Use place value understanding and properties of operations to perform multi-digit arithmetic.

4.NBT.B.4 Fluently add and subtract multi-digit whole numbers using the standard algorithm.

4.NBT.B.5 Multiply a whole number of up to four digits by a one-digit whole number, and multiply two two-digit numbers, using strategies based on place value and the properties of operations. Illustrate and explain the calculation by using equations, rectangular arrays, and/or area models.

4.NBT.B.6 Find whole-number quotients and remainders with up to four-digit dividends and one-digit divisors, using strategies based on place value, the properties of operations, and/or the relationship between multiplication and division. Illustrate and explain the calculation by using equations, rectangular arrays, and/or area models.

DOMAIN **4.NF**
NUMBER AND OPERATIONS–FRACTIONS

MAJOR CLUSTER **4.NF.A**
Extend understanding of fraction equivalence and ordering.

4.NF.A.1 Explain why a fraction $\frac{a}{b}$ is equivalent to a fraction $\frac{(n \times a)}{(n \times b)}$ by using visual fraction models, with attention to how the number and size of the parts differ even though the two fractions themselves are the same size. Use this principle to recognize and generate equivalent fractions.

4.NF.A.2 Compare two fractions with different numerators and different denominators, e.g., by creating common denominators or numerators, or by comparing to a benchmark fraction such as $\frac{1}{2}$. Recognize that comparisons are valid only when the two fractions refer to the same whole. Record the results of comparisons with symbols >, =, or <, and justify the conclusions, e.g., by using a visual fraction model.

MAJOR CLUSTER **4.NF.B**
Build fractions from unit fractions.

4.NF.B.3 Understand a fraction $\frac{a}{b}$ with $a > 1$ as a sum of fractions $\frac{1}{b}$.

4.NF.B.3a Understand addition and subtraction of fractions as joining and separating parts referring to the same whole.

4.NF.B.3b Decompose a fraction into a sum of fractions with the same denominator in more than one way, recording each decomposition by an equation. Justify decompositions, e.g., by using a visual fraction model. *Examples:* $\frac{3}{8} = \frac{1}{8} + \frac{1}{8} + \frac{1}{8}$; $\frac{3}{8} = \frac{1}{8} + \frac{2}{8}$; $2\frac{1}{8} = 1 + 1 + \frac{1}{8} = \frac{8}{8} + \frac{8}{8} + \frac{1}{8}$.

4.NF.B.3c Add and subtract mixed numbers with like denominators, e.g., by replacing each mixed number with an equivalent fraction, and/or by using properties of operations and the relationship between addition and subtraction.

4.NF.B.3d Solve word problems involving addition and subtraction of fractions referring to the same whole and having like denominators, e.g., by using visual fraction models and equations to represent the problem.

4.NF.B.4 Apply and extend previous understandings of multiplication to multiply a fraction by a whole number.

4.NF.B.4a Understand a fraction $\frac{a}{b}$ as a multiple of $\frac{1}{b}$. *For example, use a visual fraction model to represent $\frac{5}{4}$ as the product $5 \times (\frac{1}{4})$, recording the conclusion by the equation $\frac{5}{4} = 5 \times (\frac{1}{4})$.*

4.NF.B.4b Understand a multiple of $\frac{a}{b}$ as a multiple of $\frac{1}{b}$, and use this understanding to multiply a fraction by a whole number. *For example, use a visual fraction model to express $3 \times (\frac{2}{5})$ as $6 \times (\frac{1}{5})$, recognizing this product as $\frac{6}{5}$. (In general, $n \times (\frac{a}{b}) = \frac{(n \times a)}{b}$.)*

Common Core Standards

4.NF.B.4c Solve word problems involving multiplication of a fraction by a whole number, e.g., by using visual fraction models and equations to represent the problem. *For example, if each person at a party will eat* $\frac{3}{8}$ *of a pound of roast beef, and there will be 5 people at the party, how many pounds of roast beef will be needed? Between what two whole numbers does your answer lie?*

MAJOR CLUSTER **4.NF.C**
Understand decimal notation for fractions, and compare decimal fractions.

4.NF.C.5 Express a fraction with denominator 10 as an equivalent fraction with denominator 100, and use this technique to add two fractions with respective denominators 10 and 100. *For example, express* $\frac{3}{10}$ *as* $\frac{30}{100}$, *and add* $\frac{3}{10} + \frac{4}{100} = \frac{34}{100}$.

4.NF.C.6 Use decimal notation for fractions with denominators 10 or 100. *For example, rewrite 0.62 as* $\frac{62}{100}$; *describe a length as 0.62 meters; locate 0.62 on a number line diagram.*

4.NF.C.7 Compare two decimals to hundredths by reasoning about their size. Recognize that comparisons are valid only when the two decimals refer to the same whole. Record the results of comparisons with the symbols >, =, or <, and justify the conclusions, e.g., by using a visual model.

DOMAIN **4.MD**
MEASUREMENT AND DATA

SUPPORTING CLUSTER **4.MD.A**
Solve problems involving measurement and conversion of measurements

4.MD.A.1 Know relative sizes of measurement units within one system of units including km, m, cm; kg, g; lb, oz.; l, ml; hr, min, sec. Within a single system of measurement, express measurements in a larger unit in terms of a smaller unit. Record measurement equivalents in a two-column table. *For example, know that 1 ft is 12 times as long as 1 in. Express the length of a 4 ft snake as 48 in. Generate a conversion table for feet and inches listing the number pairs (1, 12), (2, 24), (3, 36), ...*

4.MD.A.2 Use the four operations to solve word problems involving distances, intervals of time, liquid volumes, masses of objects, and money, including problems involving simple fractions or decimals, and problems that require expressing measurements given in a larger unit in terms of a smaller unit. Represent measurement quantities using diagrams such as number line diagrams that feature a measurement scale.

4.MD.A.3 Apply the area and perimeter formulas for rectangles in real world and mathematical problems. *For example, find the width of a rectangular room given the area of the flooring and the length, by viewing the area formula as a multiplication equation with an unknown factor.*

SUPPORTING CLUSTER **4.MD.B**
Represent and interpret data.

4.MD.B.4 Make a line plot to display a data set of measurements in fractions of a unit ($\frac{1}{2}, \frac{1}{4}, \frac{1}{8}$). Solve problems involving addition and subtraction of fractions by using information presented in line plots. *For example, from a line plot find and interpret the difference in length between the longest and shortest specimens in an insect collection.*

ADDITIONAL CLUSTER **4.MD.C**
Geometric measurement: understand concepts of angle and measure angles.

4.MD.C.5 Recognize angles as geometric shapes that are formed wherever two rays share a common endpoint, and understand concepts of angle measurement:

4.MD.C.5a An angle is measured with reference to a circle with its center at the common endpoint of the rays, by considering the fraction of the circular arc between the points where the two rays intersect the circle. An angle that turns through $\frac{1}{360}$ of a circle is called a "one-degree angle," and can be used to measure angles.

4.MD.C.5b An angle that turns through *n* one-degree angles is said to have an angle measure of *n* degrees.

4.MD.C.6 Measure angles in whole-number degrees using a protractor. Sketch angles of specified measure.

4.MD.C.7 Recognize angle measure as additive. When an angle is decomposed into non-overlapping parts, the angle measure of the whole is the sum of the angle measures of the parts. Solve addition and subtraction problems to find unknown angles on a diagram in real world and mathematical problems, e.g., by using an equation with a symbol for the unknown angle measure.

Common Core Standards

DOMAIN **4.G.A**
GEOMETRY

ADDITIONAL CLUSTER **4.G.A**
Draw and identify lines and angles, and classify shapes by properties of their lines and angles.

4.G.A.1 Draw points, lines, line segments, rays, angles (right, acute, obtuse), and perpendicular and parallel lines. Identify these in two-dimensional figures.

4.G.A.2 Classify two-dimensional figures based on the presence or absence of parallel or perpendicular lines, or the presence or absence of angles of a specified size. Recognize right triangles as a category, and identify right triangles.

4.G.A.3 Recognize a line of symmetry for a two-dimensional figure as a line across the figure such that the figure can be folded along the line into matching parts. Identify line-symmetric figures and draw lines of symmetry.

MATHEMATICAL PRACTICES

MP.1 Make sense of problems and persevere in solving them.

MP.2 Reason abstractly and quantitatively.

MP.3 Construct viable arguments and critique the reasoning of others.

MP.4 Model with mathematics.

MP.5 Use appropriate tools strategically.

MP.6 Attend to precision.

MP.7 Look for and make use of structure.

MP.8 Look for and express regularity in repeated reasoning.

Math Practices and Problem Solving Handbook

The **Math Practices and Problem Solving Handbook** is available at SavvasRealize.com.

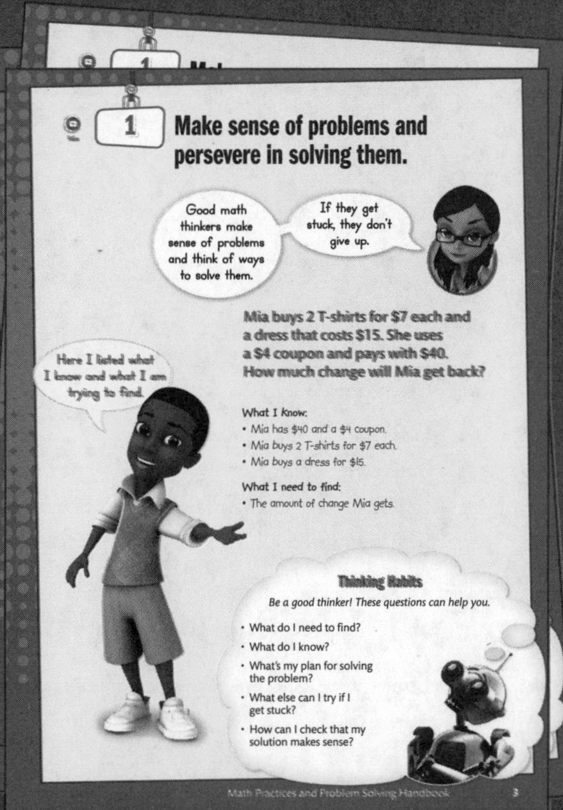

1
Make sense of problems and persevere in solving them.
Good math thinkers make sense of problems and think of ways to solve them.
If they get stuck, they don't give up.
Mia buys 2 T-shirts for $7 each and a dress that costs $15. She uses a $4 coupon and pays with $40. How much change will Mia get back?
Here I listed what I know and what I am trying to find.
What I know:
• Mia has $40 and a $4 coupon.
• Mia buys 2 T-shirts for $7 each.
• Mia buys a dress for $15.
What I need to find:
• The amount of change Mia gets.
Thinking Habits
Be a good thinker! These questions can help you.
• What do I need to find?
• What do I know?
• What's my plan for solving the problem?
• What else can I try if I get stuck?
• How can I check that my solution makes sense?
Math Practices and Problem Solving Handbook 3

Math Practices

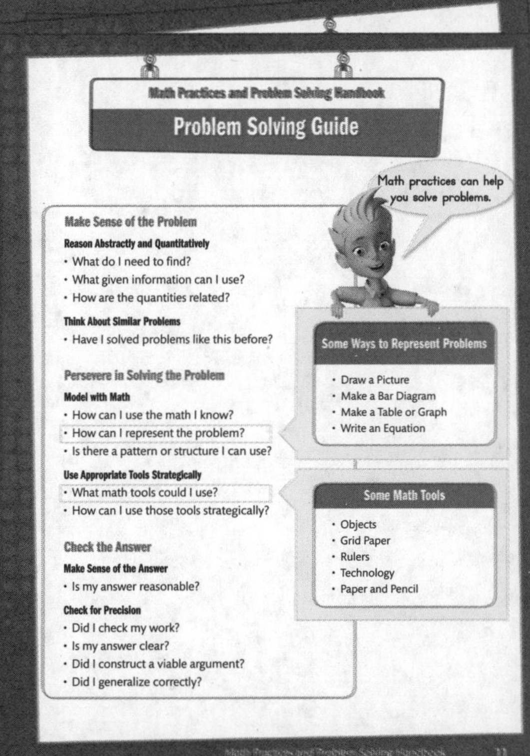

Math Practices and Problem Solving Handbook
Problem Solving Guide
Math practices can help you solve problems.
Make Sense of the Problem
Reason Abstractly and Quantitatively
• What do I need to find?
• What given information can I use?
• How are the quantities related?
Think About Similar Problems
• Have I solved problems like this before?
Persevere in Solving the Problem
Model with Math
• How can I use the math I know?
• How can I represent the problem?
• Is there a pattern or structure I can use?
Use Appropriate Tools Strategically
• What math tools could I use?
• How can I use those tools strategically?
Check the Answer
Make Sense of the Answer
• Is my answer reasonable?
Check for Precision
• Did I check my work?
• Is my answer clear?
• Did I construct a viable argument?
• Did I generalize correctly?
Some Ways to Represent Problems
• Draw a Picture
• Make a Bar Diagram
• Make a Table or Graph
• Write an Equation
Some Math Tools
• Objects
• Grid Paper
• Rulers
• Technology
• Paper and Pencil

Problem Solving Guide
Problem Solving Recording Sheet
Bar Diagrams

TOPIC 8

Extend Understanding of Fraction Equivalence and Ordering

Essential Questions: What are some ways to name the same part of a whole? How can you compare fractions with unlike numerators and denominators?

Digital Resources

Interactive Student Edition | Activity | Visual Learning | Video | Practice | Assessment | Games | Tools | Glossary

Some animals use their senses differently from humans. The entire body of a catfish is covered with taste-sensitive cells.

They use their sense of taste to locate food that is far away in the water.

Lots of animals have special ways of receiving information. Here is a project about senses.

enVision STEM Project: Senses

Do Research Use the Internet or other resources to find information about how animals use special senses, such as echolocation, electricity, or magnetism. Include information about where the animal lives and how the special sense is used.

Journal: Write a Report Include what you found. Also in your report:

- Some spiders rely on sight to receive information about food. Most spiders have 8 eyes. Draw a picture of a spider with many eyes, using some shaded circles as eyes and some empty circles as eyes.
- Write a fraction that names shaded spider eyes to total spider eyes. Write three equivalent fractions.

Name ______________________________

Review What You Know

Vocabulary

Choose the best term from the box. Write it on the blank.

- denominator
- numerator
- fraction
- unit fraction

1. A symbol, such as $\frac{2}{3}$ or $\frac{1}{2}$, used to name part of a whole, part of a set, or a location on a number line is called a ________.

2. The number above the fraction bar in a fraction is called the ________.

3. A fraction with a numerator of 1 is called a ________.

Unit Fractions

Write a fraction for each statement.

4. 2 copies of $\frac{1}{6}$ is ____.
5. 3 copies of $\frac{1}{3}$ is ____.
6. 4 copies of $\frac{1}{5}$ is ____.
7. 2 copies of $\frac{1}{10}$ is ____.
8. 7 copies of $\frac{1}{12}$ is ____.
9. 3 copies of $\frac{1}{8}$ is ____.

Fraction Concepts

Write the fraction shown by each figure.

10. 

11. 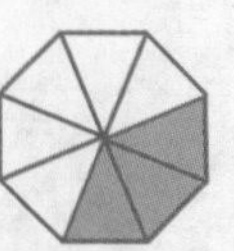

12. 

13. 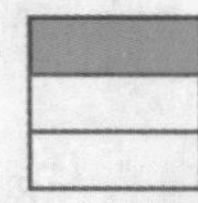

14. 

15. 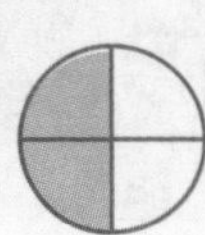

Parts of Wholes

16. **Construct Arguments** Is $\frac{1}{4}$ of the figure below green? Explain.

17. This picture shows a square. Shade in $\frac{3}{4}$ of the square.

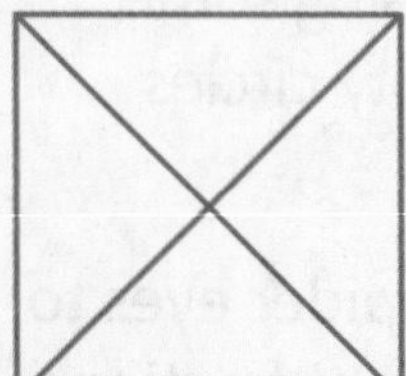

Name ___________________________

Pick a Project

PROJECT 8A

How much do you know about the Indianapolis Motor Speedway?

Project: Create a Fraction Game

PROJECT 8B

Who does all the stage work for a play or musical?

Project: Build a Model

PROJECT 8C

What is your favorite pie?

Project: Write and Perform a Skit

PROJECT 8D

How do you make clothes that could fit anyone?

Project: Create a Game

Name ________________________________

Lesson 8-1
Equivalent Fractions: Area Models

I can ...
recognize and generate equivalent fractions.

Content Standard 4.NF.A.1
Mathematical Practices MP.1, MP.2, MP.5

Solve & Share

Lena has yellow tile on $\frac{1}{4}$ of her kitchen floor. Write another fraction equivalent to $\frac{1}{4}$. ***Solve this problem any way you choose.***

Choose appropriate tools strategically. You can use area models or fraction strips to solve this problem.

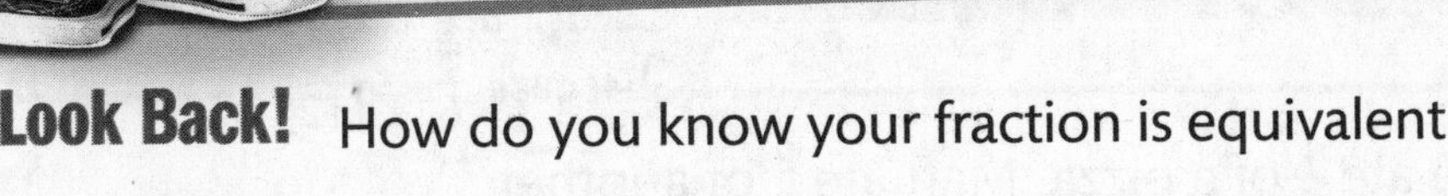

Look Back! How do you know your fraction is equivalent to $\frac{1}{4}$?

What Are Some Ways to Name the Same Part of a Whole?

Visual Learning Bridge

A

James ate part of the pizza shown in the picture at the right. He said $\frac{5}{6}$ of the pizza is left. Cardell said $\frac{10}{12}$ of the pizza is left. Who is correct?

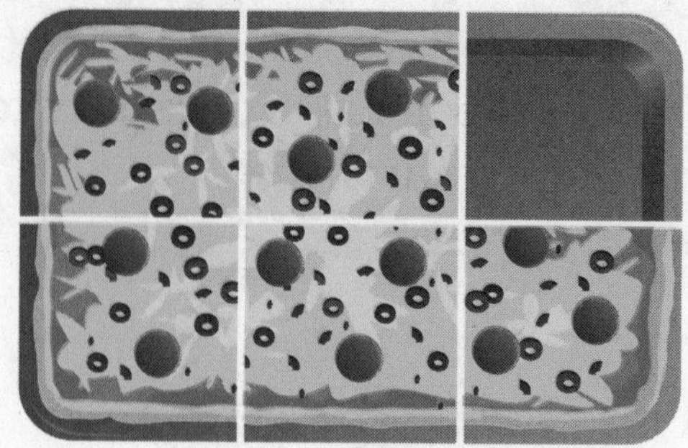

Equivalent fractions name the same part of the same whole.

fraction $\left\{\begin{matrix} 5 \\ 6 \end{matrix}\right.$ ← numerator ← denominator

B

One Way

Use an area model. Draw a rectangle and divide it into sixths. Shade $\frac{5}{6}$. Then divide the rectangle into twelfths.

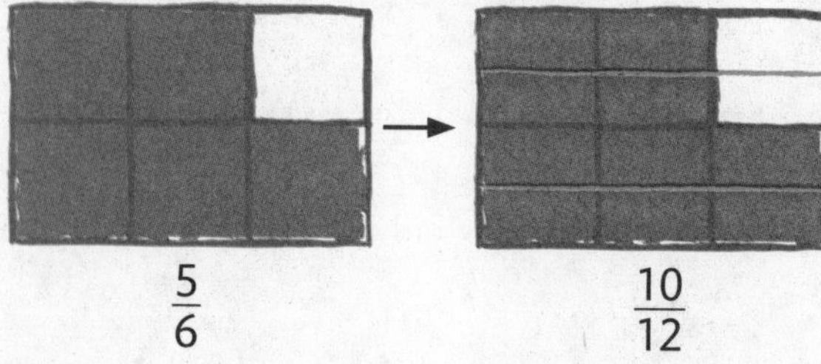

$\frac{5}{6}$ $\frac{10}{12}$

The number and size of parts differ, but the shaded part of each rectangle is the same. $\frac{5}{6}$ and $\frac{10}{12}$ are equivalent fractions.

C

Another Way

Use a different area model. Draw a circle and divide it into sixths. Shade $\frac{5}{6}$. Then divide the circle into twelfths.

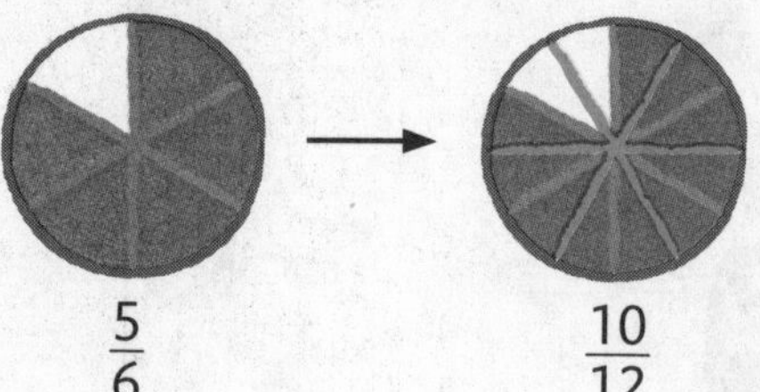

$\frac{5}{6}$ $\frac{10}{12}$

The number and size of parts differ, but the shaded part of each circle is the same. $\frac{5}{6}$ and $\frac{10}{12}$ are equivalent fractions.

Both James and Cardell are correct because $\frac{5}{6} = \frac{10}{12}$.

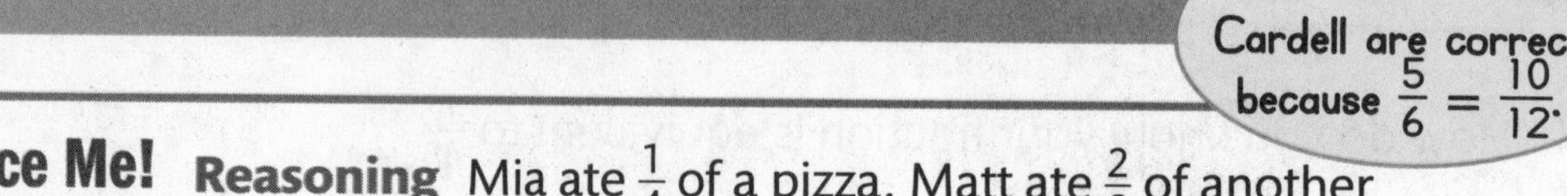

Convince Me! **Reasoning** Mia ate $\frac{1}{4}$ of a pizza. Matt ate $\frac{2}{8}$ of another pizza. Did Mia and Matt eat the same amount of pizza? Explain.

Name ____________________

Guided Practice

Do You Understand?

1. Use the area model to explain why $\frac{3}{4}$ and $\frac{9}{12}$ are equivalent.

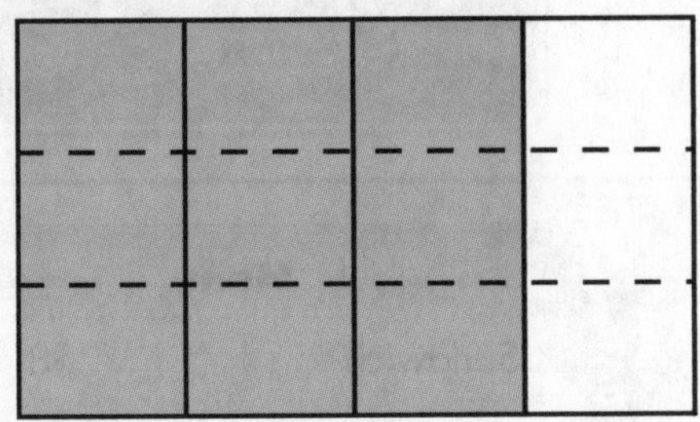

Do You Know How?

For **2–3**, use the area model to solve each problem.

2. Find the missing numerator.

$\frac{2}{4} = \frac{\square}{8}$

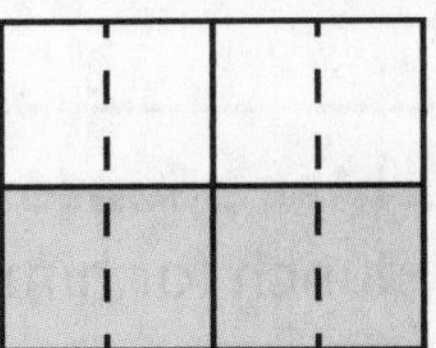

3. Find the missing numerator.

$\frac{1}{3} = \frac{\square}{6}$

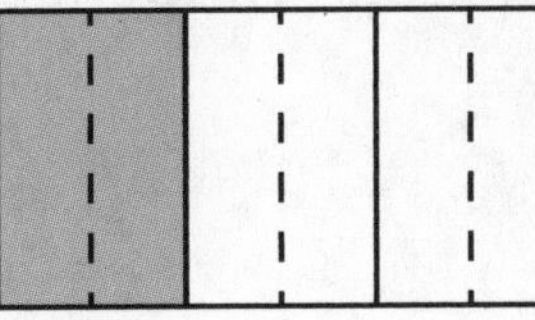

Independent Practice

4. Write a fraction equivalent to $\frac{1}{5}$.

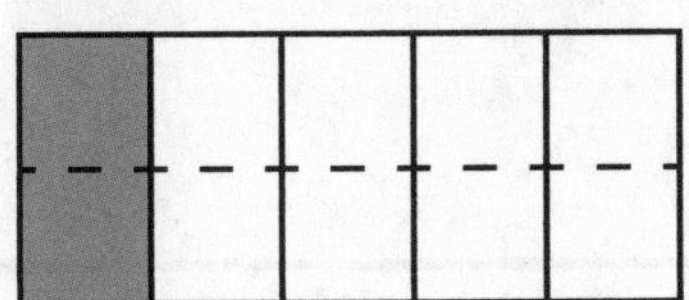

5. Write two fractions equivalent to $\frac{4}{12}$.

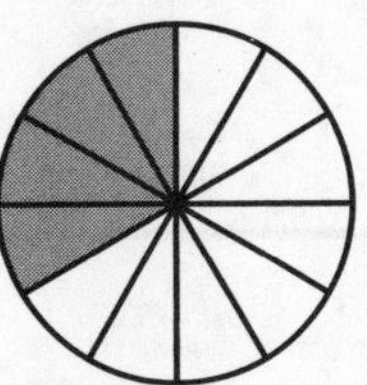

6. Write a fraction equivalent to $\frac{2}{6}$.

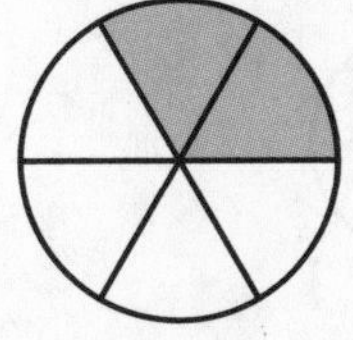

7. Write two fractions equivalent to $\frac{2}{3}$.

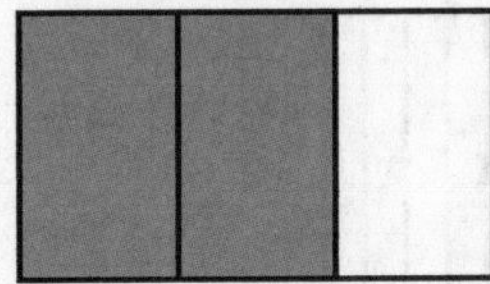

For **8–15**, draw an area model or use fraction strips to solve each problem.

8. $\frac{2}{8} = \frac{\square}{4}$

9. $\frac{2}{4} = \frac{\square}{8}$

10. $\frac{1}{2} = \frac{\square}{6}$

11. $\frac{3}{3} = \frac{6}{\square}$

12. $\frac{1}{5} = \frac{\square}{10}$

13. $\frac{5}{6} = \frac{10}{\square}$

14. $\frac{8}{12} = \frac{2}{\square}$

15. $\frac{4}{5} = \frac{8}{\square}$

Problem Solving

16. enVision® STEM Monarch butterflies migrate when they sense daylight hours are shorter and temperatures get colder. Write two equivalent fractions for the part of the migration a monarch butterfly can complete in 1 week.

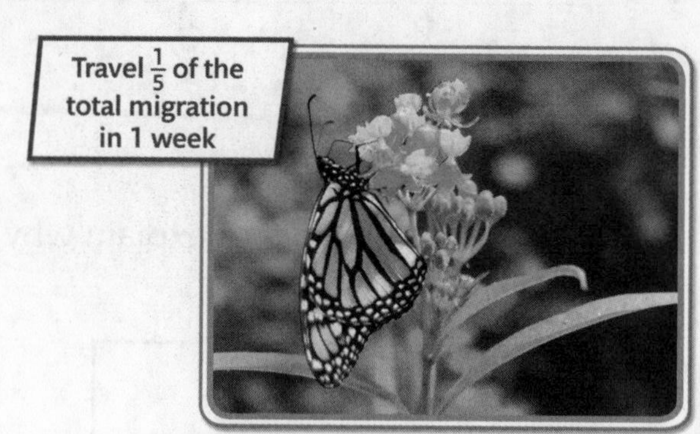

Travel $\frac{1}{5}$ of the total migration in 1 week

17. Make Sense and Persevere Garrett buys lunch for himself and his friend. He buys 2 sandwiches, 2 fries, and 2 malts. How much did Garrett spend on lunch?

DATA

Menu	
Sandwich	$8
Hot Dog	$2
Fries	$3
Soda	$2
Shake/Malt	$4

18. Connor said, "To the nearest hundred, I've attended school for 800 days of my life!" Write three numbers that could be the actual number of days Connor has attended school.

19. Higher Order Thinking Josh, Lisa, and Vicki each ate $\frac{1}{4}$ of their own pizza. Each pizza was the same size, but Josh ate 1 slice, Lisa ate 2 slices, and Vicki ate 3 slices. How is this possible?

Assessment Practice

20. Select all the fractions that are equivalent to $\frac{2}{3}$. Use the area models to help.

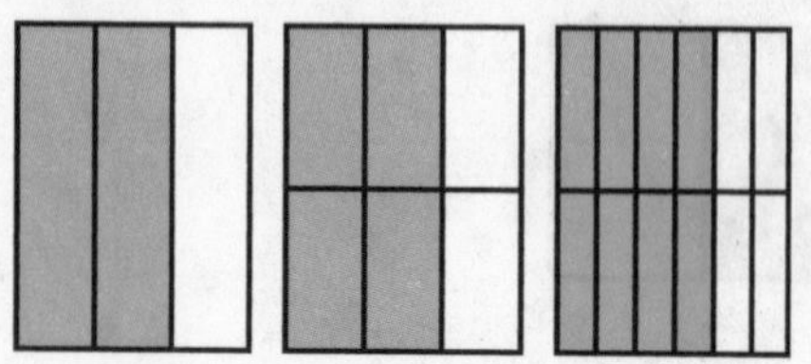

- ☐ $\frac{3}{6}$
- ☐ $\frac{8}{12}$
- ☐ $\frac{4}{8}$
- ☐ $\frac{4}{6}$
- ☐ $\frac{1}{2}$

21. Select all the pairs that are equivalent fractions. Use the area models to help.

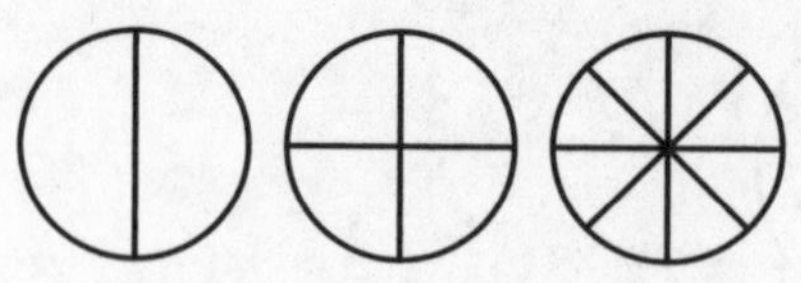

- ☐ $\frac{1}{4}, \frac{2}{8}$
- ☐ $\frac{3}{4}, \frac{6}{8}$
- ☐ $\frac{7}{8}, \frac{3}{4}$
- ☐ $\frac{8}{8}, \frac{4}{4}$
- ☐ $\frac{1}{2}, \frac{2}{2}$

Name ____________________

Activity

Lesson 8-2
Equivalent Fractions: Number Lines

I can ...

name the same point on a number line using equivalent fractions.

Content Standard 4.NF.A.1
Mathematical Practices MP.1, MP.4, MP.5

Solve & Share

Suppose you have a ruler showing fourths. Use your ruler to name a fraction that is equivalent to $\frac{2}{4}$. Tell how you know the fraction is equivalent.

You can use rulers or number lines to help solve problems.

$\frac{2}{4}$

0 1 2

INCHES

Look Back! **Model with Math** Do you think there is more than one fraction equivalent to $\frac{2}{4}$? Draw a picture to explain.

How Can You Use a Number Line to Explain Why Fractions Are Equivalent?

Visual Learning Bridge

A

Sal rode his bike $\frac{3}{4}$ mile to school. Name two fractions that are equivalent to $\frac{3}{4}$.

A number line is another appropriate tool for finding equivalent fractions.

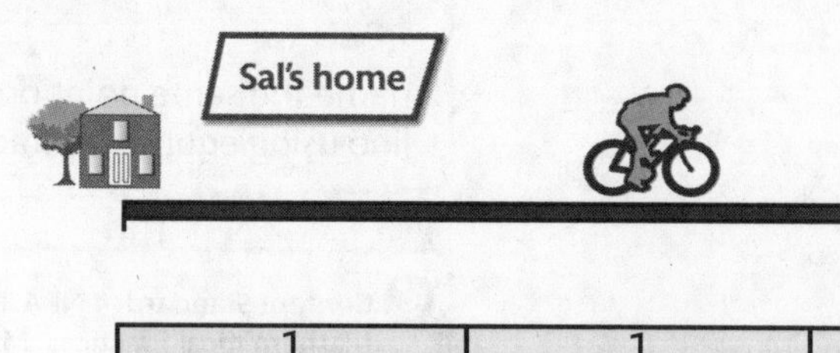

$\frac{3}{4}$ mile

$\frac{1}{4}$	$\frac{1}{4}$	$\frac{1}{4}$	$\frac{1}{4}$

0, $\frac{1}{4}$, $\frac{2}{4}$, $\frac{3}{4}$, 1

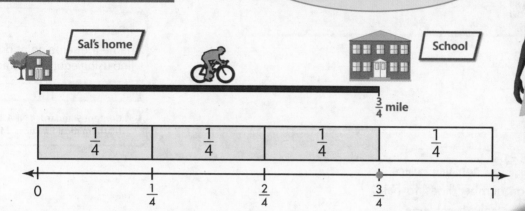

B

Show $\frac{3}{4}$ on the number line.

Divide each fourth into two equal parts to show eighths.

Divide each fourth into three equal parts to show twelfths.

$\frac{3}{4}$, $\frac{6}{8}$, and $\frac{9}{12}$ are at the same point on the number lines that are all the same length. $\frac{6}{8}$ and $\frac{9}{12}$ are equivalent to $\frac{3}{4}$.

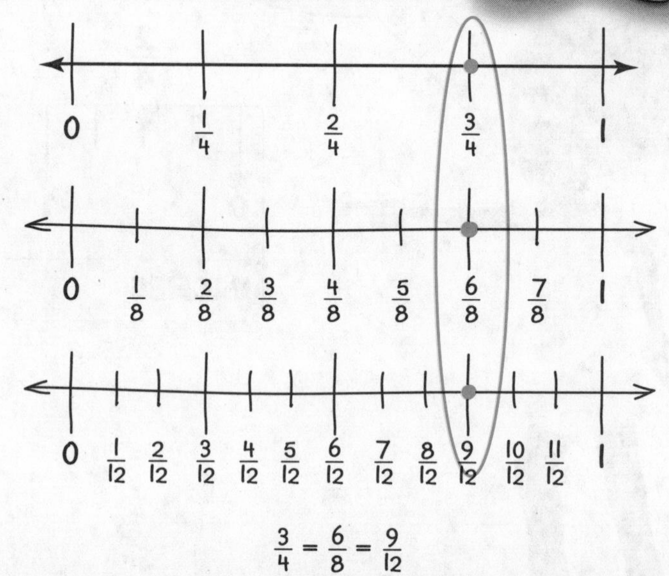

$\frac{3}{4} = \frac{6}{8} = \frac{9}{12}$

Convince Me! The number and size of each part on two number lines are different. Can the number lines show equivalent fractions? Use the number lines above to explain.

Name ____

Practice Tools Assessment

Another Example!

You can use a number line to find equivalent fractions that are greater than or equal to 1.

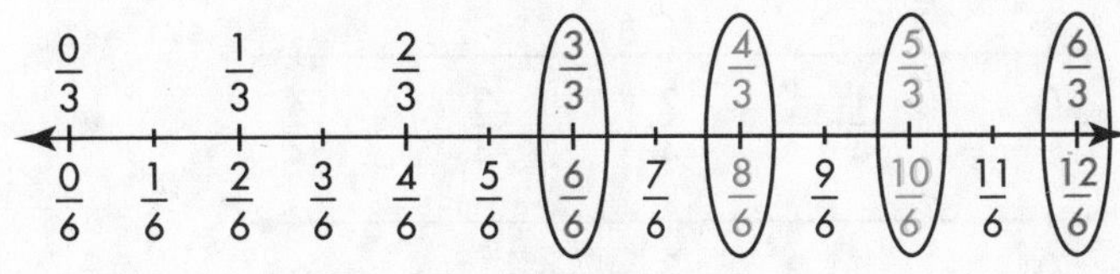

Guided Practice

Do You Understand?

1. Use the number line above to write a fraction equivalent to $\frac{9}{6}$. Why are the fractions equivalent? Explain.

Do You Know How?

For **2–3**, use the number line below.

2. Write an equivalent fraction for $\frac{1}{3}$.

3. Write an equivalent fraction for $\frac{1}{2}$.

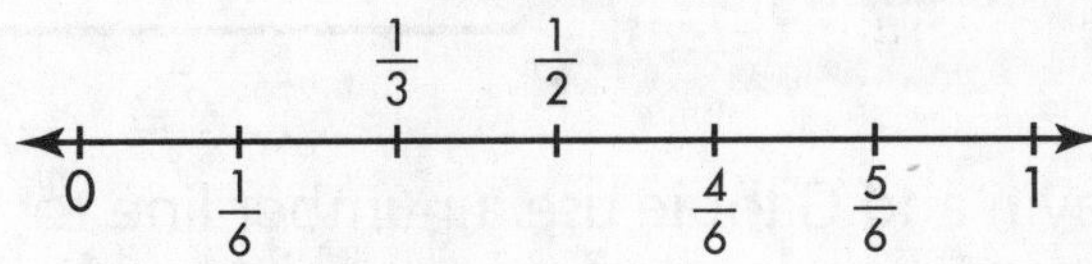

Independent Practice

For **4–7**, use the number line to find equivalent fractions. Circle the correct answers.

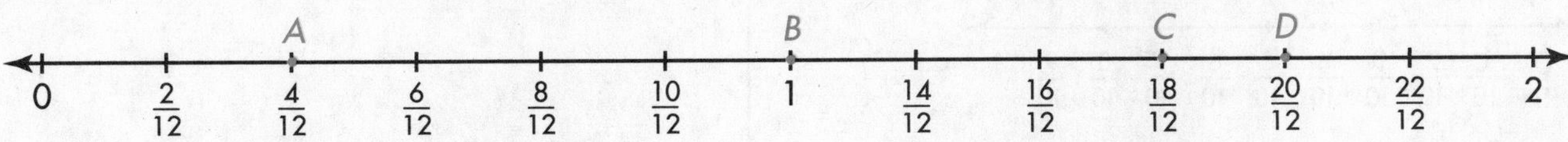

4. Which of the following fractions is an equivalent fraction for point *A*?

$\frac{1}{4}$ $\frac{1}{3}$ $\frac{2}{3}$ $\frac{1}{6}$ $\frac{2}{6}$

5. Which of the following fractions is an equivalent fraction for point *B*?

$\frac{11}{12}$ $\frac{12}{12}$ $\frac{13}{12}$ $\frac{7}{6}$ $\frac{6}{6}$

6. Which of the following fractions is an equivalent fraction for point *C*?

$\frac{8}{6}$ $\frac{2}{3}$ $\frac{1}{2}$ $\frac{3}{2}$ $\frac{6}{4}$

7. Which of the following fractions is an equivalent fraction for point *D*?

$\frac{6}{5}$ $\frac{10}{6}$ $\frac{3}{2}$ $\frac{6}{10}$ $\frac{5}{3}$

Problem Solving

8. What equivalent fractions are shown by the two number lines?

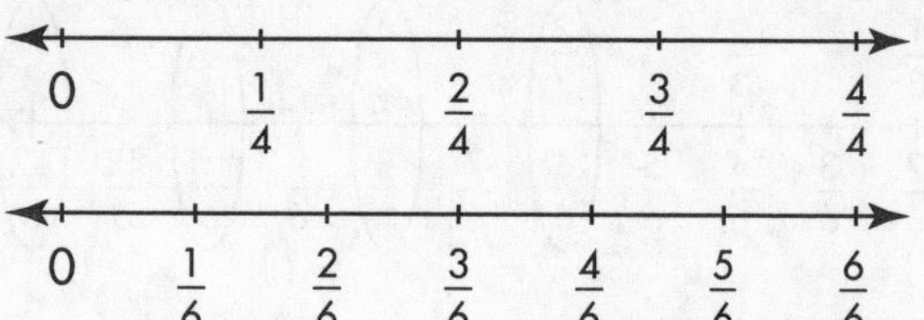

9. **Make Sense and Persevere** Randy and Carla like to walk the path around their town park. The path is 2 miles long. Last month Randy walked the path 13 times, and Carla walked it 22 times. How many more miles did Carla walk than Randy last month?

10. **Higher Order Thinking** Jarred says these number lines show $\frac{3}{4}$ is equivalent to $\frac{2}{3}$. Is Jarred correct? Explain.

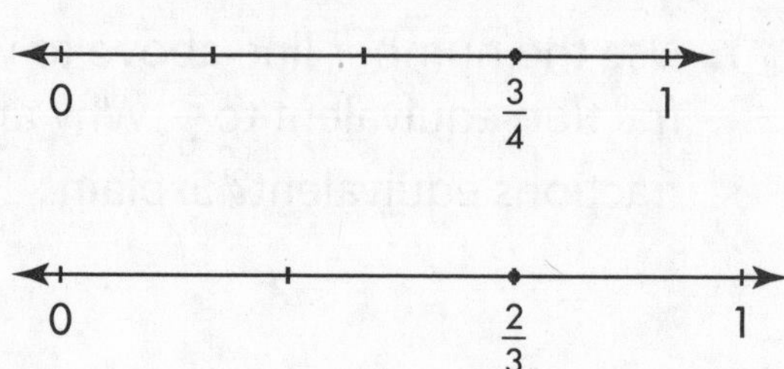

Assessment Practice

11. Kevin and Gabbie use a number line to find fractions that are equivalent to $\frac{4}{10}$. Kevin says he can find an equivalent fraction with a denominator greater than 10. Gabbie says she can find an equivalent fraction with a denominator less than 10.

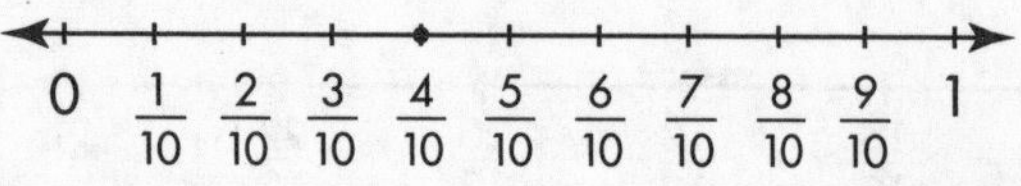

Many fractions can represent the same point on a number line. What fractions could represent 0 and 1 on the number line above?

Part A

Write to explain how Kevin can use the number line to find his equivalent fraction.

Part B

Write to explain how Gabbie can use the number line to find her equivalent fraction.

Name ____________________

Activity

Lesson 8-3

Generate Equivalent Fractions: Multiplication

I can ...

use multiplication to find equivalent fractions.

Content Standards 4.NF.A.1 Also 4.NBT.B.5
Mathematical Practices MP.2, MP.3, MP.4

Solve & Share

Wayne bought a box of muffins. Four sixths of the muffins are blueberry. Write a fraction equivalent to $\frac{4}{6}$. ***Solve this problem any way you choose.***

What can you draw to model with math to help represent the problem? *Show your work in the space below!*

Look Back! How are the numerator and denominator of your fraction related to the numerator and denominator of $\frac{4}{6}$?

Visual Learning A-Z Glossary

Essential Question

How Can You Use Multiplication to Find Equivalent Fractions?

Visual Learning Bridge

A

A librarian said $\frac{1}{2}$ of the books checked out yesterday were nonfiction. What are some fractions equivalent to $\frac{1}{2}$?

To find equivalent fractions, multiply by a fraction equal to one.

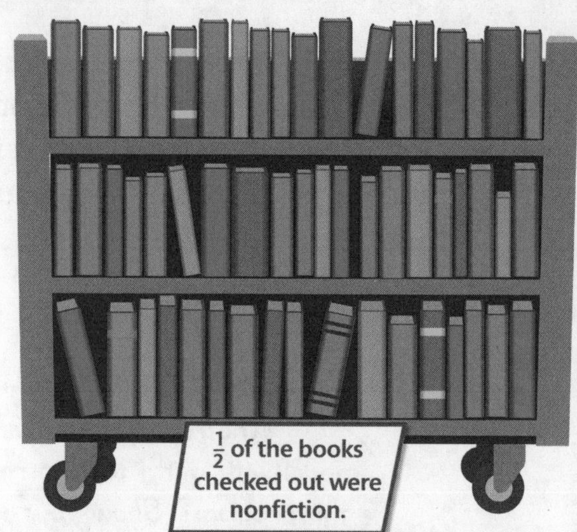

B **Multiply by $\frac{2}{2}$.**

Multiply the numerator and the denominator by 2.

$$\frac{1 \times 2}{2 \times 2} = \frac{2}{4}$$

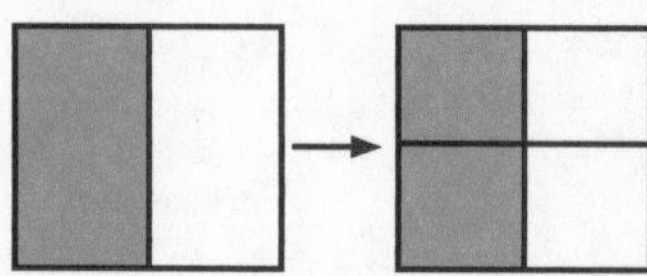

C **Multiply by $\frac{3}{3}$.**

Multiply the numerator and the denominator by 3.

$$\frac{1 \times 3}{2 \times 3} = \frac{3}{6}$$

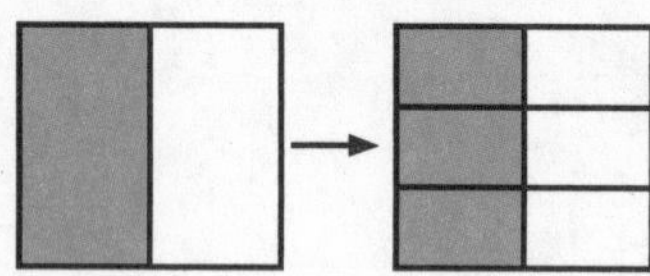

D **Multiply by $\frac{4}{4}$.**

Multiply the numerator and the denominator by 4.

$$\frac{1 \times 4}{2 \times 4} = \frac{4}{8}$$

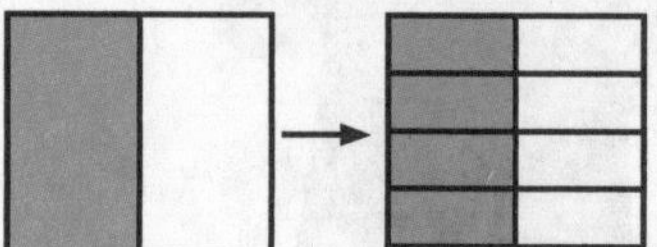

$\frac{2}{2}$, $\frac{3}{3}$, and $\frac{4}{4}$ are all equal to 1. Multiplying by 1 gives the same number.

$\frac{1}{2}$, $\frac{2}{4}$, $\frac{3}{6}$, and $\frac{4}{8}$ are equivalent fractions.

Convince Me! **Critique Reasoning** Kevin said, "In each of the examples above, all you are doing is multiplying by one. When you multiply by 1, the value doesn't change." Is Kevin correct? Explain.

Name ____________________

Guided Practice

Do You Understand?

1. Use an area model and multiplication to show why $\frac{5}{6}$ and $\frac{10}{12}$ are equivalent fractions.

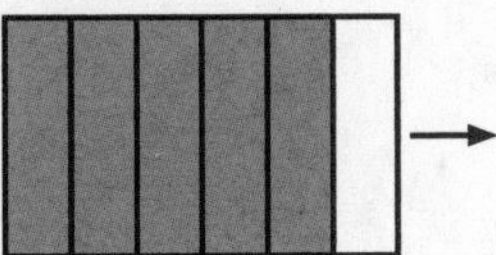

2. Use multiplication to explain why $\frac{3}{4}$ and $\frac{8}{12}$ are **NOT** equivalent fractions.

Do You Know How?

For **3–7**, multiply to find equivalent fractions.

3. 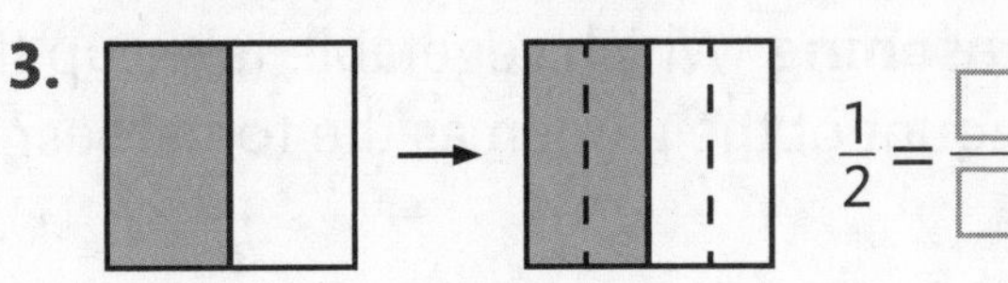 $\frac{1}{2} = \frac{\square}{\square}$

4. $\frac{3}{4} = \frac{\square}{12}$

5. $\frac{5}{5} = \frac{10}{\square}$

6. $\frac{3}{2} = \frac{6}{\square}$

7. $\frac{1}{6} = \frac{\square}{12}$

Independent Practice

Leveled Practice For **8–13**, fill in the missing numbers to find equivalent fractions.

8. 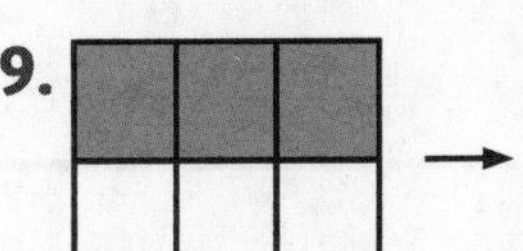 $\frac{2 \times 2}{3 \times 2} = \frac{\square}{\square}$

9. 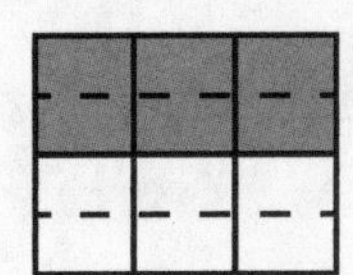 $\frac{3 \times 2}{6 \times 2} = \frac{\square}{\square}$

10. $\frac{1 \times \square}{5 \times \square} = \frac{\square}{10}$

11. $\frac{5 \times \square}{4 \times \square} = \frac{\square}{100}$

12. $\frac{7 \times \square}{4 \times \square} = \frac{\square}{12}$

13. $\frac{3 \times \square}{4 \times \square} = \frac{9}{\square}$

For **14–21**, write two equivalent fractions for each given fraction.

14. $\frac{1}{10}$

15. $\frac{4}{2}$

16. $\frac{5}{6}$

17. $\frac{1}{3}$

18. $\frac{2}{5}$

19. $\frac{3}{4}$

20. $\frac{9}{2}$

21. $\frac{7}{12}$

Problem Solving

For **22–23**, use the chart at the right.

Vegetable	Fraction of Garden Planted
Carrots	$\frac{1}{6}$
Tomatoes	$\frac{1}{4}$
Peppers	$\frac{4}{12}$
Beans	$\frac{3}{12}$

22. Write three equivalent fractions to describe the portion of the garden planted with carrots.

23. **Reasoning** Which vegetable takes up the same amount of the garden as the tomatoes? Explain.

24. Jeena has 5 packets of seeds. Each packet has 12 seeds. Jeena wants to divide the seeds evenly among 10 flower pots. How many seeds can she plant in each flower pot?

25. **Higher Order Thinking** Jen says, "I can use this equation to find equivalent fractions but *n* cannot be zero."

$$\frac{a}{b} = \frac{(n \times a)}{(n \times b)}$$

Do you agree with Jen? Explain. Give examples to support your reasoning.

Assessment Practice

26. Select the equivalent fraction.

	Fractions Equivalent to $\frac{1}{4}$	Fractions Equivalent to $\frac{2}{3}$
$\frac{4}{6}$	☐	☐
$\frac{2}{8}$	☐	☐
$\frac{8}{12}$	☐	☐
$\frac{3}{12}$	☐	☐

27. Nia found a fraction that is equivalent to $\frac{3}{8}$. Is Nia's fraction work, shown below, correct? Explain.

$$\frac{3 \times 4}{8 \times 3} = \frac{12}{24}$$

Name ______________________________________

Activity

Lesson 8-4
Generate Equivalent Fractions: Division

I can ...
use division to find equivalent fractions.

Content Standards 4.NF.A.1 Also 4.OA.B.4, 4.NBT.B.6
Mathematical Practices MP.4, MP.6, MP.7

Solve & Share Sara bought a piece of ribbon. The length of the ribbon is given in tenths. Write the length as two other equivalent fractions. ***Solve this problem any way you choose.***

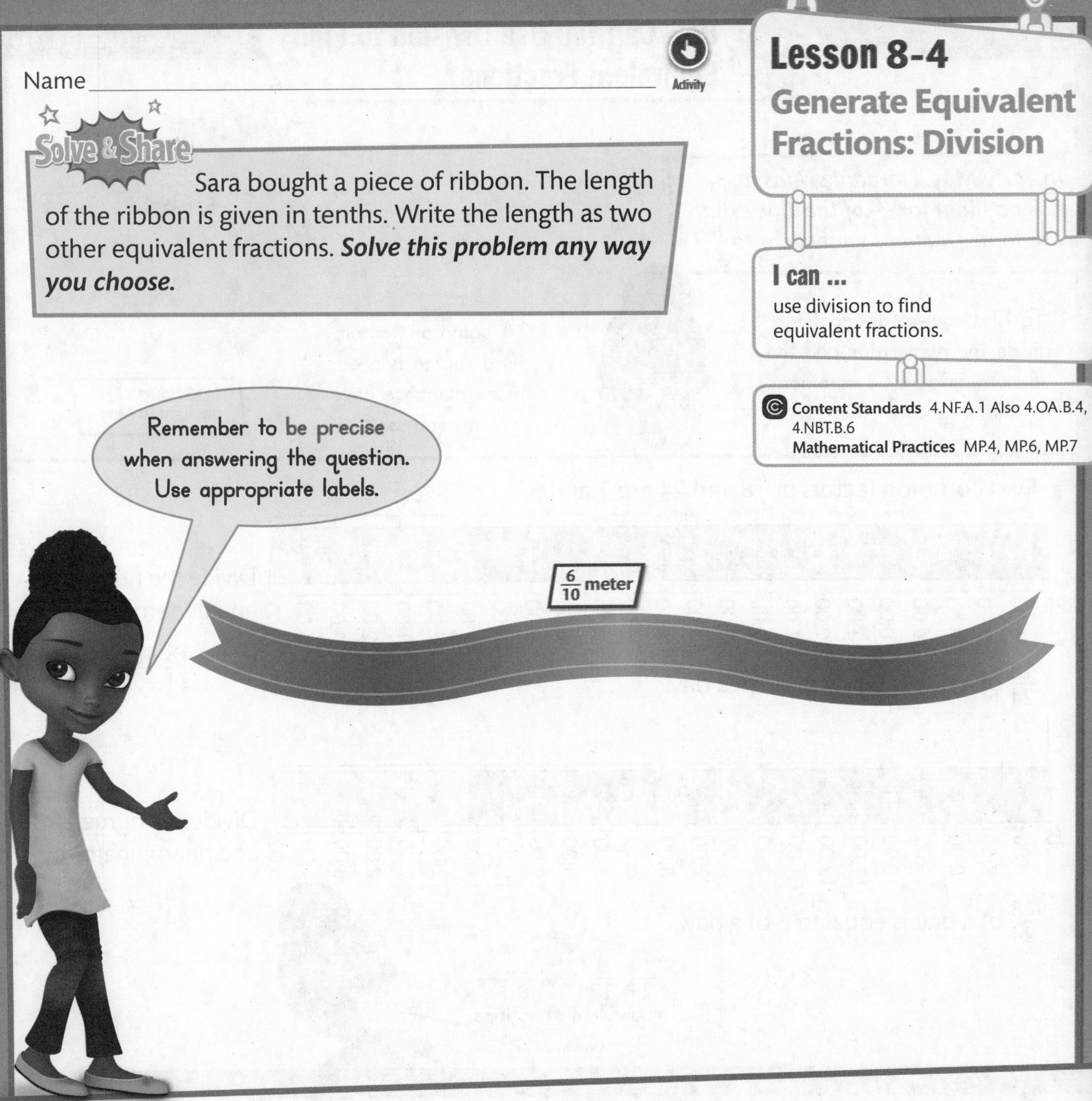

Remember to be precise when answering the question. Use appropriate labels.
$\frac{6}{10}$ meter

Look Back! Sara wrote the following equivalent fractions: $\frac{6}{10} = \frac{3}{5}$. What two operations could Sara have used to find her equivalent fractions? Explain.

Visual Learning | A-Z Glossary

Essential Question

How Can You Use Division to Find Equivalent Fractions?

Visual Learning Bridge

A

In early May, Fairbanks, Alaska, has daylight for $\frac{18}{24}$ of the day. What are some fractions equivalent to $\frac{18}{24}$?

To find equivalent fractions, divide the numerator and the denominator by a common factor greater than 1.

A common factor is a factor two or more numbers have in common.

Fairbanks

18 hours of daylight in May

B

Two common factors of 18 and 24 are 2 and 3.

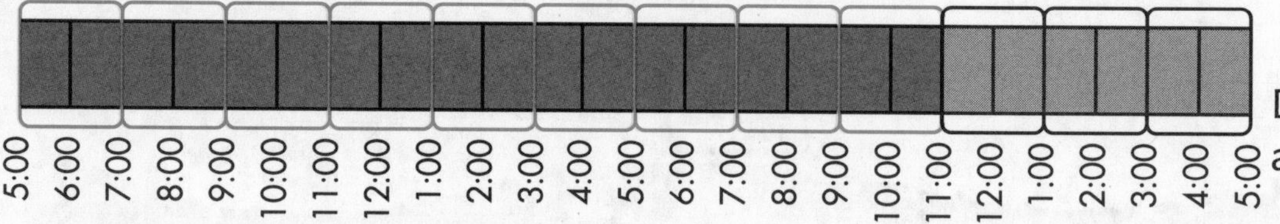

Divide the numerator and denominator by 2.

$\frac{18 \div 2}{24 \div 2} = \frac{9}{12}$

$\frac{18}{24}$ of a day is equal to $\frac{9}{12}$ of a day.

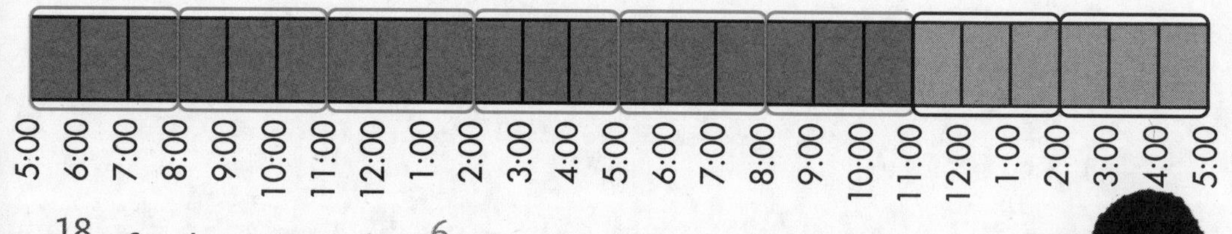

Divide the numerator and denominator by 3.

$\frac{18 \div 3}{24 \div 3} = \frac{6}{8}$

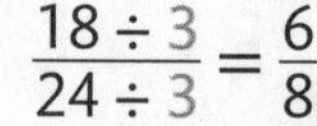

$\frac{18}{24}$ of a day is equal to $\frac{6}{8}$ of a day.

$\frac{18}{24}$, $\frac{9}{12}$, and $\frac{6}{8}$ are equivalent fractions.

Convince Me! **Model with Math** Draw a number line and label it with equivalent fractions to show $\frac{18}{24} = \frac{9}{12} = \frac{6}{8} = \frac{3}{4}$.

Name ____________________

Guided Practice

Do You Understand?

1. Use division to show $\frac{9}{12}$ and $\frac{3}{4}$ are equivalent fractions.

2. Is there a fraction with a smaller numerator and denominator that is equivalent to $\frac{4}{12}$? Explain.

Do You Know How?

For **3–8**, divide to find equivalent fractions.

3. $\frac{6}{10} = \frac{\square}{\square}$

4. $\frac{8}{12} = \frac{\square}{\square}$

5. $\frac{8}{12} = \frac{\square}{3}$

6. $\frac{10}{12} = \frac{5}{\square}$

7. $\frac{2}{10} = \frac{\square}{5}$

8. $\frac{10}{100} = \frac{\square}{10}$

Independent Practice

Leveled Practice For **9–16**, fill in the missing numbers to find equivalent fractions.

9. $\frac{6 \div 6}{12 \div 6} = \frac{\square}{\square}$

10. $\frac{70 \div 5}{10 \div 5} = \frac{\square}{\square}$

11. $\frac{2 \div 2}{6 \div 2} = \frac{\square}{\square}$

12. $\frac{50 \div 10}{100 \div 10} = \frac{\square}{\square}$

13. $\frac{9 \div \square}{6 \div \square} = \frac{3}{\square}$

14. $\frac{10 \div \square}{4 \div \square} = \frac{\square}{2}$

15. $\frac{4 \div \square}{12 \div \square} = \frac{\square}{6}$

16. $\frac{2 \div \square}{8 \div \square} = \frac{\square}{4}$

For **17–24**, divide to find two equivalent fractions.

17. $\frac{20}{100}$

18. $\frac{40}{10}$

19. $\frac{16}{12}$

20. $\frac{12}{8}$

21. $\frac{24}{12}$

22. $\frac{10}{100}$

23. $\frac{90}{10}$

24. $\frac{80}{100}$

Problem Solving

For **25–27**, use the table at the right.

Animal	Number of Hours Spent Sleeping	Fraction of the Day Spent Sleeping	Equivalent Fraction
Cat	12		
Cow	4		
Squirrel	15		
Tiger	16		

25. Complete the table at the right by writing the fraction of the day each animal sleeps and an equivalent fraction. Remember, there are 24 hours in a day.

26. Suppose the cow slept 4 more hours. What fraction of the day would the cow spend sleeping?

27. How many hours does a tiger sleep in 7 days?

28. Use Structure Ethan ate $\frac{4}{8}$ of his sandwich. Andy ate $\frac{1}{2}$ of his sandwich. The sandwiches were the same size.

a. Whose sandwich had more equal parts?

b. Whose sandwich had larger equal parts?

c. Who ate more? Explain.

29. Higher Order Thinking If the numerator and denominator of a fraction are both odd numbers, can you write an equivalent fraction with a smaller numerator and denominator? Give an example to explain.

Assessment Practice

30. Select all the equations that are correct.

- ☐ $\frac{12 \div 3}{3 \div 3} = \frac{3}{1}$
- ☐ $\frac{4 \div 2}{8 \div 2} = \frac{2}{4}$
- ☐ $\frac{5 \div 5}{10 \div 5} = \frac{1}{5}$
- ☐ $\frac{10 \div 2}{4 \div 2} = \frac{5}{2}$
- ☐ $\frac{12 \div 4}{8 \div 4} = \frac{3}{2}$

31. There are 12 students in DeLynn's class. Eight students own pets. Which pair of fractions show the fraction of the class that owns pets?

Ⓐ $\frac{8}{12}, \frac{2}{3}$

Ⓑ $\frac{1}{2}, \frac{2}{3}$

Ⓒ $\frac{6}{4}, \frac{3}{2}$

Ⓓ $\frac{12}{8}, \frac{3}{2}$

Name ______________________________ Activity

Lesson 8-5
Use Benchmarks to Compare Fractions

I can ...
use benchmarks, area models, and number lines to compare fractions.

Content Standard 4.NF.A.2
Mathematical Practices MP.2, MP.3, MP.8

Solve & Share

Color a part of each strip of paper below. Estimate what fraction of each strip is colored. Explain how you made your estimate. ***Solve this problem any way you choose.***

Compare the parts you colored to $\frac{1}{4}$, $\frac{1}{2}$, and $\frac{3}{4}$.

Look Back! **Generalize** How could you tell if a fraction is greater than, less than, or equal to $\frac{1}{2}$ just by looking at the numerator and the denominator?

How Can You Use Benchmarks to Compare Fractions?

Visual Learning Bridge

A

Robert needs $\frac{3}{8}$ stick of butter to make muffins and $\frac{2}{3}$ stick of butter to make cookies. Which recipe uses more butter?

BUTTER

You can use benchmark fractions to compare fractions. Benchmark fractions are commonly used fractions such as $\frac{1}{4}$, $\frac{1}{3}$, $\frac{1}{2}$, $\frac{2}{3}$, and $\frac{3}{4}$.

B Compare $\frac{3}{8}$ to the benchmark fraction $\frac{1}{2}$.

Muffins

$\frac{1}{2}$ 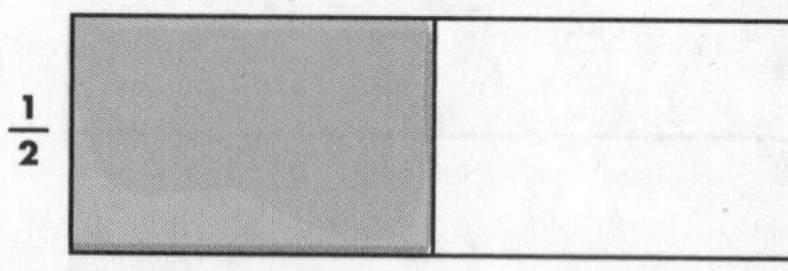

$\frac{3}{8}$ 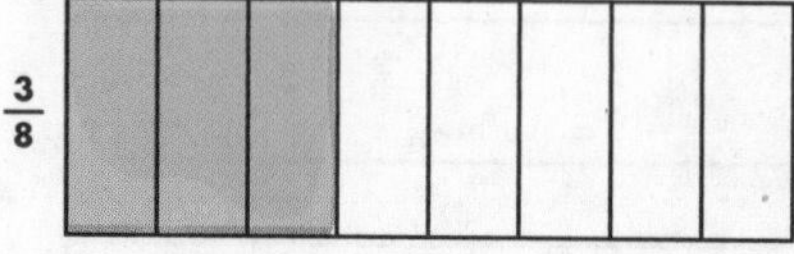

$\frac{3}{8} < \frac{1}{2}$

You can compare these fractions because they refer to the same whole, a stick of butter.

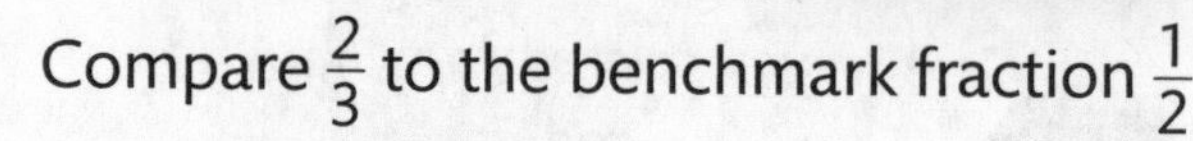

C Compare $\frac{2}{3}$ to the benchmark fraction $\frac{1}{2}$.

Cookies

$\frac{1}{2}$ 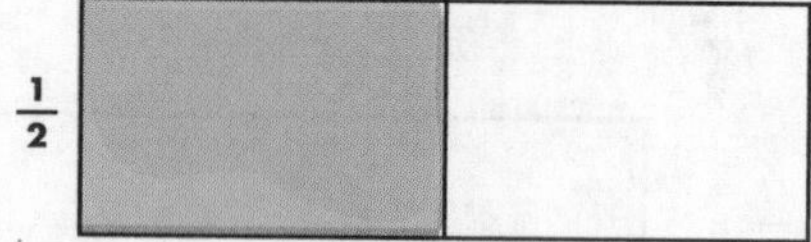

$\frac{2}{3}$ 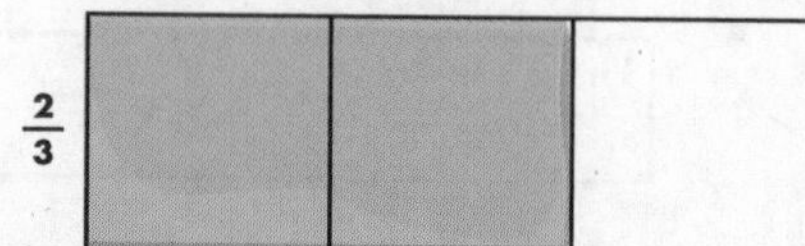

$\frac{2}{3} > \frac{1}{2}$

$\frac{3}{8} < \frac{1}{2}$ and $\frac{2}{3} > \frac{1}{2}$, so $\frac{3}{8} < \frac{2}{3}$.

The cookie recipe uses more butter.

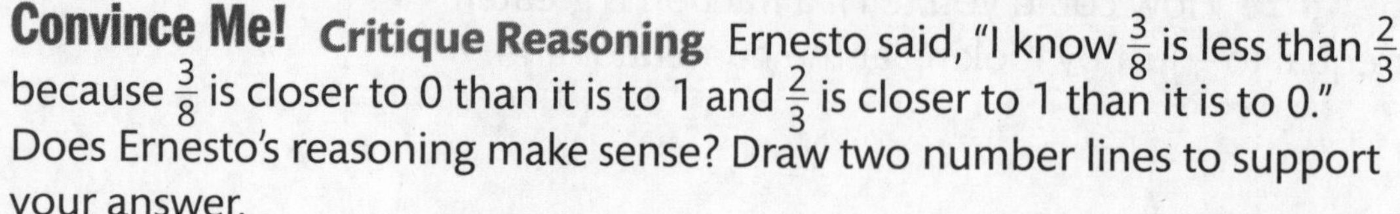

Convince Me! Critique Reasoning Ernesto said, "I know $\frac{3}{8}$ is less than $\frac{2}{3}$ because $\frac{3}{8}$ is closer to 0 than it is to 1 and $\frac{2}{3}$ is closer to 1 than it is to 0." Does Ernesto's reasoning make sense? Draw two number lines to support your answer.

Name ____________________

Another Example!

Compare $\frac{9}{10}$ and $\frac{7}{6}$. Use 1 whole as a benchmark.

$\frac{9}{10} < 1$ and $\frac{7}{6} > 1$, so $\frac{9}{10} < \frac{7}{6}$.

Guided Practice

Do You Understand?

1. Carl found $\frac{4}{8}$ is equal to $\frac{1}{2}$, and $\frac{1}{3}$ is less than $\frac{1}{2}$. How can Carl compare $\frac{4}{8}$ to $\frac{1}{3}$?

2. Write a fraction that is closer to 0 than to 1. Write another fraction that is closer to 1 than to 0. Use your fractions to complete the comparison.

Do You Know How?

For **3–4**, compare. Write <, >, or =.

3. $\frac{2}{6} \bigcirc \frac{4}{5}$

4. $\frac{11}{12} \bigcirc \frac{9}{8}$

5. Circle the fractions that are less than $\frac{1}{2}$.

$\frac{5}{4}$ $\frac{1}{4}$ $\frac{1}{5}$ $\frac{2}{3}$ $\frac{2}{12}$ $\frac{51}{100}$

6. Circle the fractions that are greater than 1.

$\frac{99}{100}$ $\frac{6}{5}$ $\frac{7}{8}$ $\frac{14}{8}$ $\frac{11}{10}$ $\frac{11}{12}$

Independent Practice

For **7–10**, circle all the fractions that match each statement.

7. Fractions less than $\frac{1}{2}$

$\frac{3}{4}$ $\frac{1}{6}$ $\frac{6}{12}$ $\frac{4}{10}$ $\frac{5}{8}$ $\frac{5}{2}$

8. Fractions greater than $\frac{1}{2}$

$\frac{5}{8}$ $\frac{1}{4}$ $\frac{6}{3}$ $\frac{7}{10}$ $\frac{5}{12}$ $\frac{6}{12}$

9. Fractions greater than 1

$\frac{5}{4}$ $\frac{2}{3}$ $\frac{6}{6}$ $\frac{1}{10}$ $\frac{15}{12}$ $\frac{7}{8}$

10. Fractions closer to 0 than to 1

$\frac{3}{4}$ $\frac{1}{8}$ $\frac{1}{4}$ $\frac{7}{5}$ $\frac{2}{4}$ $\frac{3}{10}$

For **11–18**, compare using benchmark fractions or 1. Then write >, <, or =.

11. $\frac{1}{3} \bigcirc \frac{4}{6}$

12. $\frac{4}{8} \bigcirc \frac{2}{4}$

13. $\frac{7}{5} \bigcirc \frac{7}{8}$

14. $\frac{6}{12} \bigcirc \frac{4}{5}$

15. $\frac{4}{5} \bigcirc \frac{2}{5}$

16. $\frac{6}{6} \bigcirc \frac{13}{12}$

17. $\frac{8}{10} \bigcirc \frac{1}{8}$

18. $\frac{4}{4} \bigcirc \frac{10}{10}$

Problem Solving

19. **Reasoning** Jordan has $\frac{5}{8}$ can of green paint and $\frac{3}{6}$ can of blue paint. If the cans are the same size, does Jordan have more green paint or blue paint? Explain.

20. **Vocabulary** Write two examples of a *benchmark fraction.*

21. Four neighbors each have gardens that are the same size.

    a. Which neighbors planted vegetables in less than half of their gardens?

    b. Who has a larger section of vegetables in their garden, Margaret or Wayne?

DATA

Neighbor	Fraction of Garden Planted with Vegetables
James	$\frac{5}{12}$
Margaret	$\frac{5}{10}$
Claudia	$\frac{1}{6}$
Wayne	$\frac{2}{3}$

22. Gavin bought 3 pizzas for a party. Each pizza had 8 slices. There were 8 other people at the party. Everyone ate the same number of slices. How many slices did each person eat? How many slices were left over?

23. **Higher Order Thinking** How can you tell just by looking at the numerator and denominator of a fraction if it is closer to 0 or to 1? Give some examples in your explanation.

Assessment Practice

24. Donna ate $\frac{7}{12}$ box of popcorn. Jack ate $\frac{4}{10}$ box of popcorn. The boxes of popcorn are the same size. Write to explain how to use a benchmark fraction to determine who ate more popcorn.

Name ______________________

Activity

Lesson 8-6
Compare Fractions

I can ...
use equivalent fractions to compare fractions.

Content Standards 4.NF.A.2 Also 4.NBT.B.5, 4.NF.A.1
Mathematical Practices MP.3, MP.5

Solve & Share

Juan read for $\frac{5}{6}$ of an hour. Larissa read for $\frac{10}{12}$ of an hour. Who read for a longer period of time? Explain. ***Solve this problem any way you choose.***

You can select and use appropriate tools such as drawings, number lines, or fraction strips to solve. *Show your work in the space below!*

Look Back! Carlos read for $\frac{8}{12}$ of an hour. Did Carlos read for more or less time than Juan? Write your answer as a number sentence using >, <, or =.

Visual Learning A-Z Glossary

Essential Question

How Can You Compare Fractions with Unlike Denominators?

Visual Learning Bridge

A

Isabella's father is building a model dinosaur with small pieces of wood. Compare the lengths of the pieces of wood. Compare $\frac{1}{4}$ inch and $\frac{5}{6}$ inch. Then, compare $\frac{4}{5}$ inch and $\frac{4}{10}$ inch.

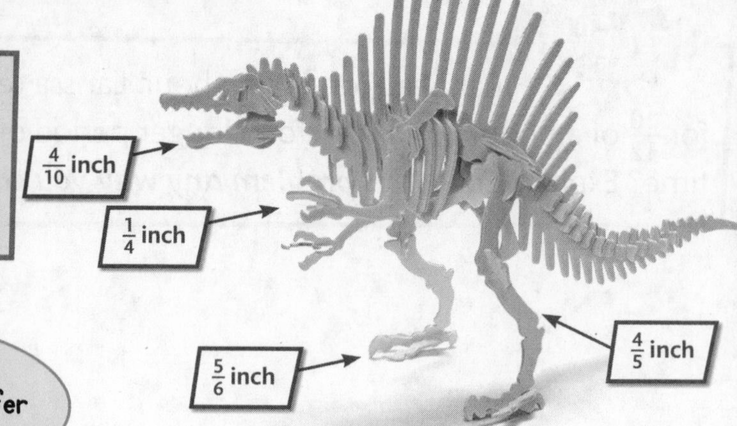

You can compare these fractions because they refer to the same whole, an inch.

B Compare $\frac{1}{4}$ and $\frac{5}{6}$ by renaming each fraction so they both have the same denominator.

$\frac{1}{4} = \frac{1 \times 3}{4 \times 3} = \frac{3}{12}$ $\frac{5}{6} = \frac{5 \times 2}{6 \times 2} = \frac{10}{12}$

Compare the numerators of the renamed fractions.

$\frac{3}{12} < \frac{10}{12}$

So, $\frac{1}{4} < \frac{5}{6}$.

C Compare $\frac{4}{5}$ and $\frac{4}{10}$ on a number line.

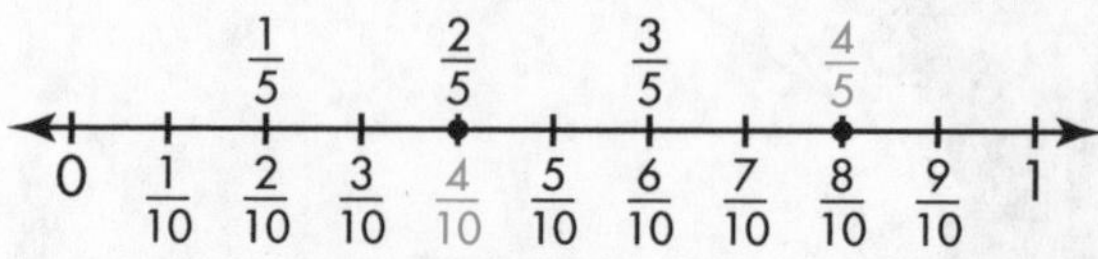

The fraction that is farther to the right on a number line is greater.

So, $\frac{4}{5} > \frac{4}{10}$.

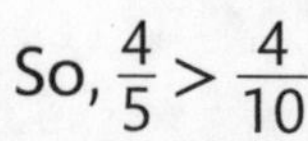

Convince Me! **Critique Reasoning** The fractions on the right refer to the same whole. Kelly said, "These are easy to compare. I just think about $\frac{1}{8}$ and $\frac{1}{6}$." Circle the greater fraction. Explain what Kelly was thinking.

$\frac{5}{8}$ $\frac{5}{6}$

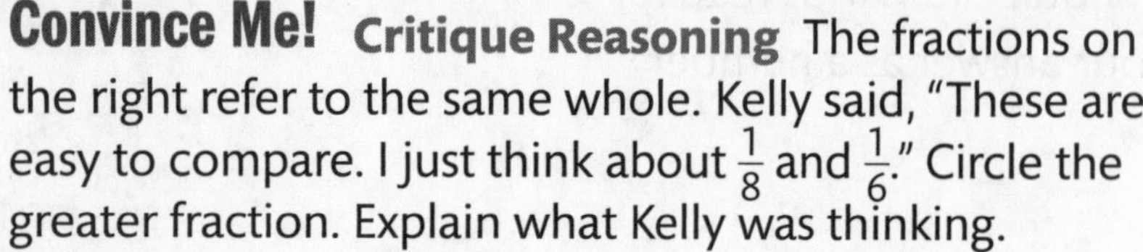

Name ____________________

Another Example!

Compare $\frac{3}{4}$ and $\frac{6}{10}$.

Create an equivalent fraction for either $\frac{3}{4}$ or $\frac{6}{10}$ so that the numerators are the same.

$\frac{6 \div 2}{10 \div 2} = \frac{3}{5}$

$\frac{3}{4} > \frac{3}{5}$, When you divide a whole into 4 equal parts, each part is larger than when you divide it into 5 equal parts.

1		
$\frac{1}{4}$	$\frac{1}{4}$	$\frac{1}{4}$
$\frac{1}{5}$	$\frac{1}{5}$	$\frac{1}{5}$

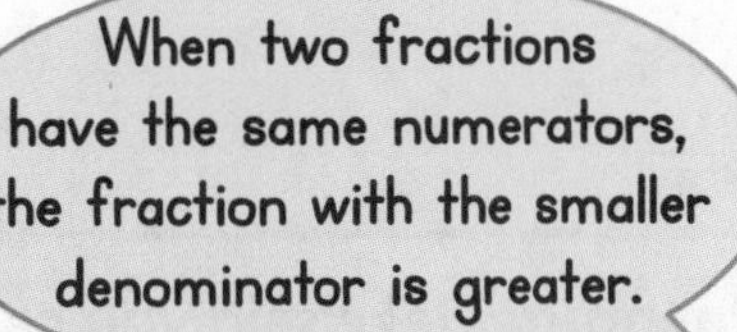

When two fractions have the same numerators, the fraction with the smaller denominator is greater.

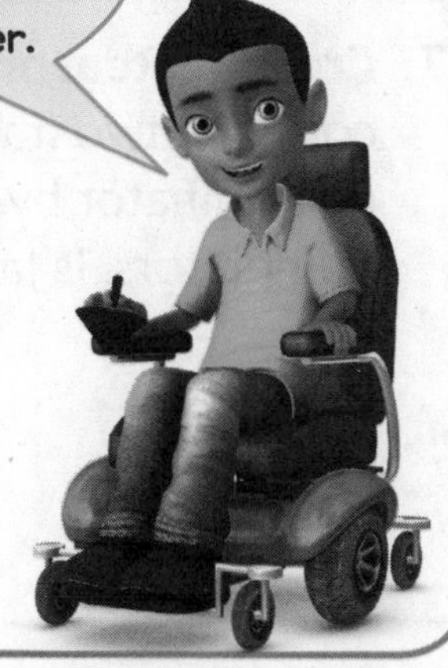

Guided Practice

Do You Understand?

1. Mary says $\frac{1}{8}$ is greater than $\frac{1}{4}$ because 8 is greater than 4. Is Mary's reasoning correct? Explain.

Do You Know How?

For **2–5**, write >, <, or =. Use number lines, fraction strips, benchmark or equivalent fractions.

2. $\frac{3}{4} \bigcirc \frac{6}{8}$

3. $\frac{1}{4} \bigcirc \frac{1}{10}$

4. $\frac{3}{5} \bigcirc \frac{5}{10}$

5. $\frac{1}{2} \bigcirc \frac{4}{5}$

Independent Practice

Leveled Practice For **6–15**, find equivalent fractions to compare. Then, write >, <, or =.

6. $\frac{7}{8} \bigcirc \frac{3}{4}$

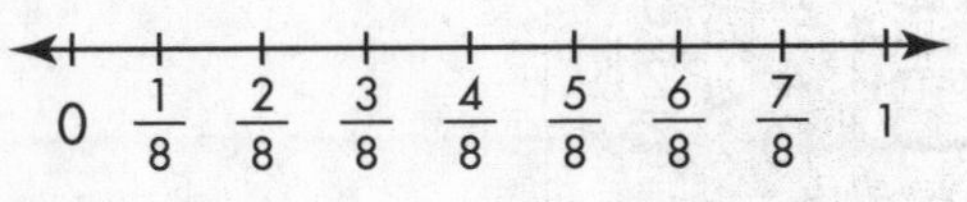

7. $\frac{5}{6} \bigcirc \frac{10}{12}$

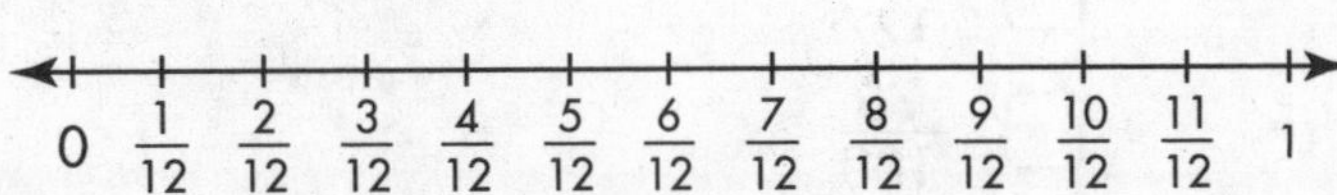

8. $\frac{7}{10} \bigcirc \frac{4}{5}$

9. $\frac{7}{12} \bigcirc \frac{1}{3}$

10. $\frac{5}{12} \bigcirc \frac{4}{5}$

11. $\frac{2}{6} \bigcirc \frac{3}{12}$

12. $\frac{6}{8} \bigcirc \frac{3}{4}$

13. $\frac{6}{10} \bigcirc \frac{3}{6}$

14. $\frac{2}{10} \bigcirc \frac{1}{6}$

15. $\frac{5}{6} \bigcirc \frac{2}{3}$

Problem Solving

16. Felicia drew the pictures at the right to show $\frac{3}{8}$ is greater than $\frac{3}{4}$. What was Felicia's mistake?

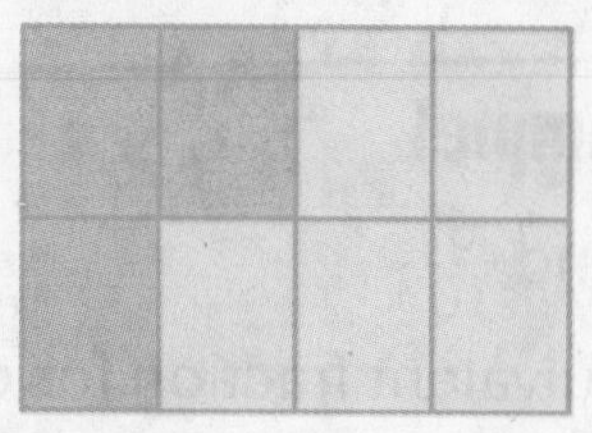

17. **Critique Reasoning** Jake said you can compare two fractions with the same denominator by only comparing the numerators. Is Jake correct? Explain.

18. Tina completed $\frac{2}{3}$ of her homework. George completed $\frac{8}{9}$ of his homework. Tina and George have the same amount of homework. Who completed a greater fraction of homework?

19. If $34 \times 2 = 68$ then what does 34×20 equal?

20. What can you conclude about $\frac{3}{5}$ and $\frac{60}{100}$ if you know $\frac{3}{5}$ is equivalent to $\frac{6}{10}$ and $\frac{6}{10}$ is equivalent to $\frac{60}{100}$?

21. Jackson played a video game for $\frac{1}{6}$ hour. Hailey played a video game for $\frac{1}{3}$ hour. Who played the video game for a greater amount of time? Explain.

22. **Higher Order Thinking** Write a fraction that is greater than $\frac{3}{12}$, is less than $\frac{75}{100}$, and has 6 as a denominator.

Assessment Practice

23. Select all fractions that would make the comparison true.

$\frac{3}{4} = \square$

- ☐ $\frac{5}{12}$
- ☐ $\frac{75}{100}$
- ☐ $\frac{9}{12}$
- ☐ $\frac{7}{10}$
- ☐ $\frac{6}{8}$

24. Select all answer choices that show a correct comparison.

- ☐ $\frac{5}{6} > \frac{7}{12}$
- ☐ $\frac{1}{2} > \frac{10}{10}$
- ☐ $\frac{4}{10} > \frac{2}{6}$
- ☐ $\frac{1}{5} < \frac{2}{3}$
- ☐ $\frac{2}{3} > \frac{9}{12}$

Name ____________________

Activity

Problem Solving

Lesson 8-7

Construct Arguments

I can ...
construct math arguments using what I know about fractions.

Mathematical Practices MP.3 Also MP.1, MP.2, MP.5
Content Standards 4.NF.A.1 Also 4.NF.A.2

Solve & Share Sherry and Karl both started their hike with a small bottle filled with water. Tia started her hike with a larger bottle that was $\frac{1}{2}$ full. At the end of the hike, Sherry and Tia's bottles were each half filled with water. Karl's bottle was $\frac{1}{3}$ filled with water. Who has the most water left? Construct a math argument to support your answer.

Sherry

Karl

Tia

Thinking Habits

Be a good thinker!
These questions can help you.

- How can I use numbers, objects, drawings, or actions to justify my argument?
- Am I using numbers and symbols correctly?
- Is my explanation clear and complete?

Look Back! Construct Arguments If Tia's bottle was $\frac{1}{3}$ filled with water at the end of the hike, would you be able to decide who had the most water left? Construct an argument to support your answer.

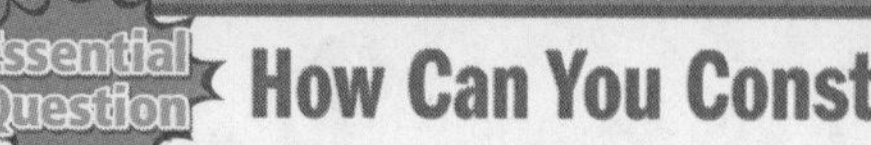

How Can You Construct Arguments?

A

Erin said $\frac{1}{2}$ is the same amount as $\frac{2}{4}$.
Matt said $\frac{1}{2}$ and $\frac{2}{4}$ can be different amounts.
Which student is correct?

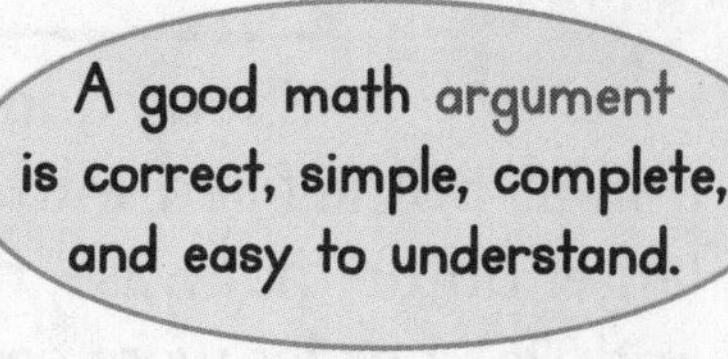

A good math argument is correct, simple, complete, and easy to understand.

What do you need to do to solve this problem?

I need to construct an argument with what I know about fraction models and ways to show $\frac{1}{2}$ and $\frac{2}{4}$.

B

How can I construct an argument?

I can

- use numbers, objects, drawings, or models to justify my arguments.
- use a counterexample in my argument.
- give an explanation of my argument that is clear and complete.

C

Here's my thinking.

I will use drawings to show which student is correct.

Both wholes are the same size. The $\frac{1}{2}$ and $\frac{2}{4}$ represent the same part of the whole.

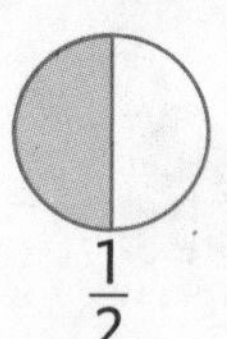
$\frac{1}{2}$

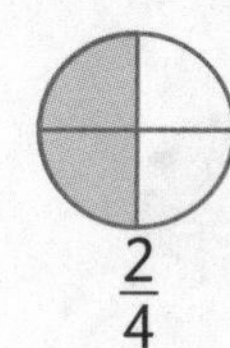
$\frac{2}{4}$

These wholes are not the same size. So, $\frac{2}{4}$ of the larger circle represents more than $\frac{1}{2}$ of the smaller circle.

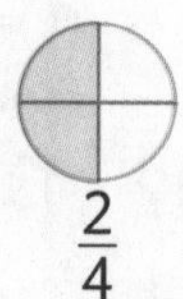
$\frac{2}{4}$

$\frac{1}{2}$

Both students are correct. $\frac{1}{2}$ and $\frac{2}{4}$ of the same-size whole are the same amount. $\frac{1}{2}$ and $\frac{2}{4}$ of different-size wholes are different amounts.

Convince Me! Critique Reasoning Erin also said $\frac{3}{6}$ and $\frac{5}{10}$ are **NOT** the same size because the denominators are not factors of each other. Is Erin's argument correct? Explain.

Name ____________________

Guided Practice

Construct Arguments

Margie and Parker ordered the same-size burritos. Margie ate $\frac{4}{6}$ of her burrito. Parker ate $\frac{4}{5}$ of his burrito. Margie concluded she ate more than Parker because the fraction of the burrito she ate has a greater denominator.

1. What is Margie's argument? How does she support her argument?

2. Does Margie's conclusion make sense?

Independent Practice

Construct Arguments

In the after-school club, Dena, Shawn, and Amanda knit scarves that are all the same size with yellow, white, and blue yarn. Dena's scarf is $\frac{3}{5}$ yellow, Shawn's scarf is $\frac{2}{5}$ yellow, and Amanda's scarf is $\frac{3}{4}$ yellow. The rest of each scarf has an equal amount of white and blue.

When you construct an argument, you need to make sure your explanation is complete.

3. Describe how Amanda could make the argument that her scarf has the most yellow.

4. How much of Dena's scarf is blue?

5. Dena has a scarf at home that is the same size as the scarf she made in the club. The scarf at home is $\frac{6}{8}$ yellow. Dena said the scarf at home has more yellow. Is she correct? Explain. Include an explanation of how you make the comparison.

Problem Solving

Performance Task

Snail Race

Mr. Aydin's science class had a snail race to see which snail would crawl the farthest from a starting line in two minutes. The table shows the distances the snails crawled.

Snail	Slimy	Slinky	Curly	Pod	Stylo	Creeper
Distance in feet	$\frac{3}{12}$	$\frac{1}{6}$	$\frac{1}{5}$	$\frac{3}{10}$	$\frac{2}{10}$	$\frac{1}{3}$

6. **Use Appropriate Tools** Curly and Stylo traveled the same distance. Justify this conjecture using a number line or fraction strips.

7. **Construct Arguments** Who traveled farther, Slimy or Slinky? Change the fractions to have the same denominator.

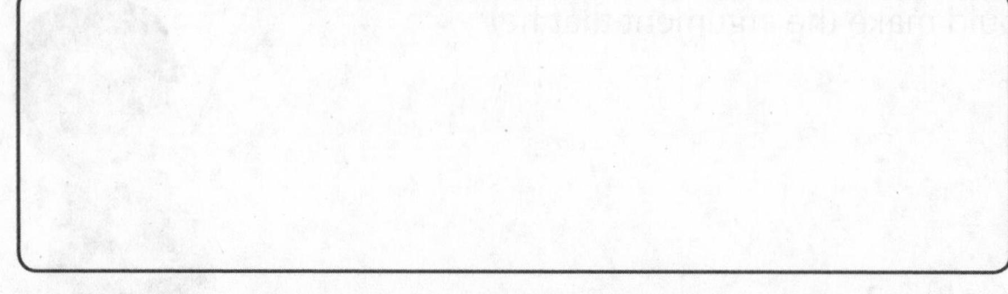

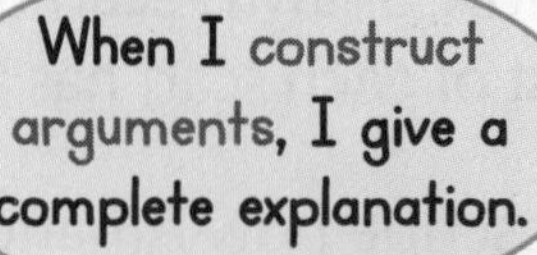
When I construct arguments, I give a complete explanation.

8. **Reasoning** Who traveled farther, Creeper or Slimy? Change the fractions to have the same numerator.

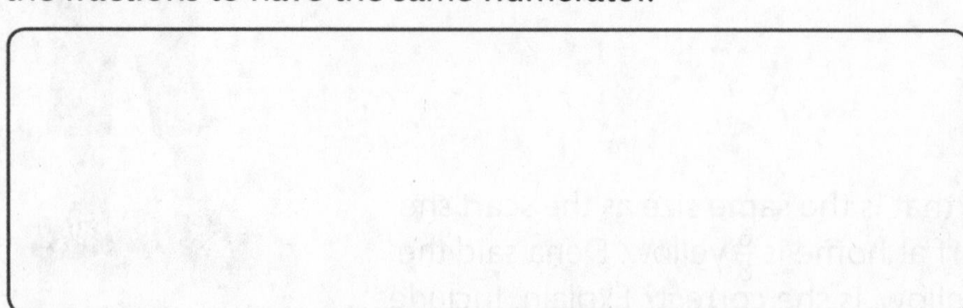

9. **Make Sense and Persevere** Who won the race?

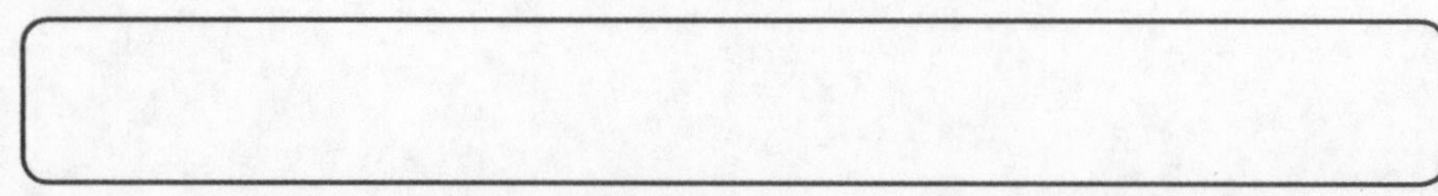

Name ______________________________

Fluency Practice Activity

Find a partner. Get paper and a pencil. Each partner chooses a different color: light blue or dark blue.

Partner 1 and Partner 2 each point to a black number at the same time. Each partner subtracts the two numbers.

If the answer is on your color, you get a tally mark. Work until one partner has twelve tally marks.

I can ...
subtract multi-digit whole numbers.

Content Standard 4.NBT.B.4
Mathematical Practices MP.3, MP.6, MP.7, MP.8

Partner 1

510

608

701

850

909

93	362	322	267
714	607	191	421
433	229	213	471
365	530	315	655
131	492	284	413
458	120	22	506

Partner 2

195

243

379

488

417

Tally Marks for Partner 1

Tally Marks for Partner 2

Word List

- benchmark fraction
- common factor
- denominator
- equivalent fractions
- fraction
- numerator

Understand Vocabulary

Choose the best term from the box. Write it on the blank.

1. A number that names part of a whole, part of a set, or a location on a number line is a(n) ______________________.

2. A commonly used fraction that helps you understand a different size or amount is called a(n) ______________________.

3. The number below the fraction bar in a fraction that shows the total number of equal parts is the ______________________.

4. Fractions that name the same part of a whole or the same location on a number line are called ______________________.

5. The number above the fraction bar that represents part of the whole is called a(n) ______________________.

For each of these terms, give an example and a non-example.

	Example	Non-example
6. Fraction	______________	______________
7. Equivalent fractions	______________	______________
8. A fraction with a common factor other than 1 for its numerator and denominator	______________	______________

Use Vocabulary in Writing

9. Explain how to compare $\frac{5}{8}$ and $\frac{3}{8}$. Use at least 3 terms from the Word List in your explanation.

Name ______________________

TOPIC 8

Reteaching

Set A pages 293–300

Use an area model to write an equivalent fraction for $\frac{1}{2}$.

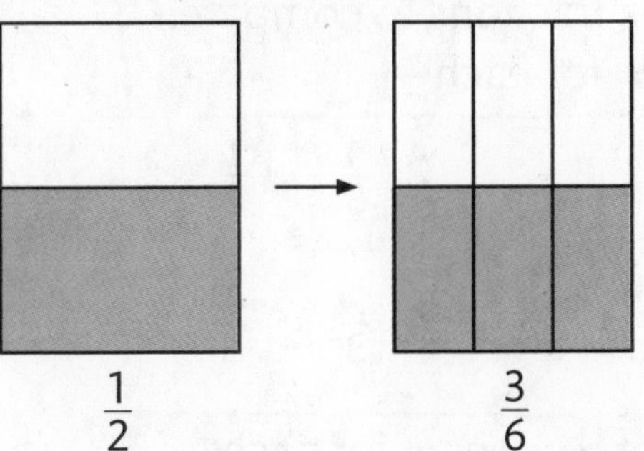

$\frac{1}{2}$ $\frac{3}{6}$

$\frac{1}{2}$ and $\frac{3}{6}$ name the same part of the whole.

$\frac{1}{2}$ and $\frac{3}{6}$ are equivalent fractions.

Use a number line to write an equivalent fraction for $\frac{1}{3}$.

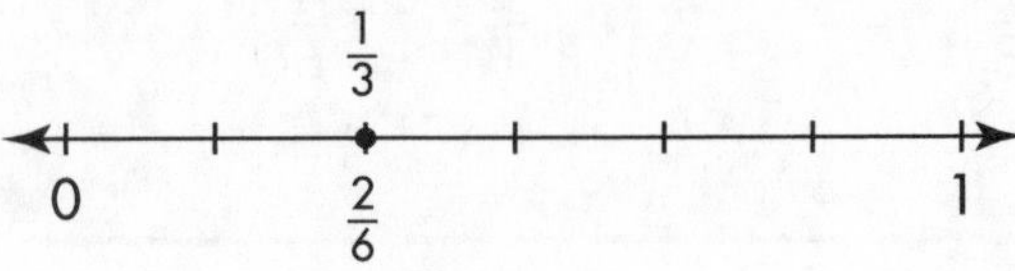

$\frac{1}{3}$ and $\frac{2}{6}$ name the same part of the whole.

$\frac{1}{3}$ and $\frac{2}{6}$ are equivalent fractions.

Remember that equivalent fractions name the same part of a whole.

Write an equivalent fraction for each fraction given.

1. $\frac{2}{8}$

2. $\frac{2}{3}$

3. $\frac{1}{4}$

4. $\frac{3}{5}$

Draw a number line to shown each fraction and an equivalent fraction.

5. $\frac{4}{6}$

6. $\frac{4}{10}$

Set B pages 301–308

Find two equivalent fractions for $\frac{1}{2}$.

$\frac{1}{2} \times \frac{2}{2} = \frac{2}{4}$ $\frac{1}{2} \times \frac{3}{3} = \frac{3}{6}$

$\frac{1}{2}, \frac{2}{4}$, and $\frac{3}{6}$ are equivalent fractions.

Find two equivalent fractions for $\frac{8}{12}$.

$\frac{8}{12} \div \frac{2}{2} = \frac{4}{6}$ $\frac{8}{12} \div \frac{4}{4} = \frac{2}{3}$

$\frac{8}{12}, \frac{4}{6}$, and $\frac{2}{3}$ are equivalent fractions.

Remember that you can multiply or divide to find equivalent fractions.

Multiply or divide to find equivalent fractions.

1. $\frac{2}{3} = \frac{8}{\square}$

2. $\frac{1}{4} = \frac{\square}{8}$

3. $\frac{1}{6} = \frac{2}{\square}$

4. $\frac{3}{5} = \frac{\square}{10}$

5. $\frac{10}{12} = \frac{5}{\square}$

6. $\frac{4}{10} = \frac{\square}{5}$

7. $\frac{2}{6} = \frac{1}{\square}$

8. $\frac{6}{10} = \frac{\square}{5}$

Set C pages 309–316

Compare $\frac{5}{8}$ and $\frac{4}{10}$. Use benchmark fractions.

$\frac{1}{2}$

$\frac{1}{8}$ $\frac{1}{8}$ $\frac{1}{8}$ $\frac{1}{8}$ $\frac{1}{8}$

$\frac{5}{8} > \frac{1}{2}$

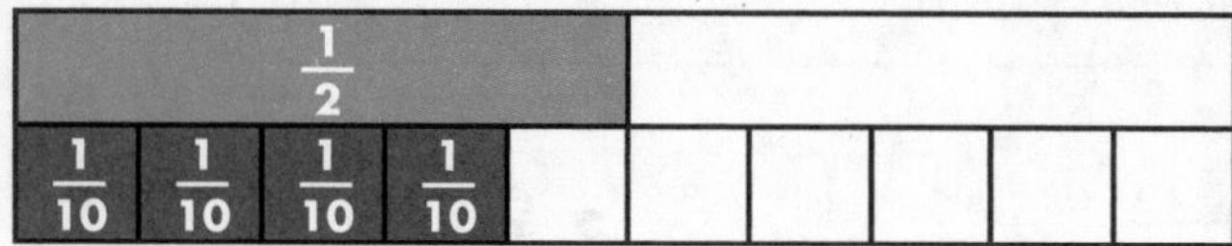

$\frac{4}{10} < \frac{1}{2}$

So, $\frac{5}{8} > \frac{4}{10}$.

Compare $\frac{4}{6}$ and $\frac{3}{4}$. Rename each fraction.

$\frac{4}{6} = \frac{4 \times 2}{6 \times 2} = \frac{8}{12}$ $\frac{3}{4} = \frac{3 \times 3}{4 \times 3} = \frac{9}{12}$

$\frac{8}{12}$ is less than $\frac{9}{12}$ so, $\frac{4}{6}$ is less than $\frac{3}{4}$.

Remember When the numerators of two fractions are the same, the fraction with the lesser denominator is greater.

Use benchmark fractions to compare. Write >, <, or = for each ○.

1. $\frac{5}{5}$ ○ $\frac{4}{6}$
2. $\frac{4}{8}$ ○ $\frac{1}{2}$
3. $\frac{5}{12}$ ○ $\frac{7}{8}$
4. $\frac{2}{3}$ ○ $\frac{4}{6}$

Compare. Write >, <, or = for each ○.

5. $\frac{3}{4}$ ○ $\frac{5}{8}$
6. $\frac{1}{5}$ ○ $\frac{2}{10}$
7. $\frac{2}{5}$ ○ $\frac{1}{4}$
8. $\frac{3}{6}$ ○ $\frac{3}{4}$
9. $\frac{2}{4}$ ○ $\frac{2}{3}$
10. $\frac{8}{10}$ ○ $\frac{4}{6}$

Set D pages 317–320

Think about these questions to help you **construct arguments.**

Thinking Habits

- How can I use numbers, objects, drawings, or actions to justify my argument?
- Am I using numbers and symbols correctly?
- Is my explanation clear and complete?

Remember you can use drawings and numbers to construct arguments.

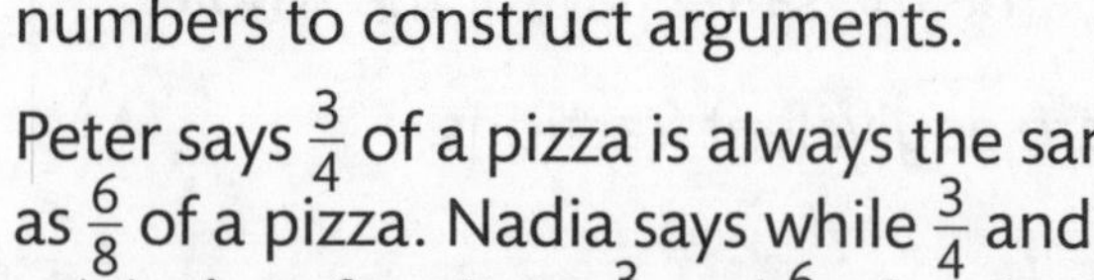

Peter says $\frac{3}{4}$ of a pizza is always the same as $\frac{6}{8}$ of a pizza. Nadia says while $\frac{3}{4}$ and $\frac{6}{8}$ are equivalent fractions, $\frac{3}{4}$ and $\frac{6}{8}$ of a pizza could represent different amounts.

1. Who is correct? Explain. Use a drawing to justify your argument.

2. Use a counterexample to explain who is correct.

Name ____________________

TOPIC 8

Assessment Practice

1. Draw a model to show that $\frac{3}{4} = \frac{6}{8}$.

2. Leslie will use more than $\frac{1}{2}$ cup but less than 1 whole cup of flour for a recipe. What fraction of a cup might Leslie use? Explain.

3. Jared has mowed $\frac{2}{5}$ of the yard. Abby says that Jared has mowed $\frac{4}{6}$ of the yard. Is Abby correct? Explain.

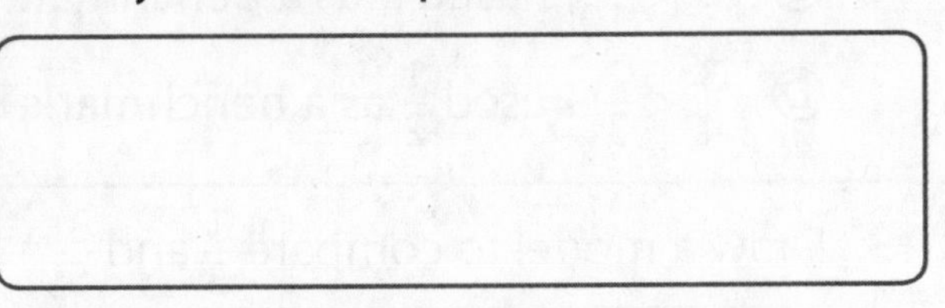

4. Explain how to use division to find an equivalent fraction for $\frac{9}{12}$.

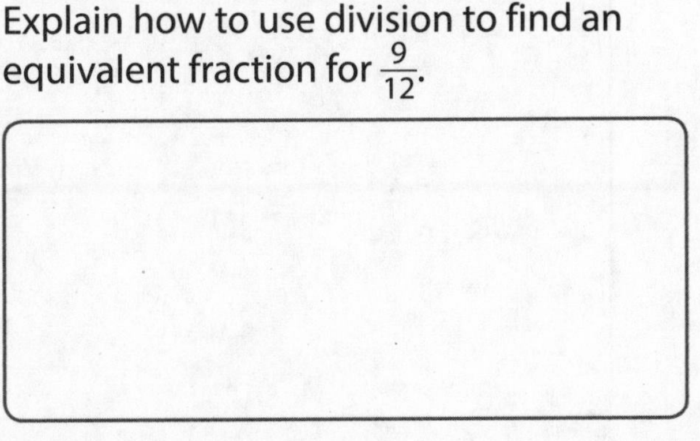

5. Write two fractions that are equivalent to $\frac{3}{6}$. Describe how you can show they are equivalent.

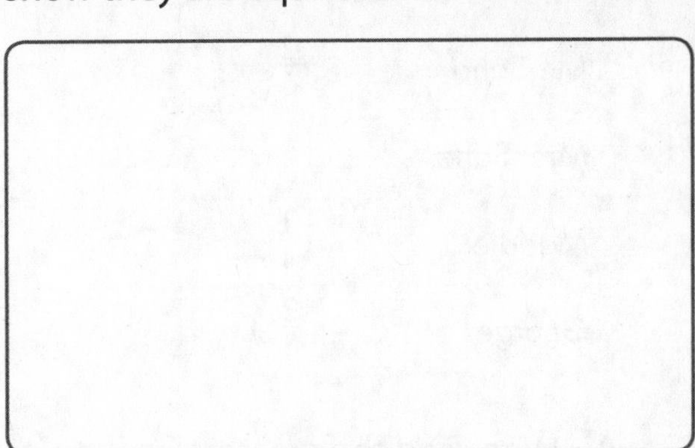

6. Compare the fractions to $\frac{1}{2}$. Write each fraction in the correct answer space.

Less Than $\frac{1}{2}$	Equal to $\frac{1}{2}$	Greater Than $\frac{1}{2}$

$\frac{5}{4}$	$\frac{5}{10}$	$\frac{2}{12}$
$\frac{6}{12}$	$\frac{3}{8}$	$\frac{2}{3}$

7. Sarah and Cole both ordered large subs for lunch. Sarah had $\frac{1}{2}$ of a sub and Cole had $\frac{2}{5}$ of a sub. Who ate more? Explain.

Ⓐ The subs are different sizes, so it is impossible to compare the fractions and tell who ate more.

Ⓑ Sarah ate more than Cole, as $\frac{2}{5} < \frac{1}{2}$.

Ⓒ Sarah's sub was bigger than Cole's, so Sarah ate more.

Ⓓ They ate the same amount because $\frac{1}{2}$ is the same as $\frac{2}{5}$.

8. The Sahas were reading a best-selling novel as a family. After the first week, they checked in with each other to see how much of the book each had read.

Fraction Read	
Mr. Saha	$\frac{2}{6}$
Mrs. Saha	$\frac{1}{3}$
Maddie	$\frac{3}{4}$
George	$\frac{2}{3}$

A. Who read the greatest fraction of the book?

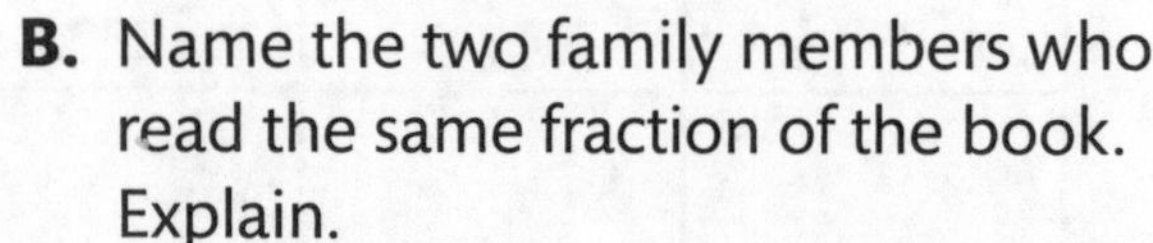

B. Name the two family members who read the same fraction of the book. Explain.

9. Johnny found a fraction equivalent to the one shown by the point on the number line. Which fraction could Johnny have found? Explain.

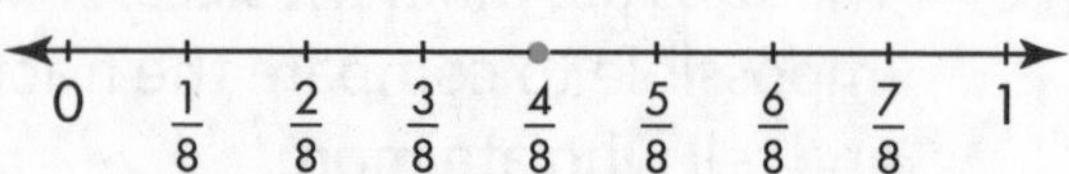

Ⓐ $\frac{1}{4}$; because $\frac{4 \div 2}{8 \div 2} = \frac{1}{4}$

Ⓑ $\frac{1}{8}$; because $\frac{4}{8} - \frac{3}{8} = \frac{1}{8}$

Ⓒ $\frac{1}{2}$; because $\frac{4 \div 4}{8 \div 4} = \frac{1}{2}$

Ⓓ $\frac{7}{8}$; because $\frac{4}{8} + \frac{3}{8} = \frac{7}{8}$

10. Bill and Gina each ate $\frac{1}{2}$ of their own pizza. Bill ate more pizza than Gina. Draw a picture and explain how that is possible.

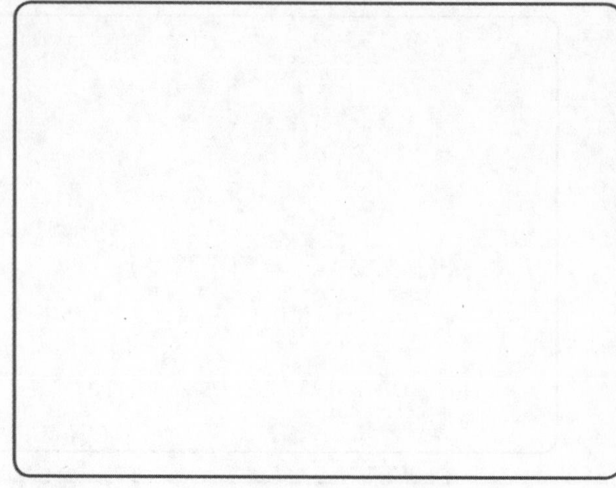

11. Order $\frac{5}{8}, \frac{1}{2}, \frac{2}{3}, \frac{2}{5}$ from least to greatest.

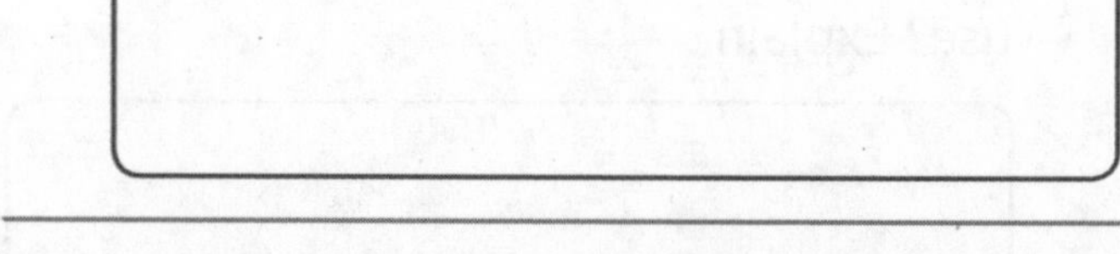

12. Only one of the comparisons below is correct. Which is correct? What benchmark was used to check your answer?

Ⓐ $\frac{2}{3} < \frac{1}{2}$; I used $\frac{1}{2}$ as a benchmark.

Ⓑ $\frac{1}{2} = \frac{3}{5}$; I used $\frac{1}{4}$ as a benchmark.

Ⓒ $\frac{2}{3} < \frac{9}{10}$; I used $\frac{3}{4}$ as a benchmark.

Ⓓ $\frac{3}{4} < \frac{2}{3}$; I used $\frac{1}{2}$ as a benchmark.

13. Draw a model to compare $\frac{1}{3}$ and $\frac{3}{5}$.

Name ____________________

TOPIC 8

Performance Task

Comparing Grasshoppers

Mrs. Rakin's class measured the lengths of some grasshoppers. The **Grasshopper Lengths** table shows the lengths they found.

Grasshopper Lengths

Grasshopper	Length (inch)
A	$\frac{5}{8}$
B	$\frac{3}{2}$
C	$\frac{7}{4}$
D	$\frac{7}{8}$
E	$\frac{3}{4}$
F	$\frac{3}{8}$

1. Mrs. Rakin asked the students to choose two grasshoppers and compare their lengths.

Part A

Henry used benchmark fractions to compare the lengths of grasshoppers A and C. Which grasshopper is longer? Explain.

Part B

Riley used a number line to compare the lengths of grasshoppers A and E. Which grasshopper is longer? Use the number line to show the comparison.

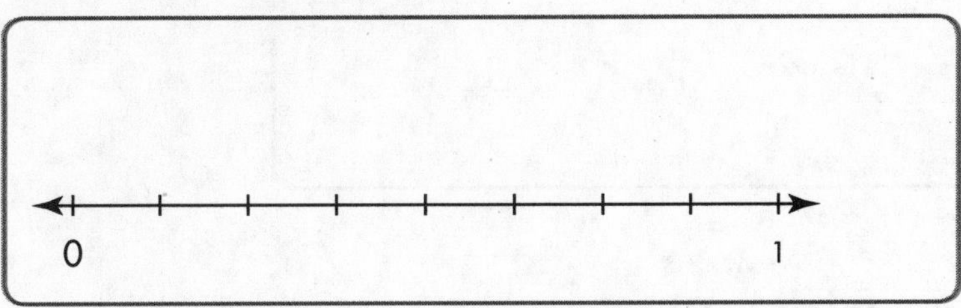

Part C

Jack compared the lengths of grasshoppers D and E. He said grasshopper D is longer. Is Jack correct? Justify the comparison using fraction strips.

2. One group of students measured the lengths of grasshoppers in centimeters, instead of inches. The **More Grasshopper Lengths** table shows the lengths they found.

More Grasshopper Lengths

Grasshopper	Length (centimeter)
G	$\frac{7}{10}$
H	$\frac{4}{5}$
I	$\frac{6}{10}$

Part A

Tommy compared the lengths of grasshoppers G and H. Which grasshopper is longer? Explain how to rename the fractions using multiplication so they have the same denominator to compare.

Part B

Venon compared the lengths of grasshoppers H and I. Which grasshopper is longer? Explain how to rename the fractions using division so they have the same denominator to compare.

Part C

Rina wants to determine if grasshopper D is longer or shorter than grasshopper G. Explain how Rina can compare the fractions.

TOPIC 9 Understand Addition and Subtraction of Fractions

Essential Questions: How do you add and subtract fractions and mixed numbers with like denominators? How can fractions be added and subtracted on a number line?

Digital Resources

Interactive Student Edition, Activity, Visual Learning, Video, Practice, Assessment, Games, Tools, Glossary

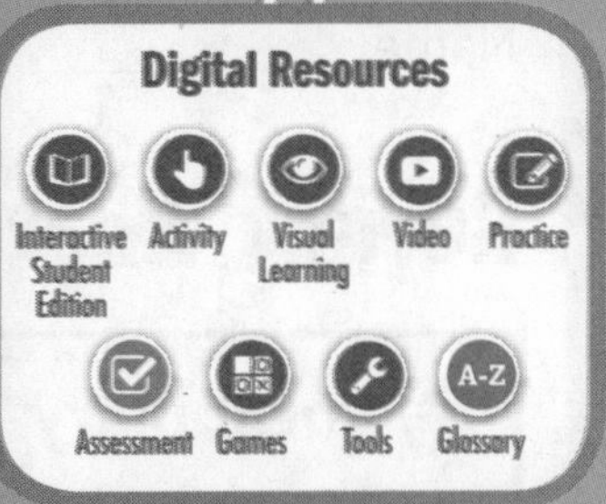

Morse code uses a special machine to transfer information using a series of tones.
A combination of dots and dashes stands for each letter, each number, and even some whole words.
How do you write, "I love math," using Morse code? Here is a project about fractions and information.

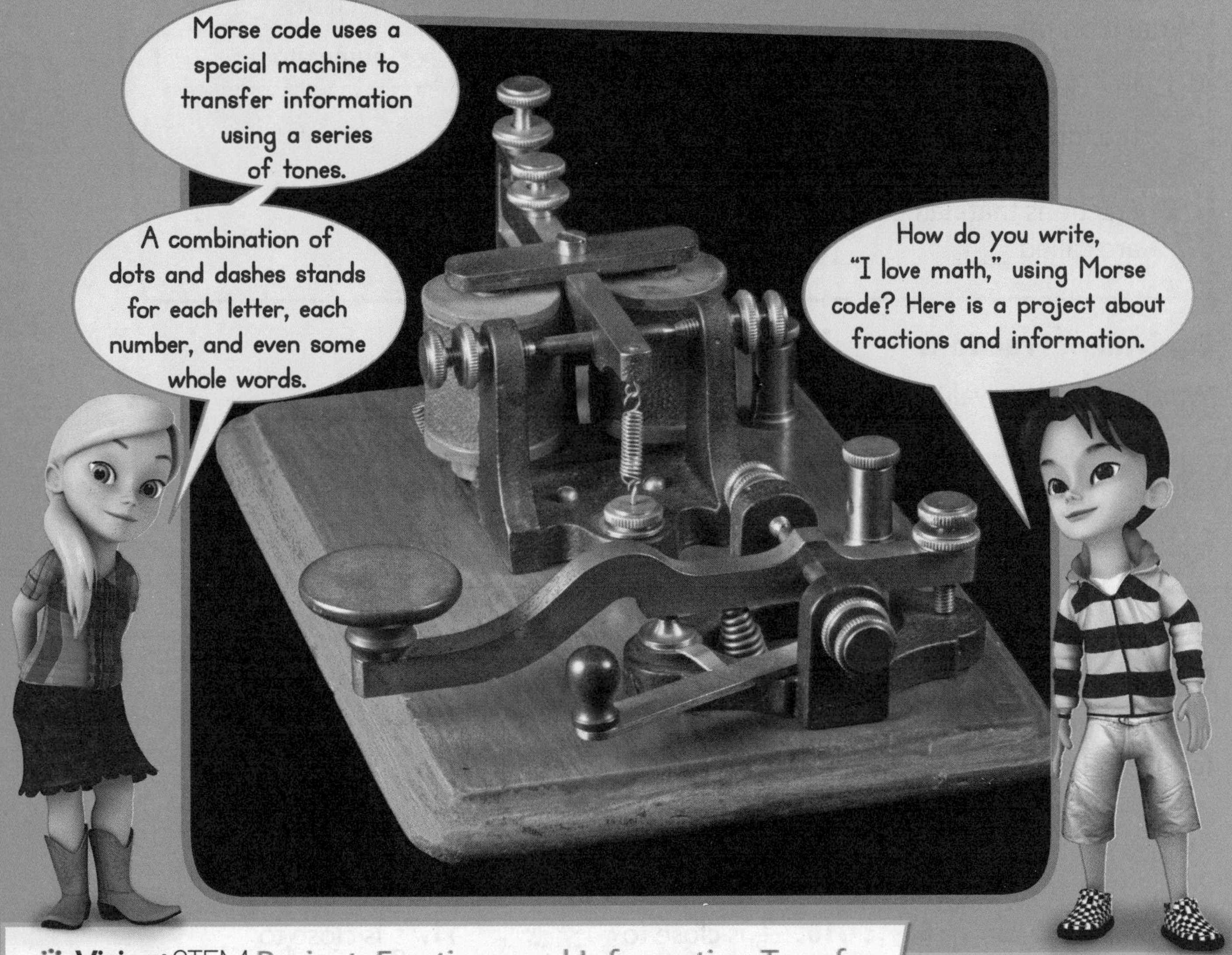

enVision® STEM Project: Fractions and Information Transfer

Do Research Morse code uses patterns to transfer information. Any word can be written using Morse code. Use the Internet or other sources to find how to write *fourth*, *grade*, and *school* using Morse code.

Journal: Write a Report Include what you found. Also in your report:

- Write *one* in Morse code. Write a fraction that tells what part of the code for *one* is dashes.
- Write *three* in Morse code. Write a fraction that tells what part of the code for *three* is dots.
- Write and solve an equation to find how much greater the fraction for dots is than the fraction for dashes in the word *three*.

Name ______________________________

Review What You Know

Vocabulary

Choose the best term from the box. Write it on the blank.

- benchmark fractions
- equivalent fractions
- denominator
- numerator

1. In $\frac{2}{3}$, 2 is the ______________ of the fraction and 3 is the ______________ of the fraction.

2. Fractions that name the same region or part of a segment are called ______________.

Equivalent Fractions

Write the missing values to show pairs of equivalent fractions.

3. $\frac{2}{3} = \frac{\square}{6}$

4. $\frac{\square}{4} = \frac{3}{12}$

5. $\frac{6}{5} = \frac{\square}{10}$

6. $\frac{1}{2} = \frac{50}{\square}$

7. $\frac{1}{5} = \frac{\square}{10}$

8. $\frac{3}{\square} = \frac{30}{100}$

Benchmark Fractions

Use the number line to find a benchmark fraction or whole number for each given fraction.

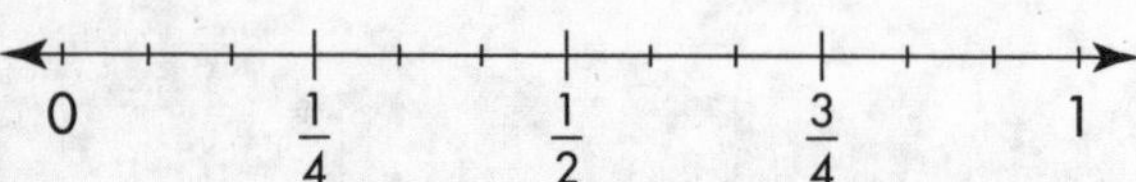

9. $\frac{11}{12}$ is close to ________.

10. $\frac{8}{12}$ is close to ________.

11. $\frac{2}{6}$ is close to ________.

Problem Solving

12. Adult admission to the dog show is \$16. Children's admission is \$9. How much would it cost 3 adults and 2 children to enter the dog show?

13. Meg saved coins she found for a year. She found a total of 95 pennies, 13 nickels, 41 dimes, and 11 quarters. She would like to evenly divide the coins into 4 piggy banks. How many coins will go in each piggy bank?

Name ______________________________

How do you follow a recipe?

Project: Exploring Recipes

Would you like to be a code breaker?

Project: Create a Fraction Code

What is a farmers' market?

Project: Write and Perform a Skit

3-ACT MATH PREVIEW

Math Modeling

Just Add Water

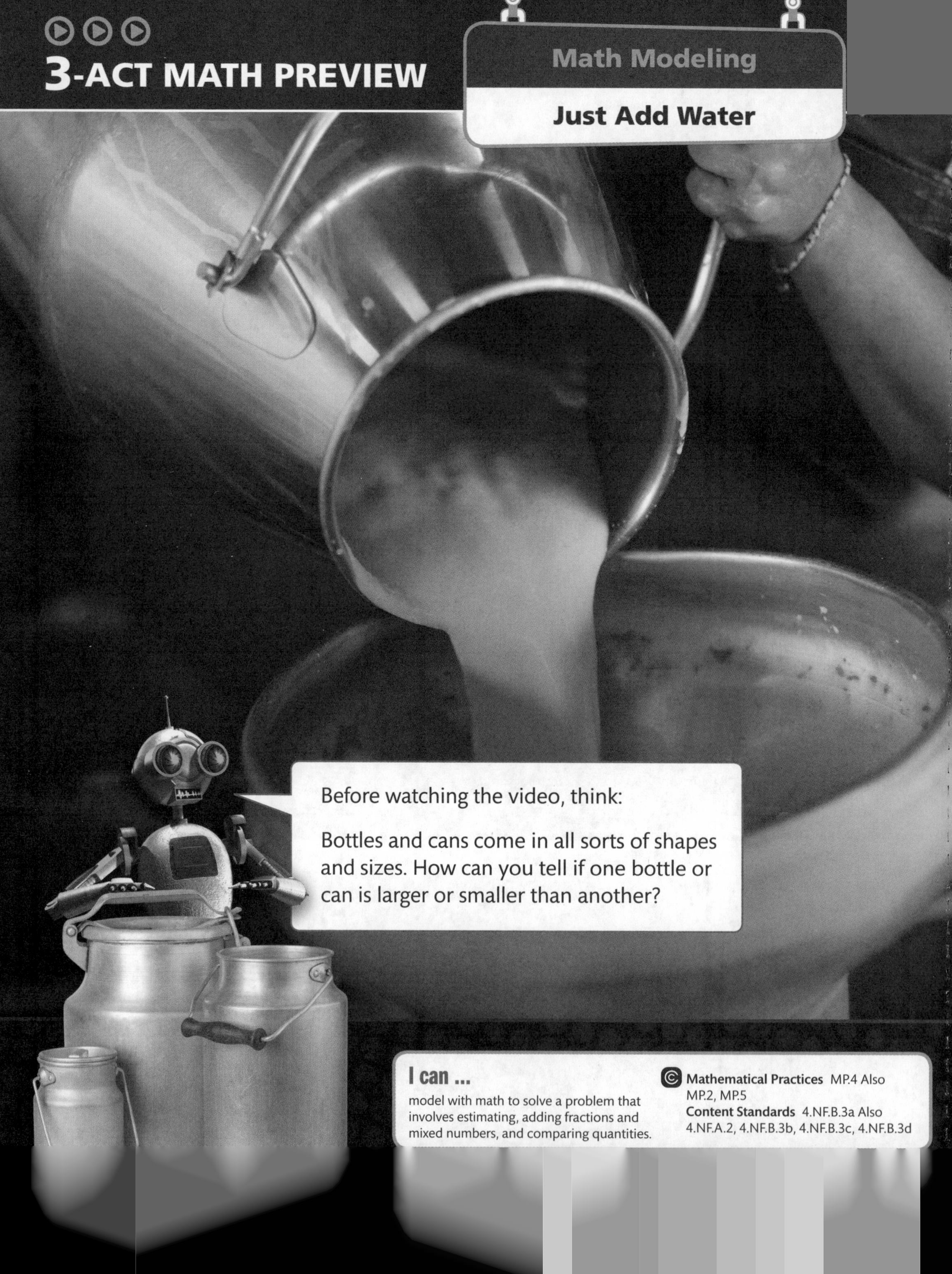

Before watching the video, think:
Bottles and cans come in all sorts of shapes and sizes. How can you tell if one bottle or can is larger or smaller than another?

I can ...

model with math to solve a problem that involves estimating, adding fractions and mixed numbers, and comparing quantities.

Mathematical Practices MP.4 Also MP.2, MP.5
Content Standards 4.NF.B.3a Also 4.NF.A.2, 4.NF.B.3b, 4.NF.B.3c, 4.NF.B.3d

Name ____________________

Activity

Lesson 9-1
Model Addition of Fractions

I can ...
use tools such as fraction strips or area models to add fractions.

Content Standards 4.NF.B.3a Also 4.NF.B.3d
Mathematical Practices MP.1, MP.5

Solve & Share Kyle and Jillian are working on a sports banner. They painted $\frac{3}{8}$ of the banner green and $\frac{4}{8}$ purple. How much of the banner have they painted? ***Solve this problem any way you choose.***

You can use drawings, area models, or fraction strips to solve this problem. *Show your work in the space below!*

Look Back! Use Appropriate Tools Kyle says $\frac{1}{8} + \frac{1}{8} + \frac{1}{8} = \frac{3}{8}$. Jillian says $\frac{1}{8} + \frac{1}{8} + \frac{1}{8} = \frac{3}{24}$. Use a tool to decide who is correct and explain.

How Can You Use Tools to Add Fractions?

A

Ten canoeing teams are racing downriver. Five teams have silver canoes and two teams have brown canoes. What fraction of the canoes are either silver or brown?

You can **use tools** such as fraction strips to add two or more fractions.

B

Find $\frac{5}{10} + \frac{2}{10}$. Use five $\frac{1}{10}$ fraction strips to show $\frac{5}{10}$ and two $\frac{1}{10}$ strips to show $\frac{2}{10}$.

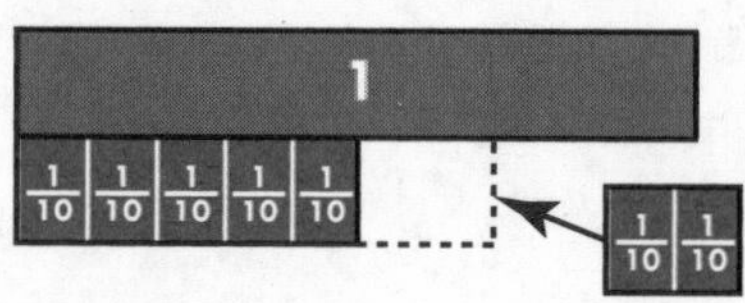

Five $\frac{1}{10}$ strips joined with two $\frac{1}{10}$ strips are seven $\frac{1}{10}$ strips.

Add the numerators. Then write the sum over the like denominator.

$$\frac{5}{10} + \frac{2}{10} = \frac{7}{10}$$

C

Find $\frac{5}{10} + \frac{2}{10}$. Mark five $\frac{1}{10}$ segments to show $\frac{5}{10}$ and two $\frac{1}{10}$ segments to show $\frac{2}{10}$.

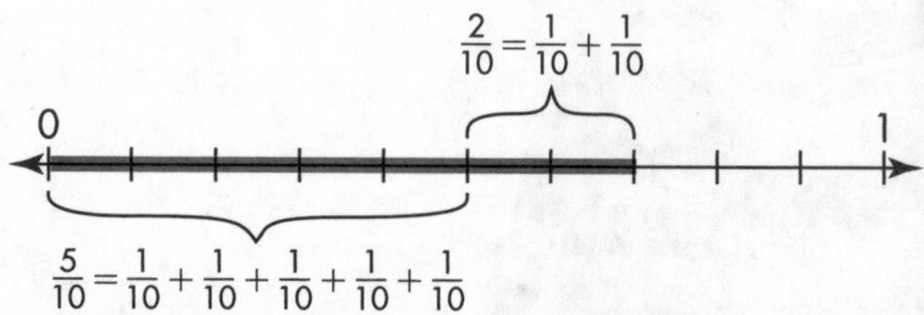

Adding $\frac{5}{10}$ and $\frac{2}{10}$ means joining five $\frac{1}{10}$ segments and two $\frac{1}{10}$ segments.

$\frac{7}{10}$ of the canoes are either silver or brown.

Convince Me! **Make Sense and Persevere** What two fractions would you add to find the fraction of the canoes that are either green or brown? What is the sum? How do you know your sum is correct?

Name ____________________

Guided Practice

Do You Understand?

1. In the problem on the previous page, would you get the same answer if you used an area model instead of fraction strips or a number line? Explain.

2. What two fractions are being added below? What is the sum?

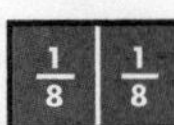

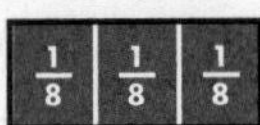

Do You Know How?

For **3–4**, find each sum.

3. $\frac{2}{5} + \frac{1}{5}$

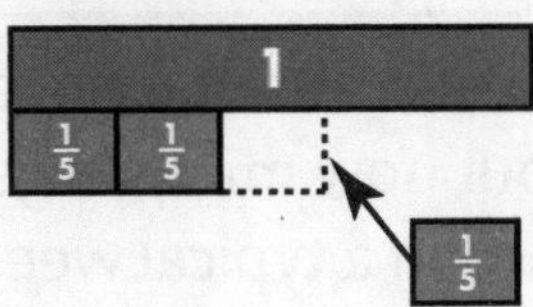

4. $\frac{1}{6} + \frac{1}{6}$

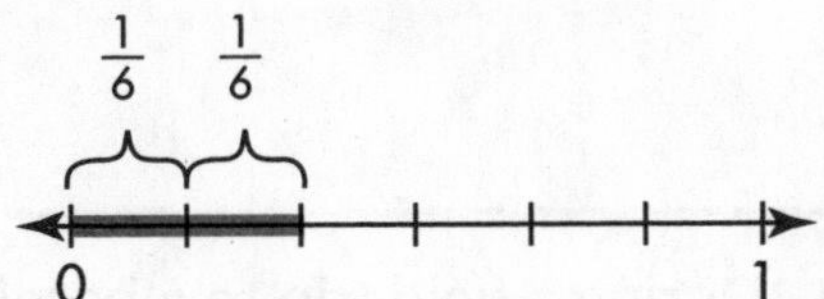

Independent Practice

Leveled Practice For **5–16**, find each sum. Use a tool as needed.

5. $\frac{3}{12} + \frac{4}{12}$

6. $\frac{4}{10} + \frac{1}{10}$

7. $\frac{2}{12} + \frac{4}{12}$

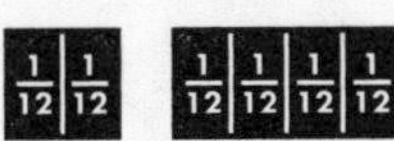

8. $\frac{1}{6} + \frac{2}{6} + \frac{3}{6}$

$\frac{1}{6}$ $\quad \frac{3}{6} = \frac{1}{6} + \frac{1}{6} + \frac{1}{6}$

0 1

$\frac{2}{6} = \frac{1}{6} + \frac{1}{6}$

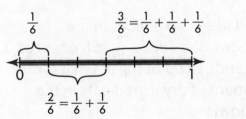

9. $\frac{1}{4} + \frac{2}{4}$

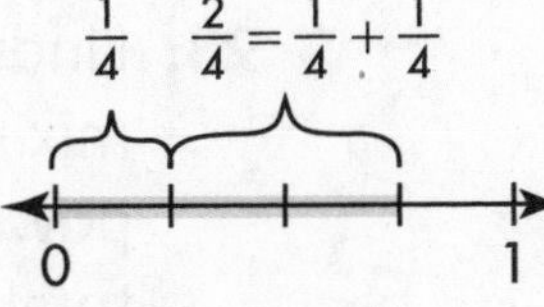

10. $\frac{1}{3} + \frac{1}{3}$

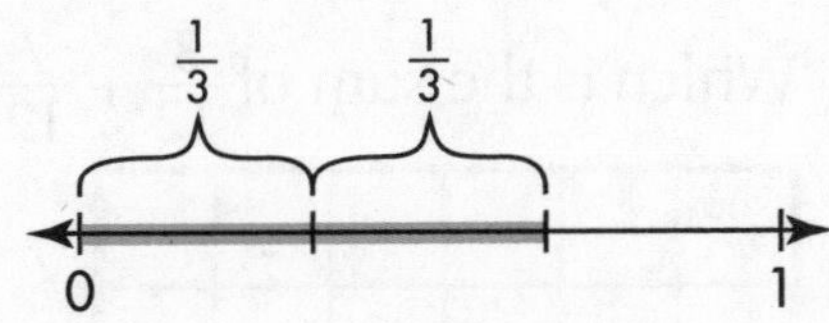

11. $\frac{5}{8} + \frac{1}{8}$

12. $\frac{1}{4} + \frac{3}{4}$

13. $\frac{7}{12} + \frac{2}{12}$

14. $\frac{1}{4} + \frac{1}{4}$

15. $\frac{2}{5} + \frac{2}{5}$

16. $\frac{1}{10} + \frac{2}{10} + \frac{1}{10}$

Problem Solving

17. Number Sense Using three different numerators, write an equation in which three fractions, when added, have a sum of 1.

18. Use Appropriate Tools Diane added $\frac{3}{8}$ to $\frac{1}{8}$. Draw a picture to show $\frac{1}{8} + \frac{3}{8} = \frac{4}{8}$.

19. A bakery sells about 9 dozen bagels per day. About how many bagels does the bakery sell in a typical week? Explain.

20. During a field trip to a baseball game, $\frac{3}{8}$ of the students are wearing red caps and $\frac{3}{8}$ are wearing blue caps. Write and solve an equation to find the number of students, *s*, who are wearing red or blue caps.

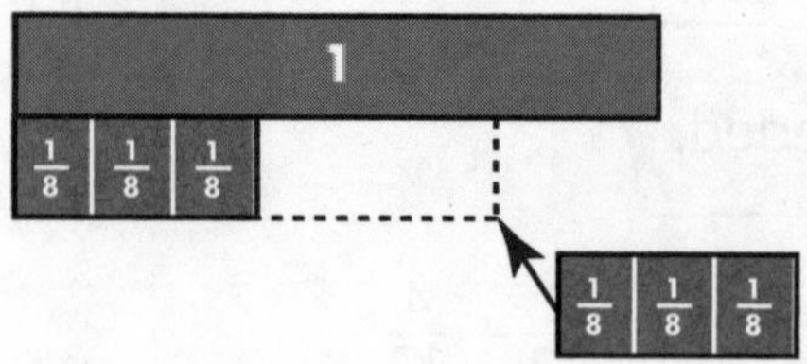

21. Higher Order Thinking Terry ran $\frac{1}{10}$ of the distance from school to home. He walked $\frac{3}{10}$ more of the distance and then skipped $\frac{2}{10}$ more of the distance. What fraction of the distance home does Terry still have to go?

Look back to see if you answered the question that was asked.

Assessment Practice

22. Which is the sum of $\frac{3}{12} + \frac{7}{12}$?

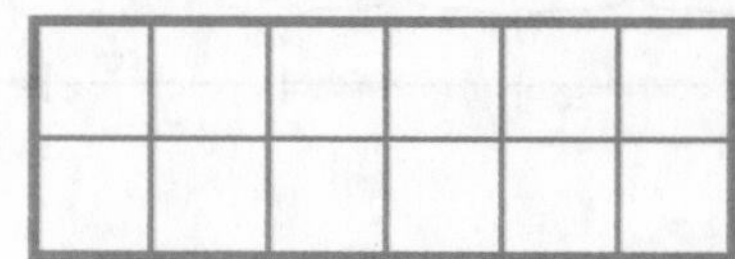

Ⓐ $\frac{11}{12}$

Ⓑ $\frac{10}{12}$

Ⓒ $\frac{8}{12}$

Ⓓ $\frac{10}{24}$

23. Lindsay had $\frac{5}{10}$ cup of flour in the mixing bowl. She added $\frac{2}{10}$ cup of cocoa powder and $\frac{3}{10}$ cup of sugar. What is the total amount of dry ingredients in the mixing bowl?

Ⓐ 1 cup

Ⓑ $\frac{7}{10}$

Ⓒ $\frac{5}{10}$

Ⓓ $\frac{1}{10}$

Name ______________________

Lesson 9-2
Decompose Fractions

I can ...
use number lines, area models, or drawings to decompose fractions.

Content Standard 4.NF.B.3b
Mathematical Practices MP.4, MP.5

Solve & Share

Karyn has $\frac{11}{8}$ pounds of chili to put into three bowls. The amount of chili in each bowl does not have to be the same. How much chili could Karyn put into each bowl? ***Solve this problem any way you choose.***

How can you model the amount of chili Karyn puts in each bowl? *Show your work in the space below!*

Look Back! Use a drawing or fraction strips to help write equivalent fractions for the amount of chili in one of the bowls.

How Can You Represent a Fraction in a Variety of Ways?

Visual Learning Bridge

A

Charlene wants to leave $\frac{1}{6}$ of her garden empty. What are some different ways Charlene can plant the rest of her garden?

Decompose means to break into parts. Compose means to combine parts. The fraction of the garden that Charlene will plant can be decomposed in more than one way.

B

One Way

Charlene could plant four $\frac{1}{6}$ sections with blue flowers and one $\frac{1}{6}$ section with red peppers.

$\frac{5}{6}$ is $\frac{4}{6}$ and $\frac{1}{6}$.

$$\frac{5}{6} = \frac{4}{6} + \frac{1}{6}$$

C

Another Way

Charlene could plant one $\frac{1}{6}$ section with green beans, one $\frac{1}{6}$ section with yellow squash, one $\frac{1}{6}$ section with red peppers, and two $\frac{1}{6}$ sections with blue flowers.

$\frac{5}{6}$ is $\frac{1}{6}$ and $\frac{1}{6}$ and $\frac{1}{6}$ and $\frac{2}{6}$.

$$\frac{5}{6} = \frac{1}{6} + \frac{1}{6} + \frac{1}{6} + \frac{2}{6}$$

Convince Me! **Use Appropriate Tools** Draw pictures or use fraction strips to show why these equations are true.

$\frac{5}{6} = \frac{3}{6} + \frac{2}{6}$ $\frac{5}{6} = \frac{1}{6} + \frac{2}{6} + \frac{2}{6}$

Name ______________________________

Another Example!

What is one way you can decompose $3\frac{1}{8}$?

$3\frac{1}{8}$ is 1 whole + 1 whole + 1 whole + $\frac{1}{8}$.

A mixed number has a whole number part and a fraction part.

Each whole can also be shown as eight equal parts.

$3\frac{1}{8} = 1 + 1 + 1 + \frac{1}{8}$

$3\frac{1}{8} = \frac{8}{8} + \frac{8}{8} + \frac{8}{8} + \frac{1}{8}$

Guided Practice

Do You Understand?

1. What is another way to decompose $3\frac{1}{8}$?

2. Look at the area model above. What fraction with a greater numerator than denominator is equivalent to $3\frac{1}{8}$? Explain.

Do You Know How?

For **3–4**, decompose each fraction or mixed number in two different ways. Use a tool if needed.

3. $\frac{3}{5} = \frac{\square}{\square} + \frac{\square}{\square}$ $\frac{3}{5} = \frac{\square}{\square} + \frac{\square}{\square} + \frac{\square}{\square}$

4. $1\frac{3}{4} = 1 + \frac{\square}{\square}$ $1\frac{3}{4} = \frac{\square}{\square} + \frac{\square}{\square}$

Independent Practice

Leveled Practice For **5–10**, decompose each fraction or mixed number in two different ways. Use a tool if needed.

5. $\frac{4}{6} =$ $\frac{4}{6} =$

6. $\frac{7}{8} =$ $\frac{7}{8} =$

7. $1\frac{3}{5} =$ $1\frac{3}{5} =$

8. $2\frac{1}{2} =$ $2\frac{1}{2} =$

9. $\frac{9}{12} =$ $\frac{9}{12} =$

10. $1\frac{1}{3} =$ $1\frac{1}{3} =$

Problem Solving

11. Jackie ate $\frac{1}{5}$ of a bag of popcorn. She shared the rest with Enrique. List three ways they could have shared the remaining popcorn.

12. Use Appropriate Tools Draw an area model to show $\frac{4}{10} + \frac{3}{10} + \frac{2}{10} = \frac{9}{10}$.

13. In a class of 12 students, 8 students are boys. Write two equivalent fractions that tell which part of the class is boys.

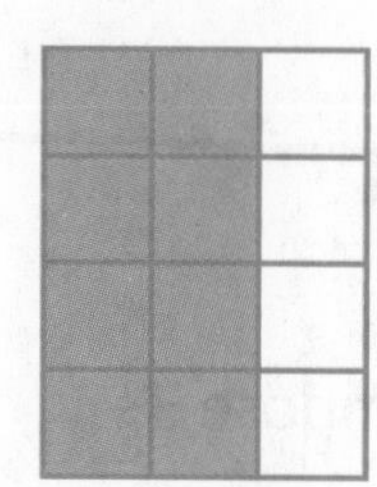

The area model shows 12 sections. Each section is $\frac{1}{12}$ of the class.

14. Use Appropriate Tools Find three different ways to decompose $1\frac{5}{6}$. Use number lines to justify your answer.

15. Higher Order Thinking Jason wrote $1\frac{1}{3}$ as the sum of three fractions. None of the fractions had a denominator of 3. What fractions might Jason have used?

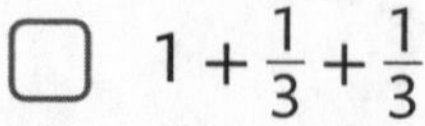

Assessment Practice

16. A teacher distributes a stack of paper to 3 groups. Each group receives a different amount of paper. Select all the ways the teacher can distribute the paper by decomposing $1\frac{2}{3}$ inches. Use a fraction model if needed.

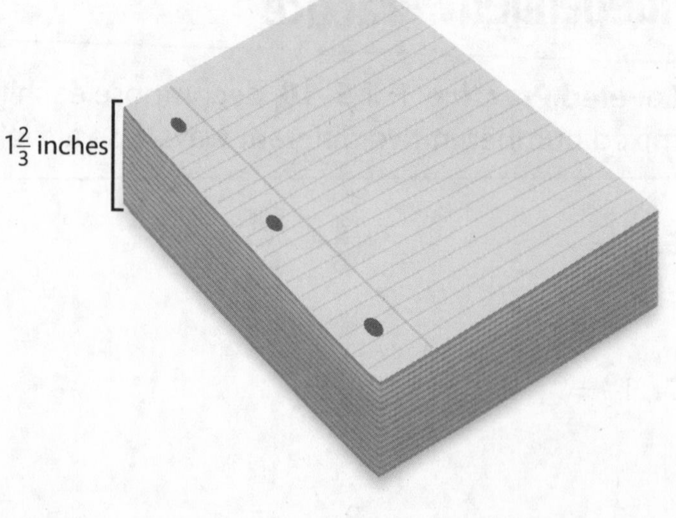

- ☐ $1 + \frac{1}{3} + \frac{1}{3}$
- ☐ $\frac{2}{3} + \frac{1}{3} + \frac{1}{3}$
- ☐ $\frac{2}{3} + \frac{2}{3} + \frac{1}{3}$
- ☐ $\frac{1}{3} + \frac{1}{3} + \frac{1}{3} + \frac{1}{3} + \frac{1}{3}$
- ☐ $1 + \frac{2}{3}$

Name ______________________________ Activity

Lesson 9-3
Add Fractions with Like Denominators

I can ...
use my understanding of addition as joining parts of the same whole to add fractions with like denominators.

Content Standards 4.NF.B.3a Also 4.NF.B.3d
Mathematical Practices MP.3, MP.4, MP.7

Solve & Share

Jonas is making nachos and tacos for a family party. He uses $\frac{2}{5}$ bag of shredded cheese for the nachos and $\frac{1}{5}$ bag for the tacos. How much of the bag of shredded cheese does Jonas use? ***Solve this problem any way you choose.***

What equation can you write to represent this problem?
Shredded Cheese

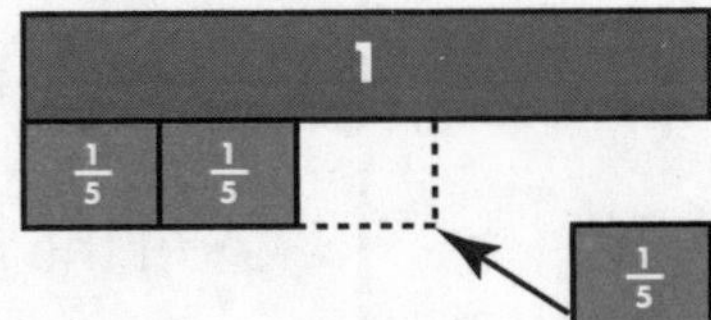
1
$\frac{1}{5}$
$\frac{1}{5}$
$\frac{1}{5}$

Look Back! Look for Relationships What do you notice about the denominators in your equation?

How Can You Add Fractions with Like Denominators?

Visual Learning Bridge

A

The table shows the results of a fourth-grade Pets Club survey. What fraction of the club members chose a hamster or a dog as their favorite pet?

Add the fractions for hamsters and dogs to find the result.

DATA

Favorite Pet	
Cat	$\frac{5}{12}$
Dog	$\frac{4}{12}$
Hamster	$\frac{2}{12}$
Parrot	$\frac{1}{12}$

B Find $\frac{2}{12} + \frac{4}{12}$ using a model.

$\frac{4}{12} = \frac{1}{12} + \frac{1}{12} + \frac{1}{12} + \frac{1}{12}$

0 ... 1

$\frac{2}{12} = \frac{1}{12} + \frac{1}{12}$

$$\frac{2}{12} + \frac{4}{12} = \underbrace{\frac{1}{12} + \frac{1}{12}}_{2} + \underbrace{\frac{1}{12} + \frac{1}{12} + \frac{1}{12} + \frac{1}{12}}_{4} = \frac{6}{12}$$

C Find $\frac{2}{12} + \frac{4}{12}$ by joining parts.

Add the numerators. Write the sum over the like denominator.

$$\frac{2}{12} + \frac{4}{12} = \frac{2+4}{12} = \frac{6}{12}$$

Convince Me! **Critique Reasoning** Frank solved the problem above and found $\frac{2}{12} + \frac{4}{12} = \frac{6}{24}$. What error did Frank make? Explain.

Name ______________________________

Another Example!

Find $\frac{4}{5} + \frac{3}{5}$.

$$\frac{4}{5} + \frac{3}{5} = \overbrace{\frac{1}{5} + \frac{1}{5} + \frac{1}{5} + \frac{1}{5}}^{4} + \overbrace{\frac{1}{5} + \frac{1}{5} + \frac{1}{5}}^{3} = \frac{7}{5}$$

Write the fraction as a mixed number. $\frac{7}{5} = \frac{5}{5} + \frac{2}{5} = 1\frac{2}{5}$

You can write the sum as a fraction or a mixed number.

Guided Practice

Do You Understand?

1. Using the survey on the previous page, what fraction of the club members chose either a bird or a cat?

2. Greg found $\frac{1}{3} + \frac{2}{3} = \frac{3}{6}$. What error did Greg make?

Do You Know How?

For **3–6**, find each sum. Use drawings or fraction strips as needed.

3. $\frac{2}{4} + \frac{1}{4}$

4. $\frac{1}{3} + \frac{2}{3}$

5. $\frac{2}{12} + \frac{11}{12}$

6. $\frac{1}{10} + \frac{4}{10}$

Independent Practice

For **7–18**, find each sum. Use drawings or fraction strips as needed.

7. $\frac{2}{8} + \frac{1}{8}$

8. $\frac{3}{6} + \frac{2}{6}$

9. $\frac{1}{8} + \frac{4}{8}$

10. $\frac{3}{10} + \frac{2}{10}$

11. $\frac{3}{10} + \frac{5}{10}$

12. $\frac{5}{12} + \frac{4}{12}$

13. $\frac{4}{5} + \frac{3}{5} + \frac{2}{5}$

14. $\frac{3}{10} + \frac{2}{10} + \frac{6}{10}$

15. $\frac{2}{6} + \frac{5}{6}$

16. $\frac{3}{6} + \frac{9}{6}$

17. $\frac{11}{10} + \frac{11}{10}$

18. $\frac{7}{8} + \frac{1}{8}$

Problem Solving

For **19–21**, use the table at the right.

19. What fraction of the set is either triangles or rectangles?

20. **Model with Math** Write and solve an equation to find what fraction, f, of the set is either circles or rectangles.

21. Which two shapes make up half of the set? Find two possible answers.

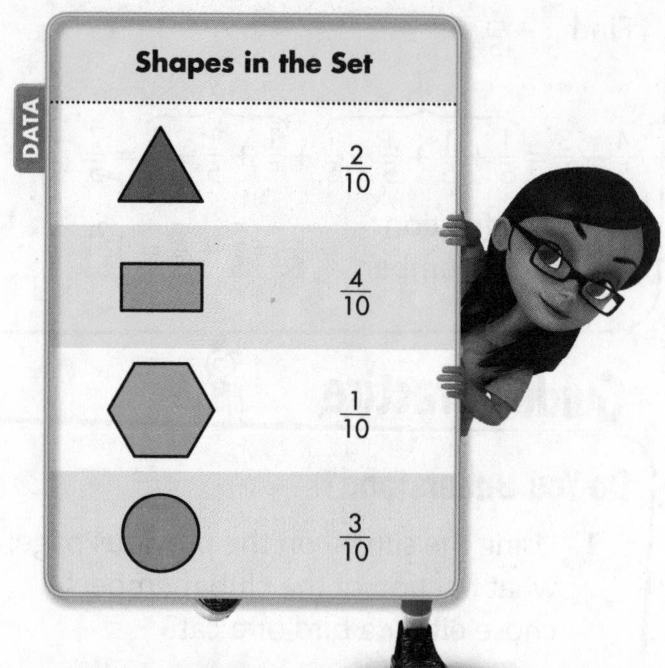

22. There are 64 crayons in each box. A school bought 25 boxes of crayons for the art classes. If the crayons are shared equally among 5 classes, how many crayons will each class receive? Explain.

23. **Higher Order Thinking** Three-tenths of Ken's buttons are blue, $\frac{4}{10}$ are green, and the rest are black. What fraction of Ken's buttons are black?

Assessment Practice

24. Match each expression with its sum.

	$\frac{6}{10}$	$\frac{7}{10}$	$\frac{9}{10}$	$1\frac{1}{10}$
$\frac{3}{10}+\frac{4}{10}$	☐	☐	☐	☐
$\frac{1}{10}+\frac{5}{10}$	☐	☐	☐	☐
$\frac{8}{10}+\frac{3}{10}$	☐	☐	☐	☐
$\frac{2}{10}+\frac{1}{10}+\frac{6}{10}$	☐	☐	☐	☐

25. Jayla did some chores in the morning. She did $\frac{3}{12}$ of her chores in the evening. By the end of the day, she had completed $\frac{7}{12}$ of her chores. What fraction of the chores c, did Jayla do in the morning?

Ⓐ $c=\frac{1}{12}$

Ⓑ $c=\frac{2}{12}$

Ⓒ $c=\frac{3}{12}$

Ⓓ $c=\frac{4}{12}$

Name ____________________

Lesson 9-4
Model Subtraction of Fractions

I can ...
use tools such as fraction strips or area models to subtract fractions with like denominators.

Content Standards 4.NF.B.3a Also 4.NF.B.3d
Mathematical Practices MP.4, MP.5, MP.6

Solve & Share

Mr. Yetkin uses $\frac{4}{6}$ of a sheet of plywood to board up a window. How much of the plywood is left? ***Solve this problem any way you choose.***

You can select tools such as fraction strips, drawings, or area models to solve this problem. *Show your work in the space below!*

Look Back! **Be Precise** Explain why $\frac{4}{6}$ is subtracted from $\frac{6}{6}$ to find how much of the plywood is left.

How Can You Use Tools to Subtract Fractions?

A

A flower garden is divided into eighths. If $\frac{2}{8}$ of the garden is used to grow yellow roses, what fraction is left to grow other flowers?

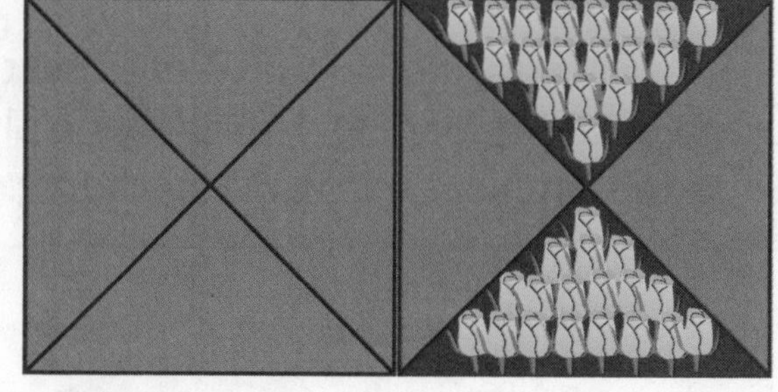

You can use tools such as fraction strips to represent subtraction.

B

One Way

Find $\frac{8}{8} - \frac{2}{8}$.

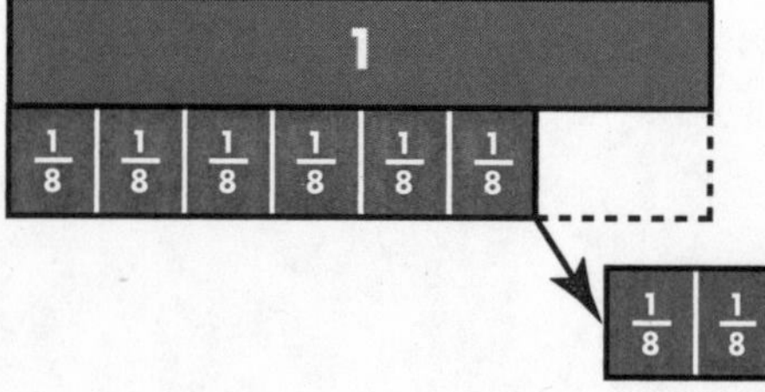

$\frac{8}{8} = \frac{1}{8} + \frac{1}{8} + \frac{1}{8} + \frac{1}{8} + \frac{1}{8} + \frac{1}{8} + \frac{1}{8} + \frac{1}{8}$

$\frac{2}{8} = \frac{1}{8} + \frac{1}{8}$

Separating the $\frac{2}{8}$ from $\frac{8}{8}$ leaves $\frac{6}{8}$.

$\frac{8}{8} - \frac{2}{8} = \frac{1}{8} + \frac{1}{8} + \frac{1}{8} + \frac{1}{8} + \frac{1}{8} + \frac{1}{8} + \cancel{\frac{1}{8}} + \cancel{\frac{1}{8}}$

$\frac{8}{8} - \frac{2}{8} = \frac{6}{8}$

C

Another Way

Find $\frac{8}{8} - \frac{2}{8}$.

$\frac{8}{8} = \frac{1}{8} + \frac{1}{8} + \frac{1}{8} + \frac{1}{8} + \frac{1}{8} + \frac{1}{8} + \frac{1}{8} + \frac{1}{8}$

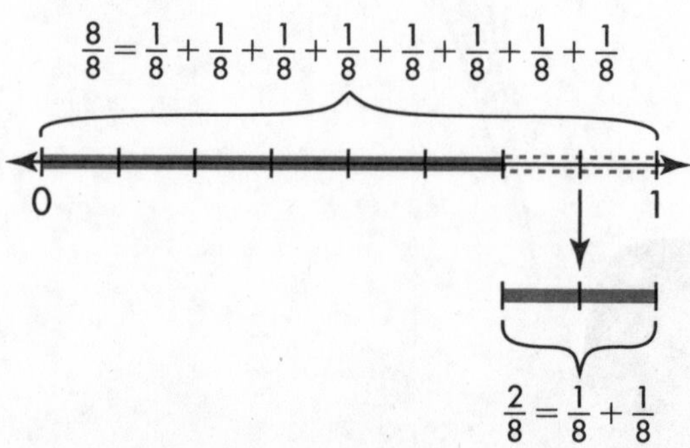

$\frac{2}{8} = \frac{1}{8} + \frac{1}{8}$

Separating the $\frac{2}{8}$ from $\frac{8}{8}$ leaves $\frac{6}{8}$.

$\frac{8}{8} - \frac{2}{8} = \frac{1}{8} + \frac{1}{8} + \frac{1}{8} + \frac{1}{8} + \frac{1}{8} + \cancel{\frac{1}{8}} + \cancel{\frac{1}{8}} + \frac{1}{8}$

$\frac{8}{8} - \frac{2}{8} = \frac{6}{8}$

Six eighths of the garden is left to grow other flowers.

Convince Me! **Use Appropriate Tools** In the problem above, suppose six sections of the garden are used for yellow roses and two other sections are used for petunias. How much more of the garden is used for yellow roses than is used for petunias? Use fraction strips or another tool to help. Write your answer as a fraction.

Name ____________________

Another Example!

Find $\frac{11}{8} - \frac{2}{8}$.

Use eleven $\frac{1}{8}$-fraction strips to show $\frac{11}{8}$. Take 2 strips away.

$\frac{11}{8} - \frac{2}{8} = \frac{9}{8}$

$\frac{9}{8} = \frac{8}{8} + \frac{1}{8} = 1\frac{1}{8}$

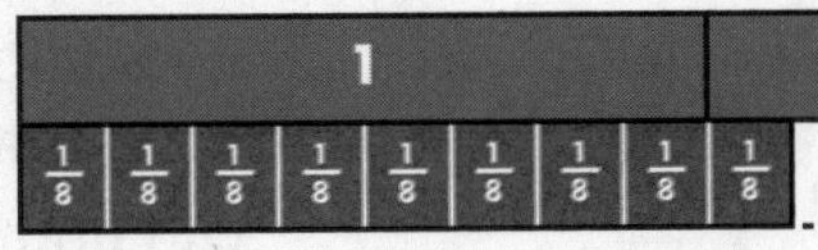

You can write the difference as a fraction or a mixed number.

Guided Practice

Do You Understand?

1. In the problem at the top of the previous page, suppose one other $\frac{1}{8}$ section was used to grow peonies. What fraction of the garden is now available for flowers?

Do You Know How?

For **2–5**, use fraction strips or other tools to subtract.

2. $\frac{1}{3} - \frac{1}{3}$

3. $\frac{5}{5} - \frac{2}{5}$

4. $\frac{7}{12} - \frac{3}{12}$

5. $\frac{7}{8} - \frac{1}{8}$

Independent Practice

Leveled Practice For **6–14**, find each difference. Use fraction strips or other tools as needed.

6. $\frac{11}{12} - \frac{5}{12}$

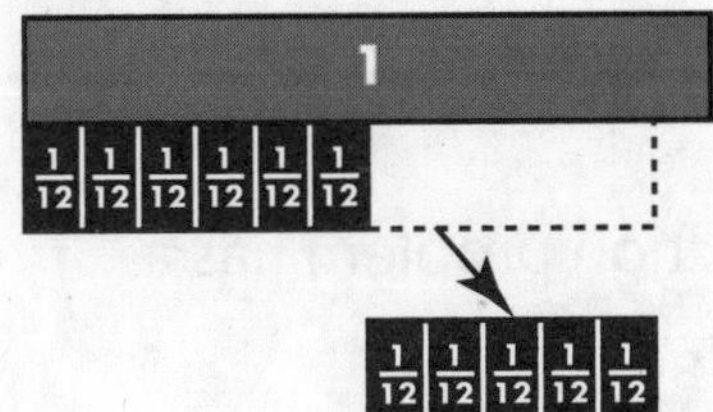

7. $\frac{2}{2} - \frac{1}{2}$

$\frac{2}{2} = \frac{1}{2} + \frac{1}{2}$

0 1

$\frac{1}{2}$

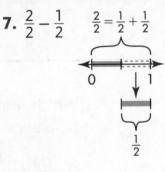

8. $\frac{2}{3} - \frac{1}{3}$

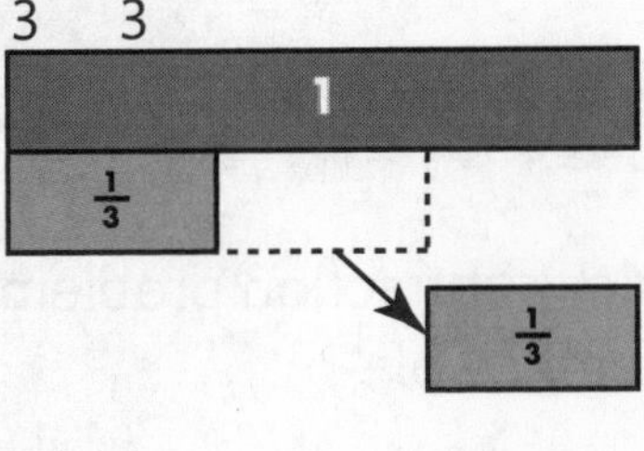

9. $\frac{4}{5} - \frac{2}{5}$

10. $\frac{17}{10} - \frac{3}{10}$

11. $\frac{8}{6} - \frac{2}{6}$

12. $\frac{9}{6} - \frac{1}{6}$

13. $\frac{21}{10} - \frac{1}{10}$

14. $\frac{1}{5} - \frac{1}{5}$

Problem Solving

15. Model with Math Leesa has $\frac{7}{8}$ gallon of juice. She shares $\frac{3}{8}$ gallon. Write and solve an equation to find j, how much juice Leesa has left.

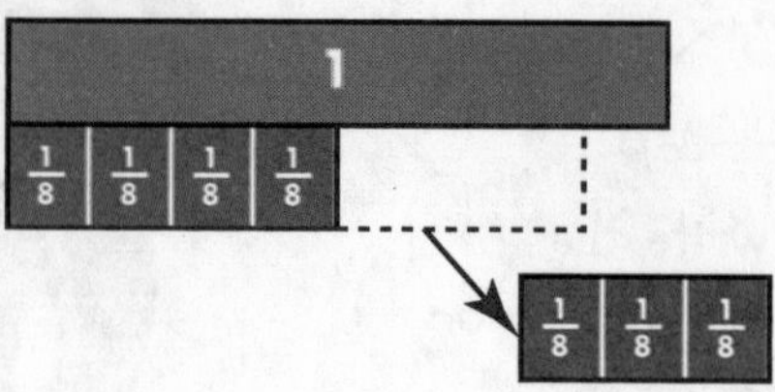

16. Higher Order Thinking Using only odd numbers for numerators, write two different subtraction problems that have a difference of $\frac{1}{2}$. Remember, you can find equivalent fractions for $\frac{1}{2}$.

17. In Kayla's class, some of the students are wearing blue shirts. $\frac{6}{8}$ of the students are **NOT** wearing blue shirts. What fraction of the students are wearing blue shirts? Show your work.

18. In Exercise 17, what number represents the whole class? How do you know what fraction to use to represent this number?

19. Rick shared his bag of grapes with friends. He gave $\frac{2}{10}$ of the bag to Melissa and $\frac{4}{10}$ of the bag to Ryan. What fraction of the bag of grapes does Rick have left? Show your work.

20. Teresa gave away 8 baseball cards and has 4 baseball cards left. Write a subtraction problem to show the fraction of the baseball cards Teresa has left.

Assessment Practice

21. Which subtraction problem has a difference of $\frac{1}{3}$?

Ⓐ $\frac{2}{2} - \frac{1}{2}$

Ⓑ $\frac{5}{3} - \frac{3}{3}$

Ⓒ $\frac{4}{3} - \frac{3}{3}$

Ⓓ $\frac{5}{3} - \frac{1}{3}$

22. Which subtraction problem has a difference of $\frac{10}{8}$?

Ⓐ $\frac{20}{8} - \frac{10}{8}$

Ⓑ $\frac{8}{10} + \frac{2}{10}$

Ⓒ $\frac{10}{8} - \frac{4}{8}$

Ⓓ $\frac{6}{8} - \frac{1}{4}$

Name ______________________

Activity

Lesson 9-5

Subtract Fractions with Like Denominators

I can ...

use my understanding of subtraction as separating parts of the same whole to subtract fractions with like denominators.

Content Standards 4.NF.B.3a Also 4.NF.B.3d
Mathematical Practices MP.2, MP.4

Solve & Share

Leah and Josh live the same direction from school and on the same side of Forest Road. Leah's house is $\frac{8}{10}$ mile from school. Josh's house is $\frac{5}{10}$ mile from school. How much farther does Leah have to walk home when she reaches Josh's house? ***Solve this problem any way you choose.***

What expression can you use to represent this problem?

Look Back! Model with Math How could you represent the problem above with a bar diagram and an equation? Tell what your variable means.

Visual
Learning

A-Z
Glossary

Essential
Question

How Can You Subtract Fractions with Like Denominators?

Visual Learning Bridge

A

Tania is squeezing lemons to make lemonade. The recipe calls for $\frac{5}{8}$ cup of lemon juice. The amount Tania has squeezed is shown at the right. What fraction of a cup of lemon juice does Tania still need to squeeze?

Subtract the fractions
to find the difference.

$\frac{3}{8}$ cup
1 cup
$\frac{3}{4}$
$\frac{5}{8}$
$\frac{1}{2}$
$\frac{3}{8}$
$\frac{1}{4}$

B

One Way

Find $\frac{5}{8} - \frac{3}{8}$ using the relationship between addition and subtraction.

$\frac{2}{8} = \frac{1}{8} + \frac{1}{8}$

0 1

$\frac{3}{8} = \frac{1}{8} + \frac{1}{8} + \frac{1}{8}$

Break $\frac{5}{8}$ apart.
Write a related addition equation:
$\frac{5}{8} = \frac{2}{8} + \frac{3}{8}$

Write a related subtraction equation:
$\frac{5}{8} - \frac{3}{8} = \frac{2}{8}$

C

Another Way

Find $\frac{5}{8} - \frac{3}{8}$ using a general method.

$$\frac{5}{8} - \frac{3}{8} = n$$

$\frac{5}{8}$ cup

$\frac{3}{8}$	n

Subtract the numerators. Write the difference over the like denominator.

$$\frac{5}{8} - \frac{3}{8} = \frac{5-3}{8} = \frac{2}{8}$$

$\frac{2}{8}$ is equivalent to $\frac{1}{4}$.
Tania needs to squeeze $\frac{1}{4}$ cup
more lemon juice.

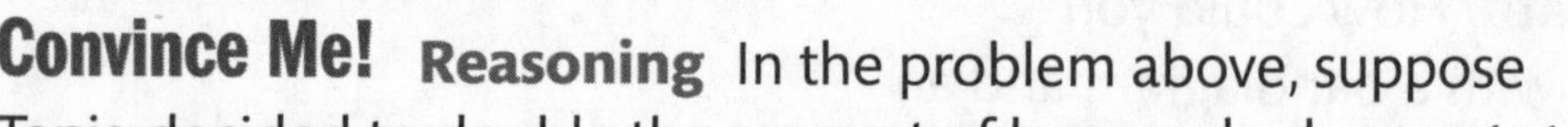

Convince Me! Reasoning In the problem above, suppose Tania decided to double the amount of lemonade she wants to make. Then how much more lemon juice would Tania need to squeeze?

Name ______________________________

Practice Tools Assessment

Guided Practice

Do You Understand?

1. Jesse has a bottle that contains $\frac{7}{10}$ liter of water. He drinks $\frac{2}{10}$ liter. Jesse says he has $\frac{1}{2}$ liter left. Is he correct? Explain.

2. What addition sentence can you use to subtract $\frac{4}{10}$ from $\frac{9}{10}$?

Do You Know How?

For **3–10**, subtract the fractions.

3. $\frac{2}{3} - \frac{1}{3}$

4. $\frac{3}{4} - \frac{2}{4}$

5. $\frac{5}{6} - \frac{2}{6}$

6. $\frac{9}{12} - \frac{3}{12}$

7. $\frac{9}{8} - \frac{3}{8}$

8. $\frac{17}{10} - \frac{9}{10}$

9. $\frac{4}{8} - \frac{1}{8}$

10. $\frac{1}{2} - \frac{1}{2}$

Independent Practice

Leveled Practice For **11–18**, subtract the fractions.

11. $\frac{5}{6} - \frac{1}{6}$

$\frac{5}{6}$

$\frac{1}{6}$ | n

12. $\frac{8}{100} - \frac{3}{100}$

$\frac{8}{100}$

$\frac{3}{100}$ | n

13. $\frac{3}{4} - \frac{1}{4}$

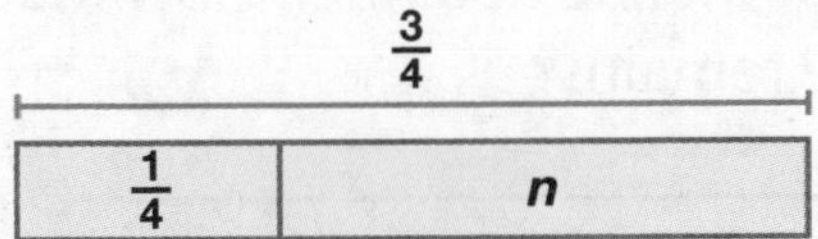

14. $\frac{6}{8} - \frac{4}{8}$

$\frac{6}{8}$

$\frac{4}{8}$ | n

15. $\frac{5}{6} - \frac{4}{6}$

16. $\frac{40}{10} - \frac{20}{10}$

17. $\frac{80}{100} - \frac{40}{100}$

18. $\frac{19}{10} - \frac{8}{10}$

Problem Solving

19. Joey ran $\frac{1}{4}$ mile in the morning and $\frac{1}{4}$ mile farther than in the morning in the afternoon. If he wants to run a full mile, how much more does Joey have to run? Write equations to explain.

20. Reasoning Explain how subtracting $\frac{4}{5} - \frac{3}{5}$ involves subtracting $4 - 3$.

21. Higher Order Thinking The flags of all 5 Nordic countries are displayed. What fraction describes how many more of the flags displayed are 2-color flags than are 3-color flags?

First find how many flags in all, then find how many 2-color and 3-color flags.

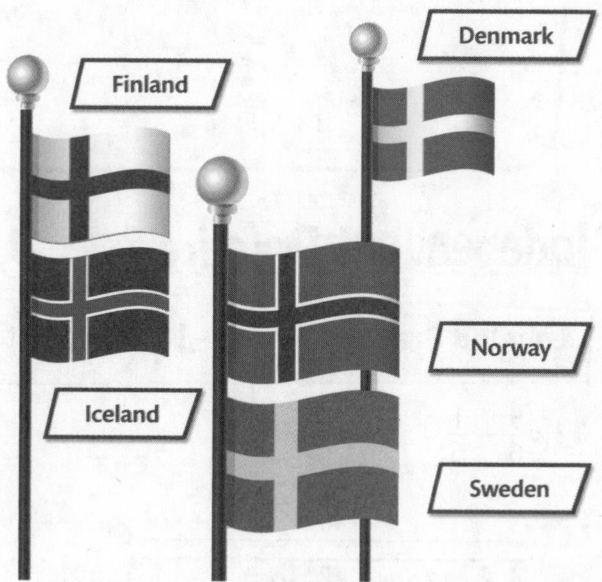

Denmark
Finland
Norway
Iceland
Sweden

Assessment Practice

22. Brian had a piece of chalk $\frac{9}{10}$ centimeter long. A piece cracked off as he was drawing on the sidewalk. Then Brian's chalk was only $\frac{6}{10}$ centimeter long. How long was the piece of chalk that cracked off?

$\frac{9}{10}$ centimeter

n	$\frac{6}{10}$

23. Marietta baked a chicken pot pie. She serves $\frac{2}{3}$ of the pie at dinner. How much of the pie remains?

Name ____________________

Activity

Lesson 9-6

Add and Subtract Fractions with Like Denominators

Solve & Share

The dirt bike track shown is $\frac{7}{8}$ of a mile long from start to finish. The track is divided into four sections. What is the length of the longest section? ***Solve this problem any way you choose.***

I can ...

use a number line to add and subtract fractions when the fractions refer to the same whole.

Content Standards 4.NF.B.3a Also 4.NF.B.3d
Mathematical Practices MP.4, MP.5

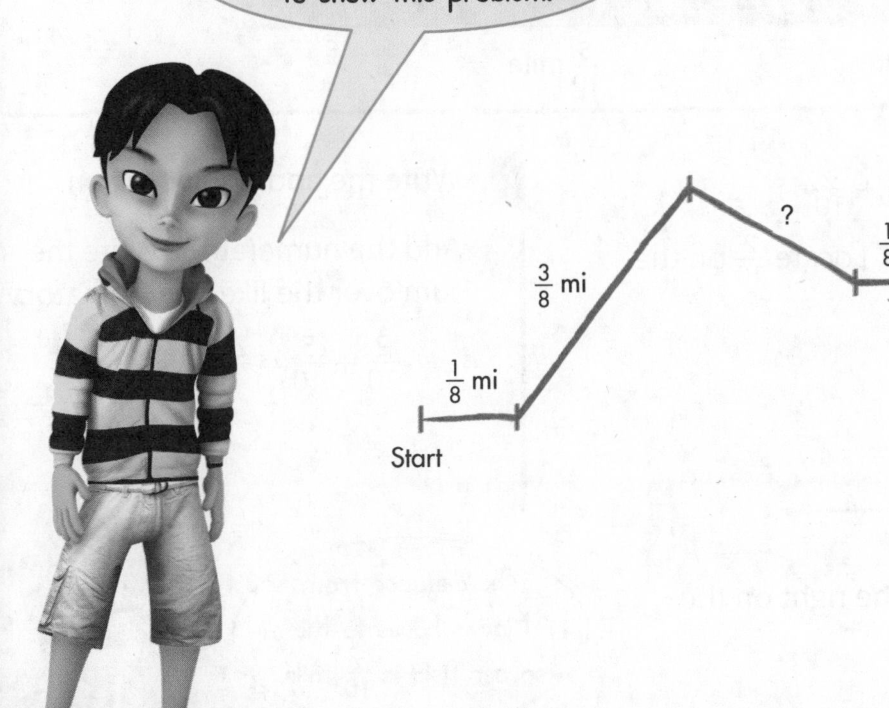

Look Back! How did you decide which section of the track was the longest?

Visual Learning

Glossary

How Do You Add and Subtract Fractions on a Number Line?

Visual Learning Bridge

A

Mary rides her bike $\frac{2}{10}$ mile to pick up her friend Marcy for soccer practice. Together, they ride $\frac{5}{10}$ mile to the soccer field. What is the distance from Mary's house to the soccer field?

You can use jumps on the number line to add or subtract fractions.

Mary's house

Marcy's house

Soccer field

$\frac{2}{10}$ mile

$\frac{5}{10}$ mile

B

Use a number line to show $\frac{2}{10} + \frac{5}{10}$.

Draw a number line for tenths. Locate $\frac{2}{10}$ on the number line.

To add, move $\frac{5}{10}$ to the right.

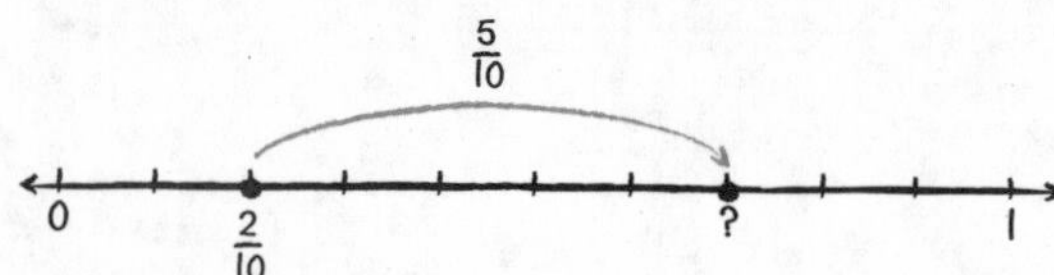

5/10
0
2/10
?
1

When you add, you move to the right on the number line.

C

Write the addition equation.

Add the numerators. Write the sum over the like denominator.

$$\frac{2}{10} + \frac{5}{10} = \frac{2+5}{10} = \frac{7}{10}$$

The distance from Mary's house to the soccer field is 7/10 mile.

Convince Me! **Use Appropriate Tools** Use the number line below to find $\frac{5}{8} + \frac{2}{8}$. Can you also use the number line to find $\frac{5}{8} - \frac{2}{8}$? Explain.

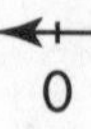
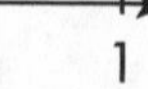

0 1

Name ____________________

Another Example!

Find $\frac{6}{8} - \frac{4}{8}$.

Start at $\frac{6}{8}$. To subtract, move $\frac{4}{8}$ to the left.

The ending point is $\frac{2}{8}$.

So, $\frac{6}{8} - \frac{4}{8} = \frac{2}{8}$.

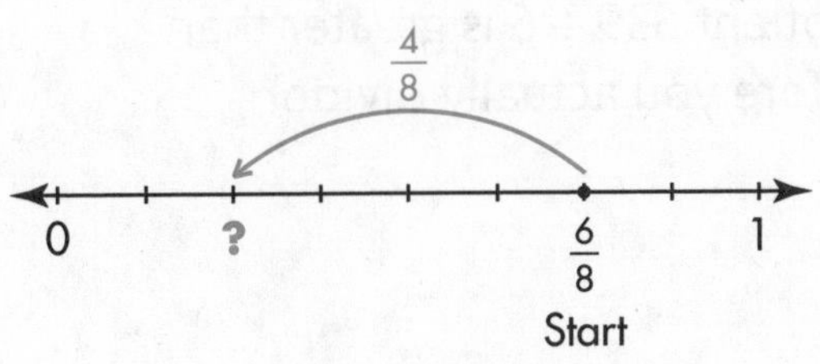

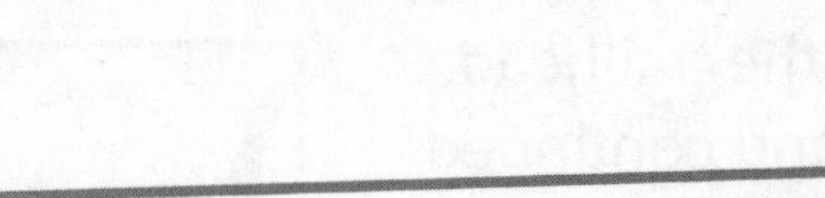

Guided Practice

Do You Understand?

1. In the example above, how is the denominator illustrated on the number line?

2. Draw a number line to represent $\frac{3}{12} + \frac{5}{12}$.

Do You Know How?

For **3–4**, write the equation shown by each number line.

3.

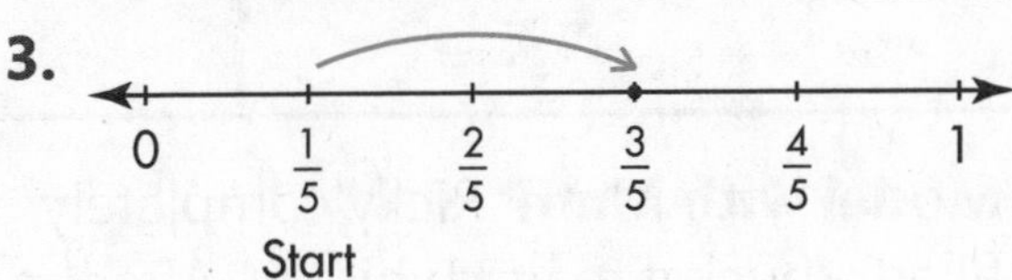

4.

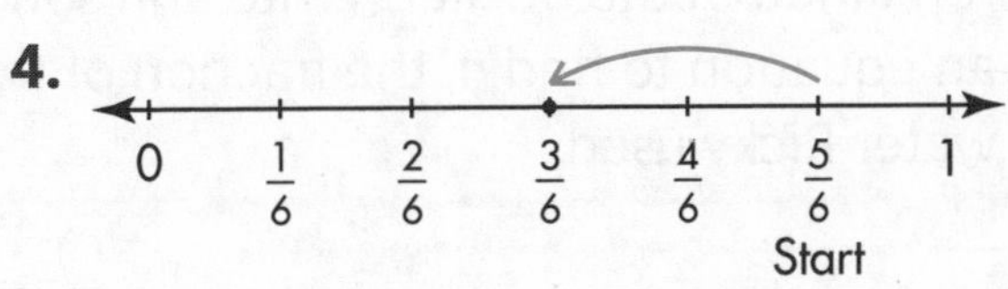

Independent Practice

For **5–8**, write the equation shown by each number line.

5.

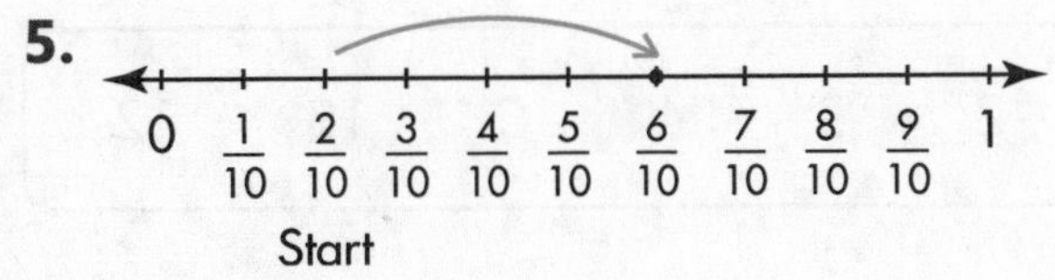

6.

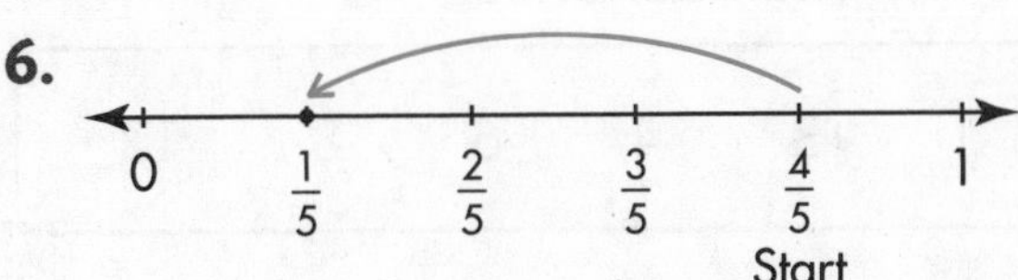

7.

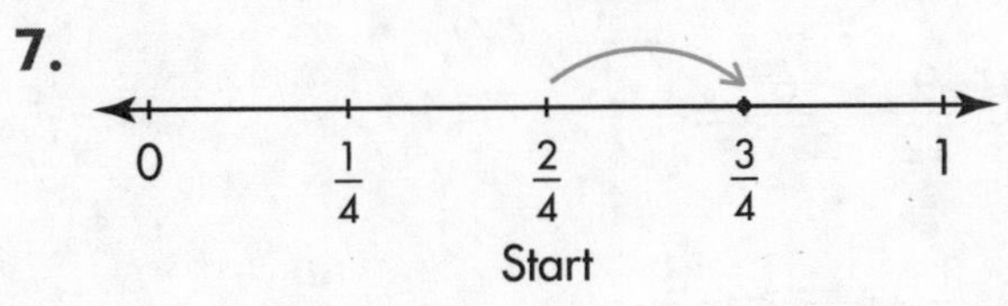

8.

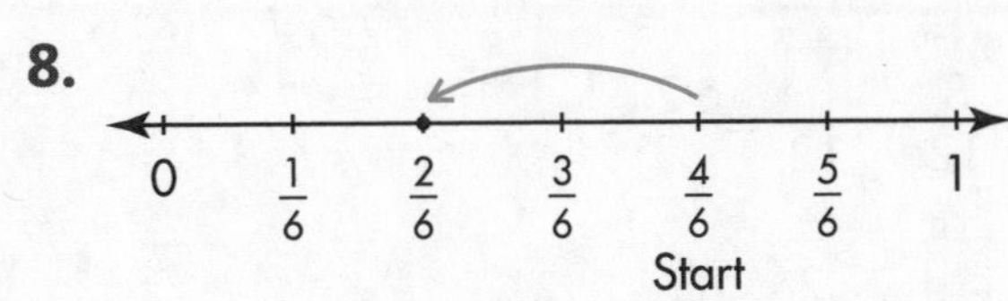

Problem Solving

9. **Number Sense** How do you know the quotient $639 \div 6$ is greater than 100 before you actually divide?

10. On average, a largemouth bass weighs about 12 pounds. Two fishermen weighed the largemouth bass they both caught and found their catch weighed 82 pounds. What is the greatest number of largemouth bass caught that are average weight?

11. Isaac started his bike ride at the trailhead. He reached the picnic area and continued to the lookout tower. If Isaac rode his bike for a total of $\frac{10}{4}$ miles, how much farther did he ride beyond the lookout tower?

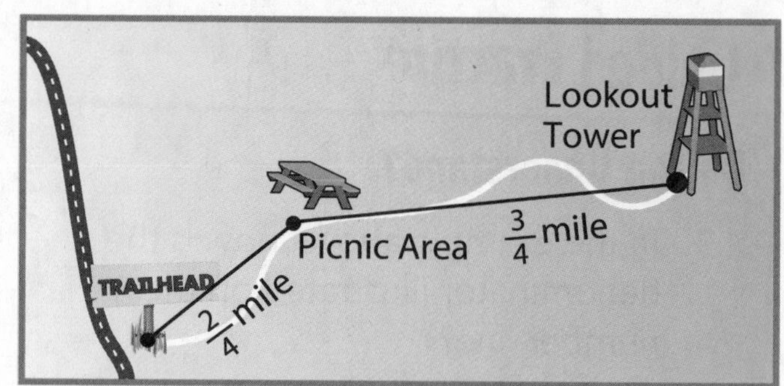

12. **Model with Math** Ricky completely filled a bucket to wash his car. After he finished washing the car, $\frac{5}{8}$ of the water remained in the bucket. Write and solve an equation to find *n*, the fraction of the water Ricky used.

13. **Higher Order Thinking** Sarah and Jenny are running an hour-long endurance race. Sarah ran $\frac{2}{6}$ hour before passing the baton to Jenny. Jenny ran $\frac{3}{6}$ hour, then passed the baton back to Sarah. What fraction of the hour does Sarah still need to run to complete the race?

Assessment Practice

14. Choose numbers from the box to fill in the missing numbers in each equation. Use each number once.

1	3	4	6	8	12

a. $\frac{\square}{4} + \frac{2}{\square} = \frac{3}{4}$

b. $\frac{8}{12} - \frac{\square}{12} = \frac{2}{\square}$

c. $\frac{\square}{8} + \frac{2}{\square} = \frac{5}{8}$

15. Choose numbers from the box to fill in the missing numbers in each equation. Use each number once.

2	3	4	6	10	12

a. $\frac{3}{10} + \frac{\square}{10} = \frac{9}{\square}$

b. $\frac{9}{12} - \frac{6}{\square} = \frac{\square}{12}$

c. $\frac{1}{4} + \frac{\square}{4} = \frac{3}{\square}$

Name ______________________________

Activity

Lesson 9-7

Model Addition and Subtraction of Mixed Numbers

I can ...

use models and equivalent fractions to help add and subtract mixed numbers.

Content Standards 4.NF.B.3c Also 4.NF.B.3d
Mathematical Practices MP.2, MP.5

Solve & Share

Tory is cutting loaves of bread into fourths. She needs to wrap $3\frac{3}{4}$ loaves to take to a luncheon and $1\frac{2}{4}$ loaves for a bake sale. How many loaves does Tory need to wrap for the luncheon and the bake sale? ***Solve this problem any way you choose.***

You can select tools such as fraction strips or number lines to add mixed numbers.

Look Back! **Reasoning** How can you estimate the sum above?

How Can You Add or Subtract Mixed Numbers?

Visual Learning Bridge

A

Bill has 2 boards to use to make picture frames. What is the total length of the two boards? How much longer is one board than the other?

$1\frac{11}{12}$ feet

$2\frac{5}{12}$ feet

You can use addition to find the total length of the two boards.

You can use subtraction to find how much longer one board is than the other.

B Use fraction strips to show $2\frac{5}{12} + 1\frac{11}{12}$.

Add the fractional parts: $\frac{5}{12} + \frac{11}{12} = \frac{16}{12}$

Rename $\frac{16}{12}$ as $1\frac{4}{12}$.

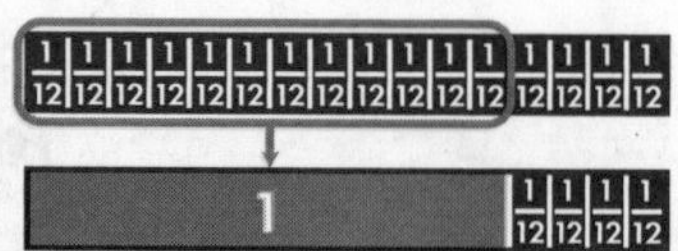

Add the whole number parts: $2 + 1 = 3$

Then add the sum of the whole number parts to the sum of the fractional parts.

$3 + 1\frac{4}{12} = 4\frac{4}{12}$

So, $2\frac{5}{12} + 1\frac{11}{12} = 4\frac{4}{12}$ feet.

C Use a number line to show $2\frac{5}{12} - 1\frac{11}{12}$.

Mark the number you are subtracting from, $2\frac{5}{12}$.

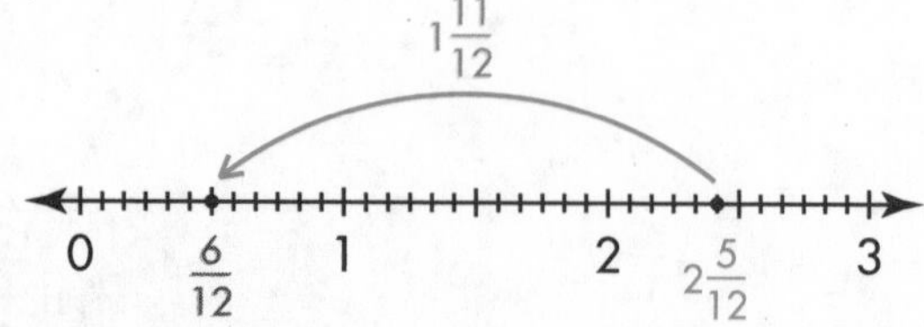

To subtract, move $1\frac{11}{12}$ to the left on the number line.

Write the difference as a fraction: $\frac{6}{12}$

So, $2\frac{5}{12} - 1\frac{11}{12} = \frac{6}{12}$ foot.

Convince Me! **Use Appropriate Tools** Suppose Bill's boards were $2\frac{11}{12}$ feet and $1\frac{5}{12}$ feet. What would be the total length of the two boards? How much longer is one board than the other? Use fraction strips or draw number lines to show your work.

Name ______________________

Practice Tools Assessment

Another Example!

Use number line to find $1\frac{1}{8} + 2\frac{4}{8}$.

Start at $1\frac{1}{8}$. Move 1 to the right 2 times. Then move $\frac{1}{8}$ to the right 4 times.

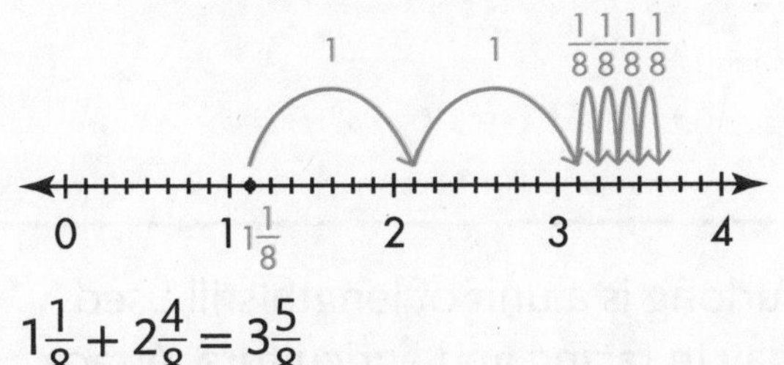

$1\frac{1}{8} + 2\frac{4}{8} = 3\frac{5}{8}$

Use fraction strip to find $2\frac{3}{5} - 1\frac{2}{5}$.

Cross out one whole. Then cross out two $\frac{1}{5}$s.

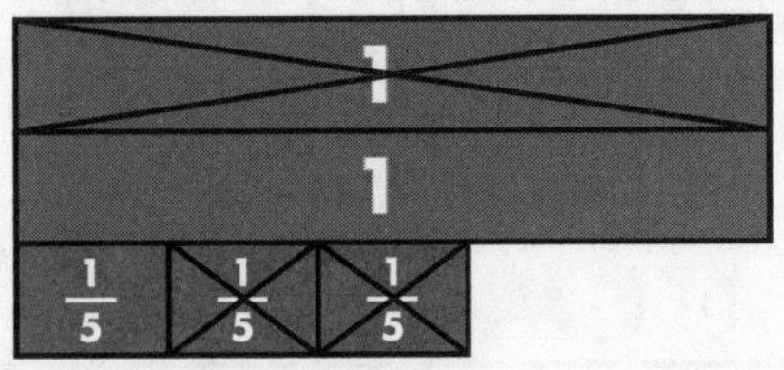

$2\frac{3}{5} - 1\frac{2}{5} = 1\frac{1}{5}$

Guided Practice

Do You Understand?

1. In the problem on the previous page, why does $\frac{16}{12} = 1\frac{4}{12}$? Use decomposing to explain.

Do You Know How?

For **2–3**, use a tool to find each sum or difference.

2. $1\frac{2}{5} + 2\frac{4}{5}$

3. $1\frac{1}{4} + 2\frac{3}{4}$

Independent Practice

For **4–11**, use a tool to find the sum or difference.

4. $2\frac{1}{4} - 1\frac{3}{4}$

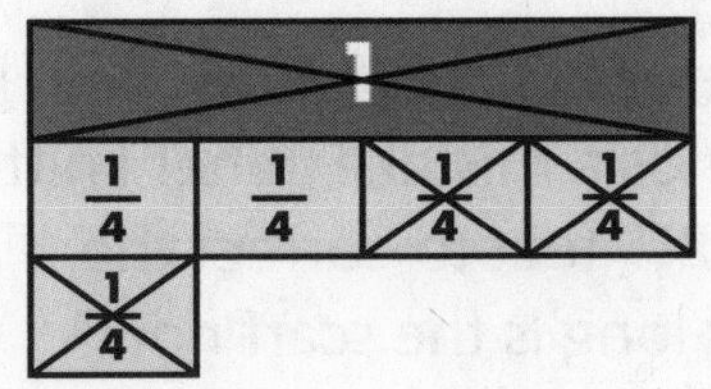

5. $1\frac{2}{3} + 2\frac{2}{3}$

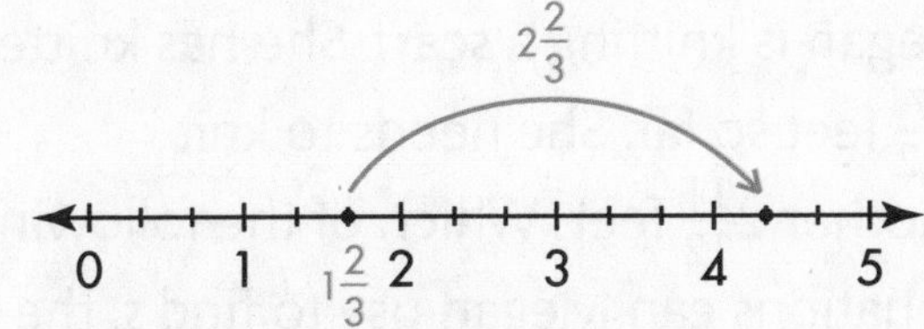

6. $2\frac{3}{4} - 1\frac{3}{4}$

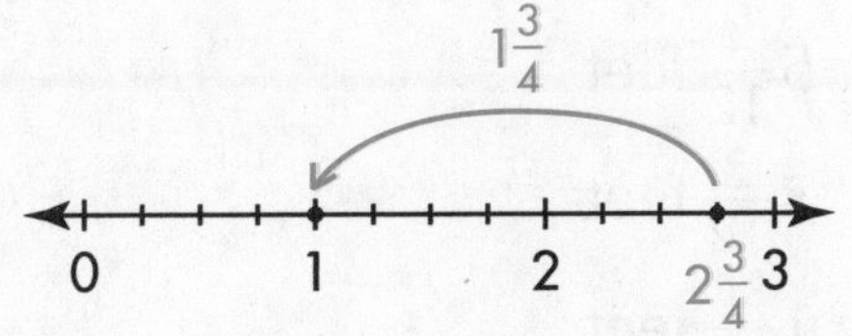

7. $1\frac{3}{6} + 1\frac{3}{6}$

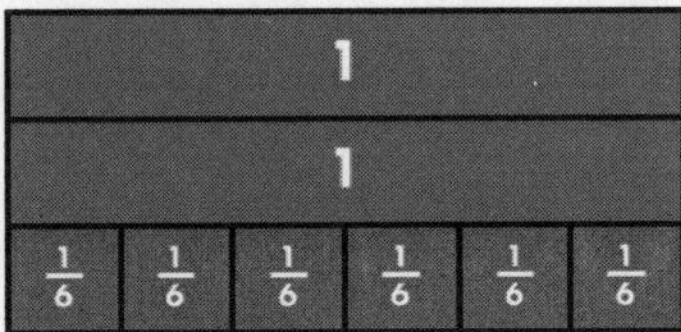

8. $2\frac{3}{5} + 1\frac{3}{5}$

9. $4\frac{5}{12} + 1\frac{7}{12}$

10. $4\frac{9}{10} + 3\frac{7}{10}$

11. $5\frac{3}{4} + 2\frac{3}{4}$

Problem Solving

12. Use Appropriate Tools Kit said, "On summer vacation, I spent $1\frac{1}{2}$ weeks with my grandma and one week more with my aunt than with my grandma." How many weeks did she spend visiting family? Use a tool to find the sum.

13. Use Appropriate Tools If Kit spent $3\frac{1}{2}$ weeks in swimming lessons, how much more time did Kit spend visiting family than in swimming lessons? Use a tool to find the difference.

14. Hannah used $1\frac{5}{8}$ gallons of paint for the ceiling. Hannah used 6 gallons of paint for the walls and ceiling combined. How much paint did Hannah use for the walls?

15. A furlong is a unit of length still used today in racing and agriculture. A race that is 8 furlongs is 1 mile. A mile is 5,280 feet. How many feet are in a furlong?

16. Higher Order Thinking A recipe calls for $1\frac{2}{3}$ cups of brown sugar for the granola bars and $1\frac{1}{3}$ cups of brown sugar for the topping. Dara has $3\frac{1}{4}$ cups of brown sugar. Does she have enough brown sugar to make the granola bars and the topping? Explain.

You can use fraction strips or a number line to compare amounts.

Assessment Practice

17. Megan is knitting a scarf. She has knitted $2\frac{7}{12}$ feet so far. She needs to knit another $2\frac{11}{12}$ feet. Which of the following equations can Megan use to find *s*, the length of the completed scarf?

Ⓐ $s = 2\frac{7}{12} + 2\frac{11}{12}$

Ⓑ $s = 2\frac{5}{12} + 2\frac{7}{12}$

Ⓒ $s = 2\frac{11}{12} - 2\frac{7}{12}$

Ⓓ $s = 4\frac{11}{12} - 2\frac{7}{12}$

18. Megan finishes the scarf. It is $5\frac{6}{12}$ feet in length. She finds a mistake in her knitting and unravels $2\frac{4}{12}$ feet to correct the mistake. How long is the scarf now?

Ⓐ $8\frac{10}{12}$ feet

Ⓑ $5\frac{4}{12}$ feet

Ⓒ $3\frac{2}{12}$ feet

Ⓓ $1\frac{4}{12}$ feet

Name ______________________________

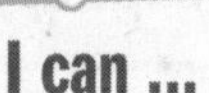

Lesson 9-8
Add Mixed Numbers

I can ...
use equivalent fractions and properties of operations to add mixed numbers with like denominators.

Content Standards 4.NF.B.3c Also 4.NF.B.3d
Mathematical Practices MP.2, MP.8

Joaquin used $1\frac{3}{6}$ cups of apple juice and $1\frac{4}{6}$ cups of orange juice in a recipe for punch. How much juice did Joaquin use? ***Solve this problem any way you choose.***

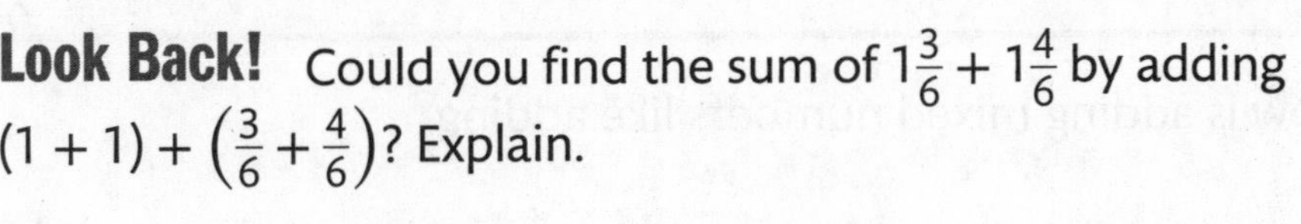

Generalize. You can use what you know about adding fractions to solve this problem.

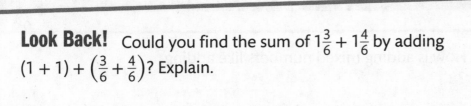

Look Back! Could you find the sum of $1\frac{3}{6} + 1\frac{4}{6}$ by adding $(1 + 1) + \left(\frac{3}{6} + \frac{4}{6}\right)$? Explain.

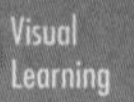
Visual Learning

Glossary

How Can You Add Mixed Numbers?

Visual Learning Bridge

A

Brenda mixes sand with $2\frac{7}{8}$ cups of potting mixture to prepare soil for her plant. After mixing them together, how many cups of soil does Brenda have?

You can use properties of operations to add mixed numbers. When you break apart a mixed number to add, you are using the Commutative and the Associative Properties.

B Find $2\frac{7}{8} + 1\frac{3}{8}$ by breaking up mixed numbers.

$$2\frac{7}{8} + 1\frac{3}{8} = (2 + 1) + \left(\frac{7}{8} + \frac{3}{8}\right)$$

Add the fractions.

$$\begin{array}{r} 2\frac{7}{8} \\ +\,1\frac{3}{8} \\ \hline \frac{10}{8} \end{array}$$

Then add whole numbers.

$$\begin{array}{r} 2\frac{7}{8} \\ +\,1\frac{3}{8} \\ \hline 3\frac{10}{8} \end{array}$$

Write the fraction as a mixed number.

$$3\frac{10}{8} = 3 + \frac{8}{8} + \frac{2}{8} = 4\frac{2}{8}$$

C Find $2\frac{7}{8} + 1\frac{3}{8}$ by adding equivalent fractions.

$$2\frac{7}{8} = 2 + \frac{7}{8} = \frac{16}{8} + \frac{7}{8} = \frac{23}{8}$$

$$1\frac{3}{8} = 1 + \frac{3}{8} = \frac{8}{8} + \frac{3}{8} = \frac{11}{8}$$

$$\frac{23}{8} + \frac{11}{8} = \frac{34}{8}$$

Write $\frac{34}{8}$ as a mixed number.

$$\frac{34}{8} = \frac{8}{8} + \frac{8}{8} + \frac{8}{8} + \frac{8}{8} + \frac{2}{8} = 4\frac{2}{8}$$

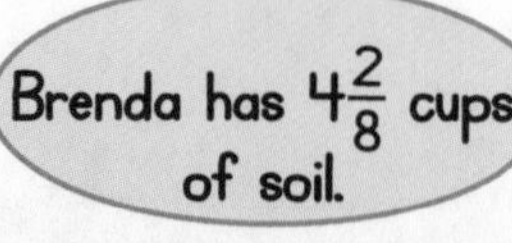

Convince Me! **Reasoning** How is adding mixed numbers like adding fractions and whole numbers?

Name ____________________

Practice Tools Assessment

Guided Practice

Do You Understand?

1. How do the Commutative and Associative Properties allow you to add the fraction parts, add the whole number parts, and then add them together? Use $2\frac{5}{10} + 1\frac{9}{10} = \left(2 + \frac{5}{10}\right) + \left(1 + \frac{9}{10}\right)$ as an example.

2. How can you use equivalent fractions to find $4\frac{2}{8} + 1\frac{1}{8}$?

Do You Know How?

For **3–8**, find each sum.

3. $1\frac{7}{8} + 1\frac{2}{8}$

4. $2\frac{4}{10} + 5\frac{5}{10}$

5. $4\frac{2}{3} + 1\frac{2}{3}$

6. $6\frac{5}{12} + 4\frac{11}{12}$

7. $2\frac{1}{3} + 2\frac{1}{3}$

8. $1\frac{9}{12} + 2\frac{5}{12}$

Independent Practice

Leveled Practice For **9–22**, find each sum by adding mixed numbers or by adding equivalent fractions.

9. a. Add the fractions.
b. Add the whole numbers.
c. Write the fraction as a mixed number.

$1\frac{3}{6} + 2\frac{4}{6} = \square = \square$

10. a. Write the mixed numbers as fractions.
b. Add the fractions.
c. Write the fraction as a mixed number.

$2\frac{1}{4} = \square$
$+ 3\frac{2}{4} = + \square$
$\square = \square$

11. $2\frac{5}{6} + 5\frac{4}{6}$

12. $2\frac{7}{10} + 1\frac{9}{10}$

13. $1\frac{7}{8} + 3\frac{5}{8}$

14. $5\frac{7}{8} + 8\frac{1}{8}$

15. $4\frac{1}{10} + 6\frac{5}{10}$

16. $1\frac{7}{12} + 4\frac{9}{12}$

17. $5 + 3\frac{1}{8}$

18. $3\frac{3}{4} + 2\frac{3}{4}$

19. $2\frac{4}{5} + 2\frac{3}{5}$

20. $3\frac{2}{6} + 2\frac{5}{6}$

21. $1\frac{7}{12} + 2\frac{10}{12}$

22. $3\frac{6}{8} + 1\frac{3}{8}$

Problem Solving

For **23**, use the map at the right.

23. a. Find the distance from the start of the trail to the end of the trail.

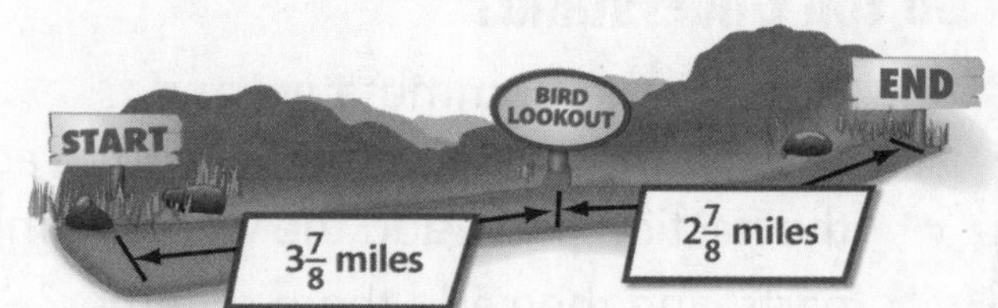

b. Linda walked from the start of the trail to the bird lookout and back. Did Linda walk more or less than if she had walked from the start of the trail to the end?

24. Joe biked $1\frac{9}{12}$ miles from home to the lake, then went some miles around the lake, and then back home. Joe biked a total of $4\frac{9}{12}$ miles. How many miles did Joe bike around the lake?

25. Reasoning The bus took $4\frac{3}{5}$ hours to get from Jim's home station to Portland and $3\frac{4}{5}$ hours to get from Portland to Seattle. How long did the bus take to get from Jim's home station to Seattle?

26. Higher Order Thinking A male Parson's chameleon is $23\frac{3}{4}$ inches long. It can extend its tongue up to $35\frac{1}{4}$ inches. What are 3 possible lengths for the chameleon when its tongue is extended?

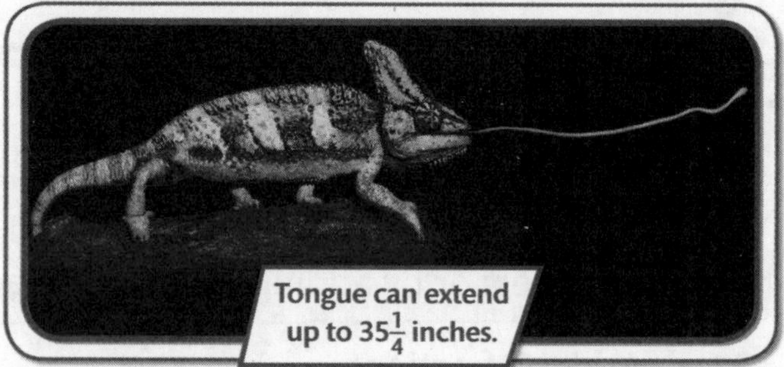

Tongue can extend up to $35\frac{1}{4}$ inches.

Assessment Practice

27. Julie attaches an extension cord that is $2\frac{6}{8}$ yards long to a cord that is $2\frac{3}{8}$ yards long. How long are the two cords together? Select all the correct ways to find the sum.

- ☐ $\frac{19}{8} + \frac{22}{8} = \frac{41}{8}$
- ☐ $\frac{19}{8} + \frac{22}{8} = \frac{41}{16}$
- ☐ $4 + \frac{9}{8}$
- ☐ $(2 + 2) + \left(\frac{3}{8} + \frac{6}{8}\right)$
- ☐ $4 + \frac{9}{16}$

28. Select all the correct sums.

- ☐ $2\frac{3}{5} + 1\frac{1}{5} = 4\frac{4}{5}$
- ☐ $2\frac{1}{3} + 1\frac{2}{3} = 4$
- ☐ $3\frac{6}{10} + 2\frac{7}{10} = 6\frac{3}{10}$
- ☐ $2\frac{3}{4} + 2\frac{2}{4} = 4\frac{1}{4}$
- ☐ $4\frac{2}{6} + 1\frac{5}{6} = 6\frac{1}{6}$

Name ____________________ Activity

Lesson 9-9
Subtract Mixed Numbers

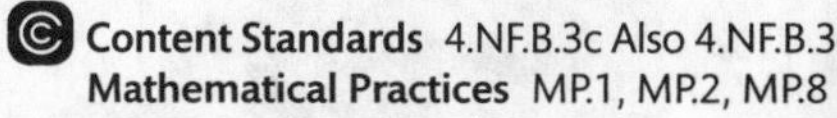

I can ...
use equivalent fractions, properties of operations, and the relationship between addition and subtraction to subtract mixed numbers with like denominators.

Content Standards 4.NF.B.3c Also 4.NF.B.3d
Mathematical Practices MP.1, MP.2, MP.8

Solve & Share

Evan is walking $2\frac{1}{8}$ miles to his aunt's house. He has already walked $\frac{6}{8}$ mile. How much farther does Evan have to go? ***Solve this problem any way you choose.***

Generalize. You can use what you know about subtracting fractions to solve this problem.

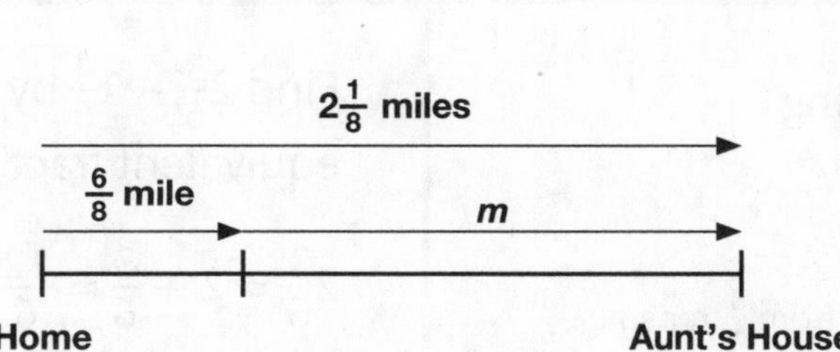

Look Back! You found $2\frac{1}{8} - \frac{6}{8} = m$. Write a related addition equation.

Visual Learning

Glossary

Essential Question

How Can You Subtract Mixed Numbers?

Visual Learning Bridge

A

A golf ball measures about $1\frac{4}{6}$ inches across the center. What is the difference between the distances across the centers of a tennis ball and a golf ball?

You can use properties of operations and the relationship between addition and subtraction to help subtract mixed numbers.

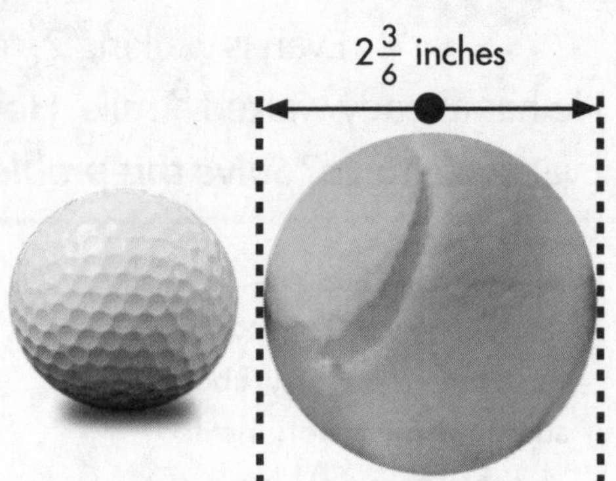
$2\frac{3}{6}$ inches

B

Find $2\frac{3}{6} - 1\frac{4}{6}$ by subtracting mixed numbers.

$$\begin{array}{r} 2\frac{3}{6} = 1\frac{9}{6} \\ -\,1\frac{4}{6} = 1\frac{4}{6} \\ \hline \frac{5}{6} \end{array}$$

To subtract $\frac{4}{6}$ from $\frac{3}{6}$, rename $2\frac{3}{6}$. Remember, $1 = \frac{6}{6}$.

$2\frac{3}{6} = 2 + \frac{3}{6} = 1 + \frac{6}{6} + \frac{3}{6} = 1\frac{9}{6}$

The tennis ball is $\frac{5}{6}$ inch wider than the golf ball.

C

Find $2\frac{3}{6} - 1\frac{4}{6}$ by subtracting equivalent fractions.

$2\frac{3}{6} = 2 + \frac{3}{6} = \frac{12}{6} + \frac{3}{6} = \frac{15}{6}$

$1\frac{4}{6} = 1 + \frac{4}{6} = \frac{6}{6} + \frac{4}{6} = \frac{10}{6}$

$\frac{15}{6} - \frac{10}{6} = \frac{5}{6}$

You can count up to check your work!
$1\frac{4}{6} + \frac{2}{6} = 2$ and $2 + \frac{3}{6} = 2\frac{3}{6}$
$\frac{2}{6} + \frac{3}{6} = \frac{5}{6}$

Convince Me! **Reasoning** Explain why you rename $4\frac{1}{4}$ to find $4\frac{1}{4} - \frac{3}{4}$.

Name ____________________

Guided Practice

Do You Understand?

1. A hole at the golf course is $3\frac{3}{6}$ inches wide. How much wider is the hole than the golf ball?

2. How could you use the relationship between addition and subtraction with counting up to find $3\frac{1}{4} - 1\frac{3}{4}$?

Do You Know How?

For **3–8**, find each difference.

3. $7\frac{5}{8} - 2\frac{4}{8}$

4. $5 - 2\frac{3}{4}$

5. $6\frac{3}{10} - 1\frac{8}{10}$

6. $9\frac{4}{12} - 4\frac{9}{12}$

7. $4\frac{5}{6} - 2\frac{1}{6}$

8. $1\frac{9}{12} - \frac{10}{12}$

Independent Practice

For **9–24**, find each difference.

9. $8\frac{7}{8} - 2\frac{4}{8}$

10. $4\frac{5}{10} - 1\frac{9}{10}$

11. $4\frac{1}{8} - 1\frac{4}{8}$

12. $6 - 2\frac{4}{5}$

13. $6\frac{1}{3} - 5\frac{2}{3}$

14. $9\frac{2}{4} - 6\frac{3}{4}$

15. $8\frac{3}{8} - 3\frac{5}{8}$

16. $7 - 3\frac{1}{2}$

17. $6\frac{1}{6} - 4\frac{5}{6}$

18. $3\frac{1}{12} - 1\frac{3}{12}$

19. $6\frac{2}{5} - 2\frac{3}{5}$

20. $4\frac{5}{10} - 1\frac{7}{10}$

21. $12\frac{9}{12} - 10\frac{7}{12}$

22. $25\frac{1}{4} - 20$

23. $7 - 2\frac{1}{8}$

24. $6\frac{3}{5} - 3\frac{4}{5}$

Problem Solving

25. The average weight of a basketball is $21\frac{1}{8}$ ounces. The average weight of a baseball is $5\frac{2}{8}$ ounces. How many more ounces does the basketball weigh?

26. What is the value of the 4 in 284,612?

27. Two of the smallest mammals on Earth are the bumblebee bat and the Etruscan pygmy shrew. How much shorter is the bat than the shrew?

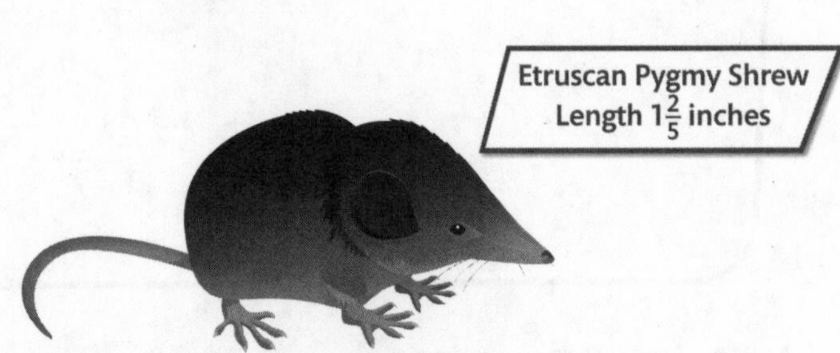

28. **Make Sense and Persevere** The average length of an adult female hand is about $6\frac{3}{5}$ inches. About how much longer is the hand than the lengths of the bat and shrew combined?

Bumblebee Bat
Length $1\frac{1}{5}$ inches

Etruscan Pygmy Shrew
Length $1\frac{2}{5}$ inches

29. Jack made $5\frac{1}{4}$ dozen cookies for the bake sale, and his sister made $3\frac{3}{4}$ dozen cookies. How many more dozen cookies did Jack make than his sister?

30. **Higher Order Thinking** Jenna has a spool that contains $5\frac{3}{4}$ meters of ribbon. She uses $3\frac{2}{4}$ meters for a school project and $1\frac{1}{4}$ meters for a bow. How much ribbon remains on the spool?

Assessment Practice

31. Last week, the office used $5\frac{1}{12}$ boxes of paper. This week, they used $1\frac{5}{12}$ boxes of paper. How many more boxes did they use last week than this week?

   Ⓐ $10\frac{6}{12}$ boxes
   Ⓑ $4\frac{8}{12}$ boxes
   Ⓒ $4\frac{4}{12}$ boxes
   Ⓓ $3\frac{8}{12}$ boxes

32. A store sold $6\frac{1}{5}$ cases of juice on Friday and $4\frac{4}{5}$ cases of juice on Saturday. How many more cases of juice did the store sell on Friday than on Saturday?

   Ⓐ 11 cases
   Ⓑ $3\frac{1}{5}$ cases
   Ⓒ $2\frac{2}{5}$ cases
   Ⓓ $1\frac{2}{5}$ cases

Name ______________________________

Activity

Problem Solving

Lesson 9-10

Model with Math

I can ...

use math I know to represent and solve problems.

Mathematical Practices MP.4 Also MP.1, MP.2
Content Standards 4.NF.B.3d Also 4.NF.B.3a, 4.NF.B.3c

Solve & Share The table shows how long Jamie studied for a math test over 3 days. How much more time did Jamie spend studying on Tuesday and Wednesday than on Thursday?

DATA

Day of the Week	Time Jamie Studied
Tuesday	$1\frac{3}{4}$ hours
Wednesday	$\frac{3}{4}$ hour
Thursday	$\frac{2}{4}$ hour

Thinking Habits

Be a good thinker! These questions can help you.

- How can I use math I know to help solve this problem?
- How can I use pictures, objects, or an equation to represent the problem?
- How can I use numbers, words, and symbols to solve the problem?

Look Back! **Model with Math** What representations can you use to help solve this problem?

How Can You Use Math to Model Problems?

Visual Learning Bridge

A

Brad and his father hiked the Gadsen Trail and the Rosebriar Trail on Saturday. They hiked the Eureka Trail on Sunday. How much farther did they hike on Saturday than on Sunday?

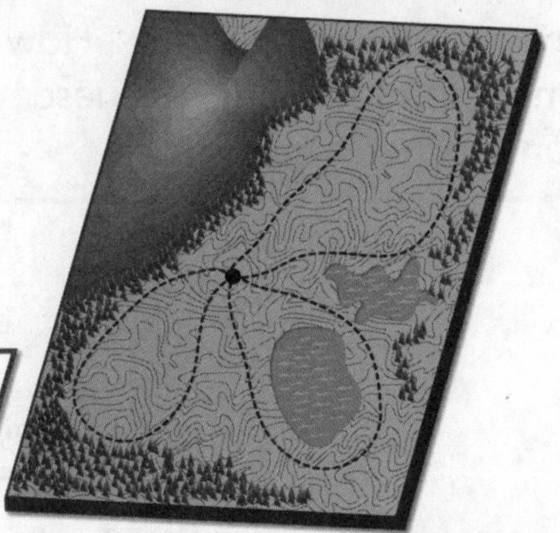

What do you need to find?

I need to find how far Brad and his father hiked on Saturday and how much farther they hiked on Saturday than on Sunday.

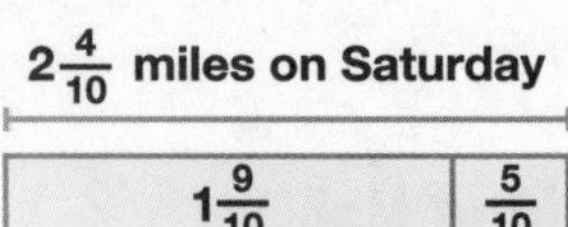

B

How can I model with math?

I can

- use previously learned concepts and skills.
- use bar diagrams and equations to represent and solve this problem.
- decide if my results make sense.

C

Here's my thinking.

Find $2\frac{4}{10} - \frac{6}{10}$.

Use a bar diagram and write an equation to solve.

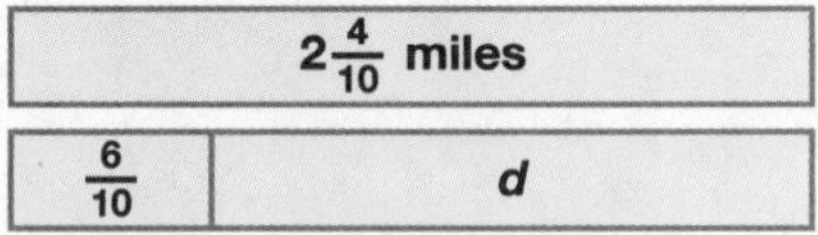

$2\frac{4}{10} - \frac{6}{10} = d \qquad d = 1\frac{8}{10}$

Brad and his father hiked $1\frac{8}{10}$ miles farther on Saturday than on Sunday.

Convince Me! Model with Math How do the bar diagrams help you decide if your answer makes sense?

Name ____________________

Guided Practice

Model with Math

Alisa hiked a trail that was $\frac{9}{10}$ mile and Joseph hiked a trail that was $\frac{5}{10}$ mile. How much farther, *d*, did Alisa hike than Joseph?

When you model with math, you use math to represent and solve a problem.

1. Draw a bar diagram to represent the problem and show the relationships among the quantities.

2. What equation can you write to represent the problem?

3. How much farther did Alisa hike than Joseph?

Independent Practice

Model with Math

The smallest female spider measures about $\frac{3}{5}$ millimeter in length. The smallest male spider measures about $\frac{1}{5}$ millimeter in length. How much longer, *n*, is the smallest female spider than the smallest male spider? Use Exercises 4–6 to answer the question.

4. Draw a picture and write an equation to represent the problem.

5. What previously learned math can you use to solve the problem?

6. How much longer is the smallest female spider than the smallest male spider?

Performance Task

On Safari

Sandra and Ron traveled in a safari car while they were in Tanzania. The diagram shows the distances in miles they traveled from start to finish. How far did Sandra and Ron travel from the leopards to the elephants?

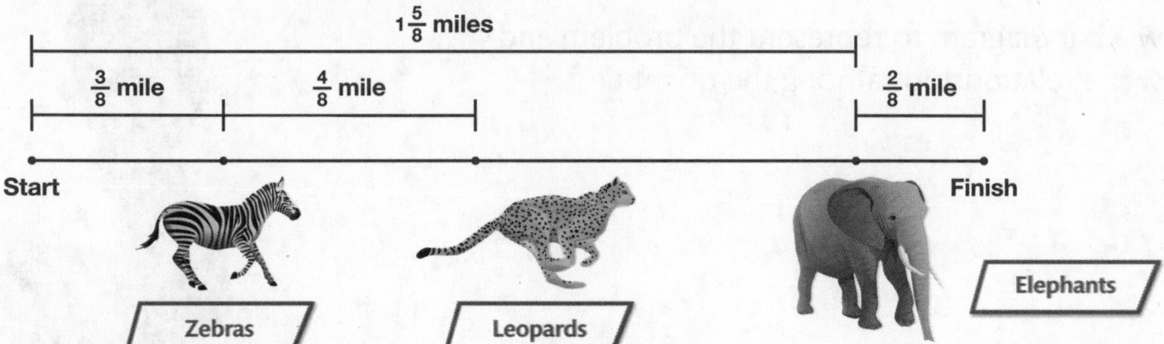

7. **Reasoning** What quantities are given in the problem and what do they mean?

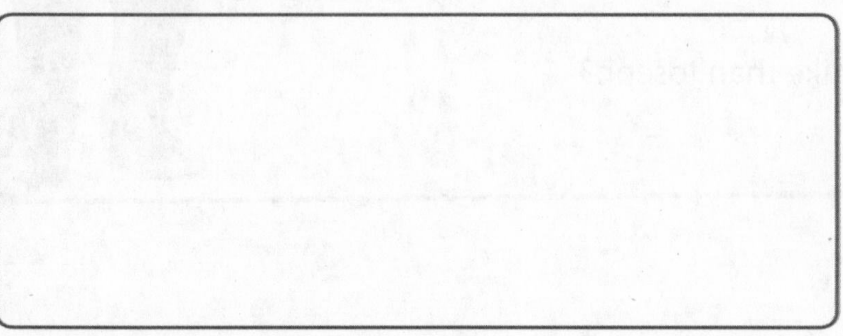

8. **Make Sense and Persevere** What is a good plan for solving the problem?

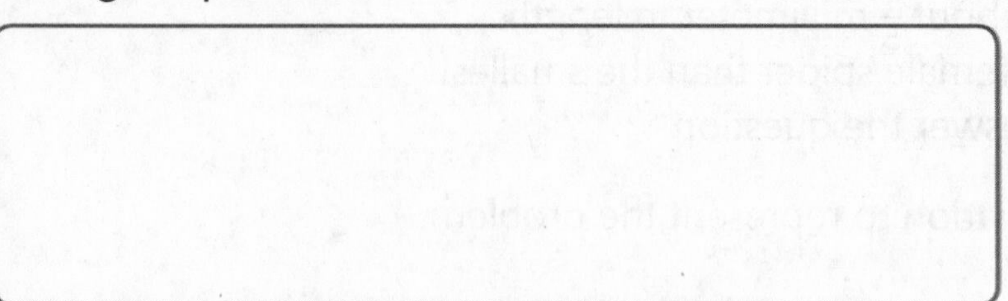

9. **Model with Math** Draw pictures and write and solve equations to find how far Sandra and Ron travel from the leopards to the elephants.

Name ____________________

Fluency Practice Activity

TOPIC 9

Find a Match

Work with a partner. Point to a clue. Read the clue.

Look below the clues to find a match. Write the clue letter in the box next to the match.

Find a match for every clue.

I can ...
add and subtract multi-digit whole numbers.

Content Standard 4.NBT.B.4
Mathematical Practices MP.3, MP.6, MP.7, MP.8

Clues

A The sum is exactly 1,000.

B The sum is exactly 1,001.

C The difference is exactly 371.

D The difference is between 40 and 45.

E The difference is exactly 437.

F The difference is between 150 and 160.

G The sum is between 995 and 1,000.

H The sum is exactly 1,899.

☐ $409 - 252$	☐ $900 - 529$	☐ $909 + 990$	☐ $506 + 494$
☐ $580 + 417$	☐ $560 - 123$	☐ $601 - 560$	☐ $309 + 692$

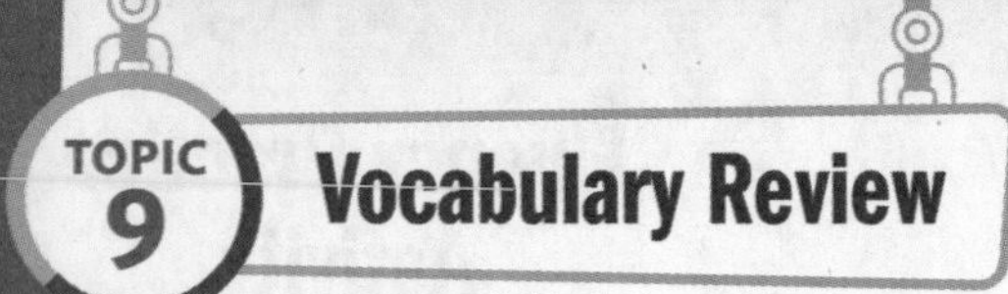

Glossary

Word List

- decompose
- denominator
- equivalent fractions
- fraction
- like denominators
- mixed number
- numerator
- whole number

Understand Vocabulary

1. Circle the label that best describes $\frac{1}{2}$.

fraction　　mixed number　　whole number

2. Circle the label that best describes $1\frac{1}{3}$.

fraction　　mixed number　　whole number

3. Circle the label that best describes 4.

fraction　　mixed number　　whole number

4. Draw a line from each term to its example.

decompose	$\frac{1}{2} = \frac{5}{10}$
denominator	$\frac{2}{3} = \frac{1}{3} + \frac{1}{3}$
equivalent fractions	$\frac{5}{6}$
like denominators	$\frac{1}{3} + \frac{2}{3} = \frac{3}{3}$
numerator	$\frac{7}{8}$

Use Vocabulary in Writing

5. Find $1\frac{1}{3} + 2\frac{2}{3}$. Use at least 3 terms from the Word List to describe how to find the sum.

Name ____________________

TOPIC 9

Reteaching

Set A pages 333–336, 341–344

Find $\frac{5}{8} + \frac{2}{8}$.

$\frac{5}{8} = \frac{1}{8} + \frac{1}{8} + \frac{1}{8} + \frac{1}{8} + \frac{1}{8}$ $\frac{2}{8} = \frac{1}{8} + \frac{1}{8}$

0 1

Add the numerators.
Keep the like denominator.

$\frac{5}{8} + \frac{2}{8} = \frac{7}{8}$

Remember you can use tools or add the numerators and write the sum over the like denoninator.

1. $\frac{2}{5} + \frac{2}{5}$
2. $\frac{2}{4} + \frac{1}{4} + \frac{1}{4}$
3. $\frac{3}{8} + \frac{4}{8}$
4. $\frac{4}{10} + \frac{2}{10} + \frac{3}{10}$
5. $\frac{4}{10} + \frac{3}{10}$
6. $\frac{7}{12} + \frac{2}{12}$

Set B pages 337–340

Decompose $1\frac{5}{6}$ two different ways.

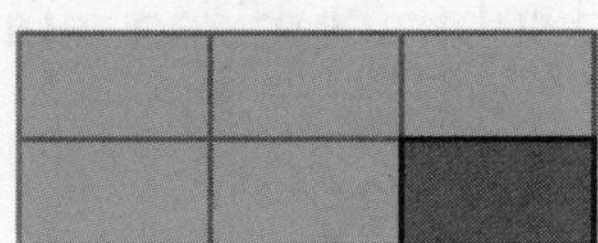

$1\frac{5}{6} = \frac{6}{6} + \frac{5}{6}$

$1\frac{5}{6} = \frac{4}{6} + \frac{4}{6} + \frac{3}{6}$

Remember you can decompose fractions in more than one way.

Decompose each fraction or mixed number in two different ways.

1. $\frac{3}{5}$
2. $\frac{9}{12}$
3. $1\frac{1}{2}$
4. $2\frac{2}{3}$

Set C pages 345–352

Find $\frac{5}{8} - \frac{2}{8}$.

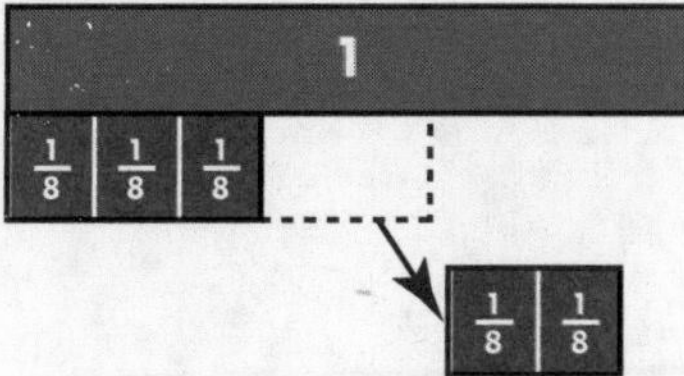

Subtract the numerators.
Keep the like denominator.

$\frac{5}{8} - \frac{2}{8} = \frac{3}{8}$

Remember you can use different tools to show how to subtract fractions.

1. $\frac{3}{3} - \frac{1}{3}$
2. $\frac{5}{6} - \frac{2}{6}$
3. $\frac{6}{8} - \frac{3}{8}$
4. $\frac{4}{10} - \frac{3}{10}$
5. $\frac{5}{5} - \frac{3}{5}$
6. $\frac{4}{6} - \frac{2}{6}$

Set D pages 353–356

Find the sum or difference shown on each number line.

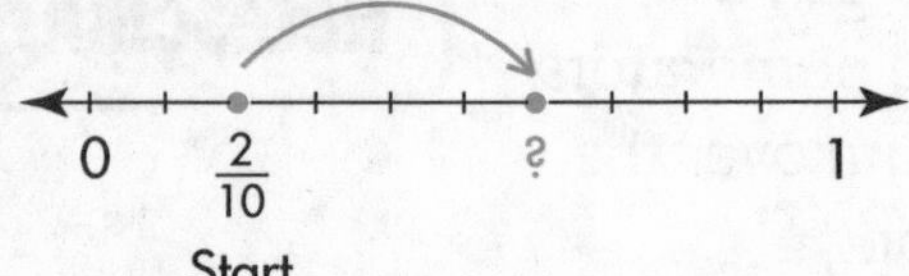

$\frac{2}{10} + \frac{4}{10} = \frac{6}{10}$

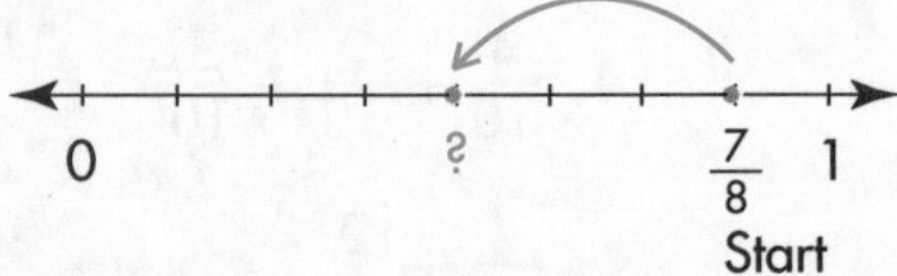

$\frac{7}{8} - \frac{3}{8} = \frac{4}{8}$

Remember you can show adding or subtracting fractions on a number line.

Write each equation shown.

1.

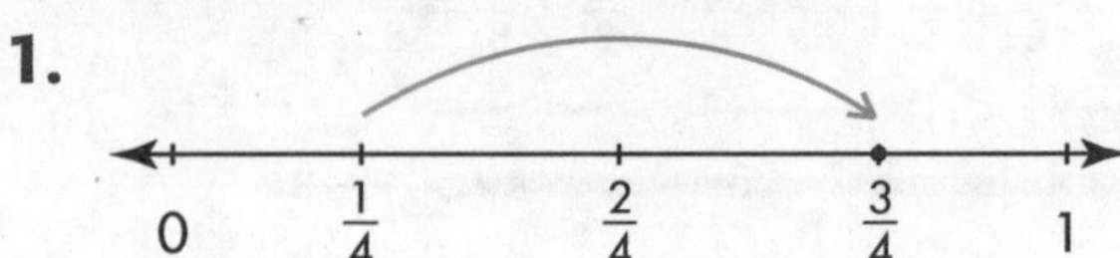

2.

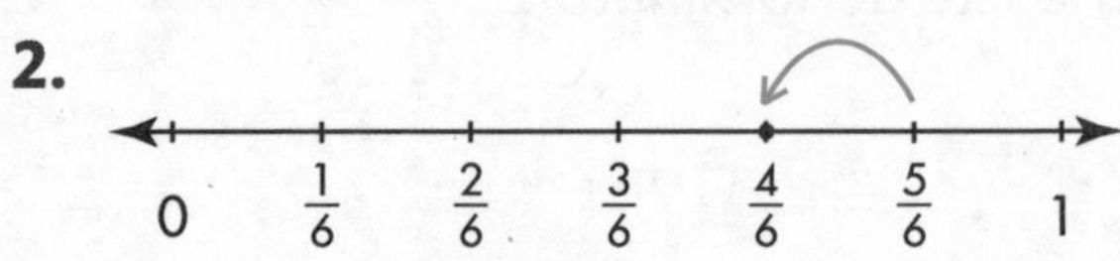

Set E pages 357–368

Find $5\frac{1}{5} - 3\frac{3}{5}$.

$$\begin{aligned} 5\tfrac{1}{5} &= 4\tfrac{6}{5} \\ -\,3\tfrac{3}{5} &= 3\tfrac{3}{5} \\ \hline &\quad 1\tfrac{3}{5} \end{aligned}$$

Find $1\frac{7}{8} + 2\frac{3}{8}$.

$$\begin{array}{r} 1\tfrac{7}{8} \\ +\,2\tfrac{3}{8} \\ \hline 3\tfrac{10}{8} = 4\tfrac{2}{8} \end{array}$$

Remember you can use different tools to add and subtract mixed numbers.

1. $5\frac{4}{8} + 2\frac{1}{8}$

2. $3\frac{3}{6} + 1\frac{5}{6}$

3. $5\frac{7}{10} + 4\frac{4}{10}$

4. $9 - 3\frac{3}{8}$

Set F pages 369–372

Think about these questions to help you **model with math**.

Thinking Habits

- How can I use math I know to help solve this problem?
- How can I use pictures, objects, or an equation to represent the problem?
- How can I use numbers, words, and symbols to solve the problem?

Remember to draw a bar diagram and write an equation to help solve a problem.

Bonnie ran $\frac{1}{4}$ mile, Olga ran $\frac{3}{4}$ mile, Gracie ran $\frac{5}{4}$ miles, and Maria ran $\frac{2}{4}$ mile. How much farther, f, did Gracie run than Bonnie and Maria combined, c?

Name ______________________________

TOPIC 9

Assessment Practice

1. Match each expression on the left to an equivalent expression.

	$\frac{5}{10}+\frac{4}{10}$	$\frac{2}{10}+\frac{3}{10}+\frac{6}{10}$	$\frac{2}{10}+\frac{1}{10}$	$\frac{16}{10}-\frac{1}{10}$
$\frac{1}{10}+\frac{1}{10}+\frac{1}{10}$	☐	☐	☐	☐
$\frac{4}{10}+\frac{5}{10}$	☐	☐	☐	☐
$\frac{2}{10}+\frac{3}{10}+\frac{6}{10}$	☐	☐	☐	☐
$\frac{11}{10}+\frac{4}{10}$	☐	☐	☐	☐

2. On Monday, $\frac{3}{12}$ of the students went on a field trip. What fraction of the students did **NOT** go on the field trip? Explain.

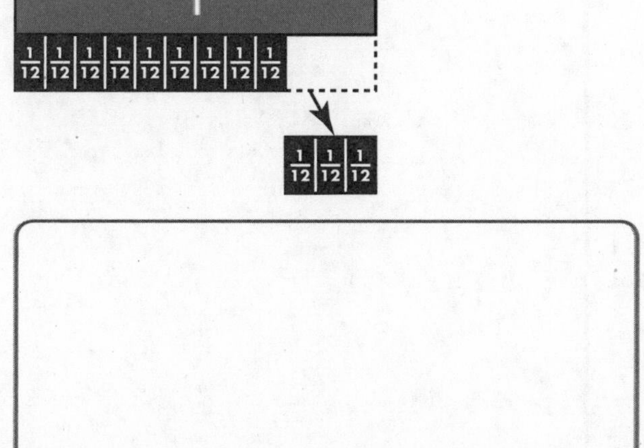

3. Riley planted flowers in some of her garden. Then, she planted vegetables in $\frac{2}{8}$ of her garden. Now, $\frac{7}{8}$ of Riley's garden is planted. What fraction of Riley's garden is planted with flowers? How much of her garden is not planted?

Ⓐ $\frac{2}{8}$ of her garden; $\frac{1}{8}$ of her garden is not planted

Ⓑ $\frac{3}{8}$ of her garden; $\frac{2}{8}$ of her garden is not planted

Ⓒ $\frac{4}{8}$ of her garden; $\frac{5}{8}$ of her garden is not planted

Ⓓ $\frac{5}{8}$ of her garden; $\frac{1}{8}$ of her garden is not planted

4. Select all the expressions that show a way to decompose $\frac{7}{8}$.

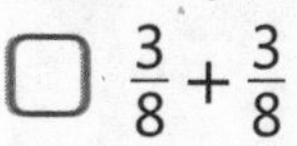

☐ $\frac{3}{8}+\frac{3}{8}$

☐ $\frac{1}{8}+\frac{1}{8}+\frac{5}{8}$

☐ $\frac{3}{4}+\frac{4}{4}$

☐ $\frac{1}{8}+\frac{3}{8}+\frac{3}{8}$

☐ $\frac{1}{8}+\frac{2}{8}+\frac{3}{8}+\frac{1}{8}$

5. Which equation is **NOT** true when $\frac{4}{12}$ is the missing number?

Ⓐ $\frac{3}{12}+\square=\frac{7}{12}$

Ⓑ $\frac{16}{12}-\square=1$

Ⓒ $1\frac{1}{12}+\square=5\frac{1}{12}$

Ⓓ $1\frac{5}{12}-\square=1\frac{1}{12}$

6. Zoe had $3\frac{1}{8}$ feet of orange ribbon. She used some ribbon to make a bow for a gift. Now she has $1\frac{3}{8}$ feet of ribbon left. How much orange ribbon did Zoe use? Use the model to write an equation, and solve.

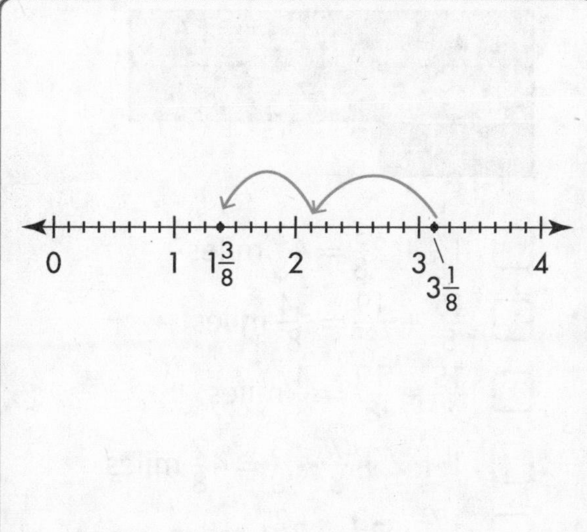

7. Roger and Sulee each decomposed $1\frac{1}{6}$. Roger wrote $\frac{1}{6} + \frac{1}{6} + \frac{2}{6} + \frac{3}{6}$. Sulee wrote $\frac{3}{6} + \frac{4}{6}$. Who was correct? Explain.

8. The number line shows which of the following equations?

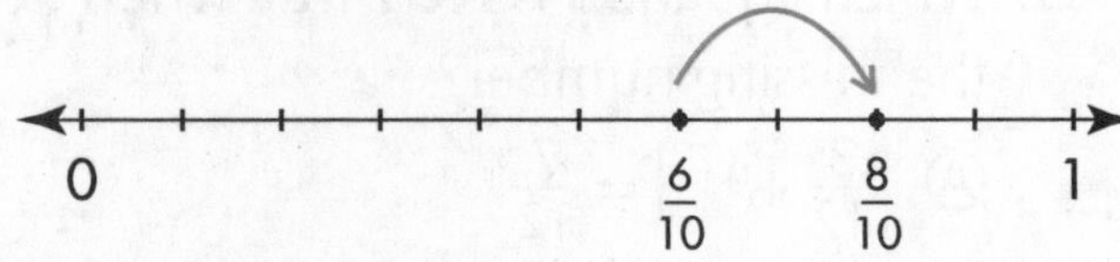

Ⓐ $0 + \frac{6}{10} = \frac{8}{10}$

Ⓑ $\frac{6}{10} + \frac{2}{10} = \frac{8}{10}$

Ⓒ $\frac{8}{10} - \frac{6}{10} = \frac{2}{10}$

Ⓓ $\frac{10}{10} - \frac{8}{10} = \frac{2}{10}$

9. Ryan kayaks $1\frac{7}{8}$ miles before lunch and $2\frac{3}{8}$ miles after lunch. Select all of the equations you would use to find how far Ryan kayacked.

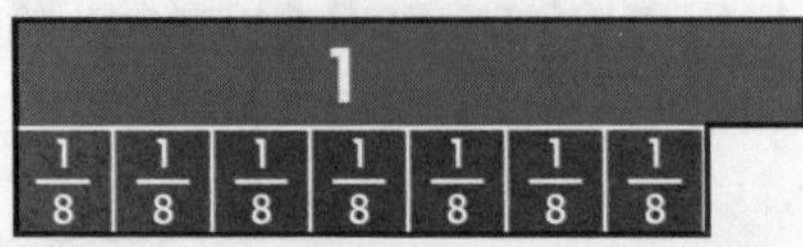

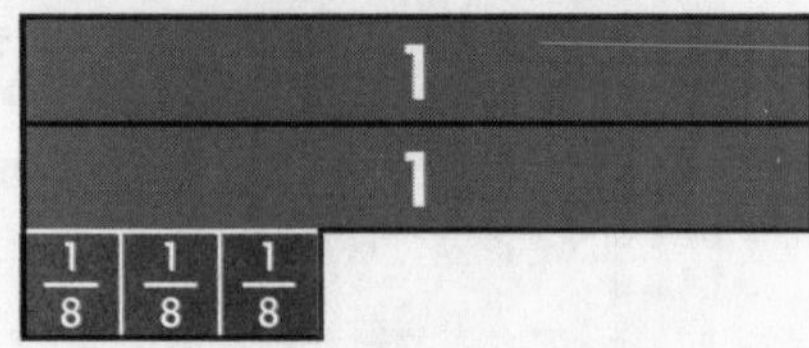

☐ $1\frac{7}{8} + 2\frac{3}{8} = 4\frac{2}{8}$ miles

☐ $\frac{15}{8} + \frac{19}{8} = \frac{34}{8}$ miles

☐ $\frac{15}{8} + \frac{19}{8} = \frac{4}{8}$ miles

☐ $1 + 2 + \frac{7}{8} + \frac{3}{8} = 4\frac{2}{8}$ miles

☐ $1\frac{7}{8} + 2\frac{3}{8} = 3\frac{21}{8}$ miles

10. The Jacobys kept track of the time they spent driving on their trip.

DATA

Driving Time

Day	Hours Driving
Monday	$5\frac{3}{4}$
Tuesday	$4\frac{3}{4}$
Wednesday	$2\frac{1}{4}$
Thursday	$6\frac{3}{4}$

A. Find how many hours the Jacobys drove on Monday and Tuesday. Draw a bar diagram to represent the problem.

B. Find how many hours the Jacobys drove in all. Explain your work.

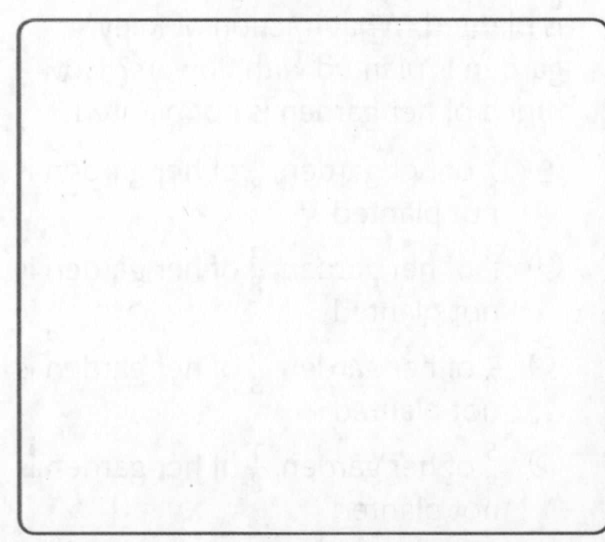

Name ______________________________

Water Race

In one of the games at the class picnic, students balanced containers filled with water on their heads. The goal was to carry the most water to the finish line. The teams are listed in the **Water Race Teams** table. The amount of water each student carried is listed in the **Water Race Results** table.

DATA

Water Race Teams	
Team	**Members**
1	Jay and Victor
2	Abbie and Shawn
3	Suki and Kira

DATA

Water Race Results	
Student	**Cups of Water**
Abbie	$\frac{5}{8}$
Jay	$\frac{6}{8}$
Kira	$\frac{5}{8}$
Shawn	$1\frac{7}{8}$
Suki	$1\frac{6}{8}$
Victor	$\frac{7}{8}$

1. Mia will hand out the prize to the winning team.

Part A

Draw a bar diagram and write an equation to find c, the cups of water Team 1 carried.

Part B

How many cups of water did Team 2 carry? Use fraction strips to show the sum.

Part C

How many cups of water did Team 3 carry? Use the number line to show the sum.

0 1 2 3

Part D

Which team carried the most water?

2. Team 1 wanted to know how they did compared to Team 2.

Part A

Draw a bar diagram and write an equation that could be used to find *m*, how much more water Team 2 carried than Team 1.

Part B

How much more water did Team 2 carry than Team 1? Explain how to solve the problem using your equation from Part A. Show your work.

Extend Multiplication Concepts to Fractions

Essential Questions: How can you describe a fraction using a unit fraction? How can you multiply a fraction by a whole number?

Light reflecting off of objects enters the eye and makes them visible.

Different kinds of flowers reflect different kinds of light, allowing them to be seen in color.

I could look at flowers all day! Here is a project about light and multiplication.

enVision® STEM Project: Light and Multiplication

Do Research Use the Internet or other sources to research the words *transparent*, *translucent*, and *opaque*. Write a definition for each word.

Journal: Write a Report Include what you found. Also in your report:

- List 1 example each of items that are transparent, translucent, or opaque.
- Suppose one-third of each of 5 same-sized posters is covered with opaque paper. What fraction of the posters are **NOT** covered by opaque paper? Explain how to use multiplication to find what part of the posters are **NOT** covered by opaque paper.

Name ____________________

Review What You Know

Vocabulary

Choose the best term from the box. Write it on the blank.

- equivalent fractions
- mixed number
- fraction
- whole number

1. A ____________ has a whole number and a fraction.

2. Fractions that name the same region, part of a set, or part of a segment are called ____________.

3. A ____________ has a numerator and a denominator.

Identifying Fractions

Write the fraction shown by each model.

4. 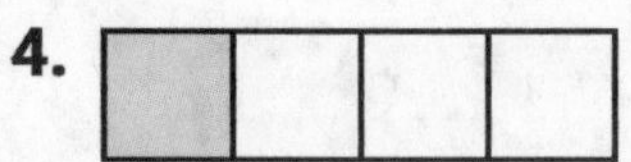

5. 

6. 

7. 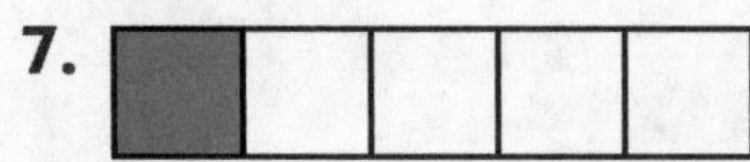

8. 

9. 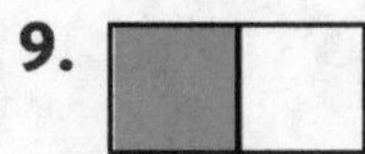

Unit Fractions

Write a fraction for each statement.

10. 3 copies of $\frac{1}{6}$ is ____.

11. 9 copies of $\frac{1}{12}$ is ____.

12. 5 copies of $\frac{1}{5}$ is ____.

13. 3 copies of $\frac{1}{10}$ is ____.

14. 6 copies of $\frac{1}{8}$ is ____.

15. 7 copies of $\frac{1}{10}$ is ____.

Equivalent Fractions

16. Draw a rectangle that shows 8 equal parts. Shade more than $\frac{3}{8}$ of the rectangle but less than $\frac{5}{8}$. What fraction did you model? Use multiplication or division to write two equivalent fractions for your model.

Name ______________________________

Pick a Project

Would you like to work with tiles?

Project: Design with Tiles

What cause would you donate your time or money to?

Project: Set Up a Charity Event

How fast can a jet aircraft travel?

Project: Write and Perform a Skit

PROJECT
10D

How would you like to run a marathon?

Project: Make a Game about Marathon Winners

Name ____________________

Lesson 10-1
Fractions as Multiples of Unit Fractions

I can ...
use fraction strips or number lines to understand a fraction as a multiple of a unit fraction.

Content Standard 4.NF.B.4a
Mathematical Practices MP.2, MP.4

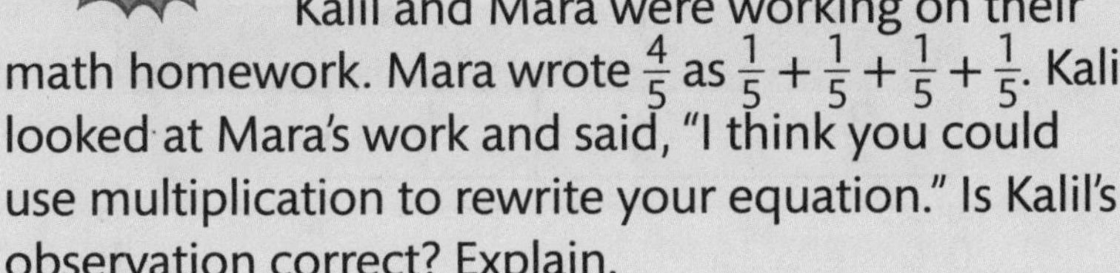

Solve & Share Kalil and Mara were working on their math homework. Mara wrote $\frac{4}{5}$ as $\frac{1}{5}+\frac{1}{5}+\frac{1}{5}+\frac{1}{5}$. Kalil looked at Mara's work and said, "I think you could use multiplication to rewrite your equation." Is Kalil's observation correct? Explain.

You can use reasoning to compare Mara's work and Kalil's observation.

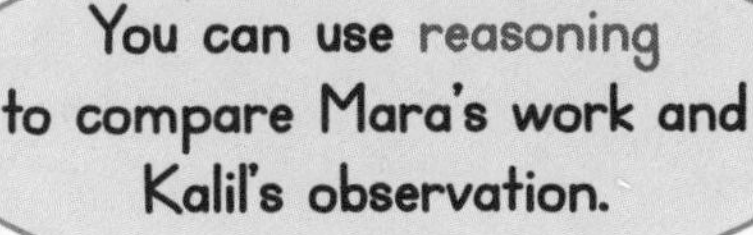

$\frac{1}{5}$	$\frac{1}{5}$	$\frac{1}{5}$	$\frac{1}{5}$

$$\frac{1}{5}+\frac{1}{5}+\frac{1}{5}+\frac{1}{5}=\frac{4}{5}$$

Look Back! Model with Math Write an equation to show the relationship between Mara's work and Kalil's observation.

How Can You Describe a Fraction Using a Unit Fraction?

Visual Learning Bridge

A

Courtney ran $\frac{3}{4}$ of the way to school. Describe $\frac{3}{4}$ using unit fractions.

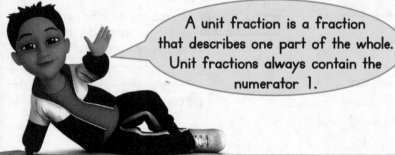

A unit fraction is a fraction that describes one part of the whole. Unit fractions always contain the numerator 1.

B

When a whole is divided into four equal parts, each part is described as the unit fraction $\frac{1}{4}$.

Decompose $\frac{3}{4}$ into unit fractions.

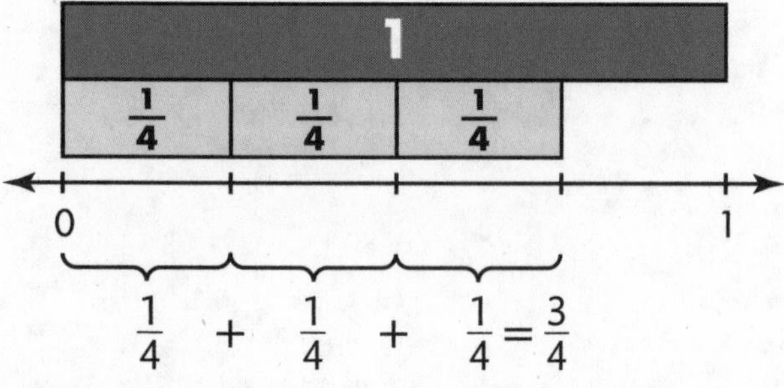

$\frac{1}{4} + \frac{1}{4} + \frac{1}{4} = \frac{3}{4}$

C

Repeated addition can be represented as multiplication.

Just as $6 + 6 + 6 = 3 \times 6$,

$\frac{1}{4} + \frac{1}{4} + \frac{1}{4} = 3 \times \frac{1}{4}$.

$\frac{3}{4} = 3 \times \frac{1}{4}$

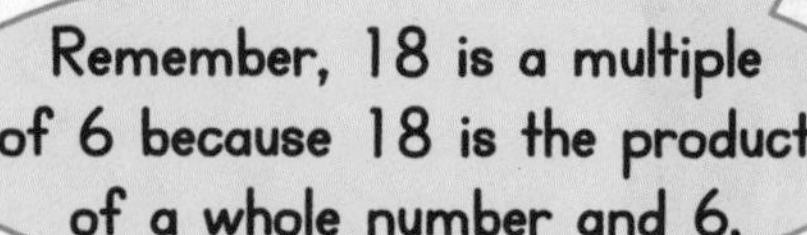

Remember, 18 is a multiple of 6 because 18 is the product of a whole number and 6.

So, $\frac{3}{4}$ is a multiple of $\frac{1}{4}$.

Convince Me! Reasoning The number $\frac{5}{8}$ is a multiple of what unit fraction? Explain.

Name ______________________

Another Example!

Describe $\frac{5}{4}$ as a multiple of a unit fraction.

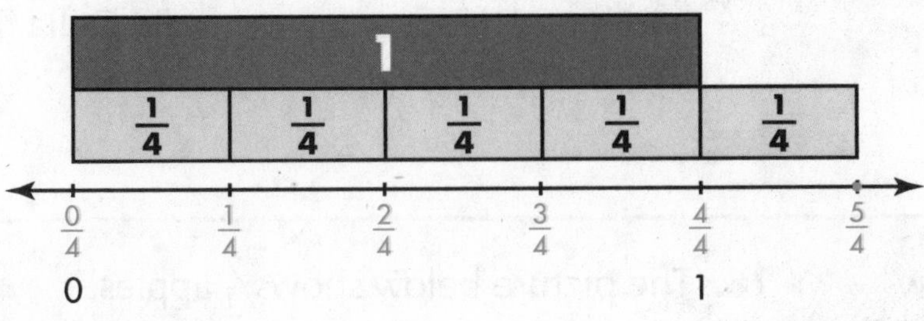

$$\frac{5}{4} = \frac{1}{4} + \frac{1}{4} + \frac{1}{4} + \frac{1}{4} + \frac{1}{4}$$
$$= 5 \times \frac{1}{4}$$

$\frac{5}{4}$ is a multiple of $\frac{1}{4}$.

Guided Practice

Do You Understand?

1. Draw a picture to explain why $\frac{3}{5} = 3 \times \frac{1}{5}$.

2. Write a multiplication equation to show each part of the following story. Mark's family ate $\frac{7}{4}$ chicken pot pies for dinner. There are 7 people in Mark's family. Each family member ate $\frac{1}{4}$ of a pie.

Do You Know How?

For **3–6**, write each fraction as a multiple of a unit fraction. Use a tool as needed.

3. $\frac{2}{3} = \square \times \frac{1}{3}$

4. $\frac{5}{6} = 5 \times \frac{1}{\square}$

5. $\frac{4}{2}$

6. $\frac{6}{5}$

Independent Practice

Leveled Practice For **7–12**, write each fraction as a multiple of a unit fraction. Use a tool as needed.

7. $\frac{7}{8} = \square \times \frac{1}{8}$

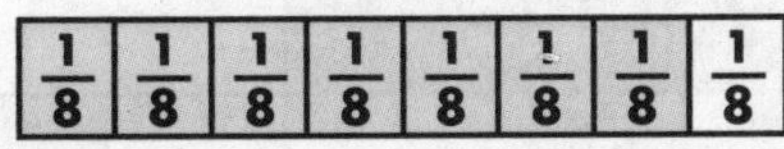

8. $\frac{3}{6} = 3 \times \frac{1}{\square}$

$\frac{1}{6}$	$\frac{1}{6}$	$\frac{1}{6}$	$\frac{1}{6}$	$\frac{1}{6}$	$\frac{1}{6}$

9. $\frac{2}{5} = \square \times \frac{1}{5}$

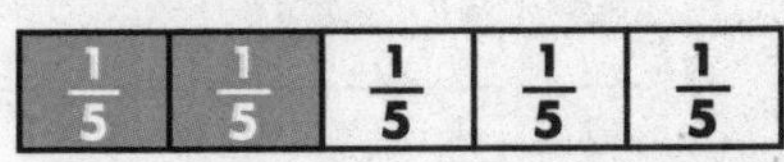

10. $\frac{6}{4}$

11. $\frac{9}{6}$

12. $\frac{8}{5}$

Problem Solving

13. Mark slices $\frac{4}{6}$ of a tomato. Each slice is $\frac{1}{6}$ of the tomato. How many slices does Mark have? Explain by writing $\frac{4}{6}$ as a multiple of $\frac{1}{6}$.

14. Delia flew 2,416 miles the first year on the job. She flew 3,719 miles the second year. Delia flew 2,076 more miles the third year than the first and second years combined. How many miles did Delia fly the third year?

15. Model with Math The picture below shows $\frac{6}{2}$ pears. Write $\frac{6}{2}$ as repeated addition and as a multiple of a unit fraction.

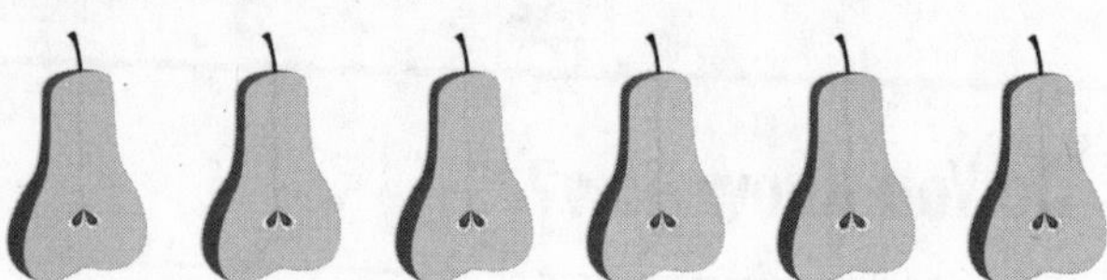

16. The picture below shows $\frac{7}{2}$ apples. Write $\frac{7}{2}$ as repeated addition and as a multiple of a unit fraction.

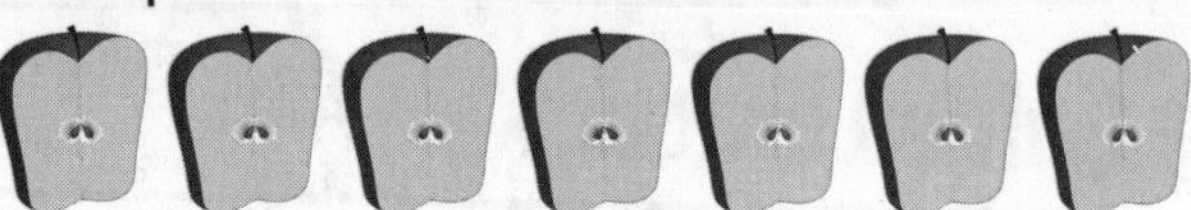

17. enVision® STEM Light travels at a speed of about 186,000 miles per second. How far does light travel in 5 seconds?

18. Higher Order Thinking Kobe drinks $\frac{1}{3}$ cup of juice each day. He has $2\frac{1}{3}$ cups of juice left. For how many days will it last? Explain by writing $2\frac{1}{3}$ as a fraction and then writing the fraction as a multiple of $\frac{1}{3}$.

Assessment Practice

19. Which multiplication equation describes the fraction plotted on the number line?

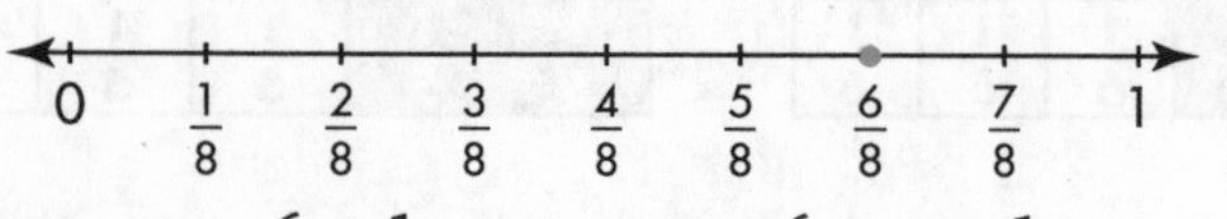

Ⓐ $6 = \frac{6}{3} \times \frac{1}{8}$

Ⓑ $\frac{6}{8} = 6 \times \frac{1}{8}$

Ⓒ $\frac{6}{8} = 8 \times \frac{1}{6}$

Ⓓ $\frac{6}{8} = \frac{1}{8} + 6$

20. Which multiplication equation describes the picture below?

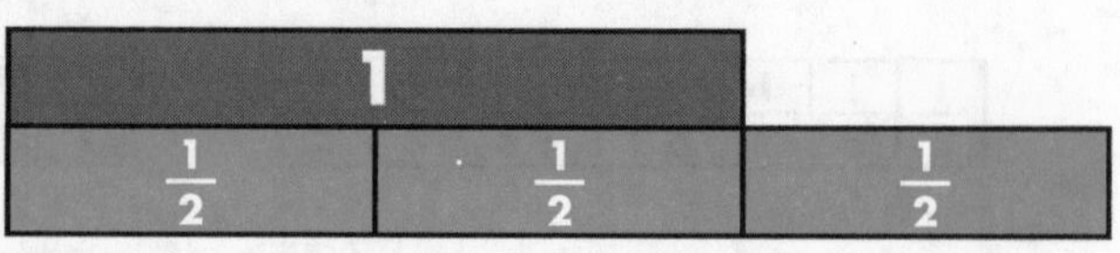

Ⓐ $\frac{3}{3} = 3 \times 1$

Ⓑ $\frac{3}{3} = \frac{1}{2} + \frac{1}{2} + \frac{1}{2}$

Ⓒ $\frac{3}{2} = 3 + \frac{1}{2}$

Ⓓ $\frac{3}{2} = 3 \times \frac{1}{2}$

Name ____________________

Activity

Solve & Share

How much tomato juice is needed for a group of 4 people if each person gets $\frac{1}{3}$ cup of juice? How much tomato juice is needed if they each get $\frac{2}{3}$ cup of juice? ***Solve these problems any way you choose.***

Lesson 10-2
Multiply a Fraction by a Whole Number: Use Models

I can ...
use drawings, area models, or number lines to multiply fractions by whole numbers.

Content Standards 4.NF.B.4b Also 4.NF.B.4a, 4.NF.B.4c
Mathematical Practices MP.4, MP.7, MP.8

You can use drawings or write equations to model with math. *Show your work in the space below!*

Look Back! Use Structure How does finding the total juice for 4 people with $\frac{2}{3}$ cup servings compare to finding it for $\frac{1}{3}$ cup servings? Why?

How Can You Multiply a Fraction by a Whole Number?

Visual Learning Bridge

A

Dori lives $\frac{1}{4}$ mile from school. If she walks to and from school each day, how far does Dori walk during a school week?

DATA

Distance Walked (in miles)

	Mon	Tues	Wed	Thurs	Fri
To School	$\frac{1}{4}$	$\frac{1}{4}$	$\frac{1}{4}$	$\frac{1}{4}$	$\frac{1}{4}$
From School	$\frac{1}{4}$	$\frac{1}{4}$	$\frac{1}{4}$	$\frac{1}{4}$	$\frac{1}{4}$

Remember, multiplication is repeated addition. So, you can use addition or multiplication to solve this problem.

B

One Way

Draw a picture to show Dori walks $\frac{1}{4}$ mile, 10 times.

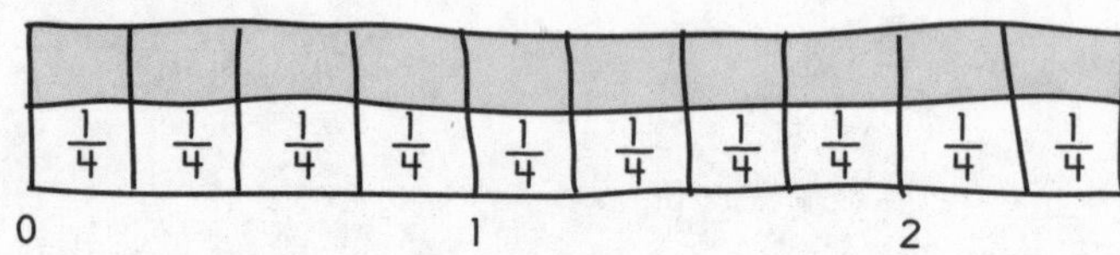

$\frac{1}{4}+\frac{1}{4}+\frac{1}{4}+\frac{1}{4}+\frac{1}{4}+\frac{1}{4}+\frac{1}{4}+\frac{1}{4}+\frac{1}{4}+\frac{1}{4}=\frac{10}{4}$

Write $\frac{10}{4}$ as a mixed number.

$\frac{10}{4}=\frac{4}{4}+\frac{4}{4}+\frac{2}{4}=2\frac{2}{4}$

C

Another Way

Draw a number line to show Dori walks $\frac{1}{4}$ mile, 10 times.

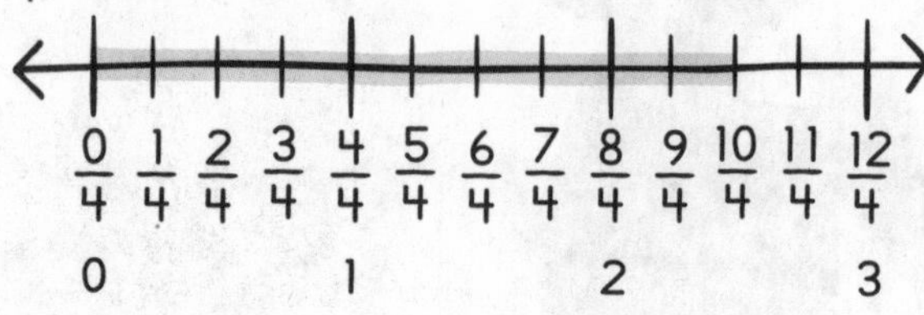

$10 \times \frac{1}{4}=\frac{10}{4}$

Write $\frac{10}{4}$ as a mixed number.

$\frac{10}{4}=\frac{4}{4}+\frac{4}{4}+\frac{2}{4}=2\frac{2}{4}$

Since $\frac{2}{4}$ is equivalent to $\frac{1}{2}$, $2\frac{2}{4}$ is equivalent to $2\frac{1}{2}$. Dori walks $2\frac{1}{2}$ miles to and from school each week.

Convince Me! Generalize Why can both addition and multiplication be used to represent the problem above? Write an equation to explain.

Name ______________________________

Another Example!

How far did Jess bike to practice if he biked $\frac{3}{5}$ mile each day for 4 days?

$\frac{1}{5}$	$\frac{1}{5}$	$\frac{1}{5}$	$\frac{1}{5}$	$\frac{1}{5}$	$\frac{1}{5}$	$\frac{1}{5}$	$\frac{1}{5}$	$\frac{1}{5}$	$\frac{1}{5}$	$\frac{1}{5}$	$\frac{1}{5}$
$\frac{3}{5}$			$\frac{3}{5}$			$\frac{3}{5}$			$\frac{3}{5}$		

Use addition.

$\frac{3}{5}+\frac{3}{5}+\frac{3}{5}+\frac{3}{5}=\frac{12}{5}=\frac{5}{5}+\frac{5}{5}+\frac{2}{5}=2\frac{2}{5}$

Jess bikes $2\frac{2}{5}$ miles.

Use multiplication.

$4\times\frac{3}{5}=\frac{12}{5}=\frac{5}{5}+\frac{5}{5}+\frac{2}{5}=2\frac{2}{5}$

Jess bikes $2\frac{2}{5}$ miles.

Guided Practice

Do You Understand?

1. Draw a picture to explain how to find $3\times\frac{2}{5}$.

Do You Know How?

For **2–3**, write and solve a multiplication equation.

2.

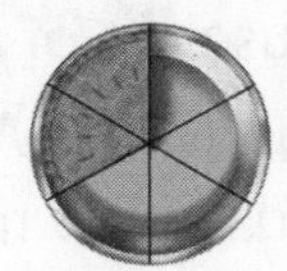
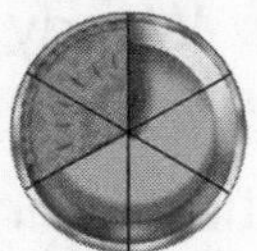

3.

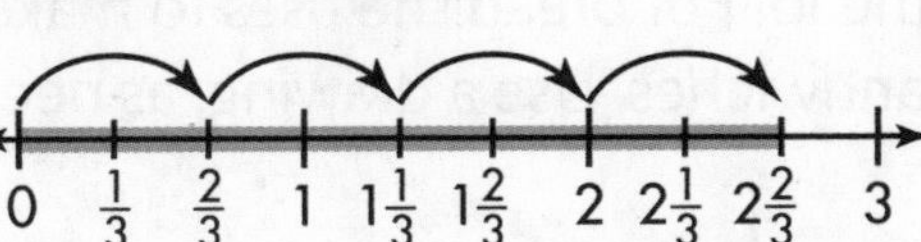

Independent Practice

For **4–7**, write and solve a multiplication equation. Use drawings or number lines as needed.

4.

$\frac{1}{8}$ mi	$\frac{1}{8}$ mi	$\frac{1}{8}$ mi	$\frac{1}{8}$ mi	$\frac{1}{8}$ mi

5.

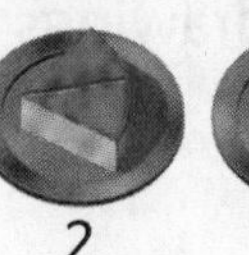

$\frac{2}{10}$ $\frac{2}{10}$ $\frac{2}{10}$

6. Calculate the distance Margo rides her bike if she rides $\frac{7}{8}$ mile each day for 4 days.

7. Calculate the distance Tom rides his bike if he rides $\frac{5}{6}$ mile each day for 5 days.

Problem Solving

8. Kiona fills a measuring cup with $\frac{3}{4}$ cup of juice 3 times to make punch. Write and solve a multiplication equation with a whole number and a fraction to show the total amount of juice Kiona uses.

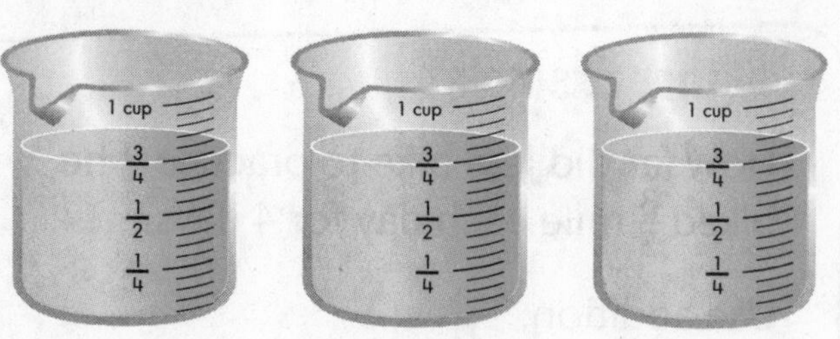

9. Each lap around a track is $\frac{3}{10}$ kilometer. Eliot walked around the track 4 times. How far did Eliot walk?

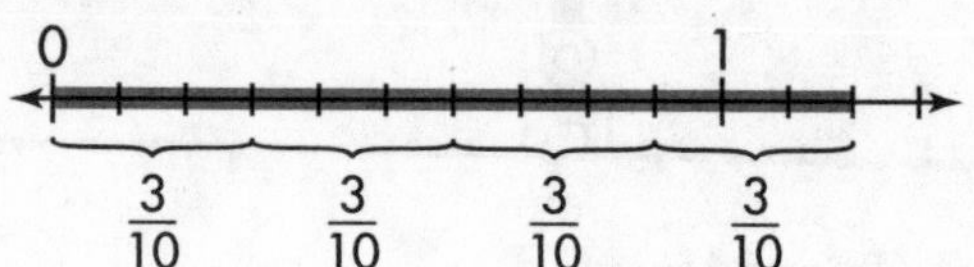

10. A chef serves $\frac{5}{6}$ of a pan of lasagna. Each piece is $\frac{1}{6}$ of the pan. How many pieces did the chef serve? Solve by writing $\frac{5}{6}$ as a multiple of $\frac{1}{6}$.

11. Model with Math Wendy uses $\frac{2}{12}$ of a loaf of bread to make one sandwich. Write and solve an equation to find *b*, how much of the loaf of bread she uses to make 4 sandwiches. Use a drawing, as needed.

12. Higher Order Thinking A baker uses $\frac{2}{3}$ cup of rye flour in each loaf of bread. How many cups of rye flour will the baker use in 3 loaves? in 7 loaves? in 10 loaves?

Assessment Practice

13. Elaine jogged $\frac{4}{5}$ mile each day for 4 days. Select all the expressions that tell how far Elaine jogged in all. Use drawings or number lines as needed.

- ☐ $4 \times \frac{4}{5}$
- ☐ $\frac{16}{5}$
- ☐ $3\frac{1}{5}$
- ☐ $4 \times \frac{1}{5}$
- ☐ $2\frac{1}{5}$

14. Freddie skated $\frac{1}{2}$ mile each day for 6 days. Select all the equations that can be used to find *s*, the total distance Freddie skated.

- ☐ $s = \frac{1}{2} + \frac{1}{2} + \frac{1}{2} + \frac{1}{2} + \frac{1}{2} + \frac{1}{2}$
- ☐ $s = 6 \times \frac{1}{2}$
- ☐ $s = 6 + \frac{1}{2}$
- ☐ $s = 6 + 2 \times \frac{1}{2}$
- ☐ $s = 6 \times 2$

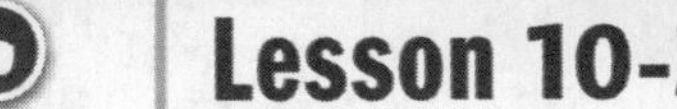

Name ____________________

Lesson 10-3
Multiply a Fraction by a Whole Number: Use Symbols

I can ...
use properties and equations to multiply a fraction by a whole number.

Content Standards 4.NF.B.4b Also 4.NF.B.4a, 4.NF.B.4c
Mathematical Practices MP.4, MP.6, MP.7

Solve & Share

A recipe for 1 gallon of fruit punch calls for $\frac{3}{4}$ cup of orange juice. How many cups of orange juice are needed to make 8 gallons of fruit punch? ***Solve this problem any way you choose.***

You can use a drawing, bar diagram, area model, or equation to model with math. *Show your work in the space below!*

Look Back! **Be Precise** Look back at your solution. What units should you use to label your answer?

How Can You Use Symbols to Multiply a Fraction by a Whole Number?

Visual Learning Bridge

A

Stanley makes ice cream sundaes. Today Stanley made 2 ice cream sundaes. How much ice cream did Stanley use? Find $2 \times \frac{3}{4}$.

You can use structure when multiplying a fraction and a whole number.

B One Way

$2 \times \frac{3}{4} = 2 \times \left(3 \times \frac{1}{4}\right)$ Write $\frac{3}{4}$ as a multiple of $\frac{1}{4}$: $\frac{3}{4} = 3 \times \frac{1}{4}$.

$= (2 \times 3) \times \frac{1}{4}$ Use the Associative Property of Multiplication.

$= 6 \times \frac{1}{4}$

$= \frac{6}{4}$

$= \frac{4}{4} + \frac{2}{4} = 1\frac{2}{4}$

So, $2 \times \frac{3}{4} = \frac{6}{4}$ or $1\frac{2}{4}$.

C Another Way

$2 \times \frac{3}{4} = \frac{2 \times 3}{4}$ Multiply the whole number and the numerator.

$= \frac{6}{4}$

$= \frac{4}{4} + \frac{2}{4} = 1\frac{2}{4}$

So, $2 \times \frac{3}{4} = \frac{6}{4}$ or $1\frac{2}{4}$

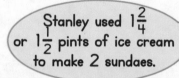

Stanley used $1\frac{2}{4}$ or $1\frac{1}{2}$ pints of ice cream to make 2 sundaes.

Convince Me! **Use Structure** Use properties of operations to calculate $3 \times \frac{3}{6}$. Show your work.

Name

Guided Practice

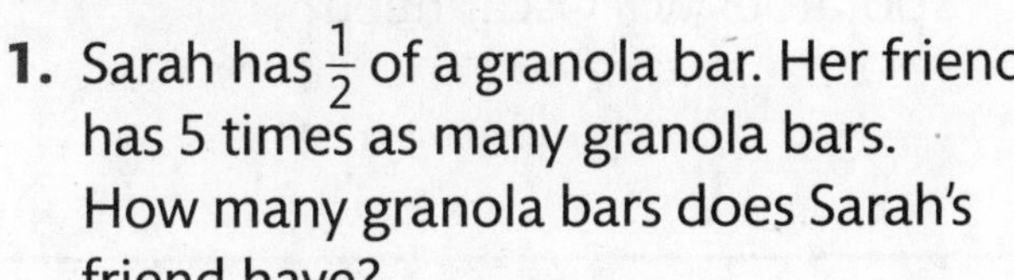

Do You Understand?

1. Sarah has $\frac{1}{2}$ of a granola bar. Her friend has 5 times as many granola bars. How many granola bars does Sarah's friend have?

2. Sue needs $\frac{5}{6}$ cup of cocoa to make one batch of chocolate pudding. She wants to make 4 batches of pudding to take to a party. Write and solve an equation to find how many cups of cocoa, *c*, Sue will need for all 4 batches of pudding.

Do You Know How?

For **3–4**, multiply.

3. $8 \times \frac{1}{2}$

4. $3 \times \frac{3}{4}$

For **5–6**, write and solve a multiplication equation.

5. Calculate the amount of medicine taken in 5 days if the dose is $\frac{3}{4}$ fluid ounce per day.

6. Calculate the total length needed to decorate 9 boxes if each box uses $\frac{2}{3}$ yard of ribbon.

Independent Practice

For **7–15**, multiply.

7. $4 \times \frac{1}{3}$

8. $6 \times \frac{3}{8}$

9. $8 \times \frac{2}{5}$

10. $2 \times \frac{5}{6}$

11. $4 \times \frac{2}{3}$

12. $5 \times \frac{7}{8}$

13. $7 \times \frac{3}{4}$

14. $9 \times \frac{3}{5}$

15. $4 \times \frac{5}{8}$

For **16–17**, write and solve a multiplication equation.

16. Calculate the total distance Mary runs in one week if she runs $\frac{7}{8}$ mile each day.

17. Calculate the length of 5 pieces of ribbon laid end to end if each piece is $\frac{2}{3}$ yard long.

Problem Solving

18. A baseball team bought 8 boxes of baseballs. If the team spent a total of \$1,696, what was the cost of 1 box of baseballs?

19. Oscar wants to make 4 chicken pot pies. The recipe requires $\frac{2}{3}$ pound of potatoes for each pot pie. How many pounds of potatoes will Oscar need?

20. It takes Mario $\frac{1}{4}$ hour to mow Mr. Harris's lawn. It takes him 3 times as long to mow Mrs. Carter's lawn. How long does it take Mario to mow Mrs. Carter's lawn? Write your answer as a fraction of an hour, then as minutes.

$\frac{1}{4}$ hour is 15 minutes.

21. **Vocabulary** Use *numerator*, *denominator*, and *whole number*.

When you multiply a fraction by a whole number, the ____________ in the product is the same as the denominator of the fraction. The ____________ in the product is the product of the ____________ and the numerator of the fraction.

22. **Model with Math** Malik swims $\frac{9}{10}$ mile each day. Write and solve an equation to find n, how many miles Malik swims in 4 days.

23. **Higher Order Thinking** Sam is making 7 fruit tarts. Each tart needs $\frac{3}{4}$ cup of strawberries and $\frac{1}{4}$ cup of blueberries. What is the total amount of fruit that Sam needs for his tarts? Use properties of operations to solve.

Assessment Practice

24. Sean is making picture frames. Each frame uses $\frac{4}{5}$ yard of wood. What is the total length of wood Sean will need to make 2 frames? Complete the equation.

$2 \times \frac{4}{5} = \frac{\square \times 4}{5} = \frac{\square}{5}$ or $1\frac{\square}{5}$ yards

25. Ellen is making plant boxes. Each box uses $\frac{3}{6}$ yard of wood. What is the total length of wood Ellen will need to make 7 plant boxes? Complete the equation.

$7 \times \frac{3}{6} = \frac{\square \times 3}{6} = \frac{\square\square}{\square}$ or $\square\frac{3}{6}$ yards

Name ______________________

Lesson 10-4

Solve Time Problems

I can ...

use addition, subtraction, multiplication, or division to solve problems involving time.

Content Standards 4.MD.A.2 Also 4.NF.B.4c, 4.NF.B.3d, 4.MD.A.1
Mathematical Practices MP.1, MP.3, MP.5

Solve & Share

The Big Sur International Marathon is run on the California coast each spring. Sean's mother was the women's overall winner. How much faster was Sean's mother than the women's winner in the Ages 65–69 group? Tell how you decided. ***Solve this problem any way you choose.***

You can use appropriate tools such as bar diagrams or number lines to solve problems involving time.

DATA

	Men	Women
Overall	2 hours 23 minutes	2 hours 50 minutes
Ages 65–69	3 hours 34 minutes	3 hours 58 minutes
Ages 70–74	4 hours 20 minutes	4 hours 34 minutes

Look Back! The men's winner in the Ages 70–74 group took $4\frac{1}{3}$ hours. Sean's grandfather, who is only 68, took $3\frac{2}{3}$ hours. How can you find the difference in these times?

How Can You Solve Problems Involving Time?

Visual Learning Bridge

A

Krystal is training for a race. She trains every day for 8 days. How many hours does Krystal train?

Krystal spends an equal amount of time sprinting, walking, and jogging. How many minutes does Krystal spend on each activity during her 8 days of training?

You can use what you know about time to help solve these problems.

Krystal trains $\frac{3}{4}$ hour per day.

B

Find how many hours Krystal trains.

Find $8 \times \frac{3}{4}$.

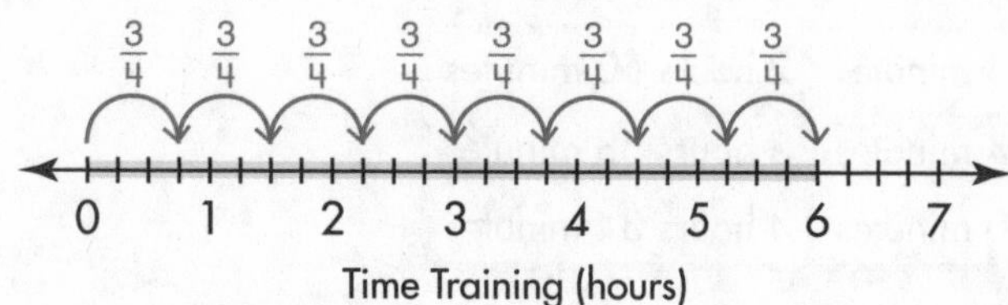

$$8 \times \frac{3}{4} = \frac{24}{4}$$
$$= \frac{4}{4} + \frac{4}{4} + \frac{4}{4} + \frac{4}{4} + \frac{4}{4} + \frac{4}{4} = 6$$

Krystal trains for 6 hours.

You can use a linear model to help solve time problems.

C

Find how many minutes Krystal spends on each activity during her training.

1 hour = 60 minutes
6×60 minutes = 360 minutes of training

In 8 days, Krystal spends 360 minutes sprinting, walking, and jogging.

Divide to find how many minutes Krystal spends on each activity. Find $360 \div 3$.

$$3\overline{)360}\ \ \text{quotient } 120$$

In 8 days, Krystal spends 120 minutes, or 2 hours, training on each activity.

Convince Me! **Construct Arguments** Why do you multiply to convert 6 hours to minutes?

Name ____________________

Practice Tools Assessment

Another Example!

Adding Time

Find 2 hours 32 minutes + 3 hours 40 minutes.

```
  2 hours 32 minutes
+ 3 hours 40 minutes
--------------------
  5 hours 72 minutes
= 6 hours 12 minutes
```

Since 72 minutes > 1 hour, regroup 60 minutes as 1 hour.

Subtracting Time

Find 5 hours 8 minutes − 2 hours 32 minutes.

```
   4        68
   5 hours  8 minutes   (5 and 8 crossed out)
 − 2 hours 32 minutes
 --------------------
   2 hours 36 minutes
```

Since 8 minutes < 32 minutes, regroup 1 hour as 60 minutes.

Guided Practice

Do You Understand?

1. How is adding and subtracting measures of time like adding and subtracting whole numbers?

Do You Know How?

For **2–3**, solve. Remember there are 60 minutes in 1 hour and 7 days in 1 week.

2. How many minutes are in a school day of 7 hours 25 minutes?

3. How much is $3\frac{2}{4}$ weeks + $2\frac{3}{4}$ weeks?

Independent Practice

For **4–7**, add, subtract, multiply, or divide.

DATA: Units of Time	
1 hour = 60 minutes	1 day = 24 hours
1 year = 12 months	1 week = 7 days

4.
```
   8 hours 30 minutes
 + 7 hours 35 minutes
 --------------------
   □ hours □ minutes  = □ hours □ minutes
```

5.
```
     □       □
   2 years 5 months
 −         9 months
 ------------------
   □ year  □ months
```

6. $8 \times \frac{1}{4}$ hour $= \frac{\square \times 1}{\square} = \frac{\square}{4} = \square$ hours

7. How long must each person work for 4 people to evenly share 48 hours of work?
$48 \div 4 = \square$ hours

Problem Solving

For **8–9**, use the table at the right.

8. How long do all of the activities at the reunion last?

9. There are 55 minutes between the time dinner ends and the campfire begins. What is the elapsed time from the beginning of dinner to the beginning of the campfire?

Suarez Family Reunion Schedule	
Trip to Scenic Lake Park	4 hours 15 minutes
Slide show	55 minutes
Dinner	1 hour 30 minutes
Campfire	1 hour 35 minutes

10. Make Sense and Persevere The band boosters spent $4,520 on airline tickets and $1,280 on hotel costs for the 8 members of the color guard. How much was spent for each member of the color guard?

11. Higher Order Thinking A boat ride at the lake lasts $2\frac{2}{4}$ hours. A canoe trip down the river lasts $3\frac{1}{4}$ hours. Show each time on the number line. How much longer is the canoe trip than the boat ride in hours? in minutes?

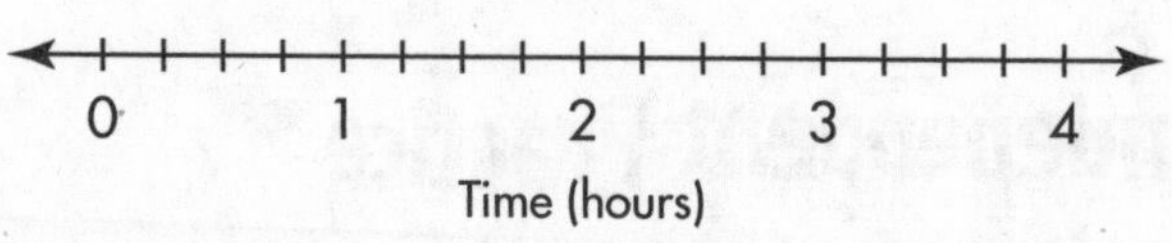

Assessment Practice

12. It takes Krys and Glen $\frac{1}{4}$ hour to walk a mile. This week Krys walked 9 miles and Glen walked 3 miles. How much longer did Krys walk than Glen?

_____ hours

13. Henry's first flight lasts 1 hour 12 minutes. The second flight lasts 2 hours 41 minutes. How much time did Henry spend on the flights?

_____ hours _____ minutes

Name ____________________ Activity

Solve & Share

Pierre's mother owns an ice cream shop. She puts $\frac{3}{12}$ cup of vanilla extract and $\frac{1}{12}$ cup of almond extract in each 10-gallon batch of ice cream. How much total extract is used to make 5 batches of ice cream? Use the bar diagrams to represent and solve this problem.

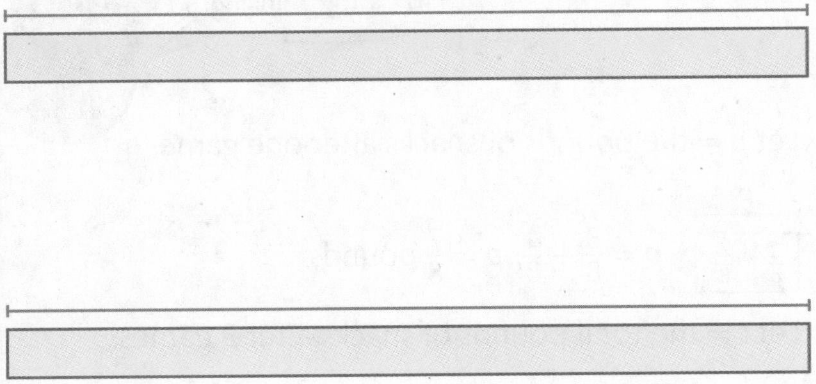

Problem Solving

Lesson 10-5

Model with Math

I can ...

use various representations to solve problems.

Mathematical Practices MP.4 Also MP.2
Content Standards 4.NF.B.4c Also 4.NF.B.3d, 4.MD.A.2

Thinking Habits

Be a good thinker!
These questions can help you.

- How can I use math I know to help solve this problem?
- How can I use pictures, objects, or an equation to represent the problem?
- How can I use numbers, words, and symbols to solve the problem?

Look Back! **Model with Math** What number sentences can you write to model the problem?

How Can You Represent a Situation with a Math Model?

Visual Learning Bridge

A

Mr. Finn gives the amount of snacks shown to the baseball team's coach every time the team wins a game. How many total pounds of snacks does Mr. Finn give the coach after the baseball team wins 3 games?

What hidden question do you need to find and solve first?

How many total pounds of snacks does Mr. Finn give the coach when the baseball team wins one game?

Here's my thinking.

B **How can I model with math?**

I can

- use previously learned concepts and skills.
- find and answer any hidden questions.
- use bar diagrams and equations to represent and solve this problem.

C Let p = the pounds of snacks after one game.

p	
$\frac{3}{8}$	$\frac{4}{8}$

$p = \frac{3}{8} + \frac{4}{8}$, $p = \frac{7}{8}$ pounds

Let t = the total pounds of snacks after 3 games.

t		
$\frac{7}{8}$	$\frac{7}{8}$	$\frac{7}{8}$

$t = 3 \times \frac{7}{8} = \frac{21}{8}$

$= \frac{8}{8} + \frac{8}{8} + \frac{5}{8}$

$t = 2\frac{5}{8}$ pounds

Mr. Finn gives the coach $2\frac{5}{8}$ pounds of snacks after the team wins 3 games.

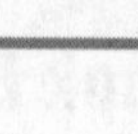

Convince Me! **Reasoning** Explain how to solve this problem another way.

Name ______________________________

Practice Tools Assessment

Guided Practice

Model with Math

Colton and his classmates are making maps of the streets where they live. How much green and black felt does his teacher need to buy so 5 groups of students can each make a map?

Felt needed for each map
$\frac{1}{6}$ sheet of white
$\frac{2}{6}$ sheet of brown
$\frac{2}{6}$ sheet of blue
$\frac{4}{6}$ sheet of green
$\frac{5}{6}$ sheet of black

1. Draw bar diagrams and write equations to find *g*, the amount of green and *b*, the amount of black felt.

2. Write and solve an equation to find *t*, the amount of green and black felt the class will use.

When you model with math, you use math you know to solve a problem.

Independent Practice

Model with Math

Moira swims $\frac{3}{6}$ hour before school 5 days a week and $\frac{5}{6}$ hour after school 4 days a week. For how long does she swim each week? Use Exercises 3–5 to answer the question.

3. Draw a bar diagram and write an equation to find *b*, how many hours Moira swims before school each week.

4. Draw a bar diagram and write an equation to find *a*, how many hours she swims after school each week.

5. Draw a bar diagram and write an equation to find *h*, how many hours Moira swims each week.

Performance Task

Seeing Orange

Perry mixed $\frac{5}{8}$ gallon of red paint and $\frac{3}{8}$ gallon of yellow paint to make the right shade of orange paint. He needs 2 gallons of orange paint to paint the basement floor. How many gallons of red and yellow paint should Perry use to make enough orange paint to cover the floor?

6. **Reasoning** What do you need to know to find how many gallons of each color Perry should use?

7. **Model with Math** Draw bar diagrams and write equations to find g, how many gallons of paint are in a batch and b, how many batches Perry needs to make.

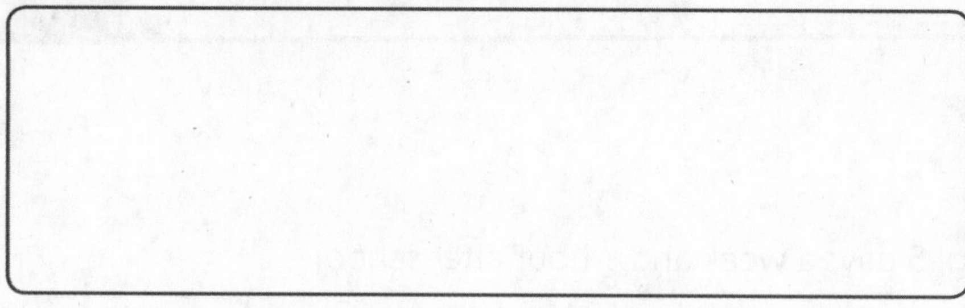

8. **Model with Math** Draw bar diagrams and write and solve equations to show how to find how many gallons of each color Perry should use. Tell what your variables represent.

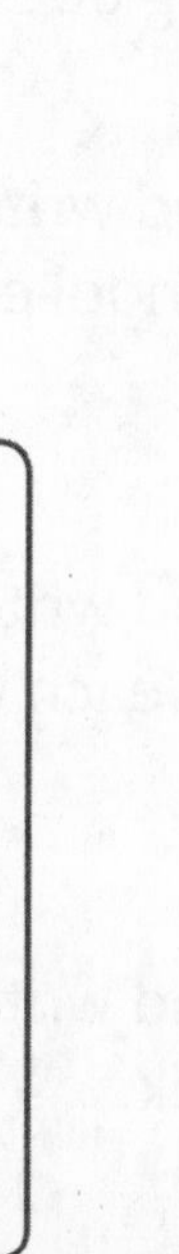

When you model with math, you use a picture to show how the quantities in the problem are related.

Name ____________________

TOPIC 10

Fluency Practice Activity

Find a partner. Get paper and a pencil. Each partner chooses a different color: light blue or dark blue.

Partner 1 and Partner 2 each point to a black number at the same time. Each partner adds the two numbers.

If the answer is on your color, you get a tally mark. Work until one partner has twelve tally marks.

I can ...
add multi-digit whole numbers.

Content Standard 4.NBT.B.4
Mathematical Practices MP.3, MP.6, MP.7, MP.8

Partner 1
2,814
3,149
4,097
5,308
6,127

3,043	5,776	4,565	6,015
6,595	3,617	6,834	3,856
3,343	6,496	5,502	5,537
3,008	3,378	4,326	4,804
4,291	3,183	5,677	3,521
3,518	6,356	3,282	4,466

Partner 2
369
194
229
468
707

Tally Marks for Partner 1	Tally Marks for Partner 2

TOPIC 10 Vocabulary Review

Glossary

Word List

- denominator
- equivalent fractions
- fraction
- mixed number
- multiple
- numerator
- unit fraction

Understand Vocabulary

Write T for *true* and F for *false*.

1. ______ The fraction $\frac{3}{4}$ is a multiple of $\frac{1}{4}$.
2. ______ Equivalent fractions are fractions where the numerator and the denominator have the same value.
3. ______ The denominator of a fraction tells the number of equal parts in the whole.
4. ______ A fraction names part of a whole, part of a set, or a location on a number line.
5. ______ The numerator is the number below the fraction bar in a fraction.

Write *always, sometimes,* or *never*.

6. A unit fraction ______________ has a numerator of 1.
7. A numerator is ______________ greater than its denominator.
8. A mixed number ______________ has just a fraction part.

Use Vocabulary in Writing

9. Samatha wrote $\frac{1}{2}$. Use at least 3 terms from the Word List to describe Samantha's fraction.

You can use most of the terms to describe Samantha's fraction.

Name

TOPIC 10

Reteaching

Set A pages 385–388

Talia used $\frac{5}{8}$ yard of ribbon.

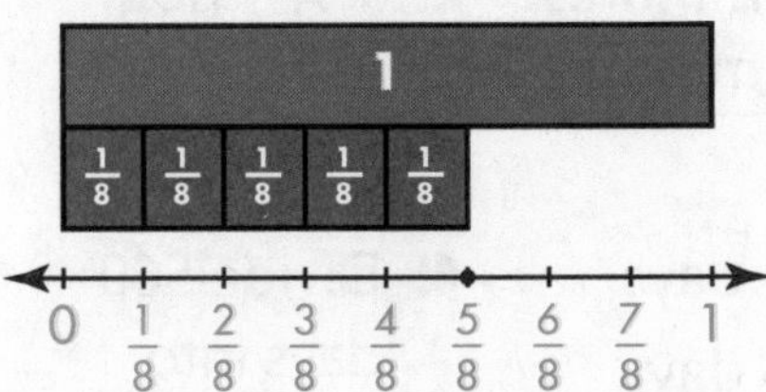

Write $\frac{5}{8}$ as a multiple of a unit fraction.

$$\frac{5}{8} = 5 \times \frac{1}{8}$$

Remember a unit fraction will always have a numerator of 1.

Write each fraction as a multiple of a unit fraction.

1. $\frac{5}{5}$

2. $\frac{3}{8}$

3. $\frac{4}{3}$

4. $\frac{6}{5}$

5. $\frac{15}{8}$

6. $\frac{7}{4}$

Set B pages 389–392

James runs $\frac{3}{5}$ mile each week. How far does James run after 2 weeks?

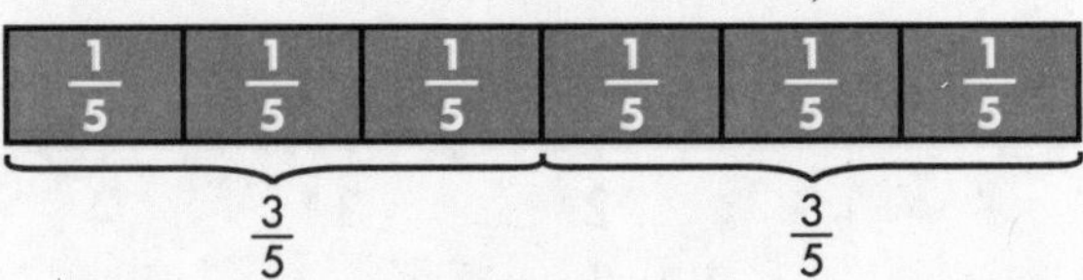

Use multiplication to find the product.

$2 \times \frac{3}{5} = \frac{3}{5} + \frac{3}{5} = \frac{6}{5} = \frac{5}{5} + \frac{1}{5} = 1\frac{1}{5}$

James ran $\frac{6}{5}$ or $1\frac{1}{5}$ miles.

Remember you can record answers as fractions or mixed numbers.

Write and solve an equation.

1. 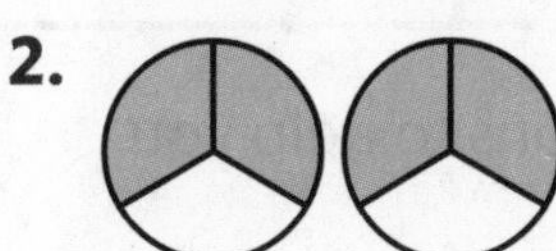

2.

Set C pages 393–396

Alisa has 7 puppies. Each puppy eats $\frac{2}{3}$ cup of food each day. How many cups of food does Alisa need to feed the puppies each day?

Multiply $7 \times \frac{2}{3}$.

Multiply the whole number and the numerator.

$$7 \times \frac{2}{3} = \frac{7 \times 2}{3}$$
$$= \frac{14}{3}$$
$$= \frac{3}{3} + \frac{3}{3} + \frac{3}{3} + \frac{3}{3} + \frac{2}{3}$$
$$= 4\frac{2}{3} \text{ cups}$$

Alisa needs $4\frac{2}{3}$ cups of food to feed the puppies each day.

Remember you multiply the whole number and the numerator and write the product above the denominator of the fraction.

1. Milo makes 5 batches of muffins. In each batch he uses $\frac{2}{3}$ bag of walnuts. How many bags of walnuts does Milo use?

2. A bird feeder can hold $\frac{7}{8}$ pound of seeds. How many pounds of seeds can 4 bird feeders hold?

Set D pages 397–400

You can add, subtract, multiply, and divide measures of time.

Units of Time	
1 hour = 60 minutes	1 day = 24 hours
1 year = 12 months	1 week = 7 days

Remember you may need to regroup when solving problems with time.

1. 7 hours 12 minutes + 3 hours 53 minutes

2. $7 \times \frac{3}{4}$ hour

3. 5 weeks 4 days − 3 weeks 6 days

4. Divide 560 days into groups of 8.

5. Li Marie practices piano $1\frac{2}{3}$ hours during the week and $2\frac{1}{3}$ hours on the weekend. Show each time on the number line. How many more hours does she practice on the weekend than the weekdays?

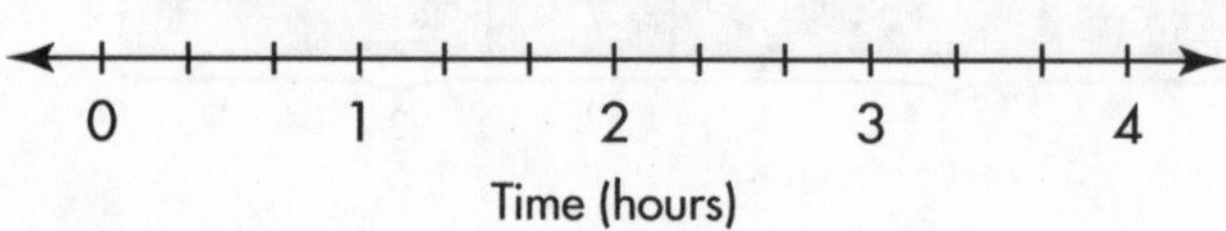

Set E pages 401–404

Think about these questions to help you **model with math.**

Thinking Habits

- How can I use math I know to help solve this problem?
- How can I use pictures, objects, or an equation to represent the problem?
- How can I use numbers, words, and symbols to solve the problem?

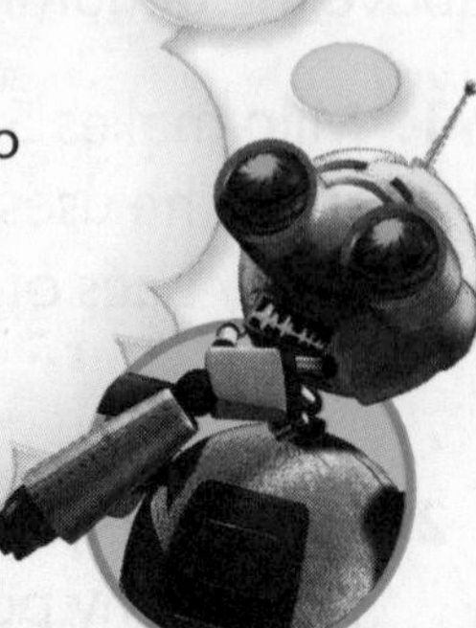

Julie makes chili with $2\frac{3}{8}$ cups of red beans, $4\frac{1}{8}$ cups of chili beans, and $\frac{7}{8}$ cup of onions. How many more cups of chili beans did Julie use than red beans and onions combined?

1. Write and solve an equation to find *r*, how many cups of red beans and onions Julie uses.

2. Write and solve an equation to find *c*, how many many more cups of chili beans Julie used than red beans and onions.

Name ____________________

1. Margo practices her flute $\frac{1}{4}$ hour each day.

Units of Time
1 week = 7 days
1 hour = 60 minutes

A. Write and solve an equation to find how many hours Margo practices her flute in 1 week.

B. Write and solve an equation to find how many minutes Margo practices her flute in 1 day. Then use that to find the number of minutes she practices in 1 week.

2. Which of the following represents the fraction $\frac{8}{9}$ as a multiple of a unit fraction?

Ⓐ $\frac{8}{9} = 1 \times \frac{8}{9}$

Ⓑ $\frac{8}{9} = 8 \times 9$

Ⓒ $\frac{8}{9} = 8 \times \frac{1}{9}$

Ⓓ $\frac{8}{9} = 4 \times \frac{2}{9}$

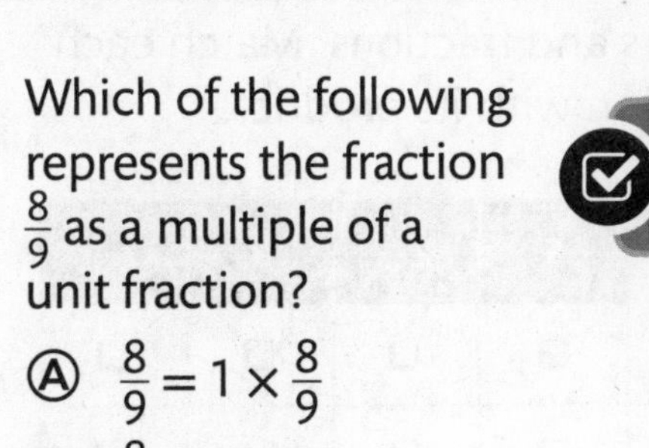

3. Ben played at a friend's house for 2 hours 35 minutes. Later he played at a park for 1 hour 10 minutes. He played for another 1 hour 20 minutes in his backyard. How long did Ben play in all?

Ⓐ 6 hours 27 minutes

Ⓑ 5 hours 15 minutes

Ⓒ 5 hours 5 minutes

Ⓓ 5 hours

4. Choose numbers from the list to fill in the missing values in the multiplication equations. Use each number once.

1 2 3 4 5 6 7 8

$\frac{7}{8} = \square \times \frac{\square}{8}$ $\quad$ $3 \times \frac{1}{\square} = \frac{\square}{4}$

$\frac{\square}{6} = 5 \times \frac{1}{\square}$ $\quad$ $8 \times \frac{1}{2} = \frac{\square}{\square}$

5. Chris found the products of whole numbers and fractions. Match each expression with its product.

	5	$2\frac{2}{8}$	3	$2\frac{2}{4}$
$5 \times \frac{2}{4}$	☐	☐	☐	☐
$6 \times \frac{5}{6}$	☐	☐	☐	☐
$6 \times \frac{3}{8}$	☐	☐	☐	☐
$5 \times \frac{3}{5}$	☐	☐	☐	☐

6. What is the product of 4 and $\frac{4}{8}$? Write another expression that is equal to the product of 4 and $\frac{4}{8}$.

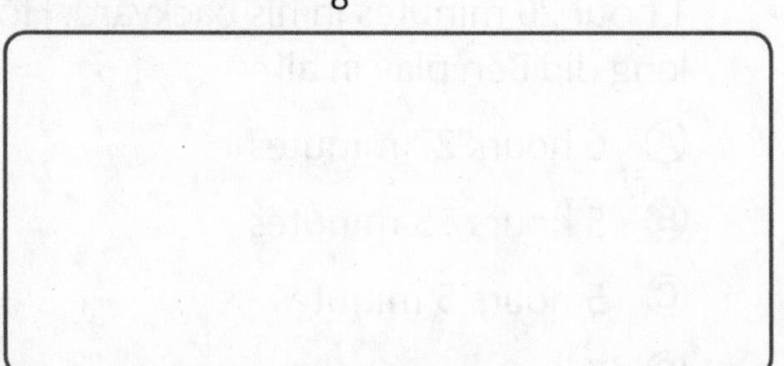

7. Complete the multiplication equation that describes what is shown by the model.

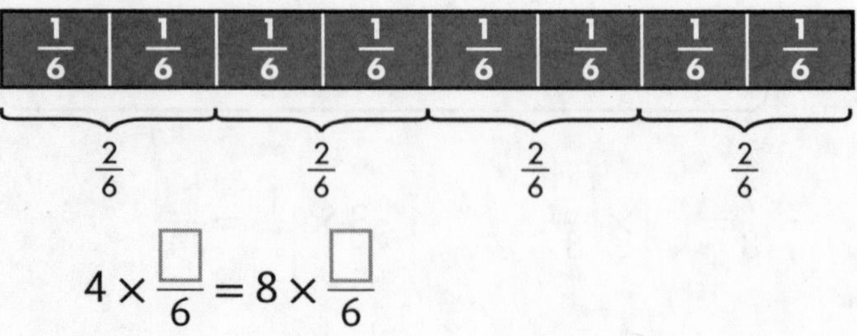

$4 \times \frac{\square}{6} = 8 \times \frac{\square}{6}$

8. Use a unit fraction and a whole number to write a multiplication equation equal to $\frac{7}{8}$.

9. Juan is making cookies. He makes 2 batches on Monday and 4 batches on Tuesday. He uses $\frac{3}{4}$ cup of flour in each batch. How much flour does Juan use? Explain.

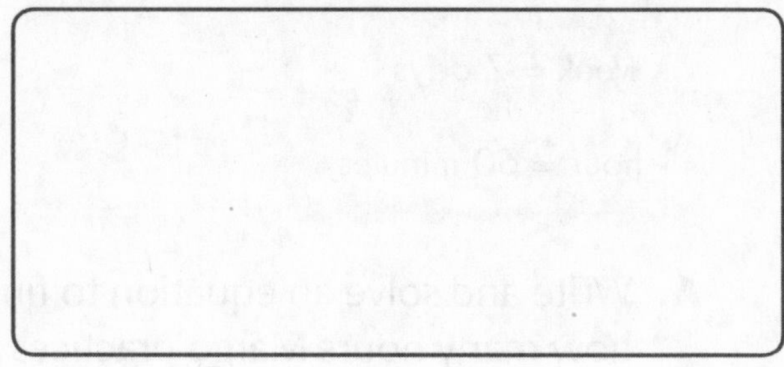

10. Lee uses $\frac{1}{5}$ yard of wire for each ornament he makes. He makes 3 ornaments for his grandmother and 2 ornaments for his mother. How many yards of wire did Lee use?

Ⓐ $\frac{3}{5}$

Ⓑ $1\frac{2}{5}$

Ⓒ $\frac{2}{5}$

Ⓓ 1

11. Lucas is making one dozen snacks for his team. He uses $\frac{1}{4}$ cup of dried cherries and $\frac{2}{4}$ cup of dried apricots for each snack. How many cups of dried fruit does Lucas need for his one dozen snacks? Remember, there are 12 snacks in one dozen. Write and solve equations to show how you found the answer.

Name ____

School Mural

Paul has permission to paint a 20-panel mural for his school. Part of the mural is shown in the **Painting a Mural** figure. Paul decides he needs help. The **Helpers** table shows how much several of his friends can paint each day and how many days a week they can paint.

Painting a Mural

Paul paints $\frac{9}{10}$ panel a day

Helpers

Friend	Panels a Day	Days a Week
Leeza	$\frac{3}{4}$	3
Kelsey	$\frac{7}{8}$	4
Tony	$\frac{5}{6}$	3

1. The students want to find how long it will take to paint the mural if each works on a different part of the panels a different number of days a week.

Part A

How many panels can Leeza paint in a week? Use fraction strips to explain.

Part B

How many panels can Kelsey paint in a week? Use equations to explain.

Part C

Paul can work 5 days a week. How many panels can Paul paint in a week? Explain.

Part D

How many panels can Tony paint in a week? Draw a bar diagram. Write and solve an equation.

2. The **Time Spent Painting Each Day** table shows how much time each of Paul's friends helped with the mural each day that they worked on it.

How much more time did Kelsey spend each day than Tony and Leeza combined? Explain.

Time Spent Painting Each Day

Friend	Time
Leeza	30 minutes
Kelsey	2 hours 30 minutes
Tony	1 hour 45 minutes

TOPIC 11

Represent and Interpret Data on Line Plots

Essential Questions: How can you solve problems using data on a line plot? How can you make a line plot?

Earthquakes occur when Earth's surface releases energy.

Many earthquakes occur near fault lines.

Cities, countries, and even schools have earthquake plans to keep everyone safe! Here is a project about safety and data.

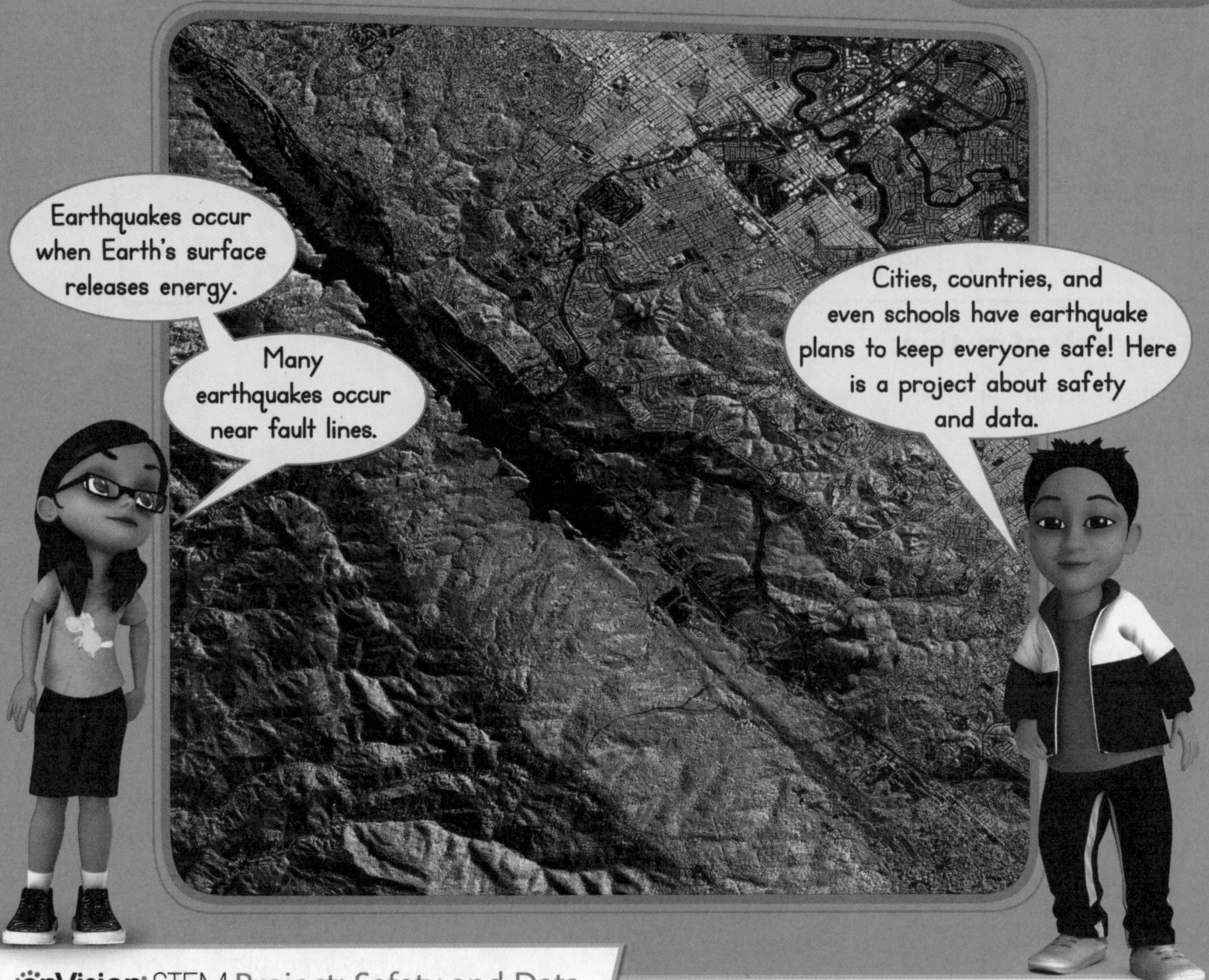

enVision® STEM Project: Safety and Data

Do Research Use the Internet or other sources to find what causes an earthquake and how the power of an earthquake is measured. Tell how people can stay safe during earthquakes.

Journal: Write a Report Include what you found. Also in your report:

- The size, or *magnitude*, of an earthquake is measured with the Richter scale. Explain how the scale is used.
- Research the magnitudes of at least 6 earthquakes that have occurred in your lifetime. Make a table showing when they occurred and their magnitudes, and then show their magnitudes on a line plot.

Name ____________________

Review What You Know

Vocabulary

Choose the best term from the box. Write it on the blank.

- compare
- data
- line plot
- scale

1. A ____________ is a way to organize data on a number line.

2. Numbers that show the units used on a graph are called a ____________.

3. ____________ are pieces of information.

Comparing Fractions

Write >, <, or = in the ○.

4. $\frac{7}{8}$ ○ $\frac{3}{4}$

5. $\frac{1}{2}$ ○ $\frac{5}{8}$

6. $\frac{1}{4}$ ○ $\frac{2}{8}$

Fraction Subtraction

Find the difference.

7. $10\frac{3}{8} - 4\frac{1}{8} =$ ____

8. $5\frac{1}{4} - 3\frac{3}{4} =$ ____

9. $7\frac{4}{8} - 2\frac{4}{8} =$ ____

Interpreting Data

Use the data in the chart to answer each exercise.

DATA

Snake Lengths (Inches)			
$12\frac{1}{2}$	$16\frac{1}{2}$	17	24
16	16	13	$12\frac{1}{2}$
$18\frac{1}{2}$	$17\frac{1}{2}$	17	16

10. What is the greatest snake length? What is the least snake length?

11. Which of the snake lengths are recorded more than once? Which length was recorded the most?

12. What is the difference between the greatest length and the shortest length recorded?

In this topic, you will use data to create line plots.

Name ______________________________

What are fun ways to get up off the couch and move?

Project: Design a Park

What are the most commonly chosen state insects?

Project: Write a Poem and Make a Graph about a State Insect

Have you ever baked a pie?

Project: Make a Pamphlet of Pie Recipes

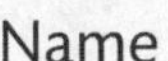

It's a Fine Line

Before watching the video, think:
A new year is a good time to start something new. I'd like to get more sleep, but I'm a robot, and we don't sleep. *Any* sleep would be more sleep!

I can ...

model with math to solve a problem that involves analyzing and interpreting data on line plots.

Mathematical Practices MP.4 Also MP.1, MP.5

Content Standards 4.NF.B.3d Also 4.NF.A.2, 4.MD.B.4

Name ____________________

Activity

Lesson 11-1

Read Line Plots

I can ...
interpret data using line plots.

Content Standards 4.MD.B.4 Also 4.NF.B.3d
Mathematical Practices MP.2 MP.4, MP.6

Solve & Share

Emily went fishing. She plotted the lengths of 12 fish caught on the line plot shown below. What was the length of the longest fish caught? What was the length of the shortest fish caught?

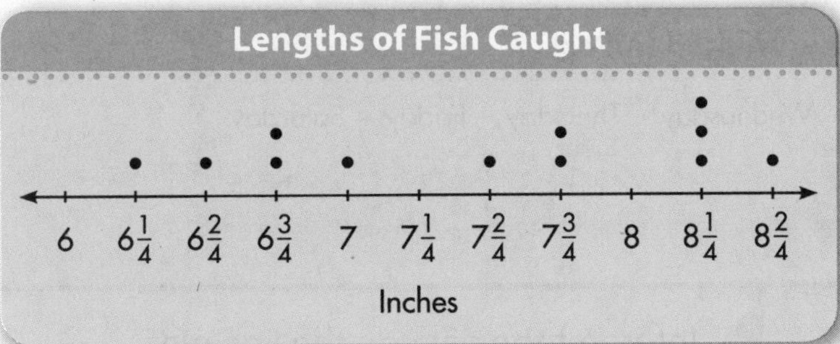

Be precise when answering questions and use appropriate labels.

Look Back! What other observations can you make from the line plot about the lengths of fish caught?

How Can You Read Data in a Line Plot?

A

A line plot shows data along a number line. Each dot above a point on the line represents one number in the data set.

The table below shows the distance Eli walked his dog each day for seven days.

Line plots make data easier to read at a glance.

DATA

Distance Walked (miles)						
Sunday	Monday	Tuesday	Wednesday	Thursday	Friday	Saturday
1	$\frac{1}{2}$	$1\frac{1}{2}$	1	$1\frac{1}{2}$	3	1

B Here is how the data look on a line plot.

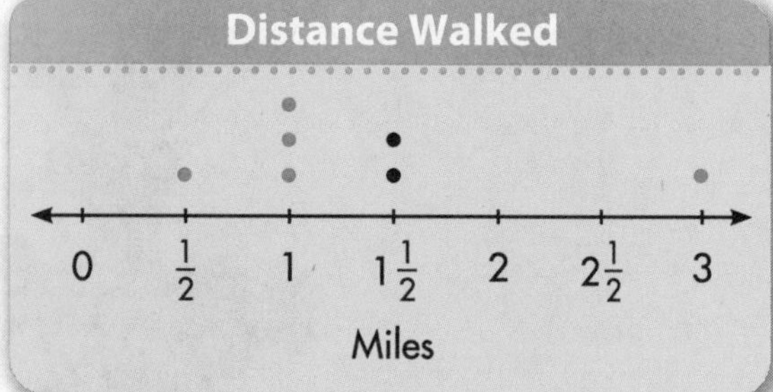

The numbers along the bottom of the line plot are the scale of the graph.

C Interpret the data on the line plot.

The most dots are above 1 on the line plot. The most common distance walked is 1 mile.

The longest distance walked is 3 miles. The shortest distance walked is $\frac{1}{2}$ mile.

What is the difference between the longest distance and the shortest distance Eli walked his dog?

$$3 - \frac{1}{2} = \frac{6}{2} - \frac{1}{2}$$
$$= \frac{5}{2} \text{ or } 2\frac{1}{2} \text{ miles}$$

Convince Me! **Model with Math** Write and solve an equation to find how many miles *m*, Eli walked his dog in all for the 7 days.

Name ____________________

Practice Tools Assessment

Guided Practice

Do You Understand?

1. How can you tell the longest distance Eli walked his dog from the line plot?

2. If a line plot represented 10 pieces of data, how many dots would it have? Explain.

Do You Know How?

For **3–5**, use the line plot below.

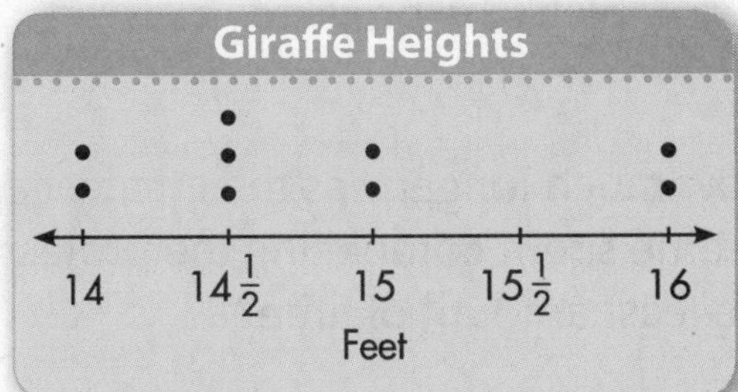

3. How many giraffes are 14 feet tall?

4. What is the most common height?

5. How tall is the tallest giraffe?

Independent Practice

For **6–10**, use the line plot at the right.

Line plot data can be recorded using Xs or dots.

6. How many people ran the 100-meter sprint?

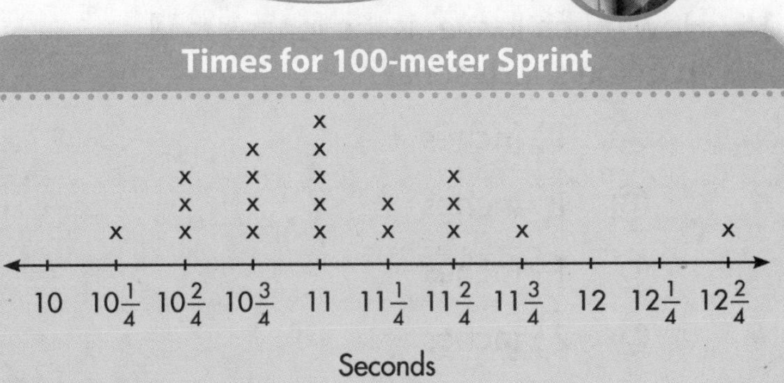

7. Which time was the most common?

8. What is the difference between the fastest sprint and the slowest sprint?

9. How many more people ran 100 meters in $11\frac{2}{4}$ seconds than in $10\frac{1}{4}$ seconds?

10. Curtis said more than half the people ran 100 meters in less than 11 seconds. Do you agree? Explain.

Problem Solving

For **11–12**, use the line plot at the right.

11. **Reasoning** Mr. Dixon recorded the times it took students in his class to complete a project. Which time was most often needed to complete the project?

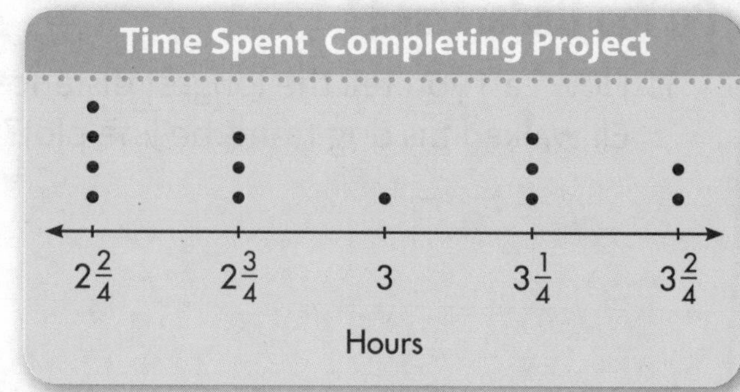

12. How much longer was the greatest amount of time spent completing the project than the least amount of time?

13. **Number Sense** Jorge collects sports cards. He displays his cards in an album. There are 72 pages in the album. Each page holds 9 cards. Explain how to decide whether or not the album holds more than 600 cards.

14. **Higher Order Thinking** Bob and 2 friends each were able to juggle with bean bags for $\frac{3}{4}$ minute. How long did they juggle altogether?

Assessment Practice

For **15–16**, use the line plot at the right.

15. How much longer is the longest nail than the shortest nail?

Ⓐ $1\frac{1}{4}$ inches
Ⓑ $1\frac{2}{4}$ inches
Ⓒ $1\frac{3}{4}$ inches
Ⓓ $2\frac{1}{4}$ inches

16. Ed measured the nails that were $2\frac{1}{4}$ inches long incorrectly. They were each actually $\frac{3}{4}$ inch longer. What was the length of the nails?

Ⓐ $\frac{3}{4}$ inch
Ⓑ $1\frac{2}{4}$ inches
Ⓒ 3 inches
Ⓓ $3\frac{1}{4}$ inches

Name ____________________

Activity

Lesson 11-2

Make Line Plots

I can ...

make a line plot to represent data.

Content Standards 4.MD.B.4 Also 4.NF.A.1, 4.NF.A.2, 4.NF.B.3d
Mathematical Practices MP.1, MP.4, MP.8

Solve & Share The manager of a shoe store kept track of the lengths of the shoes sold in a day. Complete the line plot using the data from the shoe store. What length shoe was sold the most?

A line plot can help you organize your data. *Show your work in the space below!*

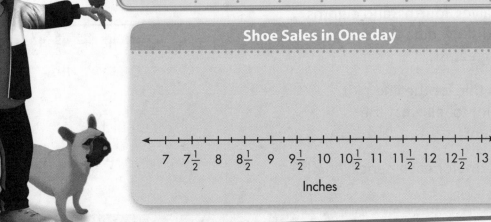

DATA

Shoe Sales in One Day

Shoe Lengths Sold (inches)	$7\frac{1}{4}$	$7\frac{3}{4}$	8	$8\frac{1}{4}$	$8\frac{1}{2}$	$9\frac{3}{4}$	10	$10\frac{1}{2}$	$12\frac{1}{2}$	$12\frac{3}{4}$
Number Sold	2	1	3	1	3	3	2	6	2	1

Shoe Sales in One day

7 $7\frac{1}{2}$ 8 $8\frac{1}{2}$ 9 $9\frac{1}{2}$ 10 $10\frac{1}{2}$ 11 $11\frac{1}{2}$ 12 $12\frac{1}{2}$ 13

Inches

Look Back! **Generalize** How can you use a line plot to find the data that occur most often?

Essential Question How Can You Make Line Plots?

A

Serena measured the lengths of her colored pencils. How can Serena make a line plot to show these lengths?

DATA

Lengths of Serena's Pencils

Color	Length
Red	5 in.
Blue	$4\frac{3}{4}$ in.
Green	$4\frac{3}{4}$ in.
Purple	$4\frac{1}{8}$ in.
Orange	$4\frac{1}{2}$ in.
Yellow	$4\frac{3}{4}$ in.

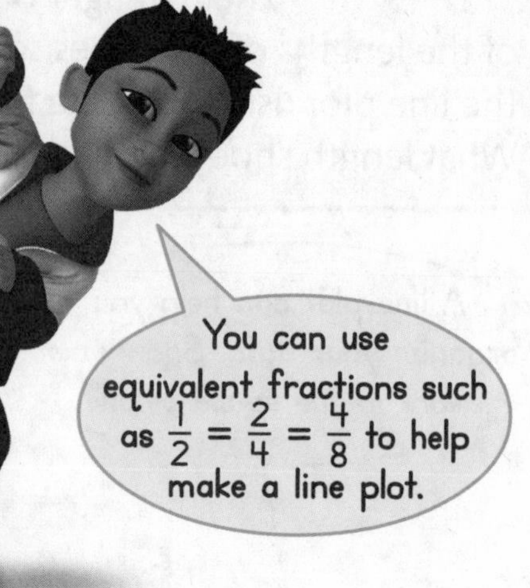

You can use equivalent fractions such as $\frac{1}{2} = \frac{2}{4} = \frac{4}{8}$ to help make a line plot.

B

Making a Line Plot

Step 1 Draw a number line and choose a scale based on the lengths of Serena's pencils. Mark halves, fourths, and eighths. The scale should show data values from the least to the greatest.

Step 2 Write a title for the line plot. Label the line plot to tell what the numbers represent.

Step 3 Draw a dot for each pencil length.

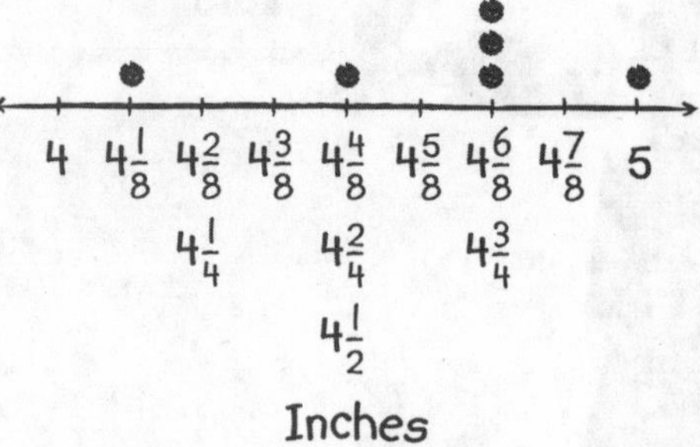

Convince Me! **Model with Math** Write and solve an equation to find the difference *d*, in length between Serena's two shortest colored pencils.

Name ________________

Practice Tools Assessment

Guided Practice

Do You Understand?

1. The scale of the line plot, Lengths of Serena's Pencils, goes from 4 to 5 by eighths. Why is this a good scale to use?

2. Use the table shown at the right to compare the lengths of Sandy's pencils with the lengths of Serena's pencils shown on the previous page. Who has more pencils that are the same length, Serena or Sandy? Which set of data was easier to compare? Why?

Do You Know How?

3. Complete the line plot.

DATA

Lengths of Sandy's Pencils

Color	Length
Red	$6\frac{1}{4}$ in.
Blue	$5\frac{1}{4}$ in.
Green	$6\frac{3}{4}$ in.
Purple	$5\frac{3}{4}$ in.
Orange	$6\frac{3}{4}$ in.
Yellow	$6\frac{1}{2}$ in.

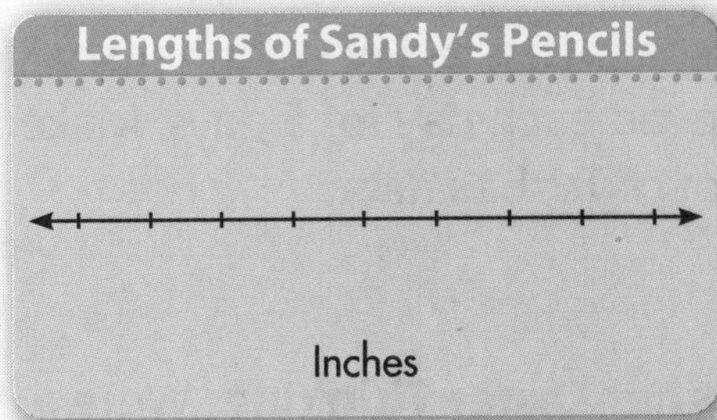

Independent Practice

Leveled Practice For **4–5**, use the table at the right.

4. Use the data in the table to make a line plot.

You can use dots or Xs to record data in a line plot.

DATA

Bracelet Lengths

8 in.	$8\frac{1}{2}$ in.
$6\frac{1}{2}$ in.	8 in.
$7\frac{1}{2}$ in.	$6\frac{1}{2}$ in.
8 in.	$7\frac{1}{2}$ in.
$6\frac{1}{2}$ in.	8 in.

5. What is the length of the longest bracelet? What is the shortest length? What is the difference?

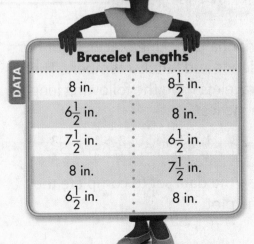

Problem Solving

6. Nora weighed each of the 7 beefsteak tomatoes she picked from her garden. The total weight of the 7 tomatoes was $10\frac{3}{4}$ pounds. Her line plot shows only 6 dots. What was the weight of the missing tomato?

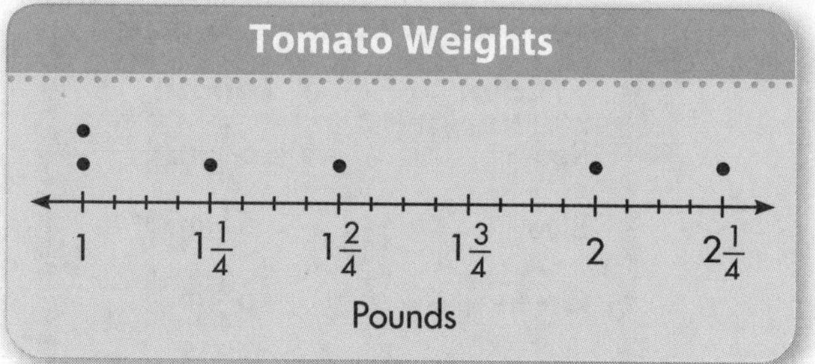

7. **Make Sense and Persevere** Alyssa made a pink-and-white-striped blanket for her bed. There are 7 pink stripes and 6 white stripes. Each stripe is 8 inches wide. How wide is Alyssa's blanket? Explain.

For **8–9**, use the table at the right.

8. Trisha measured how far her snail moved each day for 5 days. Make a line plot of Trisha's data.

Make sure to include a title and labels for the values on the line plot.

9. **Higher Order Thinking** Write a question that would require addition or subtraction to solve using Trisha's data. What is the answer?

DATA

Day	Distance
Monday	$1\frac{4}{8}$ inches
Tuesday	$1\frac{3}{8}$ inches
Wednesday	$1\frac{1}{8}$ inches
Thursday	$2\frac{1}{8}$ inches
Friday	$1\frac{1}{8}$ inches

Assessment Practice

10. Brianna is making bracelets for her friends and family members. The bracelets have the following lengths in inches:

$6, 6\frac{3}{4}, 6\frac{1}{4}, 5\frac{3}{4}, 5, 6, 6\frac{2}{4}, 6\frac{1}{4}, 6, 5\frac{3}{4}$

Use the data set to complete the line plot.

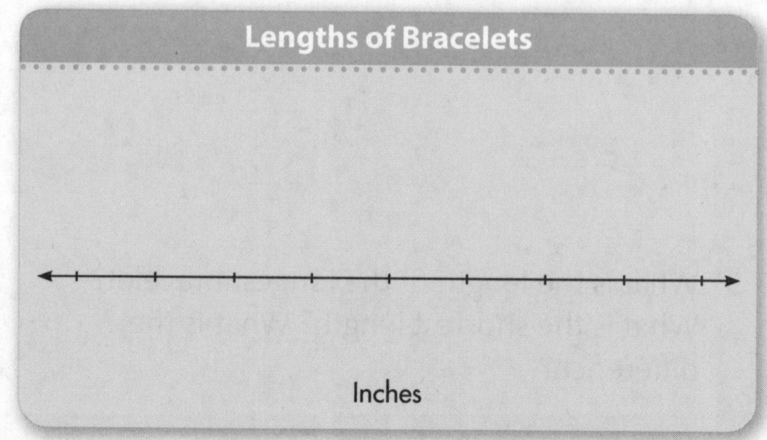

Name ____________________  Activity

Lesson 11-3
Use Line Plots to Solve Problems

I can ...
use line plots to solve problems involving fractions.

Content Standards 4.MD.B.4 Also 4.NF.B.3d
Mathematical Practices MP.1, MP.5

Solve & Share

Ms. Earl's class measured the lengths of 10 caterpillars in the school garden. The caterpillars had the following lengths in inches:

$$\frac{3}{4}, 1\frac{1}{4}, 1\frac{3}{4}, 1\frac{1}{2}, 1, 1, \frac{3}{4}, 1\frac{1}{4}, 1\frac{3}{4}, 1\frac{1}{2}$$

Plot the lengths on the line plot. Write and solve an equation to find the difference in length between the longest and shortest caterpillars.

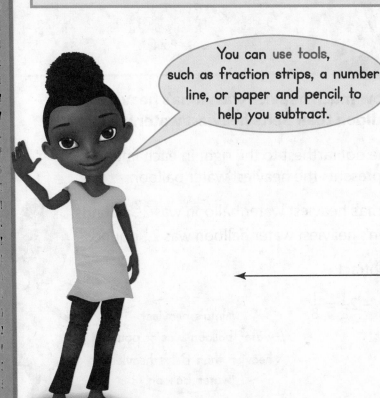

You can use tools, such as fraction strips, a number line, or paper and pencil, to help you subtract.

Look Back! How can a line plot be used to find the difference between the greatest and least values?

How Can You Use Line Plots to Solve Problems Involving Fractions?

Visual Learning Bridge

A

Alma and Ben are filling water balloons. The line plots show the weights of their water balloons. Who filled more water balloons? How many more? How much heavier was Alma's heaviest water balloon than Ben's heaviest water balloon?

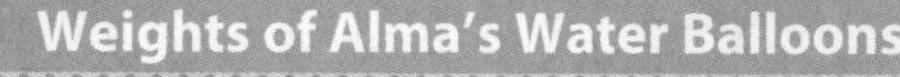

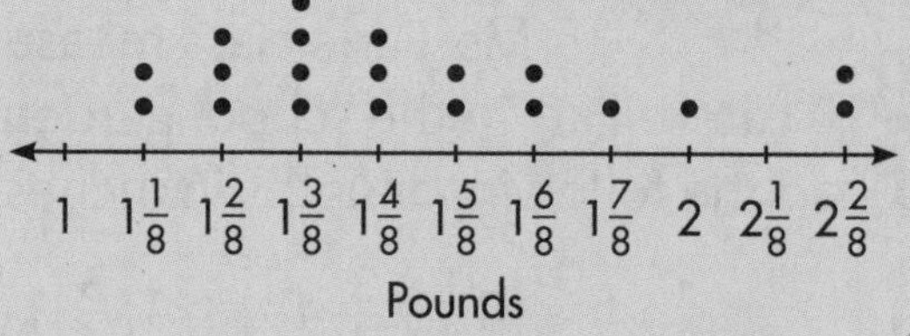

Weights of Ben's Water Balloons

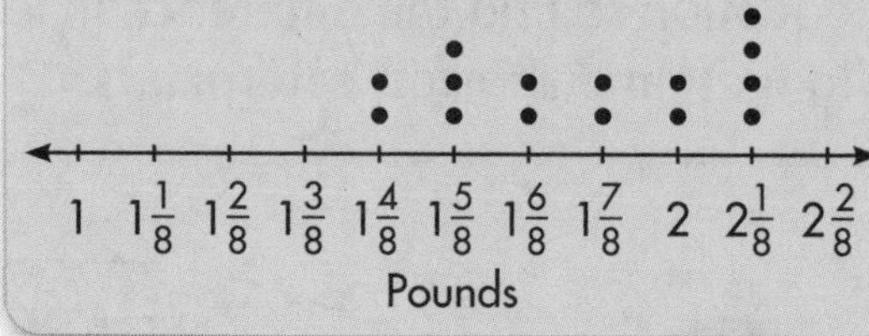

You can find the information you need by reading the line plots.

B

Who filled more water balloons? How many more?

Each dot in the line plots represents 1 water balloon.

Alma filled 20 water balloons. Ben filled 15 water balloons.

$20 - 15 = 5$

Alma filled 5 more water balloons than Ben.

C

How much heavier was Alma's heaviest water balloon than Ben's heaviest water balloon?

The dot farthest to the right in each line plot represents the heaviest water balloon.

Alma's heaviest water balloon was $2\frac{2}{8}$ pounds. Ben's heaviest water balloon was $2\frac{1}{8}$ pounds.

Subtract.

$2\frac{2}{8} - 2\frac{1}{8} = \frac{1}{8}$

Alma's heaviest water balloon was $\frac{1}{8}$ pound heavier than Ben's heaviest water balloon.

Convince Me! **Make Sense and Persevere** How much heavier was Alma's heaviest water balloon than her lightest water balloon? How much heavier was Ben's heaviest water balloon than his lightest water balloon? Write and solve equations.

Name ______________________________

Another Example!

Rowan's class measured the snowfall for 5 days. The line plot shows the heights of snowfall they recorded. How many inches of snow were recorded? What amount of snowfall occurred most often?

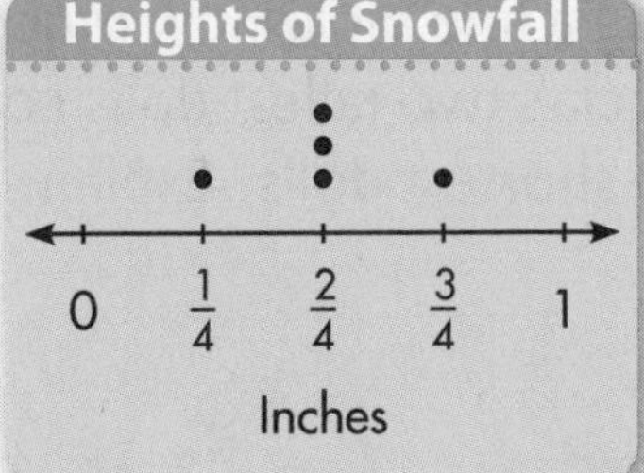

Find the total number of inches of snowfall recorded.

$\frac{1}{4} + \frac{2}{4} + \frac{2}{4} + \frac{2}{4} + \frac{3}{4} = \frac{10}{4} = 2\frac{2}{4}$ inches

The amount of snowfall that occurred most often was $\frac{2}{4}$ inch.

The value with the greatest number of dots is the value that occurs the most.

Guided Practice

Do You Understand?

1. **Use Structure** How could you use the Commutative and Associative Properties of Addition to make the addition in the Another Example easier?

Do You Know How?

For **2–3**, use the example on the previous page.

2. Who filled more water balloons over 2 pounds?

3. How much heavier were Alma's two heaviest water balloons than Ben's two heaviest?

Independent Practice

For **4–5**, use the line plot at the right.

4. What is the difference in height between the tallest and shortest patients?

5. Oscar says 5 feet is the most common height Dr. Chen measured. Do you agree? Explain.

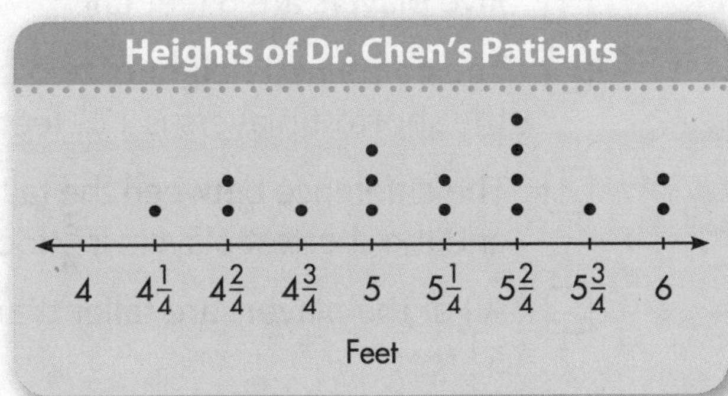

Problem Solving

6. Make Sense and Persevere Marcia measured her dolls and showed the heights using a line plot. How much taller are Marcia's two tallest dolls combined than her two shortest dolls? Explain.

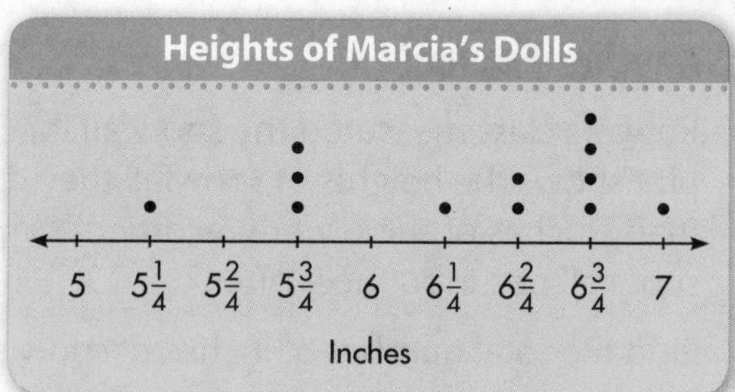

7. Higher Order Thinking Marlee is knitting a scarf. The line plot shows the length she knits each day. How many more inches does Marlee need to knit so the scarf is 30 inches long?

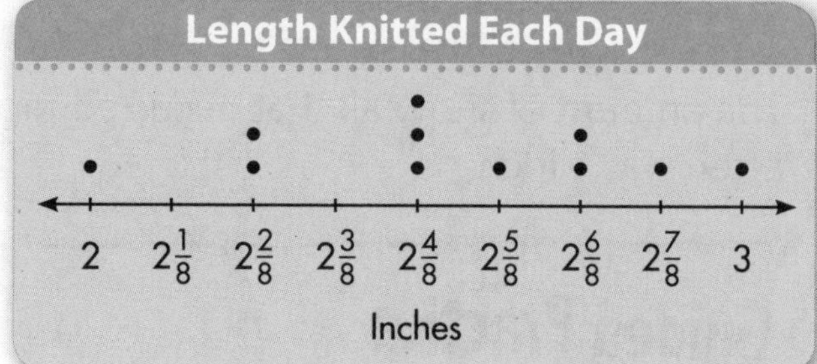

Assessment Practice

For **8–9**, use the line plot.

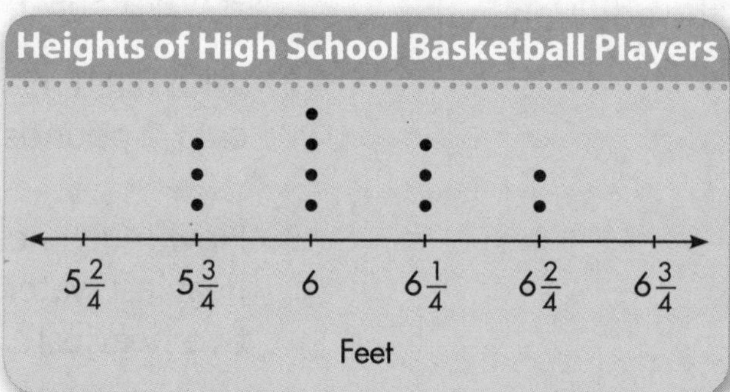

8. Which of the following statements are true? Select all that apply.

- ☐ Most of the players are 6 feet or taller.
- ☐ Five players are 6 feet tall.
- ☐ The combined height of two of the shortest players is $11\frac{1}{2}$ feet.
- ☐ The difference between the tallest and the shortest players is $\frac{3}{4}$ foot.
- ☐ All of the players are taller than $5\frac{3}{4}$ feet.

9. If one of the shortest players grew $\frac{3}{4}$ foot before the next season started, how tall would the player be?

Ⓐ $\frac{6}{4}$ feet

Ⓑ $5\frac{3}{4}$ feet

Ⓒ 6 feet

Ⓓ $6\frac{2}{4}$ feet

Name ________________________________

Problem Solving

Lesson 11-4

Critique Reasoning

I can ...
use what I know about line plots to critique the reasoning of others.

Mathematical Practices MP.3 Also MP.2, MP.4
Content Standards 4.MD.B.4 Also 4.NF.B.3c, 4.NF.B.3d

Solve & Share A class made a line plot showing the amount of snowfall for 10 days. Nathan analyzed the line plot and said, "The difference between the greatest amount of snowfall recorded and the least amount of snowfall recorded is 3 because the first measurement has one dot and the last measurement has 4 dots." How do you respond to Nathan's reasoning?

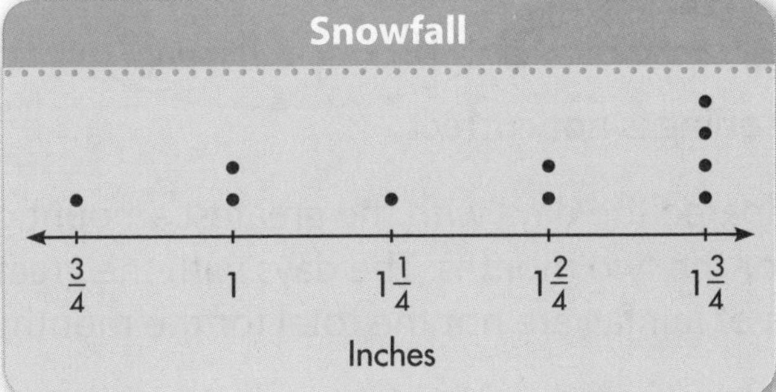

Thinking Habits

Be a good thinker! These questions can help you.

- What questions can I ask to understand other people's thinking?
- Are there mistakes in other people's thinking?
- Can I improve other people's thinking?

Look Back! Critique Reasoning Millie said that the total amount of snowfall for the 5 days above was 10 inches. Is Millie correct?

 Visual Learning  Glossary

How Can You Critique the Reasoning of Others?

Visual Learning Bridge

A

The line plots show the amount of rainfall for two months.

Val said, "The total rainfall for February was greater than the total rainfall for January because $\frac{7}{8} + \frac{7}{8}$ equals $\frac{14}{8}$, and the highest rainfall in January was $\frac{5}{8}$."

Rainfall in January

$\frac{1}{8}$ $\frac{2}{8}$ $\frac{3}{8}$ $\frac{4}{8}$ $\frac{5}{8}$

Inches

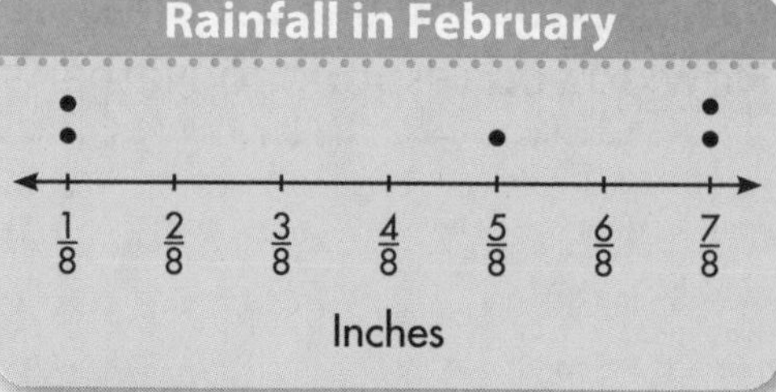

What is Val's reasoning?

Val compared the two highest amounts of rainfall for each month.

Here's my thinking.

B

How can I critique the reasoning of others?

I can

- ask questions for clarification.
- decide if the strategy used makes sense.
- look for flaws in estimates or calculations.

C

Val's reasoning is not correct.

She compared the days with the greatest amount of rainfall for the two months. The days with the greatest amounts of rainfall are not the total for the months.

Val should have added the amounts for each month. Then she could compare the amounts.

January: $\frac{1}{8} + \frac{1}{8} + \frac{1}{8} + \frac{3}{8} + \frac{3}{8} + \frac{3}{8} + \frac{5}{8} = \frac{17}{8}$ inches

February: $\frac{1}{8} + \frac{1}{8} + \frac{5}{8} + \frac{7}{8} + \frac{7}{8} = \frac{21}{8}$ inches

During February, there was $\frac{21}{8} - \frac{17}{8} = \frac{4}{8}$ inch more rain than January.

Convince Me! **Critique Reasoning** Bev thought January had more rainfall because it rained on 7 days and February only had rain on 5 days. How do you respond to Bev's reasoning?

Name ____

Guided Practice

Critique Reasoning

At a dog show, a judge wrote down the heights of 12 dogs. Cole made a line plot of the heights, shown to the right. He concluded, "The height with the most dots is $1\frac{1}{4}$ feet, so that is the greatest height of the dogs at the dog show."

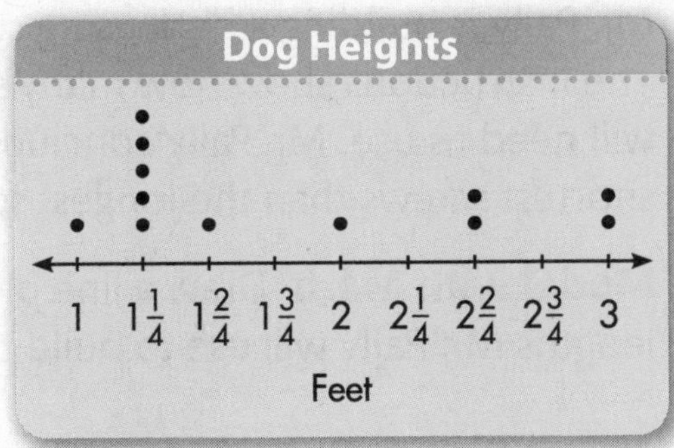

1. What is Cole's conclusion? How did he reach this conclusion?

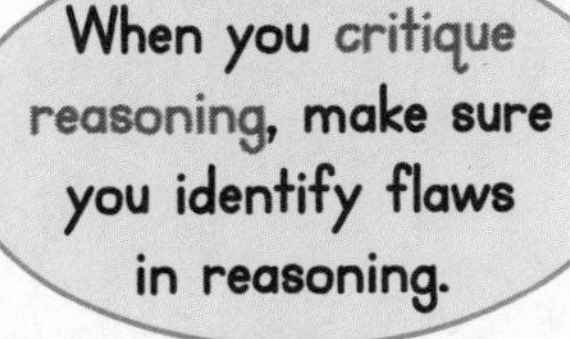

When you critique reasoning, make sure you identify flaws in reasoning.

2. Is Cole's conclusion correct? Explain.

Independent Practice

Critique Reasoning

Natasha keeps a log of the total amount of time her students practiced on their violins outside of their weekly lesson. She creates the line plot shown. Each dot represents one student who practices a specific amount of time in one week. Natasha says that 5 of her students' practice times combined is $1\frac{1}{4}$ hours because there are 5 dots above $1\frac{1}{4}$.

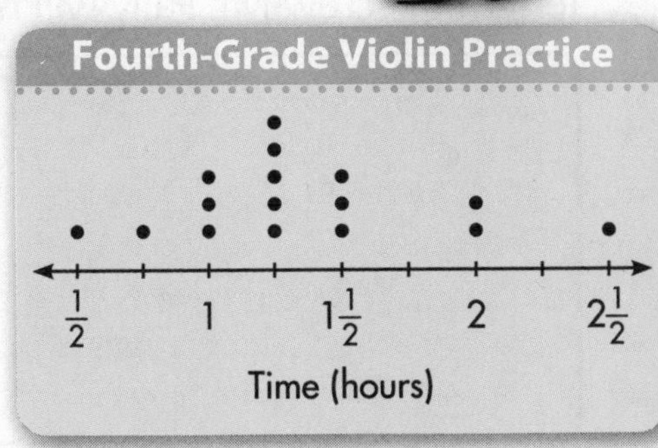

3. What is Natasha's argument? How does she support it?

4. Critique Natasha's reasoning.

Performance Task

Taking Inventory

Mr. Pally is building a desk using screws of different lengths. The instructions show how many screws of each length he will need to use. Mr. Pally concludes he will use more of the shortest screws than the longest screws.

DATA

Screw Lengths (inches)			
$\frac{3}{8}$	1	$\frac{6}{8}$	$\frac{3}{8}$
$\frac{7}{8}$	$1\frac{4}{8}$	$\frac{7}{8}$	$\frac{3}{8}$
$1\frac{4}{8}$	$\frac{6}{8}$	$\frac{3}{8}$	1
$\frac{3}{8}$	$\frac{3}{8}$	$\frac{7}{8}$	$1\frac{4}{8}$

5. **Model with Math** Draw a line plot to show the screw lengths Mr. Pally will use to build the desk.

6. **Reasoning** How can you use the line plot to find which length of screw Mr. Pally will need the most?

7. **Critique Reasoning** Is Mr. Pally's conclusion correct? How did you decide? If not, what can you do to improve his reasoning?

When you critique reasoning, ask questions to help you understand someone's thinking.

Name ____________________

Fluency Practice Activity

Find a Match

Work with a partner. Point to a clue.

Read the clue.

Look below the clues to find a match. Write the clue letter in the box next to the match.

Find a match for every clue.

I can ...
add and subtract multi-digit whole numbers.

Content Standard 4.NBT.B.4
Mathematical Practices MP.3, MP.6, MP.7, MP.8

Clues

A The sum is between 3,510 and 3,520.

B The difference is exactly 3,515.

C The sum is between 3,560 and 3,570.

D The difference is between 3,530 and 3,540.

E The sum is exactly 3,584.

F The difference is between 3,590 and 3,600.

G The sum is exactly 3,987.

H The difference is between 1,000 and 2,000.

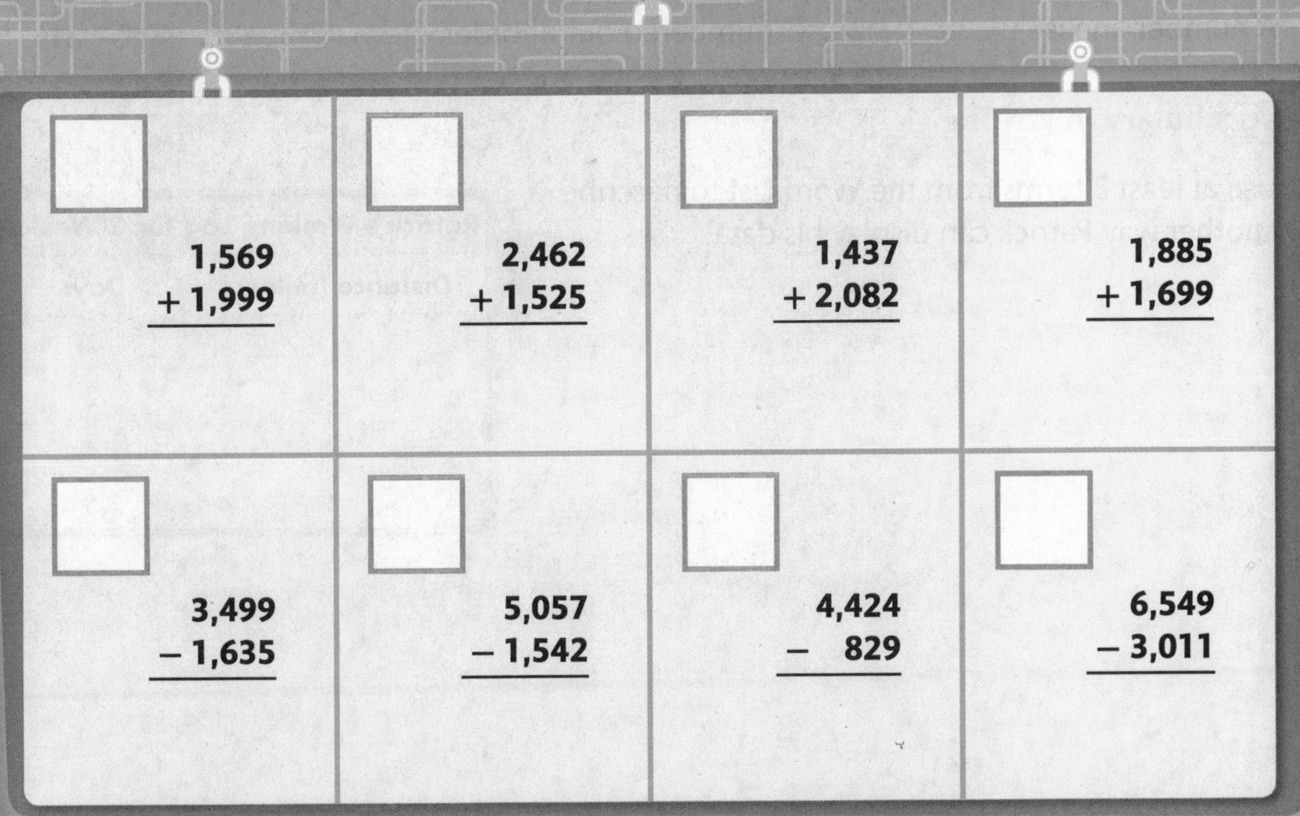

☐ $1{,}569 + 1{,}999$	☐ $2{,}462 + 1{,}525$	☐ $1{,}437 + 2{,}082$	☐ $1{,}885 + 1{,}699$
☐ $3{,}499 - 1{,}635$	☐ $5{,}057 - 1{,}542$	☐ $4{,}424 - 829$	☐ $6{,}549 - 3{,}011$

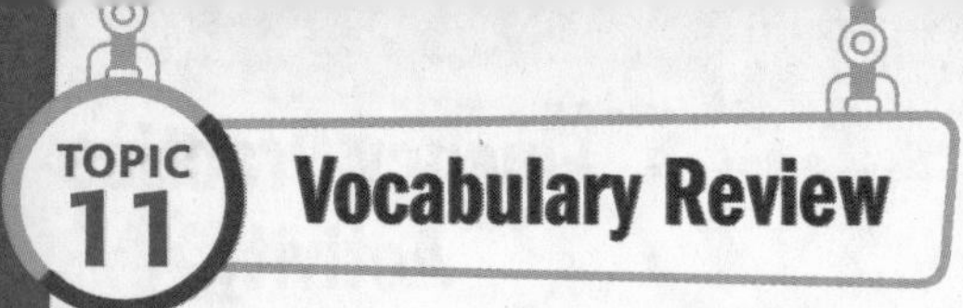

Vocabulary Review

Word List

- data set
- graph
- line plot
- number line
- scale
- table

Understand Vocabulary

Write T for *true* and F for *false*.

1. ______ Graphs are used to display and represent data.

2. ______ A data set is a collection of pieces of information.

3. ______ A table is never used to display data.

4. ______ A line plot shows data along a number line.

5. ______ A line plot may have more points than there are numbers in the data set.

Write *always*, *sometimes*, or *never*.

6. A line plot ______________ displays data.

7. The scale on a line plot is ______________ numbered using fractions.

8. A number line is ______________ numbered out of order.

Use Vocabulary in Writing

9. Use at least 3 terms from the Word List to describe another way Patrick can display his data.

DATA

Patrick's Walking Log for 2 Weeks

Distance (miles)	Days
1	3
2	2
3	4
4	5

Name ____

TOPIC 11

Reteaching

Set A pages 417–420

The line plot shows the number of hours Mrs. Mack was at the gym each day, during a two week period.

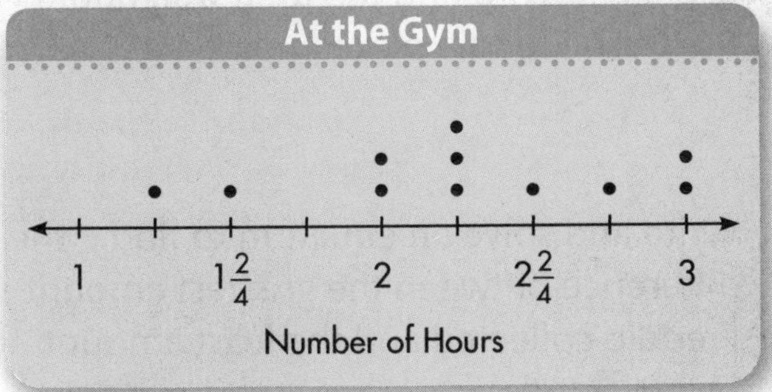

Remember each dot above the line plot represents one value in the data set.

1. How many days did Mrs. Mack go to the gym?

2. What is the least amount of time Mrs. Mack spent at the gym?

3. How many hours was Mrs. Mack at the the gym during the two weeks?

Set B pages 421–424

Lilly measured the lengths of the ribbons in her craft kit and drew a line plot.

Lengths of Lilly's Ribbons

DATA

Ribbon Colors	Length
Red	$5\frac{1}{2}$ in.
Blue	4 in.
White	$5\frac{1}{2}$ in.
Yellow	$4\frac{1}{4}$ in.
Pink	$4\frac{3}{4}$ in.

Lengths of Lilly's Ribbons

4 $4\frac{1}{4}$ $4\frac{2}{4}$ $4\frac{3}{4}$ 5 $5\frac{1}{4}$ $5\frac{2}{4}$

$4\frac{1}{2}$ $5\frac{1}{2}$

Inches

The number line shows the lengths from least to greatest. The labels show what the dots represent.

Remember to choose a reasonable scale for your number line.

A zoo in Australia studied platypuses. Their masses are recorded below.

Platypus Masses (kg)

DATA

$1\frac{6}{8}$	2	$2\frac{2}{8}$	$2\frac{4}{8}$	$1\frac{6}{8}$
$2\frac{6}{8}$	2	2	2	$1\frac{6}{8}$
$1\frac{7}{8}$	$1\frac{5}{8}$	$2\frac{2}{8}$	$1\frac{7}{8}$	$2\frac{4}{8}$

1. Draw a line plot for the data set.

2. What is the difference in mass of the platypus with the greatest mass and the platypus with the least mass?

Set C pages 425–428

Carly and Freddie pick up trash. The line plots show how much they picked up each day for 14 days. What is the difference between the greatest and least amounts Carly picked up?

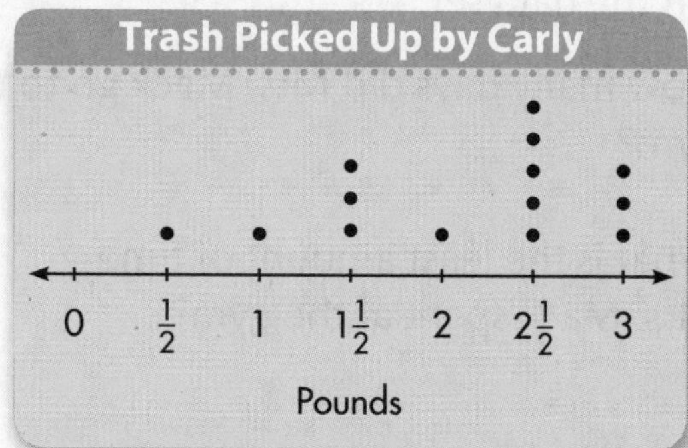

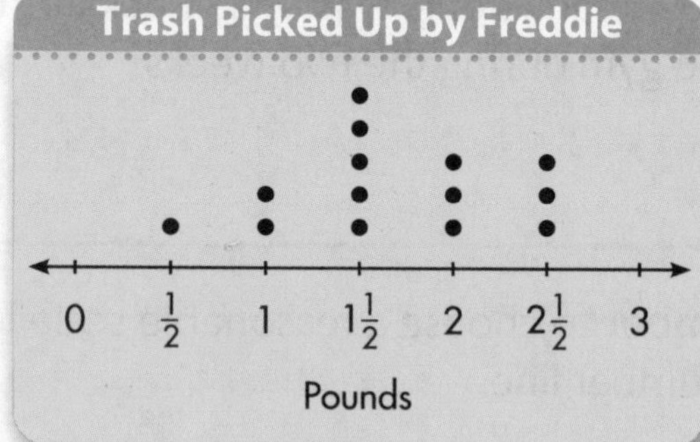

The greatest amount of trash Carly picked up was 3 pounds. The least amount was $\frac{1}{2}$ pound.

Subtract. $3 - \frac{1}{2} = 2\frac{1}{2}$ pounds

Remember you can use equations to help solve problems with data from line plots.

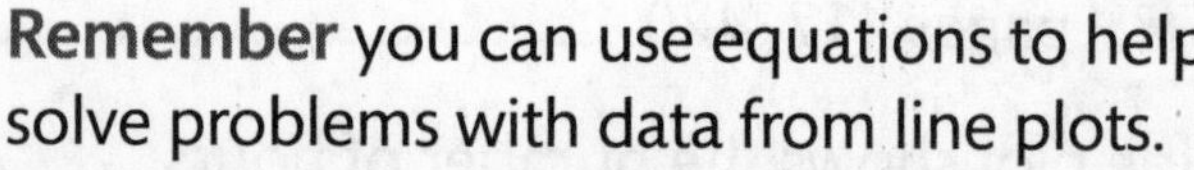

For **1–3**, use the line plots at the left.

1. Explain how to find the total weight of the trash Freddie picked up.

2. Write and solve an equation to find *t*, the difference between the greatest amount Freddie collected and the least amount he collected.

3. What is the sum of Carly's most frequent weight and Freddie's most frequent weight? Explain.

Set D pages 429–432

Think about these questions to help you **critique the reasoning** of others.

Thinking Habits

- What questions can I ask to understand other people's thinking?
- Are there mistakes in other people's thinking?
- Can I improve other people's thinking?

Remember you can use math to identify mistakes in people's thinking.

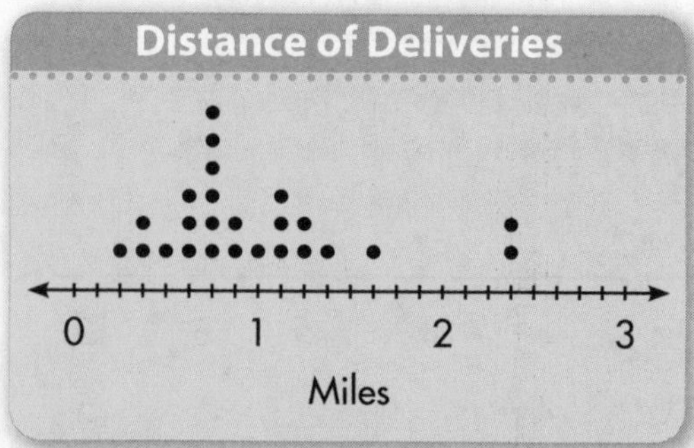

1. Spencer says $2\frac{3}{8}$ miles is the most common delivery distance. Do you agree? Explain.

Name ____________________

Assessment Practice

1. What is the difference between the heaviest and lightest weights?

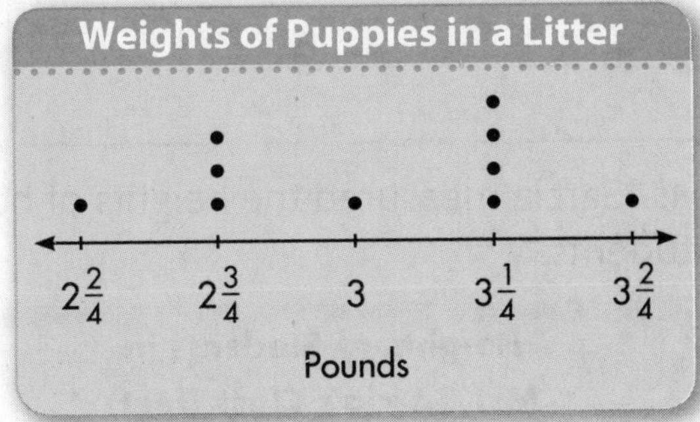

2. How many dots would be placed above $1\frac{3}{4}$ in a line plot of these data?

Glasses of Water

$1\frac{1}{2}$	$2\frac{1}{2}$	$1\frac{3}{4}$	2	$1\frac{3}{4}$
$2\frac{1}{4}$	3	$1\frac{1}{2}$	$2\frac{1}{2}$	$3\frac{1}{2}$
$1\frac{3}{4}$	2	$3\frac{1}{2}$	$1\frac{1}{4}$	$2\frac{1}{4}$

Ⓐ 3 dots
Ⓑ 2 dots
Ⓒ 1 dot
Ⓓ 0 dots

3. Which is the most common length of snail Fred has in his backyard?

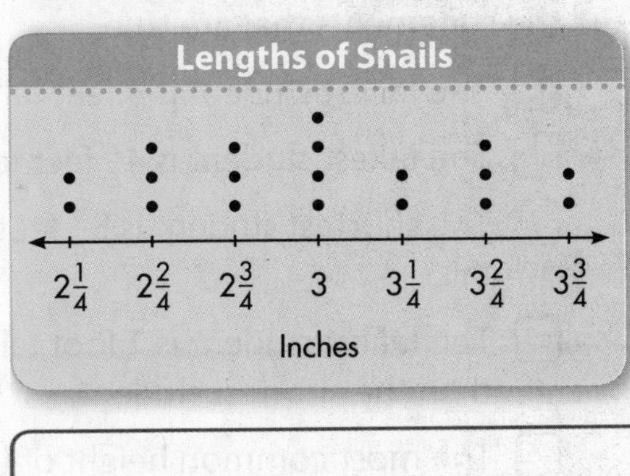

4. During a sleep study, the number of hours 15 people slept was recorded in the table below.

Hours of Sleep in One Night

9	6	7	$6\frac{1}{2}$	$5\frac{1}{2}$
8	$7\frac{1}{2}$	8	$7\frac{1}{2}$	7
6	$5\frac{1}{2}$	$7\frac{1}{2}$	$8\frac{1}{2}$	$6\frac{1}{2}$

A. Use the data in the table to draw a line plot.

B. How many more hours did the person who slept the greatest number of hours sleep than the person who slept the least number of hours? Explain.

5. Use the line plot below. Select all the true statements.

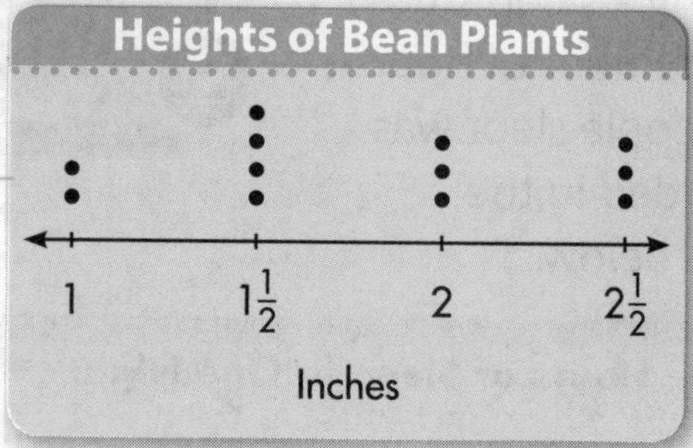

☐ The greatest height is $2\frac{1}{2}$ inches.

☐ More plants have a height of 2 inches than $1\frac{1}{2}$ inches.

☐ There are 3 plants with a height of 1 inch.

☐ There are 3 plants with a height of 2 inches and 3 plants with a height of $2\frac{1}{2}$ inches.

☐ The tallest plant is $1\frac{1}{2}$ inches taller than the shortest plant.

6. Mr. Tricorn's class measured the lengths of crayons. How many crayons did they measure? Use the line plot.

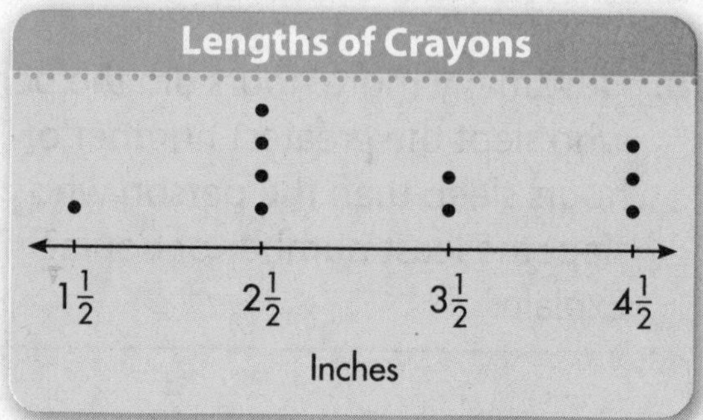

7. Use the line plot from Exercise 6. How many crayons were greater than 3 inches long?

Ⓐ 9 Ⓒ 5

Ⓑ 6 Ⓓ 3

8. Ms. Garcia measured the heights of her students.

DATA

Heights of Students in Ms. Garcia's Class (feet)				
4	$3\frac{3}{4}$	$4\frac{1}{4}$	$4\frac{2}{4}$	4
$3\frac{3}{4}$	$3\frac{2}{4}$	$4\frac{2}{4}$	4	$3\frac{3}{4}$
4	$4\frac{1}{4}$	$4\frac{1}{4}$	4	$4\frac{2}{4}$

A. Use the data in the table to draw a line plot.

B. Use the data in Exercise 8. Select all of the statements that are true.

☐ The tallest student is 4 feet tall.

☐ The tallest student is $4\frac{2}{4}$ feet tall.

☐ The shortest student is $3\frac{3}{4}$ feet tall.

☐ The tallest student is 1 foot taller than the shortest student.

☐ The most common height of the students was 4 feet tall.

Name ______________________________

Measuring Pumpkins

Mr. Chan's class picked small pumpkins from the pumpkin patch and then weighed their pumpkins.

1. The class made the **Pumpkin Weights** line plot of the data.

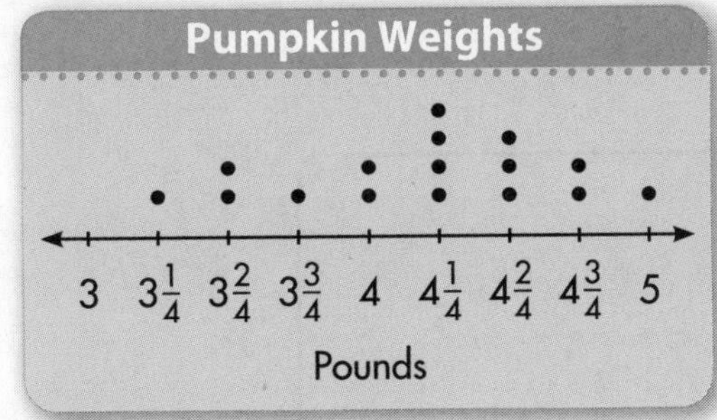

Part A

What is the most common weight of the pumpkins?

Part B

Write and solve an equation to find p, how much more the heaviest pumpkin weighs than the lightest pumpkin.

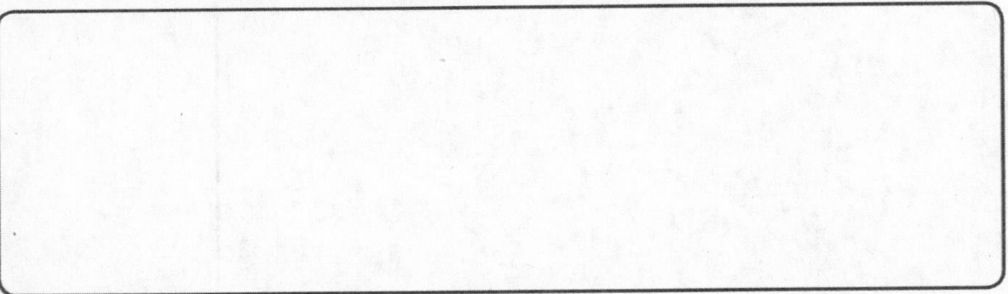

Part C

Ayana said 3 pumpkins weigh $4\frac{2}{4}$ pounds.
Critique Ayana's reasoning. Is she correct?

2. The class also measures the distance around their pumpkins to the nearest half-inch. They recorded their data in the **Pumpkin Size** list.

Pumpkin Size: $19\frac{1}{2}$, $20\frac{1}{2}$, $19\frac{1}{2}$, 20, $20\frac{1}{2}$, $21\frac{1}{2}$, 20, 21, 22, $19\frac{1}{2}$, $20\frac{1}{2}$, $21\frac{1}{2}$, 21, 21, $21\frac{1}{2}$, $20\frac{1}{2}$

Part A

Draw a line plot of **Pumpkin Size** data.

Part B

Drew says 1 more pumpkin was $20\frac{1}{2}$ inches around than was $19\frac{1}{2}$ inches around because $20\frac{1}{2} - 19\frac{1}{2} = 1$. Critique Drew's reasoning.

Part C

What is *d*, the difference between the longest distance and the shortest distance? Write and solve an equation.

TOPIC 12

Understand and Compare Decimals

Essential Questions: How can you write a fraction as a decimal? How can you locate points on a number line? How do you compare decimals?

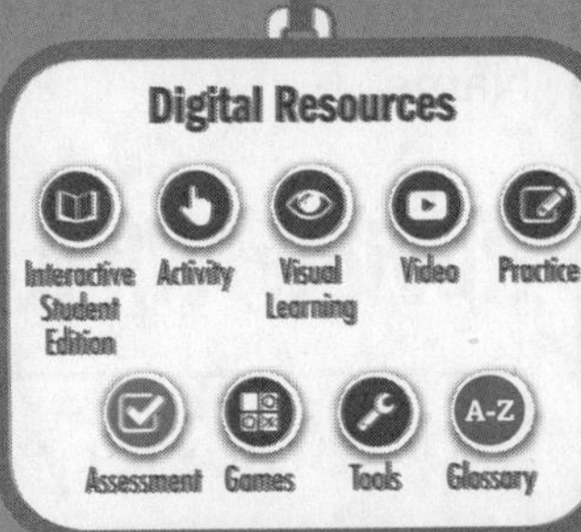

Curling is an Olympic sport that uses special stones and a target.

Players can make their stones move the other team's stones by transferring energy when they collide.

Curling must take a lot of energy! Here is a project about energy and decimals.

enVision® STEM Project: Energy and Decimals

Do Research Use the Internet or other sources to research other sports or games where players transfer energy to cause collisions in order to score points and win.

Journal: Write a Report Include what you found. Also in your report:

- Explain how the transfer of energy helps the player or team score.
- A game of curling is broken into ten rounds called *ends*. Suppose a team wins 6 of the 10 ends. Write a fraction with a denominator of 10 and an equivalent fraction with a denominator of 100. Then, write an equivalent decimal that represents the same value.

Name ______________________________

Review What You Know

Vocabulary

Choose the best term from the box. Write it on the blank.

- hundredth
- tens
- place value
- tenth

1. A ______________ is one of 10 equal parts of a whole, written as $\frac{1}{10}$.

2. ______________ is the position of a digit in a number that is used to determine the value of the digit.

3. A ______________ is one of 100 equal parts of a whole, written as $\frac{1}{100}$.

Comparing Fractions

Write >, <, or = in the ◯.

4. $\frac{5}{100}$ ◯ $\frac{5}{10}$

5. $\frac{1}{10}$ ◯ $\frac{1}{100}$

6. $\frac{2}{10}$ ◯ $\frac{20}{100}$

Parts of a Whole

Complete each fraction to represent the shaded part of the whole.

7. $\frac{\square}{10}$

8. $\frac{\square}{10}$

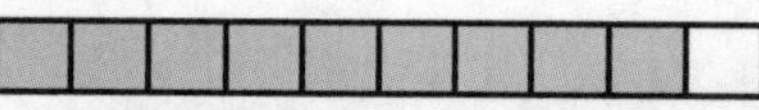

9. $\frac{\square}{10}$

Shade the part of the whole that represents the fraction.

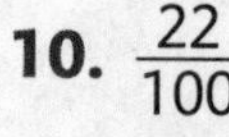

10. $\frac{22}{100}$

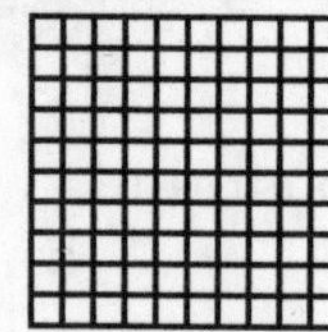

11. $\frac{79}{100}$

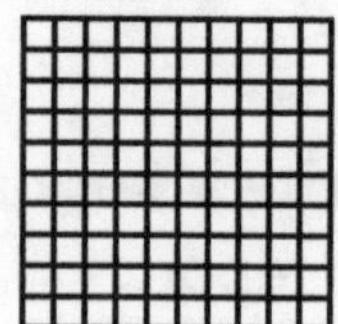

12. $\frac{37}{100}$

Problem Solving

13. Reasoning Rob walked $\frac{2}{10}$ block. Drew walked $\frac{5}{10}$ block. Write a comparison for the distance Rob and Drew each walked.

Name ____________________

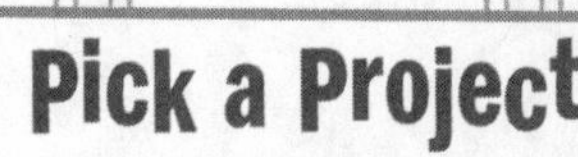

How much will it cost to visit a national park?

Project: Write a Travel Journal

How do you know who won the event?

Project: Compare Olympic Racing Times

Would you like to win an award for a presentation?

Project: Make a Presentation about Adding Fractions

PROJECT
12D

How did railroads help build Florida?

Project: Build a Miniature Railroad

Name ____________________ Activity

Lesson 12-1
Fractions and Decimals

I can ...
relate fractions and decimals.

Content Standard 4.NF.C.6
Mathematical Practices MP.2, MP.3, MP.4

Solve & Share

According to a survey, 7 out of 10 pet owners have a dog. Represent this in a drawing.

How can you model 7 out of 10? Think about the definition of a fraction.

Look Back! How many pet owners do **NOT** have a dog? Write your answer as a fraction.

How Can You Write a Fraction as a Decimal?

A

On Kelsey Street, 6 out of 10 houses have swing sets. Write $\frac{6}{10}$ as a decimal.

A decimal is another representation for a fraction and also names parts of wholes. A decimal is a number with one or more digits to the right of the decimal point.

Fractions with denominators of 10 and 100 may be written as decimals.

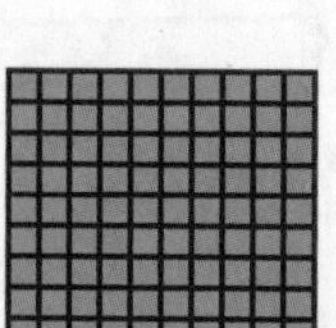

1 whole

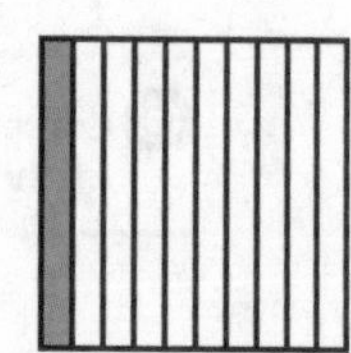

$\frac{1}{10}$, 0.1 one tenth

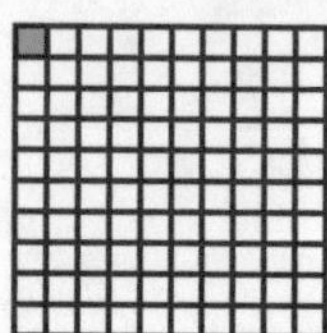

$\frac{1}{100}$, 0.01 one hundredth

B

Sixth tenths or $\frac{6}{10}$ of the houses have swing sets.

You can write $\frac{6}{10}$ as a decimal by putting a 6 in tenths place. The tenths place is to the right of the decimal point.

$\frac{6}{10} = 0.6$

decimal point

C

$\frac{6}{10}$ and $\frac{60}{100}$ are equivalent.

You can write $\frac{60}{100}$ as a decimal by using tenths and hundredths places. The hundredths place is to the right of tenths place.

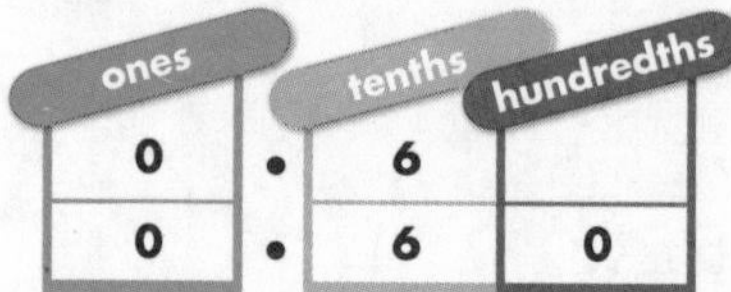

So, 0.6 or 0.60 of the houses have swing sets.

Convince Me! **Reasoning** In the Kelsey Street neighborhood, 75 out of 100 houses are two-story homes. Write $\frac{75}{100}$ as a decimal. Shade the grid to show the equivalent fraction and decimal.

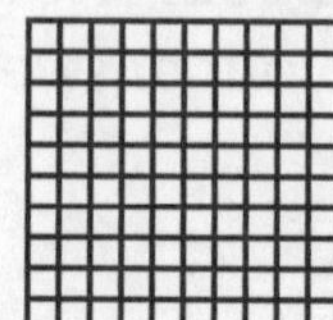

Name ____________________

Another Example!

You can use grids to show how money relates to fractions and decimals.

Cents are hundredths of a dollar, so amounts of money are written to the hundredths place.

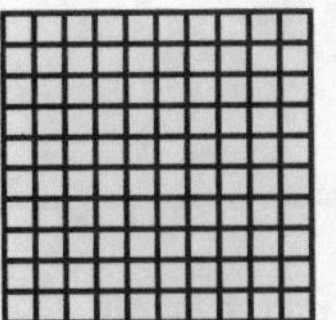
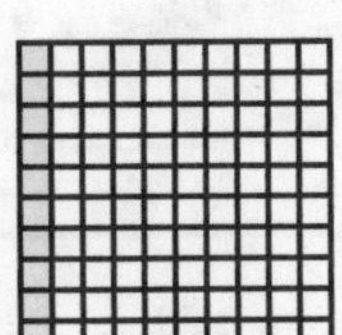
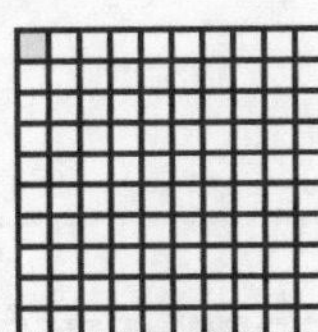

Dollar

Dime

Penny

$\$1.00 = \frac{100}{100}$ $\$0.10 = \frac{10}{100} = \frac{1}{10}$ $\$0.01 = \frac{1}{100}$

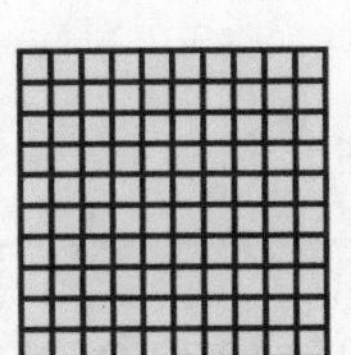
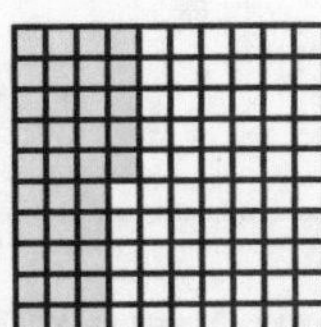

$\$2.35 = \frac{100}{100} + \frac{100}{100} + \frac{30}{100} + \frac{5}{100} = \frac{235}{100} = 2\frac{35}{100}$

$\$2.35 = \frac{235}{100}$ or $2\frac{35}{100}$

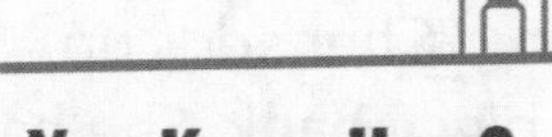

Guided Practice

Do You Understand?

1. How can you use grids to represent $4.71?

Do You Know How?

2. Write a decimal and a fraction for the part of the grid that is shaded.

Independent Practice

For **3–6**, write a decimal and fraction for each diagram.

3. 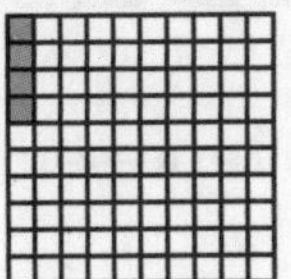

4. 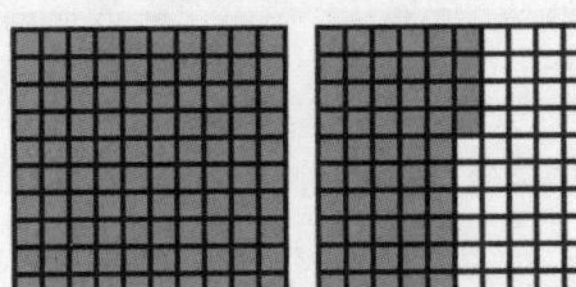

5. 

6.

Problem Solving

7. The arena of the Colosseum in Rome was about $\frac{15}{100}$ of the entire Colosseum. Write this amount as a decimal.

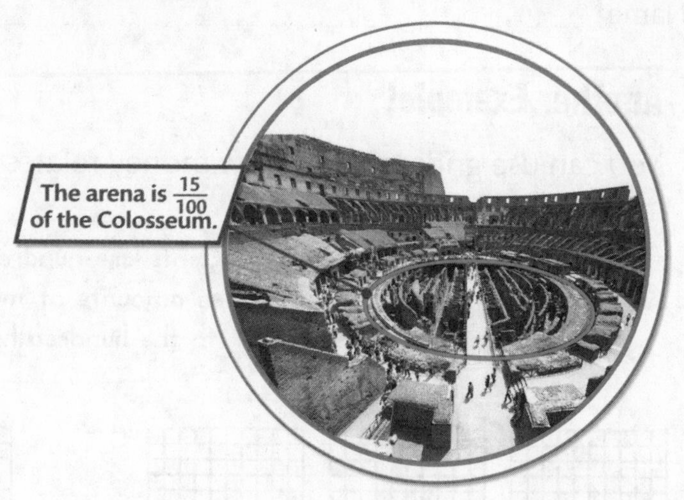

The arena is $\frac{15}{100}$ of the Colosseum.

8. What fraction of the Colosseum was **NOT** the arena? Write and solve an equation.

9. **Vocabulary** Write the vocabulary word that best completes the sentence:

Jelena says, "One dime is one ________ of a dollar."

10. **Number Sense** About how much of the rectangle is shaded green? Write this amount as a fraction and as a decimal.

11. **Critique Reasoning** Cher adds up the money in her piggy bank. She has a one-dollar bill and 3 dimes. Did Cher write the amount of money correctly? If not, what mistake did Cher make?

$1.3

12. **Higher Order Thinking** The diagram models the plants in a vegetable garden. Write a fraction and a decimal for each vegetable in the garden.

■ radishes ■ corn
■ carrots ■ lettuce

Assessment Practice

13. Which decimal represents $\frac{5}{100}$?

Ⓐ 0.05
Ⓑ 0.5
Ⓒ 0.50
Ⓓ 0.95

14. Which fraction and decimal represent twenty-nine hundredths?

Ⓐ 0.29 and $\frac{29}{10}$
Ⓑ 0.29 and $\frac{100}{29}$
Ⓒ 2.9 and $\frac{29}{100}$
Ⓓ 0.29 and $\frac{29}{100}$

Name ______________________________ Activity

Lesson 12-2
Fractions and Decimals on the Number Line

Solve & Share

Name the fractions and/or decimals of each lettered point on the number lines. Tell how you decided.

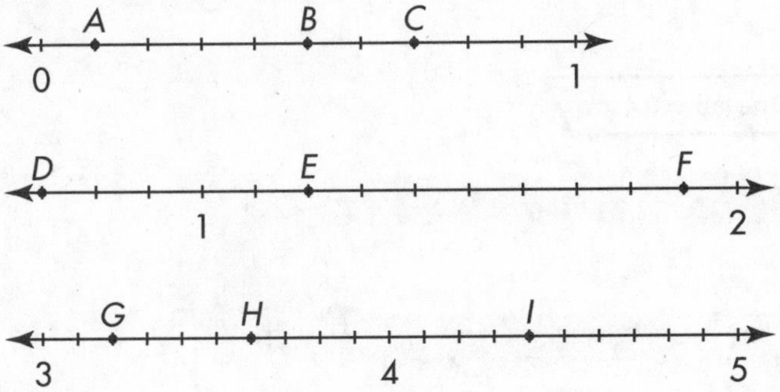

A
B
C
0
1
D
E
F
1
2
G
H
I
3
4
5

I can ...
locate and describe fractions and decimals on number lines.

Content Standards 4.NF.C.6 Also 4.MD.A.2
Mathematical Practices MP.1, MP.6, MP.7

You can use structure. The number of spaces between whole numbers can help you name each point on the number lines.

Look Back! Is the name for point *B* above different from the name for point *B* on the number line below? Explain.

A
B
C
0
1

How Can You Locate Points on a Number Line?

Visual Learning Bridge

A

In long-track speed skating, each lap is $\frac{4}{10}$ kilometer. During practice, Elizabeth skated 3.75 kilometers. Draw a number line to show $\frac{4}{10}$ and 3.75.

You can use a number line to locate and describe fractions and decimals.

B

Locate $\frac{4}{10}$ on a number line.

Draw a number line and divide the distance from 0 to1 into 10 equal parts to show tenths.

The distance from 0 to 0.4 is four tenths the distance from 0 to 1.

Draw a point at $\frac{4}{10}$.

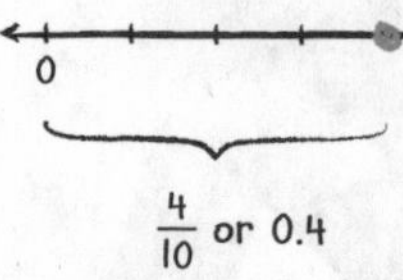

C

Locate 3.75 on a number line.

You can show 3.75 on a number line divided into tenths by plotting a point halfway between 3.7 and 3.8.

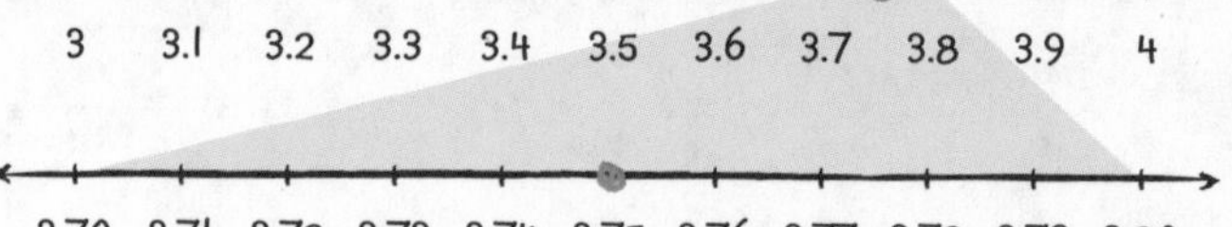

You can use a second number line to show the interval between 3.7 and 3.8. The points on both number lines are at 3.75.

Convince Me! **Be Precise** Which decimal shown on the number line is not placed in the correct location? Explain.

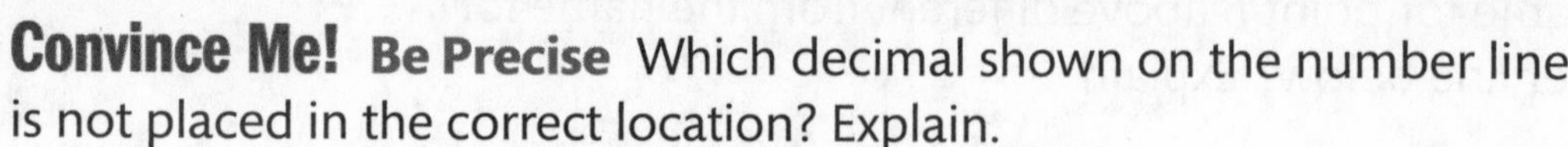

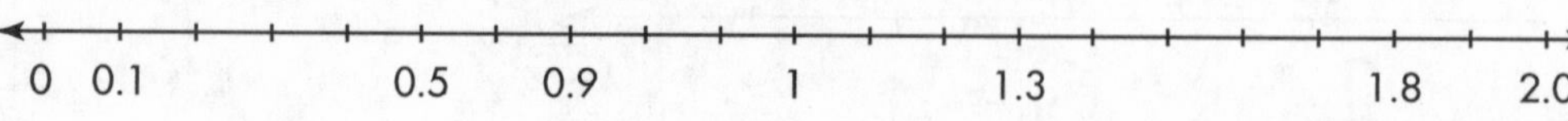

Name ______________________________

Another Example!

Fractions and decimals can name the same points on a number line.

$\frac{1}{10}$ $\frac{2}{10}$ $\frac{3}{10}$ $\frac{4}{10}$

0.1 0.2 0.3 0.4

Mixed numbers and decimals can name the the same points on a number line.

$1\frac{1}{100}$ $1\frac{2}{100}$ $1\frac{3}{100}$ $1\frac{4}{100}$

1.01 1.02 1.03 1.04

Guided Practice

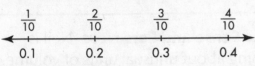

Do You Understand?

1. Locate $\frac{45}{100}$ on the number line.

$\frac{40}{100}$ $\frac{50}{100}$

2. Draw a number line to represent both the decimal and fraction for eight tenths.

Do You Know How?

For **3–6**, name the decimal and fraction for each point on the number line.

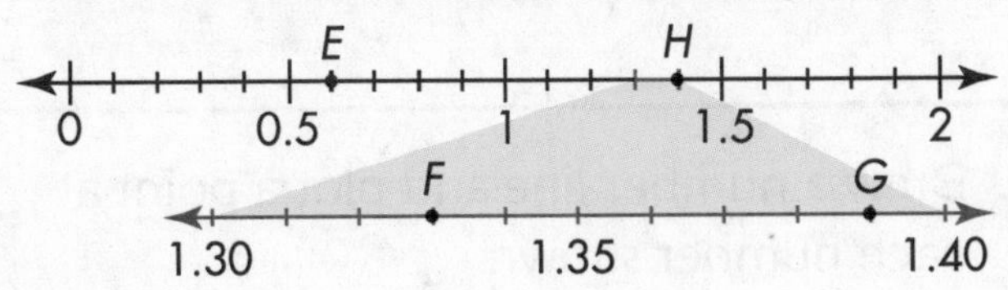

3. *E* **4.** *H*

5. *F* **6.** *G*

Independent Practice

For **7–8**, label the number lines with the given fractions and decimals.

7. Represent the decimals and fractions from 3.08 to 3.13.

8. Represent the fractions and decimals from $\frac{4}{10}$ to 1.

For **9–16**, name the decimal and fraction for each point on the number line.

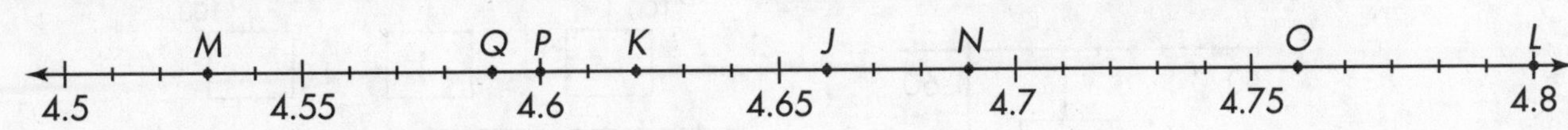

9. *J* **10.** *K* **11.** *L* **12.** *M*

13. *N* **14.** *O* **15.** *P* **16.** *Q*

Problem Solving

17. Write the five missing decimals on the number line.

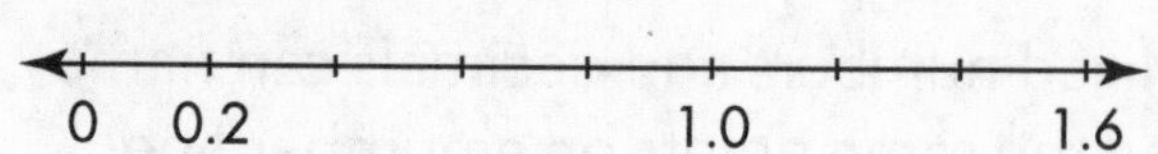

18. Write the five missing fractions on the number line.

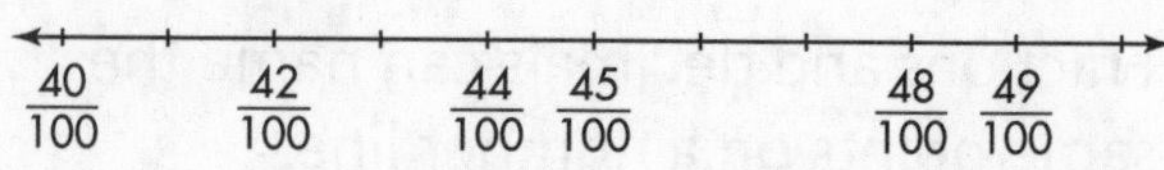

19. Draw a number line to show 60 cents. Use the number line to write 60 cents as a fraction and as a decimal.

20. Make Sense and Persevere Neil is learning about unusual units of volume. There are 2 pecks in 1 kenning. There are 2 kennings in 1 bushel. There are 8 bushels in 1 quarter. There are 5 quarters in 1 load. Write a number sentence to show how many pecks are in 1 load.

21. Draw a number line and plot a point at each number shown.

$2\frac{71}{100}$ 2.6 $2\frac{82}{100}$

22. Higher Order Thinking Use a number line to name two numbers that are the same distance apart as 3.2 and 3.8.

Assessment Practice

23. What decimals or fractions do the points on the number lines show? Choose the decimals and fractions from the box to label the number lines.

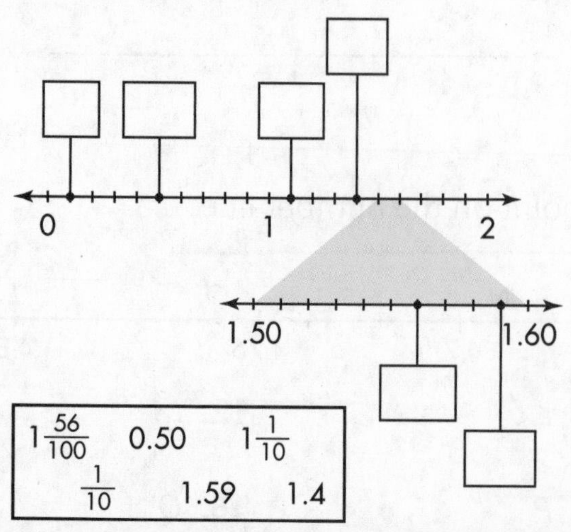

$1\frac{56}{100}$	0.50	$1\frac{1}{10}$
$\frac{1}{10}$	1.59	1.4

24. What decimals or fractions do the points on the number lines show? Choose the decimals and fractions from the box to label the number lines.

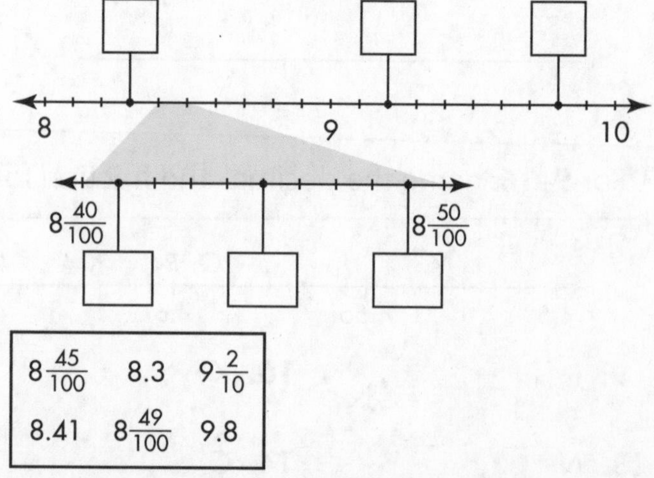

$8\frac{45}{100}$	8.3	$9\frac{2}{10}$
8.41	$8\frac{49}{100}$	9.8

Name ____________________

Activity

Lesson 12-3
Compare Decimals

I can ...
compare decimals by reasoning about their size.

Content Standards 4.NF.C.7 Also 4.MD.A.2
Mathematical Practices MP.2, MP.3, MP.5

Solve & Share

A penny made in 1982 weighs about 0.11 ounce. A penny made in 2013 weighs about 0.09 ounce. Which penny weighs more? ***Solve this problem any way you choose.***

Thinking about what you know about place value can help justify your reasoning.

Look Back! Construct Arguments Simon and Danielle are eating oranges. Danielle says, "Because we each have 0.75 of an orange left, we have the same amount left to eat." Do you agree with Danielle? Explain.

How Do You Compare Decimals?

Visual Learning Bridge

A

Donovan ran the 100-meter race in 10.11 seconds. Sal ran the same race in 10.09 seconds. Who had the faster time?

There is more than one way to compare decimals.

B

One Way

Use hundredths grids.

The whole numbers are the same. Compare the digits in the tenths place.

10.11 10.09

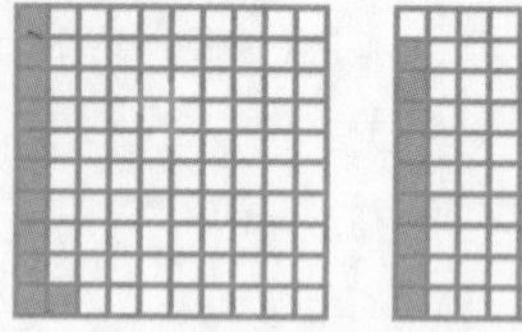

10.11 > 10.09

Sal had the faster time.

C

Another Way

Use place value.

The whole number parts are the same.

The decimal parts are both to the hundredths.

11 hundredths is greater than 9 hundredths.

10.11 > 10.09

Sal had the faster time.

D

Another Way

Start at the left.

Compare each place value. Look for the first place where the digits are different.

10.11 10.09

1 tenth > 0 tenths

10.11 > 10.09

Sal had the faster time.

Convince Me! **Reasoning** Write four different digits in the blank spaces to make each comparison true. Explain your reasoning.

0. ____ 8 < 0. ____ 7 0. 5 ____ > 0. ____ 9

Name ______________________

Another Example!

You can also use place-value blocks or number lines to compare.

0.23 < 0.32

0.23 0.32

0.20 0.25 0.30 0.35 0.40

0.23 < 0.32

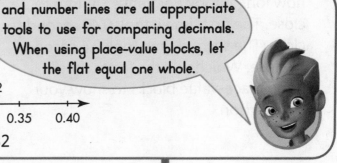

Grids, place-value blocks, and number lines are all appropriate tools to use for comparing decimals. When using place-value blocks, let the flat equal one whole.

Guided Practice

Do You Understand?

1. Cy says, "0.20 is greater than 0.2 because 20 is greater than 2." Do you agree? Explain.

Do You Know How?

For **2–5**, write >, <, or = in each ◯. Use an appropriate tool as needed to compare.

2. 0.70 ◯ 0.57
3. 0.41 ◯ 0.14
4. 6.28 ◯ 7.31
5. 1.1 ◯ 1.10

Independent Practice

Leveled Practice For **6–14**, write >, <, or = in each ◯. Use an appropriate tool as needed to compare.

6. 0.16 0.18 0.20 0.22

0.15 0.17 0.19 0.21 0.23

0.17 ◯ 0.2

7. 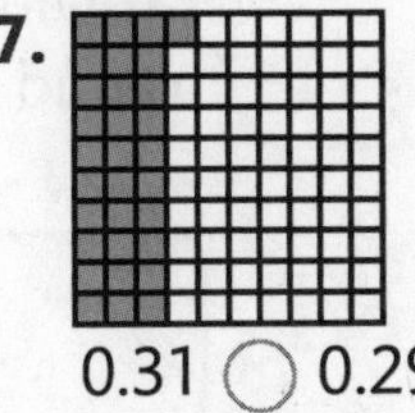 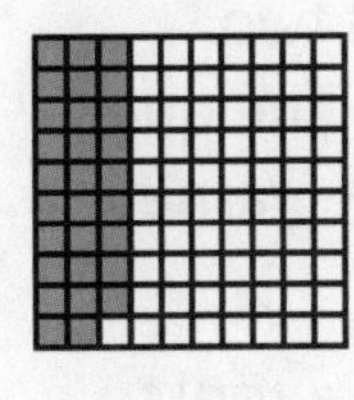

0.31 ◯ 0.29

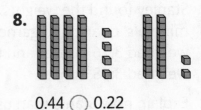

8. 0.44 ◯ 0.22

9. 0.1 ◯ 0.10
10. $2.98 ◯ $2.56
11. 7.01 ◯ 7.1
12. 0.08 ◯ 0.7
13. 3.40 ◯ 3.4
14. $21.50 ◯ $20.99

For **15–20**, write a decimal to make each comparison true.

15. ______ < 0.23
16. 8.60 = ______
17. ______ > 4.42
18. 13.2 > ______
19. 5.2 < ______
20. 6.2 = ______

Problem Solving

21. Use Appropriate Tools Maria timed how long it took her Venus Fly Trap to close. The first time it took 0.43 second to close. The second time took 0.6 second to close. Which was the faster time? Draw place-value blocks to show your comparison.

22. Fishing lures have different weights. Which lure weighs more?

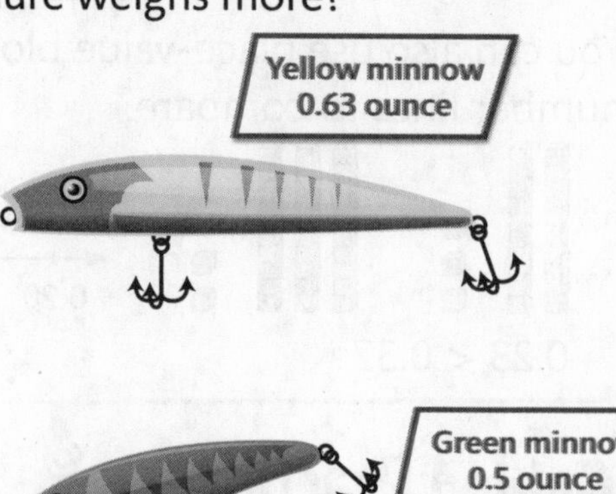

23. Number Sense Ellen wants to give 100 toys to each of 9 charities. In one week, she collects 387 toys. The next week, she collects 515 toys. Has Ellen reached her goal? Use an estimate to explain.

24. Higher Order Thinking Tori has two different-sized water bottles. In the larger bottle, she has 0.81 liter of water. In the smaller bottle, she has 1.1 liters of water. Can you tell whether one bottle has more water? Explain.

Assessment Practice

25. Stanley found the weights of two minerals, quartz and garnet. The quartz weighed 3.76 ounces and the garnet weighed 3.68 ounces.

Explain how Stanley can use a tool to find which mineral weighed more.

Explain how Stanley can use place value to find which mineral weighed less.

Name ______________________

Activity

Solve & Share

The mural is divided into 100 equal parts. Marilyn's class painted $\frac{3}{10}$ of the mural, and Cal's class painted $\frac{27}{100}$ of the mural. How much of the mural have the two classes painted? ***Solve this problem any way you choose.***

Lesson 12-4

Add Fractions with Denominators of 10 and 100

I can ...

use equivalence to add fractions with denominators of 10 and 100.

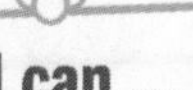

Content Standard 4.NF.C.5
Mathematical Practices MP.1, MP.3, MP.5

You can use appropriate tools. Think about how you can use the grid to find how much of the mural the two classes painted. *Show your work in the space above!*

Look Back! How much of the mural remains to be painted? Write the amount as a decimal.

How Can You Add Fractions with Denominators of 10 and 100?

Visual Learning Bridge

A

Steve and Jana collected money for an animal shelter. Steve collected $\frac{4}{10}$ of their goal while Jana collected $\frac{5}{100}$. How much of their goal did Jana and Steve collect?

B

The red shows $\frac{4}{10}$ of the goal, and the blue shows $\frac{5}{100}$ of the goal.

The amount they collected can be written as $\frac{4}{10} + \frac{5}{100}$.

You can use equivalent fractions to write tenths as hundredths.

C

Rename $\frac{4}{10}$ as an equivalent fraction with a denominator of 100.

Multiply the numerator and denominator by 10.

$$\frac{4 \times 10}{10 \times 10} = \frac{40}{100}$$

D

Add the numerators and write the sum over the like denominator.

$$\frac{40}{100} + \frac{5}{100} = \frac{45}{100}$$

Jana and Steve collected $\frac{45}{100}$ of their goal.

Convince Me! **Construct Arguments** In the problem above, why is the denominator of the total 100 and not 200?

Name ____________________

Practice Tools Assessment

Guided Practice

Do You Understand?

1. Suppose Jana collected another $\frac{25}{100}$ of their goal. What fraction of the goal have they now collected?

2. Write a problem that represents the addition shown below, then solve.

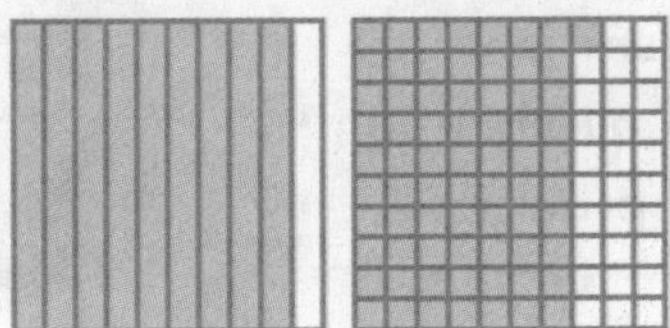

Do You Know How?

For **3–8**, add the fractions.

3. $\frac{3}{10} + \frac{4}{100}$

4. $\frac{71}{100} + \frac{5}{10}$

5. $\frac{4}{100} + \frac{38}{10}$

6. $\frac{90}{100} + \frac{1}{10}$

7. $\frac{8}{10} + \frac{1}{10} + \frac{7}{100}$

8. $\frac{38}{100} + \frac{4}{10} + \frac{2}{10}$

Independent Practice

Leveled Practice For **9–23**, add the fractions.

9. $\frac{21}{100} + \frac{2}{10} = \frac{21}{100} + \frac{\square}{100}$

10. $\frac{\square}{10} + \frac{68}{100} = \frac{30}{100} + \frac{68}{100}$

11. $\frac{4}{10} + \frac{60}{100} = \frac{\square}{10} + \frac{\square}{10}$

12. $\frac{32}{100} + \frac{28}{100} + \frac{6}{10}$

13. $\frac{11}{10} + \frac{41}{100}$

14. $\frac{72}{100} + \frac{6}{10}$

15. $\frac{5}{10} + \frac{3}{10} + \frac{18}{100}$

16. $\frac{7}{100} + \frac{6}{10}$

17. $\frac{9}{10} + \frac{4}{100}$

18. $\frac{30}{100} + \frac{5}{10}$

19. $\frac{39}{100} + \frac{2}{10}$

20. $\frac{8}{10} + \frac{9}{100}$

21. $\frac{44}{100} + \frac{34}{100} + \frac{9}{10}$

22. $\frac{70}{10} + \frac{33}{100}$

23. $\frac{28}{10} + \frac{72}{10} + \frac{84}{100}$

Problem Solving

24. Algebra A mail carrier made a total of 100 deliveries in a day. $\frac{76}{100}$ of the deliveries were letters, $\frac{2}{10}$ were packages, and the rest were postcards. Write and solve an equation to find the fraction that represents how many of the deliveries were letters and packages.

25. Make Sense and Persevere Balloons are sold in bags of 30. There are 5 giant balloons in each bag. How many giant balloons will you get if you buy 120 balloons? Explain.

26. Higher Order Thinking Of the first 100 elements on the periodic table, $\frac{13}{100}$ were discovered in ancient times, and $\frac{21}{100}$ were discovered in the Middle Ages. Another $\frac{5}{10}$ were discovered in the 1800s. What fraction of the first 100 elements was discovered *after* the 1800s? Explain.

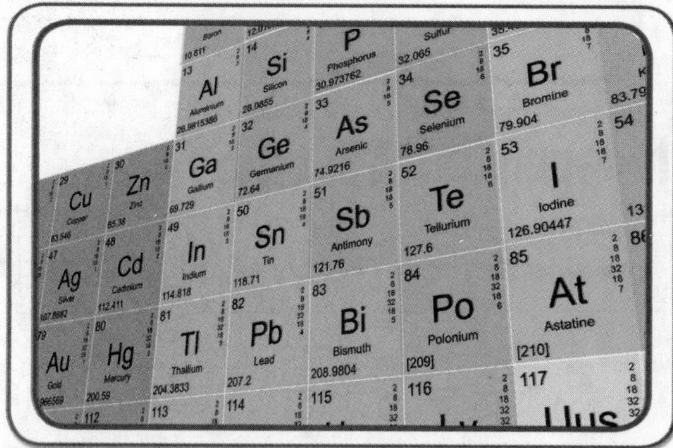

Assessment Practice

27. Delia hiked $\frac{7}{10}$ mile one day and $\frac{67}{100}$ mile the next. She wanted to know how far she hiked in all. Her work is shown below.

$$\frac{7}{10} + \frac{67}{100}$$

$$\frac{70}{100} + \frac{67}{100} = \frac{137}{100}$$

Is Delia's work correct? Explain.

Name ______________________

Activity

Lesson 12-5
Solve Word Problems Involving Money

I can ...
use fractions or decimals to solve word problems involving money.

Content Standard 4.MD.A.2
Mathematical Practices MP.1, MP.7, MP.8

Solve & Share

A flash drive costs $24, including tax. A customer purchases 3 flash drives and pays the cashier $80. How much change should the cashier give back to the customer? ***Solve this problem any way you choose.***

What do you need to do first to answer the question?

Look Back! Generalize How can you estimate and check if your solution is reasonable?

How Can You Solve Word Problems Involving Money?

Visual Learning Bridge

A

Marcus buys a toy airplane and a toy car. How much does Marcus spend? How much more does the toy airplane cost than the toy car?

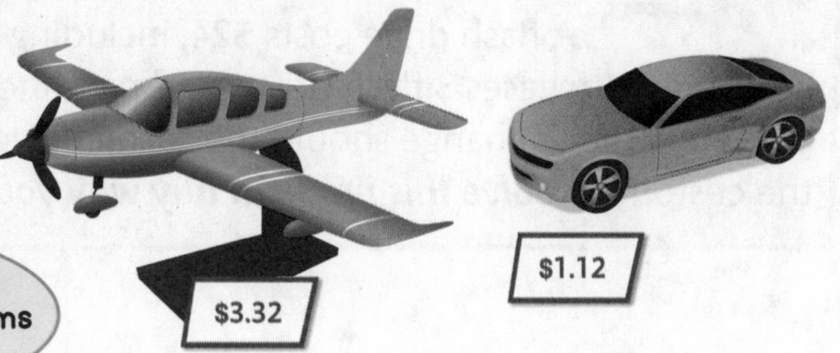

You can draw or use bills and coins to solve problems involving money.

B Find \$3.32 + \$1.12.

Cost of Airplane

Cost of Car

Add the bills, then count on to add each type of coin.

\$4.00 + \$0.40 + \$0.04 = \$4.44

Marcus spent \$4.44.

C Find \$3.32 – \$1.12.

Start with the cost of the airplane, then subtract the cost of the car.

Count the remaining bills and coins.

\$2.00 + \$0.20 = \$2.20

The toy airplane costs $2.20 more than the toy car.

Convince Me! **Use Structure** In the examples above, how can you use place value to help add or subtract?

Name ______________________________

Another Example!

Find $6.33 ÷ 3. Draw or use bills and coins.

You can use multiplication or division to solve problems involving money.

$6.33 divided into 3 equal groups:
$6.33 ÷ 3 = $2.11

3 groups of $2.11:
3 × $2.11 = $6.33

Guided Practice

Do You Understand?

1. Write a fraction and a decimal to describe how the quantities are related.

 $= \frac{1}{10}$ of a dollar = $0.10

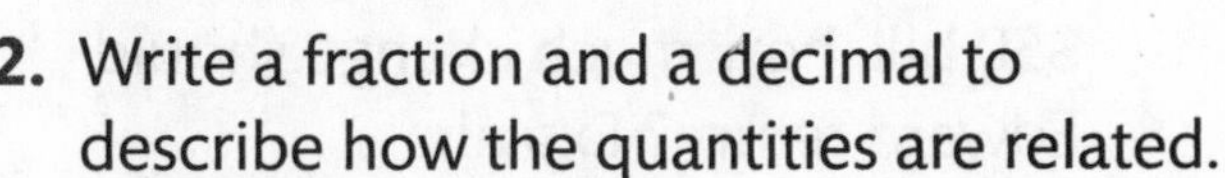
= ______ (Fraction) = ______ (Decimal)

2. Write a fraction and a decimal to describe how the quantities are related.

 $= \frac{1}{100}$ of a dollar = $0.01

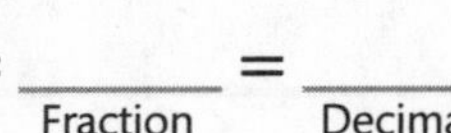
= ______ (Fraction) = ______ (Decimal)

Do You Know How?

For **3**, use the bills and coins to solve.

3. Marcus has $15.00. He buys a movie ticket for $11.25. How much money does Marcus have left?

Independent Practice

For **4–5**, you may draw or use bills and coins to solve.

4. Sarah bought 3 wool scarves. The price of each scarf was $23.21. How much did 3 scarves cost?

5. Carlos spends $14.38 on equipment. How much change should Carlos receive if he gives the clerk $20.00?

Problem Solving

6. **Use Structure** Leo went to lunch with his parents. The bill was $17.85. Complete the table to show two different combinations of coins and bills that can represent $17.85.

One Way		Another Way	
Coins and Bills	Value	Coins and Bills	Value
Total	$17.85	Total	$17.85

7. Kenya purchases a new tablet for $109.78. She pays with six $20 bills. Show how you would estimate how much change Kenya should receive.

8. **Algebra** Marco paid $12 for 3 jump ropes. If each jump rope costs the same amount, how much does 1 jump rope cost? Write and solve an equation.

9. **Number Sense** Jiang has a collection of 3,788 toy building bricks. He used 1,229 bricks to build a city. About how many bricks does Jiang have left? Explain how you estimated.

10. **Higher Order Thinking** Edward bought 7 concert tickets for himself and six friends for a total of $168. Each friend paid Edward back for his or her ticket. If one of Edward's friends gave him a $50 bill, how much change should Edward return? Explain.

Assessment Practice

11. Rajeev bought a skateboard for $37.74. How much change should Rajeev receive if he gave the cashier $40.00? You may draw or use bills and coins to solve.

Ⓐ $2.26

Ⓑ $2.74

Ⓒ $3.26

Ⓓ $3.74

12. Genevieve bought a catcher's mitt for $30.73 and a bat for $19.17. How much did Genevieve spend? You may draw or use bills and coins to solve.

Ⓐ $11.56

Ⓑ $49.17

Ⓒ $49.90

Ⓓ $50.73

Name ____________________________ Activity

Solve & Share

Three people hiked the same 1-mile trail. The distance for each hiker is represented in the drawings. Show about where the 1-mile mark should be on each drawing. Explain.

Start 0.5 mi

Start 0.25 mi

Start 0.75 mi

Problem Solving

Lesson 12-6

Look For and Use Structure

I can ...
use the structure of the place-value system to solve problems.

Mathematical Practices MP.7 Also MP.1, MP.2, MP.4, MP.6
Content Standards 4.NF.C.7 Also 4.MD.A.2

Thinking Habits

Be a good thinker!
These questions can help you.

- What patterns can I see and describe?
- How can I use the patterns to solve the problem?
- Can I see expressions and objects in different ways?

Look Back! Look For Relationships The three drawings represent 0.5, 0.25, and 0.75 mile with equivalent lengths. How does this affect where 1-mile is located on each drawing?

How Can You Look for and Make Use of Structure to Solve Problems?

Visual Learning Bridge

A

Maps from two different ski resorts show a 1-mile cross-country ski trail for beginners. Show about where to mark 0.25, 0.5, and 0.75 mile on each trail.

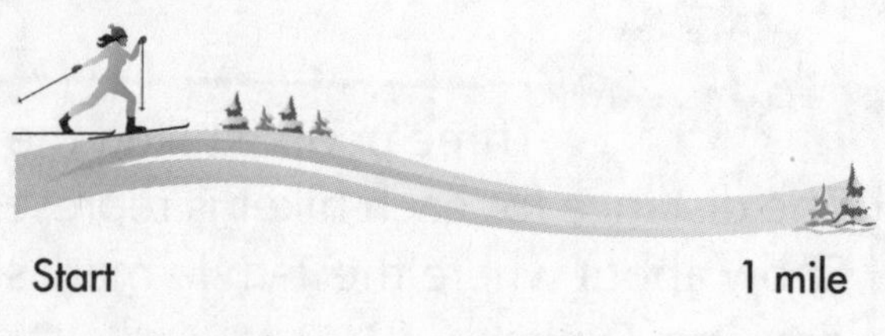

How can you determine where to mark the points on each drawing?

I need to analyze each drawing and decide about where the given decimals should be located on each.

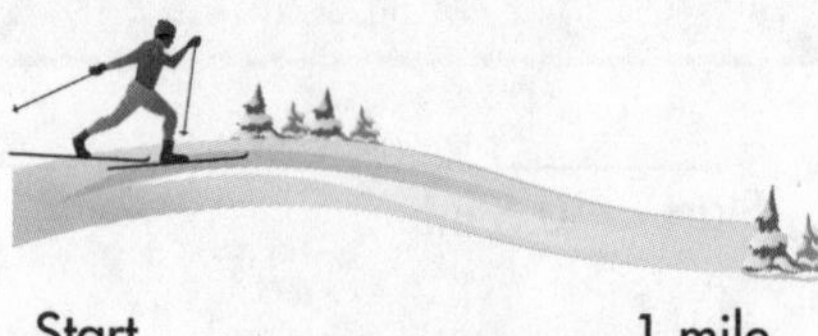

B

How can I make use of structure to solve this problem?

I can

- break the problem into simpler parts.
- use what I know about decimal meanings to locate the points.
- use equivalent forms of numbers.

C

Here's my thinking.

The size of a decimal depends on the size of the whole. The size of the whole is not the same for each drawing. Divide each whole in half to show **0.5** on each whole.

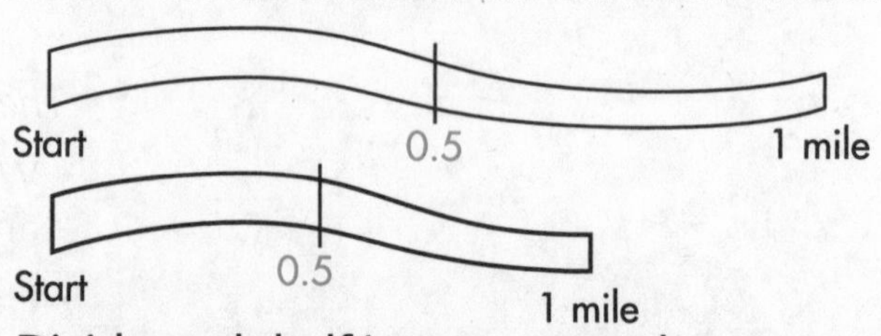

Divide each half into two equal parts to show **0.25** and **0.75** on each whole.

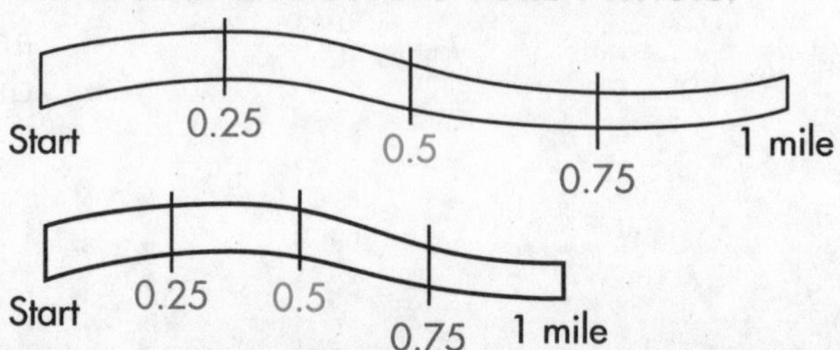

Convince Me! **Use Structure** Use the drawing of the trail shown. Where is the 1.5-mile mark on the trail? How did you decide?

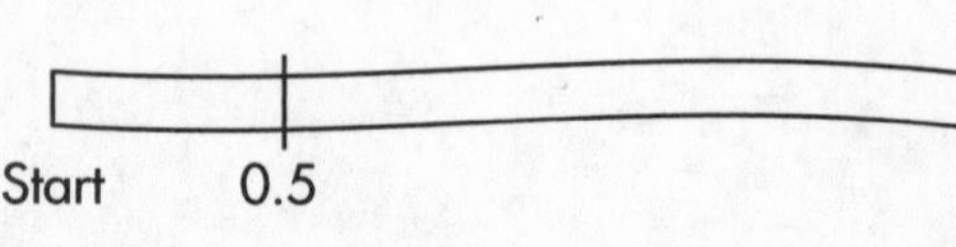

Name ______________________

Practice
Tools
Assessment

Guided Practice

Use Structure

Margie painted 0.4 of her banner blue. Helena painted 0.5 of her banner blue.

1. Complete the drawings to show the whole, or 1, for each banner.

2. Explain how you determined where to draw 1 whole for each banner.

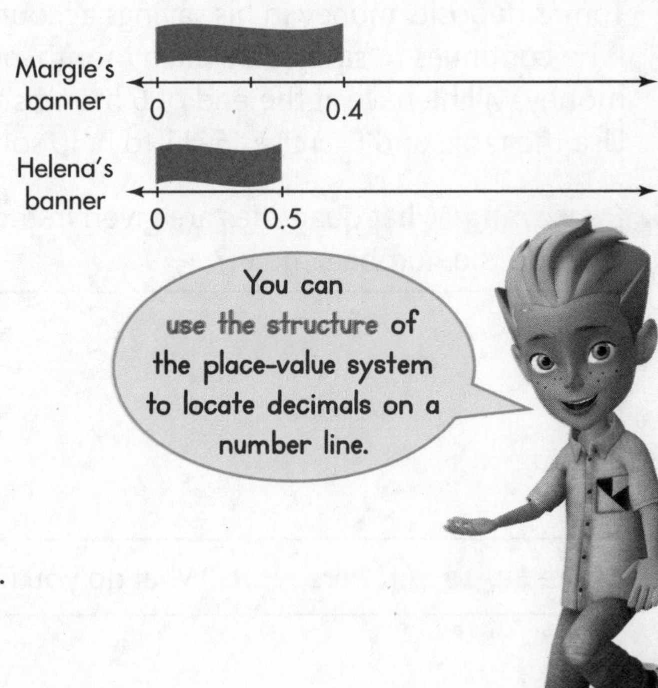
Margie's banner
0
0.4
Helena's banner
0
0.5
You can use the structure of the place-value system to locate decimals on a number line.

3. Do the drawings show 0.4 < 0.5? Explain.

Independent Practice

Use Structure

Kaitlin is making a map for the walk/run race. She wants the water stops to be at 0.5 mile, 0.3 mile, and 0.85 mile from the start.

Start ———————— End

4. Label 0.25, 0.5, 0.75 on the number line as a scale reference. Explain how you decided where to mark the number line.

5. Estimate where 0.3 and 0.85 are located compared to the other points. Mark the points 0.3 and 0.85. Explain how you estimated.

Problem Solving

Performance Task

Watching Savings Grow

Tomas deposits money in his savings account every month. If he continues to save $3.50 each month, how much money will he have at the end of 6 months? 12 months? Use the table and Exercises 6–11 to help solve.

Month	Money in Savings Account
0	$10.00
1	$13.50
2	$17.00
3	$20.50

6. Reasoning What quantities are given in the problem and what do the numbers mean?

7. Make Sense and Persevere What do you need to find?

8. Use Structure What is the relationship between the amount of money Tomas will have in his savings account in the fourth month and the amount in the third month?

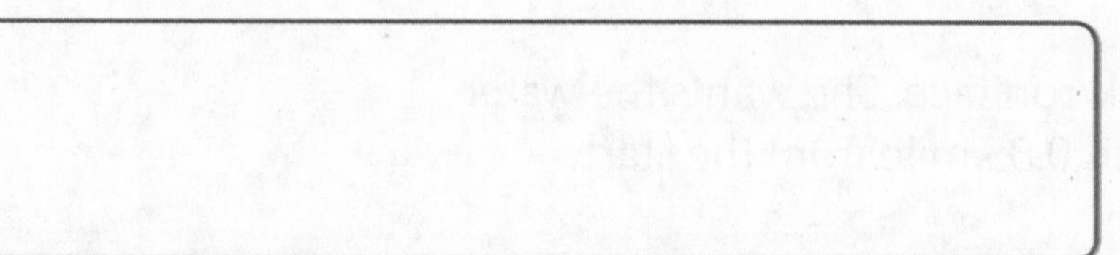

9. Model with Math Write an expression that can be used to find the amount saved at the end of 6 months.

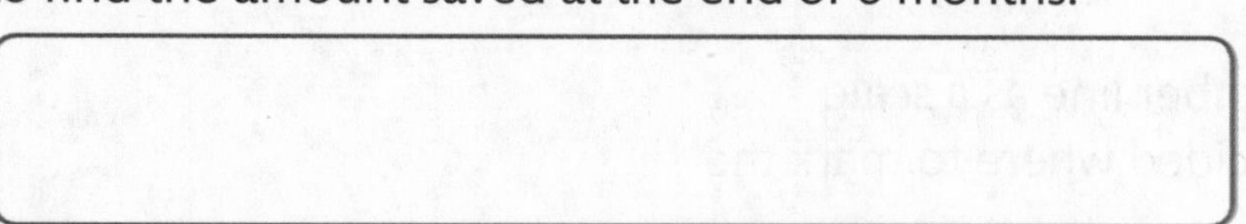

10. Model with Math Complete the table to find how much Tomas will have saved in 6 months.

11. Be Precise Use the answers from the table to find how much money Tomas will have at the end of 12 months. Show your work.

When you look for and make use of structure, you break a problem into simpler parts.

Name ______________________________

TOPIC 12

Fluency Practice Activity

Shade a path from **Start** to **Finish**. Follow the sums or differences that round to 2,000 when rounded to the nearest thousand. You can only move up, down, right, or left.

I can ...
add and subtract multi-digit whole numbers.

Content Standard 4.NBT.B.4
Mathematical Practices MP.2, MP.6, MP.7

Start				
954 + 871	2,000 − 1,876	3,887 + 369	2,195 − 737	2,698 + 400
8,998 − 7,399	1,810 + 789	8,917 − 5,252	6,295 − 3,290	8,506 − 3,282
1,789 + 210	1,340 − 771	2,615 + 347	9,000 − 6,233	5,896 + 5,601
6,726 − 4,309	1,199 + 468	3,300 − 298	9,444 + 9,444	3,922 − 923
3,856 + 1,144	4,239 − 2,239	5,999 − 4,370	5,607 − 3,605	2,203 + 122
				Finish

TOPIC 12 Vocabulary Review

Glossary

Word List

- decimal
- decimal point
- equivalent
- fraction
- greater than symbol (>)
- hundredth
- less than symbol (<)
- tenth

Understand Vocabulary

Choose the best term from the box. Write it on the blank.

1. A dot used to separate dollars from cents or ones from tenths in a number is called a ____________________.

2. One part of 100 equal parts of a whole is called a ____________________.

3. Numbers that name the same amount are ____________________.

4. A symbol, such as $\frac{2}{3}$, $\frac{5}{1}$, or $\frac{8}{5}$, used to name part of a whole, part of a set, or a location on a number line is called a ____________________.

5. One out of ten equal parts of a whole is called a ____________________.

For each of these terms, give an example and a non-example.

	Example	Non-example
6. greater than symbol (>)	__________	__________
7. less than symbol (<)	__________	__________
8. decimal	__________	__________

Use Vocabulary in Writing

9. Krista wrote $\frac{75}{100}$ and 0.75. Use at least 3 terms from the Word List to describe Krista's work.

Name ______________________________

Reteaching

Set A pages 445–448

The essay question on a 100-point test was worth 40 points. Write this part as a fraction and a decimal.

There are 100 points, so each point is $\frac{1}{100}$. $\frac{40}{100}$ is 0.40.

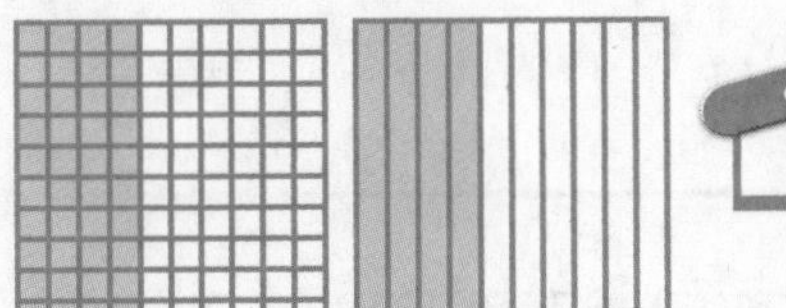

$\frac{40}{100} = \frac{4}{10}$ and $0.40 = 0.4$

Remember that the name of a fraction can help you write it as a decimal.

Write a decimal and a fraction for each model.

1. 

2. 

3. Donnie has 4 dollars, 6 pennies, and 9 dimes. Write a decimal for the amount of money Donnie has.

Set B pages 449–452

Locate 0.8 and 0.62 on a number line.

The distance from 0 to 0.8 is eight-tenths the distance from 0 to 1.

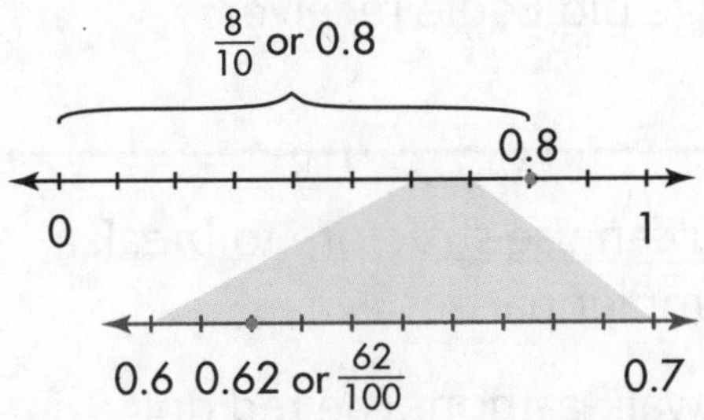

Draw a number line showing hundredths. 0.62 is between 0.6 and 0.7.

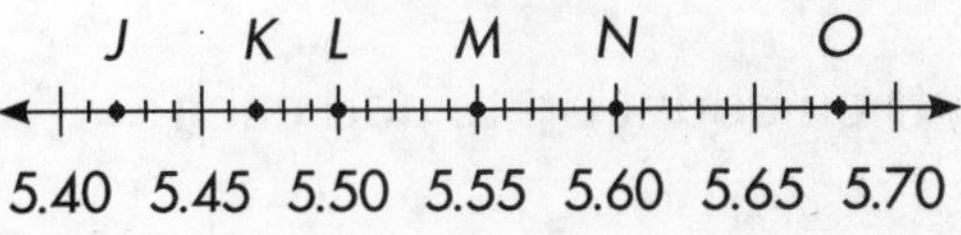

Name the decimal and fraction at each point.

1. *K*
2. *M*
3. *O*
4. *N*
5. *L*
6. *J*

Set C pages 453–456

Compare 1.74 and 1.08.

The digits in the ones place are the same, so look at the digits after the decimal point to compare.

1.74 1.08
7 tenths > 0 tenths
1.74 > 1.08

Remember you can use tools such as place-value blocks, number lines, or grids to compare decimal amounts.

Write >, <, or = in each ◯.

1. \$4.13 ◯ \$4.32
2. 0.6 ◯ 0.60
3. 5.29 ◯ 52.9
4. 12.91 ◯ 12.19

Set D pages 457–460

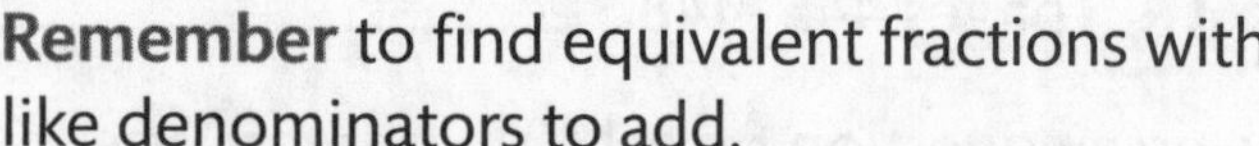

Find $\frac{9}{10} + \frac{49}{100}$.

Rewrite $\frac{9}{10}$ as an equivalent fraction with a denominator of 100.

$\frac{9 \times 10}{10 \times 10} = \frac{90}{100}$

$\frac{90}{100} + \frac{49}{100} = \frac{139}{100}$ or $1\frac{39}{100}$

Remember to find equivalent fractions with like denominators to add.

Add. Use grids or place-value blocks as needed to help.

1. $\frac{8}{10} + \frac{40}{100}$
2. $\frac{24}{100} + \frac{6}{10}$

Set E pages 461–464

Find $5.21 + $1.52.

Add the bills, then count on to add each type of coin.

$6.00 + $0.50 + $0.20 + $0.03 = $6.73

Remember to take away each type of bill and coin when subtracting money.

1. Chelsea had $71.18. She bought a new pair of glasses for $59.95. Can she buy a case that costs $12.95? Explain.
2. Eddie bought 3 train tickets for $17.00 each. If he paid with three $20 bills, how much change did Eddie receive?

Set F pages 465–468

Think about these questions to help you **look for and make use of structure.**

Thinking Habits

- What patterns can I see and describe?
- How can I use the patterns to solve the problem?
- Can I see expressions and objects in different ways?

Remember you can use structure to break a problem into simpler parts.

Raven joined a walk-a-thon. The red dot shows how far Raven walked in one hour.

1. Complete the number line below.

0 ____ ____ ____ ____ 1.25 ____ ____ 2

Miles

2. Estimate how far Raven walked in the first hour. Explain.

Name ____________________

TOPIC 12

Assessment Practice

1. Which represent the decimal 0.7? Select all that apply.

☐ 0.07 ☐ 7.00
☐ $\frac{7}{10}$ ☐ $\frac{70}{10}$
☐ $\frac{70}{100}$

2. Select all the statements that correctly compare two numbers.

☐ 29.48 > 29.69
☐ 29.48 < 29.69
☐ 15.36 > 15.39
☐ 16.99 < 17.99
☐ 21.30 = 21.03

3. Lucy buys a puzzle for \$3.89, a model airplane for \$12.75, and a stuffed animal for \$2.50. How much money did she spend in all? Draw or use bills and coins to solve.

Ⓐ \$19.14 Ⓒ \$19.00
Ⓑ \$16.64 Ⓓ \$16.00

4. Which point is incorrectly labeled? Explain.

A (3.75) B (4.5) C (4.9)

3 4 5

5. Catalina takes the money shown to the bookstore.

DATA

New Releases	
A Story of Two Towns	\$14.95
Good Morning, Sun	\$16.55
The History of Italy	\$16.00

A. Does Catalina have enough for all three books? If not, how much more money does Catalina need? Explain. Draw or use bills and coins to solve.

B. Catalina chooses to buy only 2 of the books. Choose two books for Catalina to buy, and then find how much money she will have left. Draw or use bills and coins to solve.

6. Write a fraction and a decimal that represent the part of the grid that is green.

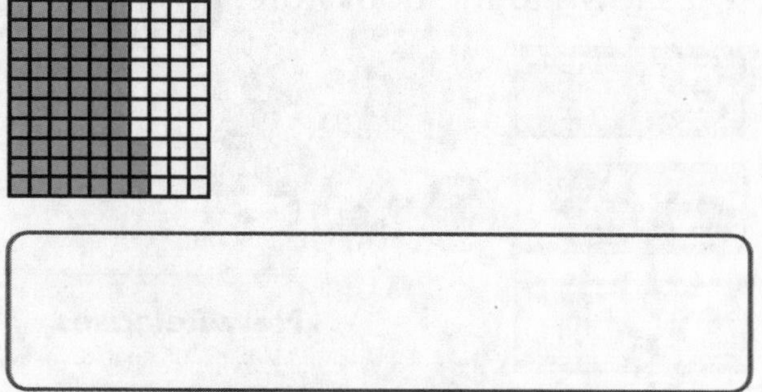

7. Match each number on the left to its equivalent fraction.

	$\frac{200}{100}$	$\frac{200}{10}$	$\frac{20}{100}$	$\frac{2}{100}$
20	❑	❑	❑	❑
2	❑	❑	❑	❑
0.02	❑	❑	❑	❑
0.20	❑	❑	❑	❑

8. Select all the statements that correctly compare two numbers.

- ☐ 7.27 > 74.7
- ☐ 1.24 < 1.42
- ☐ 58.64 > 48.64
- ☐ 138.5 < 13.85
- ☐ 12.56 > 12.65

9. What fraction is equivalent to 0.4?

10. Explain how to find the sum of $\frac{3}{10} + \frac{4}{100}$.

11. Use the table below.

DATA	
A	6.89
B	6.95
C	7.09
D	6.98

Create a number line and plot the value of each letter.

12. What decimal represents $\frac{44}{100}$?

Name ____________________

TOPIC 12

Performance Task

Nature Club

The nature club at the school devoted a month to learning about different local birds. The **Bird Traits** photos show information about several birds they observed.

Bird Traits

Red-tailed Hawk
Mass: 0.78 kg
Wingspan: 1.2 m

Great Horned Owl
Mass: 1.8 kg
Wingspan: 1.3 m

Blue Jay
Mass: 0.08 kg
Wingspan: 0.28 m

Sandpiper
Mass: 0.06 kg
Wingspan: 0.2 m

1. The club leader asked students to analyze and compare the measures from the **Bird Traits** photos.

Part A

Randall was asked to write the mass of a red-tailed hawk as a fraction. Label the mass on the number line and write the equivalent fraction.

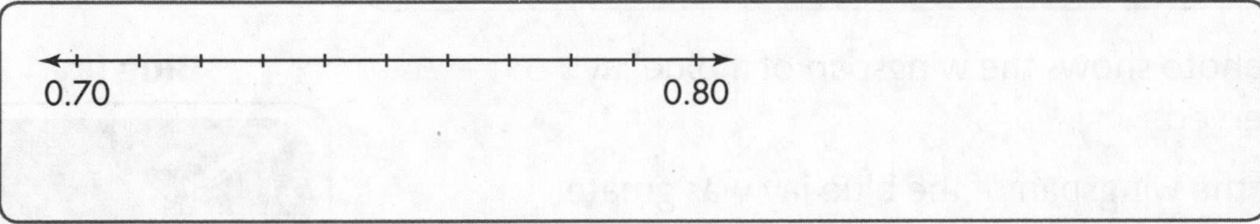

Part B

Melanie was assigned to compare the wingspans of the blue jay and the sandpiper. Which bird had a greater wingspan? Show the decimals on the grids, and write the comparison using symbols.

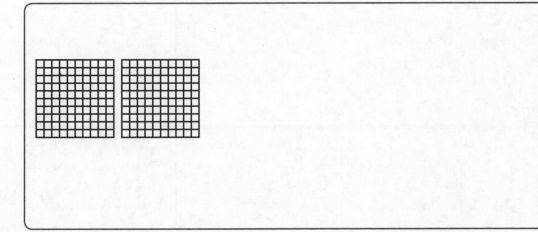

Part C

Mila compared the wingspans of the red-tailed hawk and the great horned owl. Explain how to use place value to find the greater wingspan. Show the comparison using symbols.

2. Gerald found the mass of a great horned owl and a sandpiper combined. Show how to write each mass as a fraction and then write and solve an addition equation.

3. The **Blue Jay** photo shows the wingspan of a blue jay Susannah observed.

Susannah said the wingspan of the blue jay was greater than the wingspan of the great horned owl since 1.4 > 1.3. Do you agree? Explain.

Blue Jay

Wingspan: 1.4 ft

TOPIC 13

Measurement: Find Equivalence in Units of Measure

Essential Questions: How can you convert from one unit to another? How can you be precise when solving math problems?

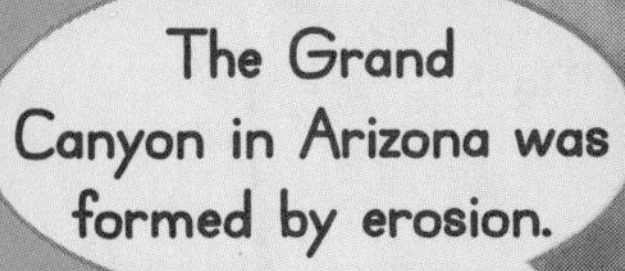

The Grand Canyon in Arizona was formed by erosion.
The Colorado River cut through the layers of rock. In some places, the canyon is more than a mile deep!
Imagine how it will look in the future! Here is a project on erosion and measurement.

ënVision® STEM **Project:** Erosion and Measurement

Do Research The Colorado River has played a large part in shaping North America. Use the Internet and other resources to research the states through which the river travels.

Journal: Write a Report Include what you found. Also in your report:

- Look up *geology* and *geometry* in the dictionary. Write the definitions and explain how these words are related. What does the prefix "geo" mean in both words?
- A.J. takes a 4-mile tour of the Grand Canyon. Explain how to convert the length of A.J.'s tour from miles to feet.

Name ____________________

Review What You Know

Vocabulary

Choose the best term from the box. Write it on the blank.

- capacity
- gram
- liter
- mass

1. The amount of liquid a container can hold is called its __________.

2. __________ is the amount of matter that something contains.

3. One metric unit of capacity is a __________.

Perimeter

Find the perimeter of each shape.

4.

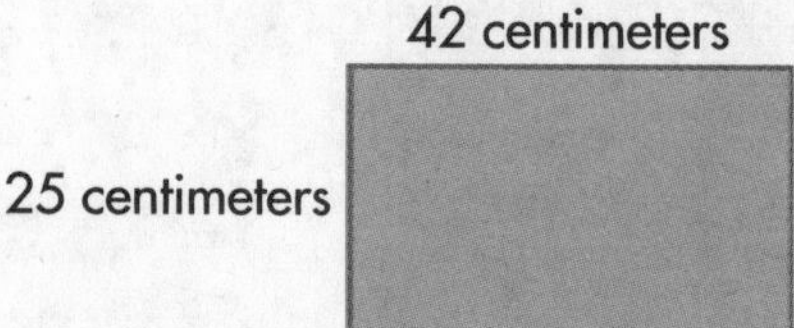

5.

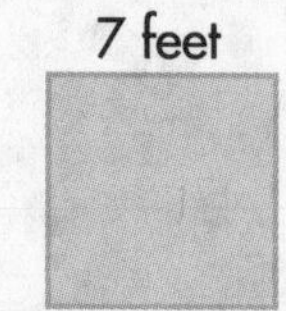

6.

7. 17 inches, 12 inches, 12 inches, 21 inches

8.

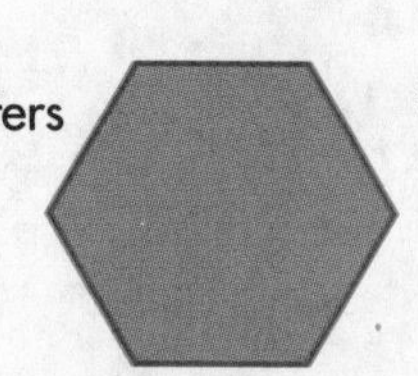

9. $19\frac{11}{12}$ feet, $7\frac{5}{12}$ feet

Area

Find the area of each shape.

10. 5 yards, 2 yards

11.

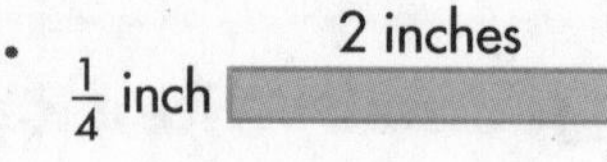

12. 7 centimeters, 3 centimeters

Problem Solving

13. **Make Sense and Persevere** A league is a nautical measurement equal to about 3 miles. If a ship travels 2,000 leagues, about how many miles does the ship travel?

Name ___________________________________

What makes the St. Johns River special?

Project: Make a Travel Brochure About Rivers in Your Home State

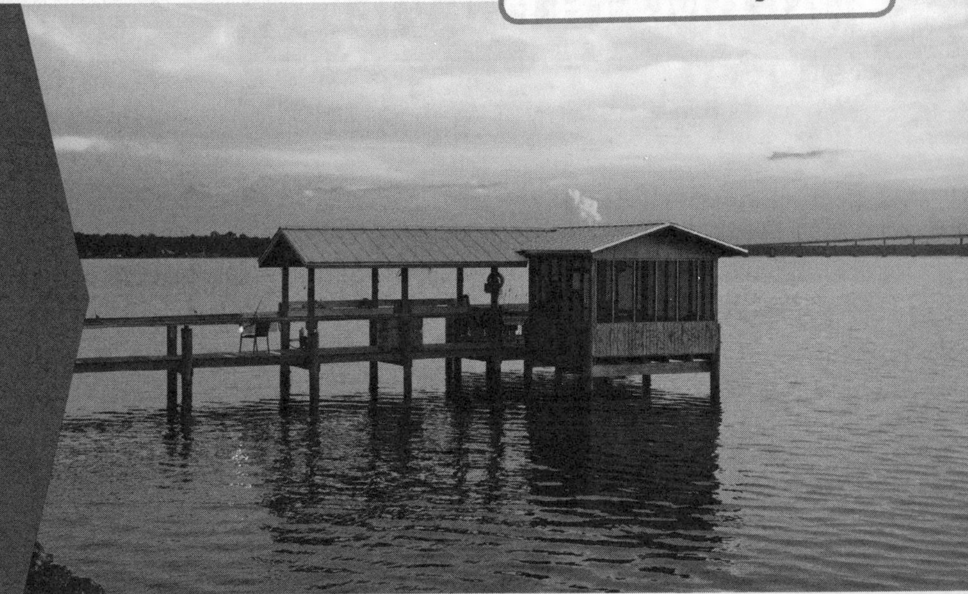

How are tin cans useful?

Project: Cooking on a Budget

Who invented the jigsaw puzzle?

Project: Make Your Own Jigsaw Puzzle

3-ACT MATH PREVIEW

Math Modeling

A Pint's a Pound

Before watching the video, think:

Most water towers hold about 50 times as much water as a swimming pool. I got all geared up, and now I can't figure out how to get in!

I can ...

model with math to solve a problem that involves estimating and computing with units of weight and capacity.

Mathematical Practices MP.4 Also MP.2, MP.5
Content Standards 4.NBT.B Also 4.MD.A.1, 4.MD.A.2

Name ___________________________ Activity

Lesson 13-1
Equivalence with Customary Units of Length

I can ...
convert customary units of length from one unit to another and recognize the relative size of different units.

Content Standards 4.MD.A.1, 4.MD.A.2
Also 4.OA.A.3, 4.NF.B.3d, 4.NF.B.4c
Mathematical Practices MP.6, MP.7, MP.8

Solve & Share

Jeremy jogged 75 yards from his house to school. How many feet did Jeremy jog? ***Solve this problem any way you choose.***

Be sure to calculate correctly and use the right units. *Show your work in the space below!*

3 feet = 1 yard

50 yd 60 yd 70 yd 80 yd

Look Back! **Look for Relationships** What do you notice about the relationship between the number of yards and the number of feet Jeremy jogged?

Essential Question

How Can You Convert from One Unit of Length to Another?

Visual Learning Bridge

A

Maggie has a tree swing. How many inches long is each rope from the bottom of the branch to the swing?

This table shows the relative sizes of customary units of length. 1 foot is 12 times as long as 1 inch.

DATA

Customary Units of Length
1 foot (ft) = 12 inches (in.)
1 yard (yd) = 3 ft = 36 in.
1 mile (mi) = 1,760 yd = 5,280 ft

Swing: $2\frac{1}{4}$ ft from ground

B

Step 1

Find the length of the rope in feet.

$r = 10 - 2\frac{1}{4}$

10 ft	
r	$2\frac{1}{4}$ ft

$$\begin{array}{rcr} 10 & = & 9\frac{4}{4} \\ -\,2\frac{1}{4} & = & -\,2\frac{1}{4} \\ \hline & & 7\frac{3}{4} \end{array}$$

Each rope is $7\frac{3}{4}$ feet long.

C

Step 2

Convert the length of the rope to inches.

DATA

Feet	Inches
1	12
2	24
3	36
4	48
5	60
6	72
7	84
$7\frac{3}{4}$	93

There are 12 inches in a foot.

Find 7×12.

$7 \times 12 = 84$ inches

Find $\frac{3}{4} \times 12$.

$\frac{3}{4} \times 12 = \frac{3 \times 12}{4}$

$= \frac{36}{4}$ or 9 inches

$84 + 9 = 93$

Each rope is 93 inches long.

Convince Me! **Generalize** How do you know the answer is reasonable when converting a larger unit to a smaller unit?

Name ___________________________________

Practice Tools Assessment

Another Example!

Mark moved forward $\frac{5}{6}$ yard when doing a back flip. Daisy moved forward $3\frac{1}{6}$ feet. How much more did Daisy move forward than Mark? One yard is 3 times as long as a foot.

$$\frac{5}{6} \times 3 = \frac{15}{6} = \frac{6}{6} + \frac{6}{6} + \frac{3}{6} = 2\frac{3}{6}$$

↑ Number of yards ↑ Feet per yard

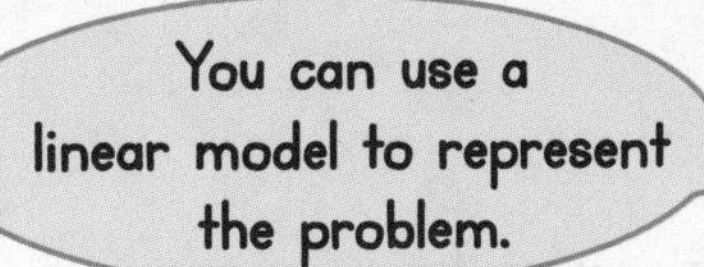

You can use a linear model to represent the problem.

Mark moved forward $2\frac{3}{6}$ feet.

$3\frac{1}{6} - 2\frac{3}{6} = 2\frac{7}{6} - 2\frac{3}{6} = \frac{4}{6}$

Daisy moved forward $\frac{4}{6}$ foot more than Mark.

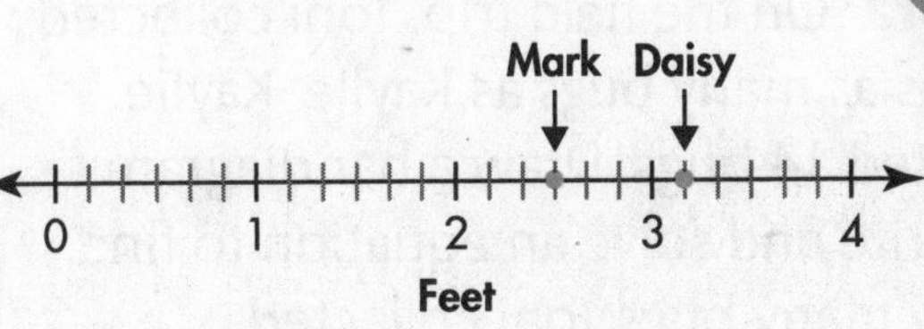

Guided Practice

Do You Understand?

1. Does it take more inches or feet to equal a given length? Explain.

2. Which is a greater distance, 9 yards or 9 miles?

Do You Know How?

For **3–4**, convert each unit.

3. 2 miles = __________ yards

4. $\frac{2}{3}$ yard = __________ feet

Independent Practice

In **5–7**, write > or < in each ◯ to compare the measures.

5. 6 inches ◯ 6 feet

6. 2 yards ◯ 7 feet

7. 4 yards ◯ 100 inches

For **8–11**, convert each unit.

8. 8 yards = __________ inches

9. 28 yards = __________ feet

10. 18 feet = __________ inches

11. 7 miles = __________ yards

Problem Solving

12. Be Precise Lou cuts 3 yards from a 9-yard roll of fabric. Then he cuts 4 feet from the roll. How many feet of fabric are left on the roll?

13. What customary units would you use to measure the length of a praying mantis? Explain.

14. Algebra On the field trip, Toni collected 4 times as many bugs as Kaylie. Kaylie collected 14 bugs. Draw a bar diagram, and write and solve an equation to find *b*, how many bugs Toni collected.

15. Which is greater, 3 miles or 5,000 yards? How much greater? Explain.

16. Higher Order Thinking Jenna uses $\frac{1}{2}$ yard of ribbon for each box she wraps. How many inches of ribbon does she need to wrap 4 boxes? Use the linear model to help solve.

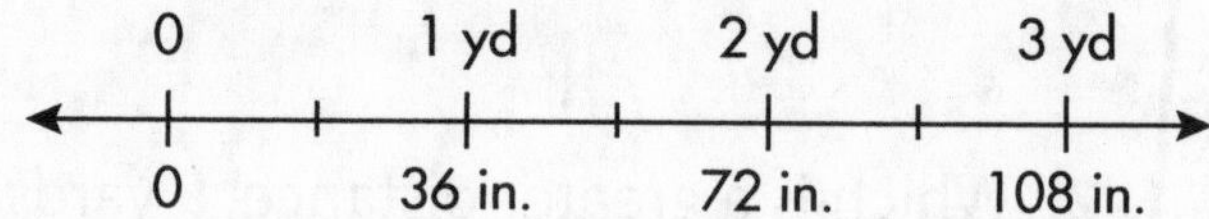

Assessment Practice

17. Connor has $3\frac{3}{4}$ feet of brown fabric and $\frac{3}{4}$ yard of green to make a costume for the school play. How many more feet of brown than green fabric does Connor have? Show both measures with points on the number line.

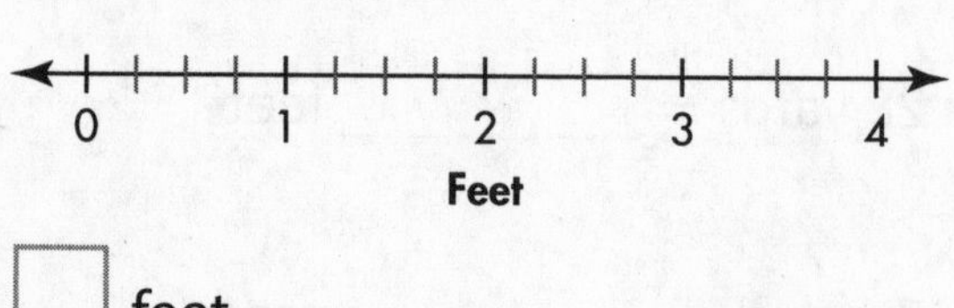

☐ feet

18. Charlotte made $\frac{11}{12}$ yard of a paper chain for the school dance. Josh made $4\frac{1}{12}$ feet, and Mika made $3\frac{4}{12}$ feet. How many feet of chain did they make in all?

Ⓐ $8\frac{4}{12}$ feet

Ⓑ $9\frac{4}{12}$ feet

Ⓒ $10\frac{2}{12}$ feet

Ⓓ $10\frac{4}{12}$ feet

Name ____________________

Activity

Lesson 13-2

Equivalence with Customary Units of Capacity

I can ...

convert customary units of capacity from one unit to another and recognize the relative size of different units.

Content Standards 4.MD.A.1, 4.MD.A.2
Also 4.OA.A.3, 4.NF.B.3d, 4.NF.B.4c
Mathematical Practices MP.1, MP.2, MP.8

Solve & Share

Casey has $\frac{1}{2}$ gallon of juice. How many 1-pint containers can he fill? ***Solve this problem any way you choose.***

Use what you know about converting a larger unit to a smaller unit. *Show your work in the space below!*

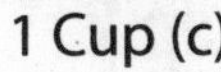

8 Fluid Ounces (fl oz)
8 fl oz = 1 c

1 Cup (c)

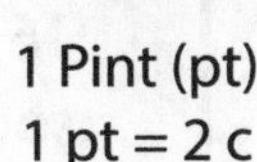

1 Pint (pt)
1 pt = 2 c

1 Quart (qt)
1 qt = 2 pt = 4 c

1 Gallon (gal)
1 gal = 4 qt = 8 pt

Look Back! Generalize How did you convert from a larger unit of capacity to a smaller unit of capacity? Did you use the same process you used to convert from a larger unit of length to a smaller unit of length? Explain.

How Can You Convert from One Unit of Capacity to Another?

Visual Learning Bridge

A

Ms. Nealy's class needs 5 gallons of punch for family math night. How much of each ingredient is needed to make enough punch with the recipe shown?

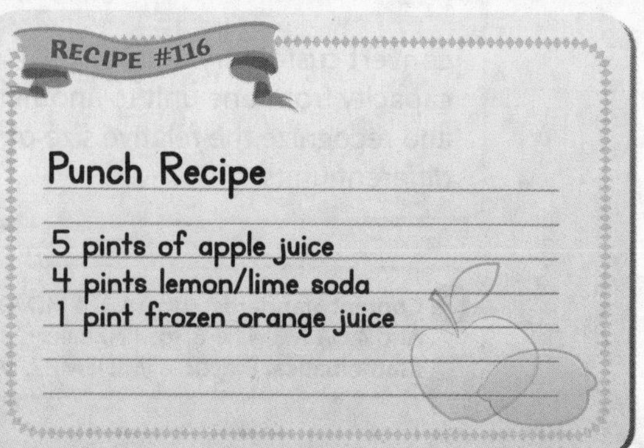

RECIPE #116
Punch Recipe
5 pints of apple juice
4 pints lemon/lime soda
1 pint frozen orange juice

Units of capacity include gallons, quarts, pints, cups, and fluid ounces.

Capacity is how much liquid a container can hold. This diagram shows the relative sizes of customary units of capacity. 1 gallon is 4 times as much as 1 quart.

1 gal															
1 qt				1 qt				1 qt				1 qt			
1 pt		1 pt		1 pt		1 pt		1 pt		1 pt		1 pt		1 pt	
1 c	1 c	1 c	1 c	1 c	1 c	1 c	1 c	1 c	1 c	1 c	1 c	1 c	1 c	1 c	1 c

B

Step 1

Convert 5 gallons to pints.

DATA

Gallons	Quarts	Pints
1	4	8
2	8	16
3	12	24
4	16	32
5	20	40

5 gallons = 40 pints

C

Step 2

Add the number of pints in the recipe to find how many batches the class needs to make.

$5 + 4 + 1 = 10$

$10 \times n = 40$

$n = 4$

The class needs to make 4 batches of the recipe.

D

Step 3

Find how much of each ingredient is in 4 batches.

$4 \times 5 = 20$ pints
$4 \times 4 = 16$ pints
$4 \times 1 = 4$ pints

20 pints of apple juice, 16 pints of lemon/lime soda, and 4 pints of frozen orange juice are needed.

Convince Me! **Reasoning** Complete the sentence below.

One gallon equals ____ quarts, ____ pints, or ____ cups.

Name ____________________

Practice Tools Assessment

Guided Practice

Do You Understand?

1. How many cups of punch does 5 gallons of the punch from the previous page make?

2. Which size container holds more, 3 pints or 3 quarts?

Do You Know How?

For **3–5**, convert each unit.

3. 2 cups = ________ fluid ounces

4. $\frac{1}{2}$ gallon = ________ pints

5. 5 pints = ________ cups

Independent Practice

In **6–8**, write > or < in each ◯ to compare the measures.

6. 2 pints ◯ 2 gallons

7. 5 quarts ◯ 8 pints

8. 10 cups ◯ 2 quarts

For **9–12**, convert each unit.

9. 7 quarts = ________ cups

10. 12 gallons = ________ quarts

11. 7 pints = ________ fluid ounces

12. $\frac{3}{4}$ gallon = ________ pints

For **13–14**, convert each unit.

13.

Pints	Fluid Ounces
$\frac{1}{2}$	
1	
2	
4	

14.

Gallons	Cups
1	
2	
3	
4	

Problem Solving

15. enVision® STEM Scientists measure how much water and debris flow past a river station at different times of the year. The water and debris are called discharge. The table shows the average discharge at the Camp Verde station on the Verde River in two months. How many more quarts of discharge per second are there in December than November?

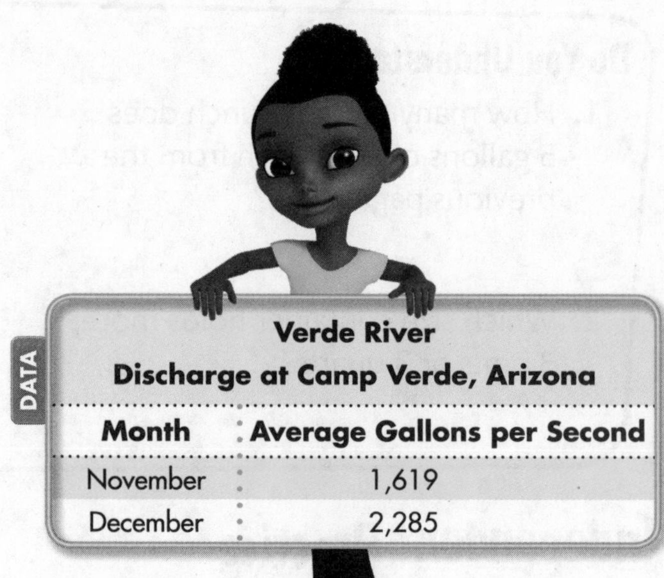

DATA

Verde River
Discharge at Camp Verde, Arizona

Month	Average Gallons per Second
November	1,619
December	2,285

16. How many quarts of discharge per second were recorded in November and December?

17. Make Sense and Persevere Annabelle had the following containers of paint left over: $\frac{1}{2}$ gallon, $\frac{3}{4}$ quart, and $\frac{1}{4}$ gallon. How many quarts of paint does Annabelle have left over? Explain.

18. Higher Order Thinking A caterer combines 3 quarts of orange juice, 5 pints of milk, and 5 cups of pineapple juice to make smoothies. How many cups can be filled with smoothies? Explain.

Assessment Practice

19. Which equals 3 quarts?

Ⓐ 6 cups
Ⓑ 12 cups
Ⓒ 12 pints
Ⓓ 3 gallons

20. Select all the comparisons that are true.

- ☐ 4 cups (<) 4 pints
- ☐ 7 pints (>) 7 fluid ounces
- ☐ 2 gallons (>) 9 quarts
- ☐ 3 quarts (<) 14 cups
- ☐ 3 gallons (<) 18 pints

Name ______________________________________

Lesson 13-3
Equivalence with Customary Units of Weight

I can ...

convert customary units of weight from one unit to another and recognize the relative size of different units.

Content Standards 4.MD.A.1, 4.MD.A.2
Also 4.OA.A.3, 4.NF.B.3d, 4.NF.B.4c
Mathematical Practices MP.6, MP.8

Solve & Share

When Lori's puppy, Bay, was born she weighed $\frac{3}{8}$ pound. What was Bay's weight in ounces? ***Solve this problem any way you choose.***

You use what you know about converting from a larger unit of measurement to a smaller unit to convert from pounds to ounces.

A hummingbird might weigh 1 ounce (oz).

A kitten might weigh 1 pound (lb).

1 lb = 16 oz

A horse might weigh 1 ton (T).

1 T = 2,000 lb

Look Back! Be Precise How did you know you needed to convert units to solve the problem above?

How Can You Convert from One Unit of Weight to Another?

Visual Learning Bridge

A

Mark made dinner for his family using the ingredients shown. How many 6-ounce servings did Mark make?

8 ounces of tomato sauce

$\frac{2}{5}$ pound of pasta

$\frac{3}{5}$ pound of meatballs

Weight is how heavy an object is. Units of weight include ounces, pounds, and tons.

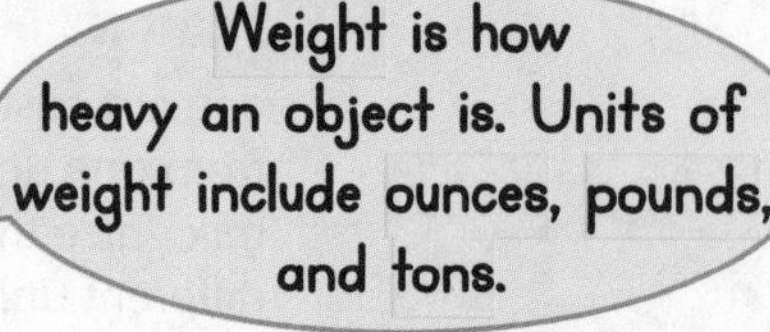

This table shows the relative sizes of customary units of weight. 1 pound is 16 times as heavy as 1 ounce.

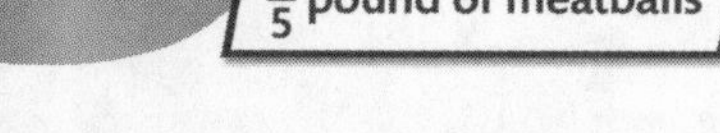

DATA

Customary Units of Weight
1 pound (lb) = 16 ounces (oz)
1 ton (T) = 2,000 lb

B To convert the weight of the pasta and the meatballs to ounces, multiply each weight by 16.

Pasta:

$\frac{2}{5} \times 16 = \frac{32}{5}$

$= 6\frac{2}{5}$ ounces

Meatballs:

$\frac{3}{5} \times 16 = \frac{48}{5}$

$= 9\frac{3}{5}$ ounces

C Add the weights of all the ingredients to find the total ounces.

$6\frac{2}{5}$ Pasta

$9\frac{3}{5}$ Meatballs

$+ 8$ Tomato Sauce

$23\frac{5}{5} = 24$

The weight of all the ingredients is 24 ounces.

D Divide to find s, the number of servings.

24 oz

6 oz — s

$24 \div 6 = s$

$s = 4$

Mark made four 6-ounce servings.

Convince Me! Generalize How do you convert a larger unit of weight to a smaller unit of weight?

Name

Practice Tools Assessment

Guided Practice

Do You Understand?

1. Would it make sense to describe the total weight of Mark's dinner in tons? Why or why not?

Do You Know How?

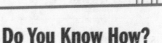

For **2–4**, convert each unit.

2. 9 tons = ________ pounds

3. $\frac{3}{4}$ pound = ________ ounces

4. 17 pounds = ________ ounces

Independent Practice

In **5–7**, write > or < in each ◯ to compare the measures.

5. 6 ounces ◯ 6 pounds
6. 3 pounds ◯ 40 ounces
7. 5,000 pounds ◯ 2 tons

For **8–13**, convert each unit.

8. 15 pounds = ________ ounces
9. 7 tons = ________ pounds
10. 46 pounds = ________ ounces
11. $\frac{1}{8}$ pound = ________ ounces
12. 6 tons = ________ pounds
13. 3 pounds = ________ ounces

For **14–15**, complete each table.

14.

Tons	Pounds
1	2,000
2	
3	

15.

Pounds	Ounces
$\frac{1}{2}$	
1	
2	

Problem Solving

For **16–19**, use the line plot at the right.

16. Be Precise What is the total weight in ounces of the three kittens that weigh the least?

17. Higher Order Thinking Two kittens had a total weight of $3\frac{1}{4}$ pounds. What could their individual weights have been?

18. Algebra How many more pounds did the heaviest kitten weigh than the lightest kitten?

19. Each of the greatest number of kittens weighed how many pounds?

---

20. About how many pounds does this African elephant weigh? Complete the table to solve.

Tons	$\frac{1}{2}$	1	2	3	4	5
Pounds		2,000				

This male African elephant weighs about 5 tons.

Assessment Practice

21. Which is most likely to weigh 3 ounces?

Ⓐ A shoe
Ⓑ A large spider
Ⓒ A box of cereal
Ⓓ A loaded pick-up truck

22. Which comparison is true?

Ⓐ 7,000 pounds $<$ 3 tons
Ⓑ 5 pounds $>$ 85 ounces
Ⓒ 50 ounces $>$ 3 pounds
Ⓓ 4 pounds $<$ 60 ounces

Name ______________________________

Activity

Lesson 13-4
Equivalence with Metric Units of Length

I can ...
convert metric units of length from one unit to another and recognize the relative size of different units.

Content Standards 4.MD.A.1, 4.MD.A.2 Also 4.OA.A.3, 4.NF.C.7
Mathematical Practices MP.3, MP.5, MP.6

Solve & Share

Find the length of the marker shown in both centimeters and millimeters. Describe the relationship between the two units.

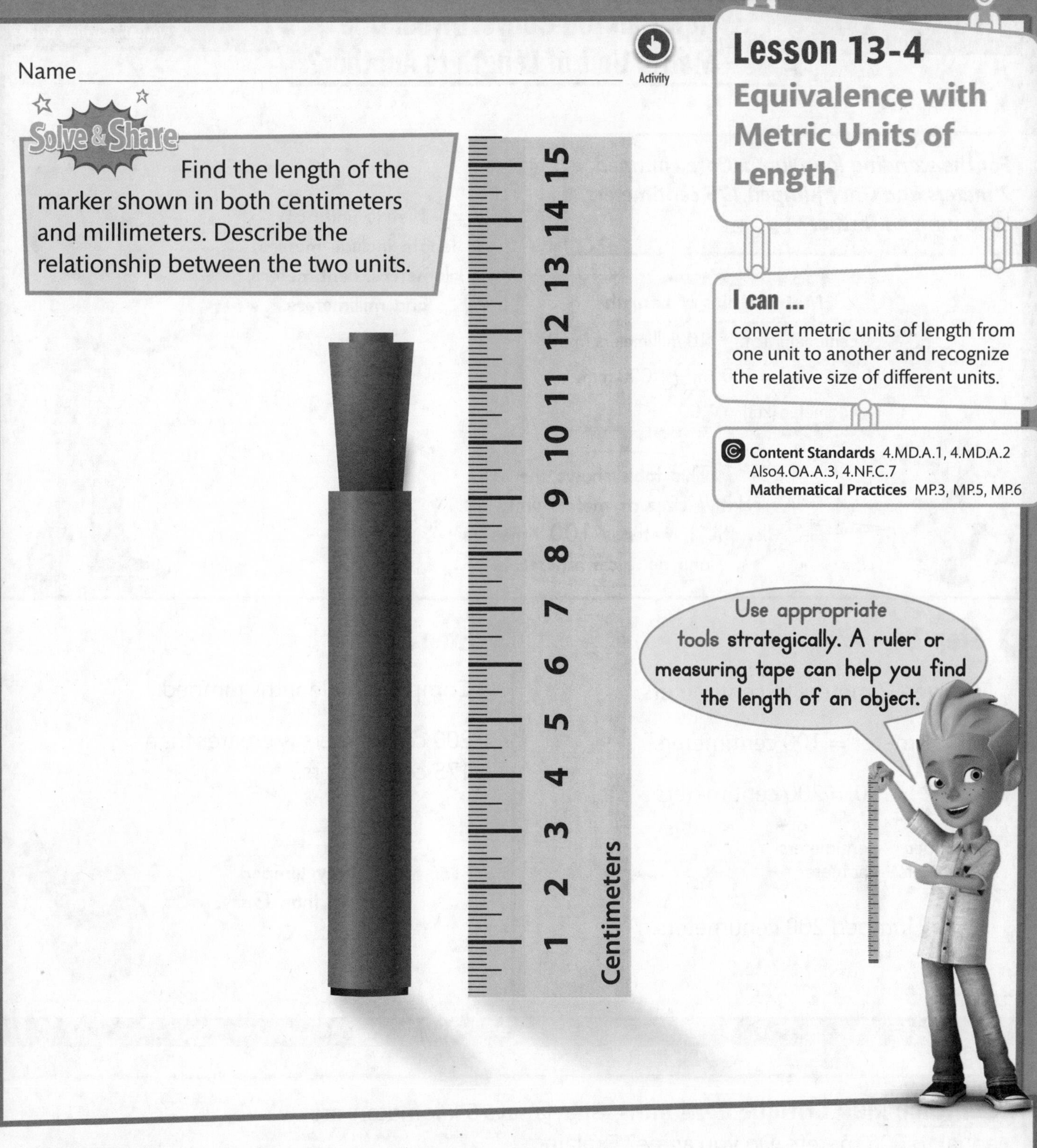

1 2 3 4 5 6 7 8 9 10 11 12 13 14 15
Centimeters
Use appropriate tools strategically. A ruler or measuring tape can help you find the length of an object.

Look Back! The length of Toby's giant pencil is 25 centimeters. How could you find the length of his pencil in millimeters?

How Can You Convert from One Metric Unit of Length to Another?

Visual Learning Bridge

A

For the standing long jump, Corey jumped 2 meters and Gary jumped 175 centimeters. Who jumped farther?

DATA

Metric Units of Length
1 centimeter (cm) = 10 millimeters (mm)
1 meter (m) = 100 cm = 1,000 mm
1 kilometer (km) = 1,000 m

This table shows the relative sizes of metric units of length. 1 meter is 100 times as long as 1 centimeter.

Step 1

Convert 2 meters to centimeters.

1 meter = 100 centimeters

$2 \times 100 = 200$ centimeters

↑ Number of meters ↑ Centimeters per meter

Corey jumped 200 centimeters.

Step 2

Compare the lengths jumped.

200 centimeters is greater than 175 centimeters.

Convince Me! Critique Reasoning Shayla says 5 kilometers are equal to 500 meters. Do you agree? Explain.

Name ______________________________________

Another Example!

Kendra and LiLi measured the length of several rosebuds. The longest one Kendra measured was 2.4 centimeters long. The longest one LiLi measured was 1.8 centimeters. Who measured the longest rosebud? Use a linear model to help explain.

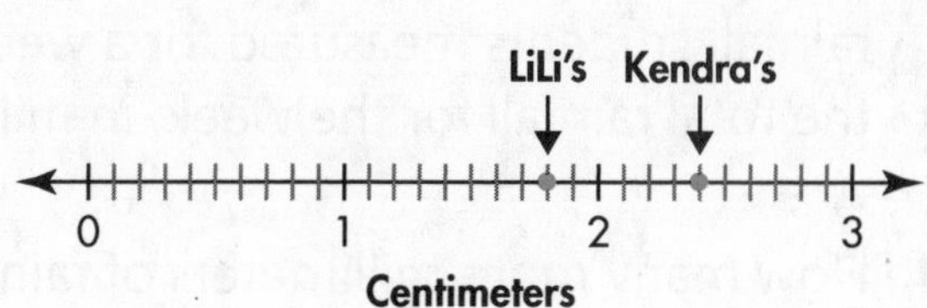

Since 2.4 cm > 1.8 cm, Kendra measured the longest rosebud.

Guided Practice

Do You Understand?

1. What metric unit would you use to measure the length of a field?

Do You Know How?

For **2–3**, convert each unit.

2. 5 kilometers = ________ meters

3. 75 centimeters = ________ millimeters

Independent Practice

In **4–6**, tell what metric unit you would use to measure each.

4. The length of your math book

5. The distance between cities

6. The length of a fly

For **7–8**, complete each table.

7.

Meters	Millimeters
1	1,000
2	
3	

8.

Centimeters	Millimeters
1	10
2	
3	

Problem Solving

For **9–10**, use the table at the right.

9. Be Precise The table shows the amount of rainfall students measured for a week. What was the total rainfall for the week, in millimeters?

10. How many more millimeters of rain fell on Thursday than on Monday and Wednesday combined?

DATA

Rainfall Students Measured	
Monday	3 cm
Tuesday	0 cm
Wednesday	1 cm
Thursday	5 cm
Friday	2 cm

11. Which is greater, 2,670 meters or 2 kilometers? Explain.

12. Critique Reasoning Milo thinks 8 hours is greater than 520 minutes. Is Milo correct? Remember 1 hour is equal to 60 minutes.

13. Algebra Leah ran around the track 8 times. She ran a total of 2,000 meters. How many meters equal 1 lap? Use the bar diagram to write an equation which can be used to find *m*, the meters in one lap.

2,000 m							
m	*m*	*m*	*m*	*m*	*m*	*m*	*m*

14. Higher Order Thinking Signs are placed at the beginning and at the end of a 3-kilometer hiking trail. Signs are also placed every 500 meters along the trail. How many signs are along the trail? Explain.

Assessment Practice

15. Select all the true statements.

- ☐ 14 meters = 1,400 centimeters
- ☐ 10 centimeters = 1,000 millimeters
- ☐ 55 kilometers = 5,500 meters
- ☐ 3 meters = 3,000 millimeters
- ☐ 5 meters = 500 centimeters

16. Select all the true statements.

- ☐ 3 meters $>$ 3,000 centimeters
- ☐ 2 kilometers $<$ 2,500 meters
- ☐ 4 centimeters $>$ 38 millimeters
- ☐ 3.5 meters $<$ 3.2 meters
- ☐ 5 kilometers $<$ 5,200 meters

Name ________________________________

Lesson 13-5
Equivalence with Metric Units of Capacity and Mass

I can ...
convert metric units of capacity and mass from one unit to another and recognize the relative size of different units.

Content Standards 4.MD.A.1, 4.MD.A.2
Also 4.OA.A.3
Mathematical Practices MP.2, MP.6, MP.8

Solve & Share

Jenny has 3 liters of water. How many milliliters of water does she have, and what is the mass of the water in grams? ***Solve this problem any way you choose.***

You can generalize about how you change larger units to smaller units when working with customary units or metric units of capacity or mass.

Some water bottles hold 1 liter or 1,000 milliliters of water.
1 liter of water has a mass of 1 kilogram or 1,000 grams.

Look Back! Why did you need to convert units to solve the problem above?

Visual Learning

Glossary

How Can You Convert from One Metric Unit of Capacity or Mass to Another?

Visual Learning Bridge

A

Louis needs 8 liters of apple juice. He has 5,000 milliliters of juice. Does Louis have enough apple juice?

Metric Units of Capacity and Mass
1 liter (L) = 1,000 milliliters (mL)
1 gram (g) = 1,000 milligrams (mg)
1 kilogram (kg) = 1,000 g

Metric units of capacity include liters and milliliters. Metric units of mass include kilograms, grams, and milligrams.

The table shows the relative sizes of measurement units. 1 liter is 1,000 times as great as 1 milliliter and 1 kilogram is 1,000 times as great as 1 gram.

B

Step 1

Find how many milliliters of apple juice Louis needs.

1 liter = 1,000 milliliters

$8 \times 1{,}000 = 8{,}000$ milliliters

↑ Number of liters ↑ Milliliters per liter

Louis needs 8,000 milliliters of juice.

C

Step 2

Compare to find if Louis has enough apple juice.

8,000 milliliters $>$ 5,000 milliliters

Louis does not have enough apple juice. How much more does he need?

$8{,}000 - 5{,}000 = 3{,}000$

Louis needs 3,000 milliliters more.

Convince Me! **Be Precise** Why did you need to convert liters to milliliters?

Name ____________________

Another Example!

How many grams of apples are needed to make 1 liter of apple juice?

1 kilogram = 1,000 grams

2 kilograms = 2 × 1,000 grams
= 2,000 grams

2,000 grams of apples make 1 liter of apple juice.

Mass is the amount of matter that something contains.

Guided Practice

Do You Understand?

1. What metric unit would you use to measure your mass? the amount of blood in your body? Explain.

Do You Know How?

For **2–3**, convert each unit.

2. 6 grams = ________ milligrams

3. 9 liters = ________ milliliters

Independent Practice

In **4–6**, tell what metric unit you would use to measure each.

4. Medicine in a pill

5. Ink in a pen

6. The mass of a pencil

For **7–10**, convert each unit.

7. 5 kilograms = ________ grams

8. 2 liters = ________ milliliters

9. 4 grams = ________ milligrams

10. 9 kilograms = ________ grams

Problem Solving

11. Reasoning A cardboard box has a mass of 800 grams. When 4 books of equal mass are put into the box, the filled box has a mass of 8 kilograms. What is the mass of each book in grams? Explain.

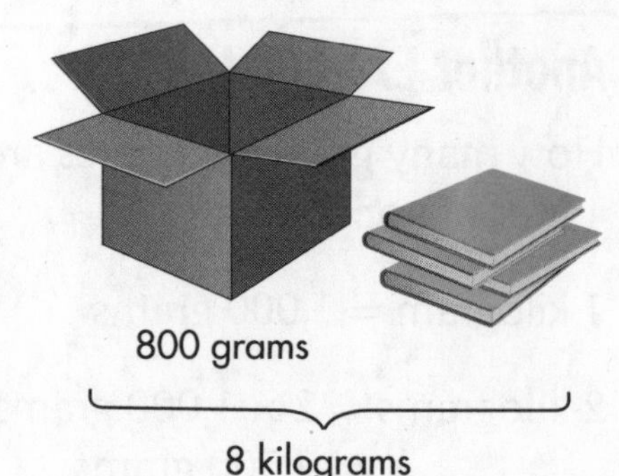

12. enVision® STEM The Cape Hatteras Lighthouse was a kilometer from the shore in 1870. How far was the lighthouse from the shore in 1970? Explain.

The beach near Cape Hatteras Lighthouse in North Carolina has eroded about 8 meters each year.

13. The mass of 4 large zucchini is about 2 kilograms. About how many grams will 1 large zucchini have?

14. Higher Order Thinking A small sofa has a mass of 30 kilograms. A pillow on the sofa has a mass of 300 grams. How many pillows would it take to equal the mass of the sofa?

 **Assessment Practice**

15. Which shows a correct comparison?

Ⓐ 5 milliliters $>$ 50 liters

Ⓑ 2 liters $<$ 200 milliliters

Ⓒ 100 liters $<$ 1,000 milliliters

Ⓓ 3,200 milliliters $>$ 3 liters

16. Write the missing numbers in the table.

Kilograms	Grams
1	1,000
2	
	3,000
4	

Name ____________________ Activity

Lesson 13-6
Solve Perimeter and Area Problems

I can ...
find the unknown length or width of a rectangle using a known area or perimeter.

Content Standards 4.MD.A.3 Also 4.OA.A.3, 4.NF.B.4c, 4.MD.A.2
Mathematical Practices MP.1, MP.2, MP.3

Solve & Share

A can of paint is used to cover all 168 square feet of a wall. The wall is 8 feet high. Tape is placed along the top, bottom, and sides of the wall. What is the width of the wall? How much tape is needed? ***Solve this problem any way you choose.***

A = ☐ square feet

☐ feet

☐ feet

You can use reasoning to find the width and the perimeter of the wall. *Show your work in the space above!*

Look Back! Describe the steps you would use to solve the problem.

How Can You Use Perimeter and Area to Solve Problems?

Visual Learning Bridge

A

The state park shown has a perimeter of 36 miles. What is the area of the state park?

Use formulas or equations that use symbols to relate two or more quantities to solve this problem.

The formula for perimeter is: $P = (2 \times \ell) + (2 \times w)$

The formula for area is: $A = \ell \times w$

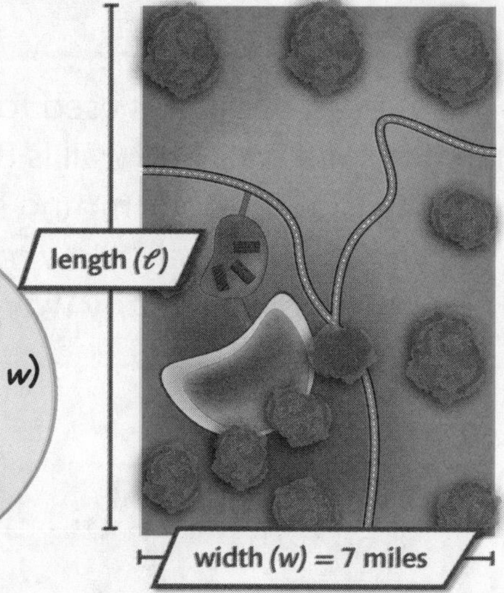

B

Step 1

Find the length of the state park.

Use the perimeter, 36 miles, and the width, 7 miles, to find the length.

Opposite sides of a rectangle are the same length, so multiply the width by 2.	$7 \times 2 = 14$
Subtract 14 from the perimeter.	$36 - 14 = 22$
22 miles is the length of two sides of the park. Divide 22 by 2 to find the length of one side.	$22 \div 2 = 11$

The length of the park is 11 miles.

C

Step 2

Find the area of the state park.

$w = 7$ miles

$\ell = 11$ miles

$A = \ell \times w$

$= 11 \times 7$

$= 77$

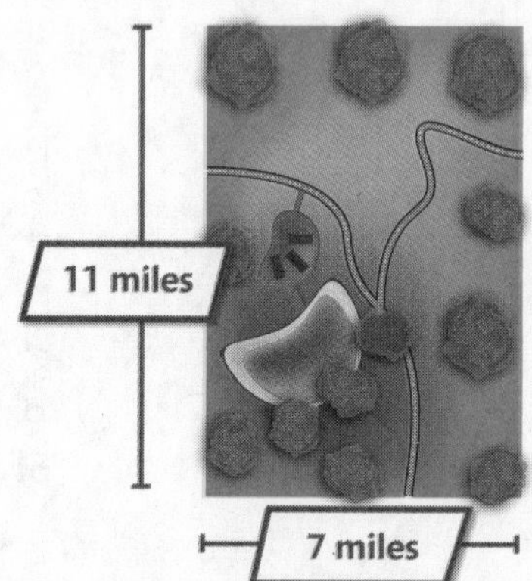

The area of the state park is 77 square miles.

Convince Me! **Make Sense and Persevere** If the area of another state park is 216 square miles, and the park has a width of 8 miles, what is the park's length? What is the perimeter of this state park?

Name ______________________________

Guided Practice

Do You Understand?

1. A sandbox is shaped like a rectangle. The area is 16 square feet. The side lengths are whole numbers. What are the possible dimensions of the sandbox? Do all possible dimensions make sense?

2. Write and solve an equation to find the width of a room if the length of the floor is 8 feet and the area of the room is 96 square feet.

Do You Know How?

For **3–5**, complete each calculation.

3. Find *n*. Perimeter = 46 in.

4. Find *n* and *A*. Perimeter = 26 cm

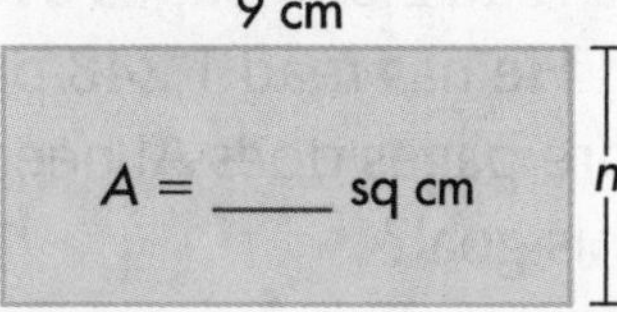

5. Find the perimeter.

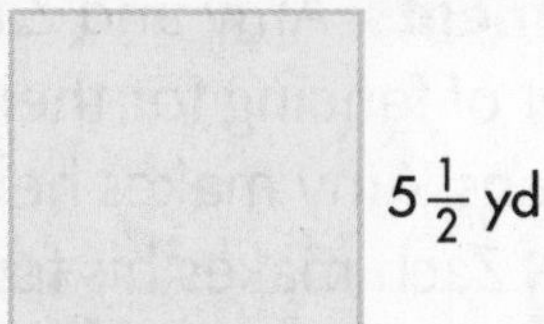

Independent Practice

For **6–9**, find the missing dimension.

6. Find *n*.

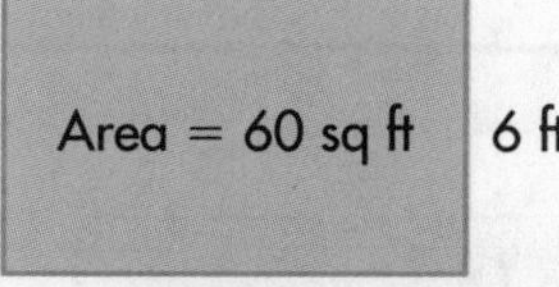

7. Find *n*. Perimeter = 65 in.

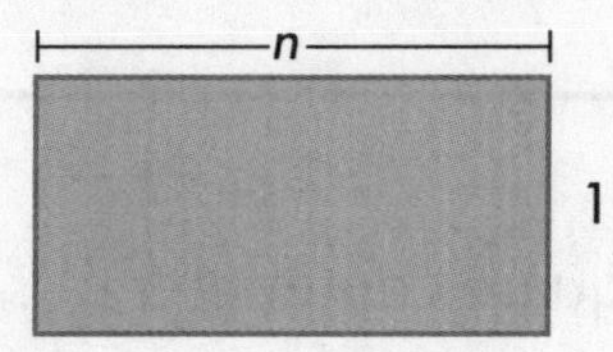

8. Find *n*. Perimeter = 84 yd

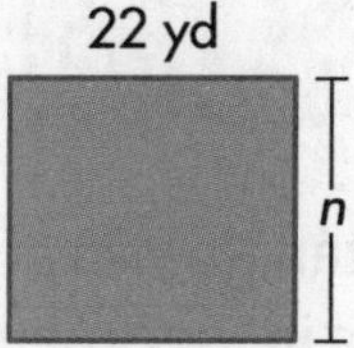

9. A rectangle has a length of 9 millimeters and an area of 270 square millimeters. What is the width? What is the perimeter?

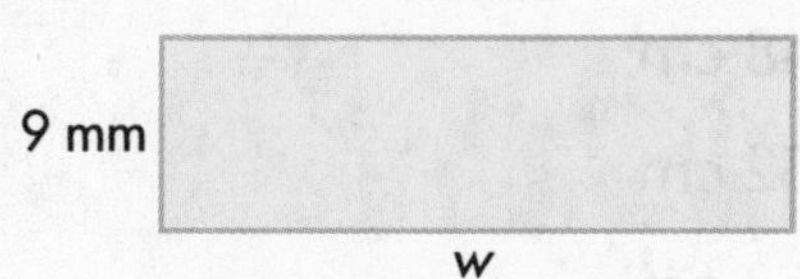

Problem Solving

10. Greg built the picture frame shown to the right. It has a perimeter of $50\frac{2}{4}$ inches. How wide is the picture frame?

11. Greg covered the back of the picture with a piece of felt. The picture is $1\frac{1}{4}$ inches shorter than the frame and 1 inch less in width. What is the area of the felt?

12. Al has a goal to read 2,000 pages over summer break. He has read 1,248 pages. How many more pages does Al need to read to reach his goal?

13. The area of a tabletop is 18 square feet. The perimeter of the same table is 18 feet. What are the dimensions of the tabletop?

14. Construct Arguments Amy and Zach each have 24 feet of fencing for their rectangular gardens. Amy makes her fence 6 feet long. Zach makes his fence 8 feet long. Whose garden has the greater area? How much greater? Explain.

15. Higher Order Thinking Nancy made a table runner that has an area of 80 square inches. The length and width of the table runner are whole numbers. The length is 5 times greater than the width. What are the dimensions of the table runner?

Assessment Practice

16. The rectangle has an area of 144 square centimeters. Which is its perimeter?

Ⓐ 26 cm

Ⓑ 48 cm

Ⓒ 52 cm

Ⓓ 72 cm

Name ______________________ Activity

Problem Solving

Lesson 13-7

Precision

I can ...
be precise when solving math problems.

Mathematical Practices MP.6 Also MP.2, MP.4
Content Standards 4.MD.A.3 Also 4.OA.A.3, 4.NF.B.4c, 4.MD.A.2

Solve & Share Mr. Beasley's science class wants to decorate one wall in the classroom like an underwater scene. They use sheets of blue poster board that are 2 feet long and 2 feet wide. How many sheets of blue poster board are used to cover the entire area of the wall? Use math words and symbols to explain how you solve.

Thinking Habits

Be a good thinker!
These questions can help you.

- Am I using numbers, units, and symbols appropriately?
- Am I using the correct definitions?
- Am I calculating accurately?
- Is my answer clear?

Look Back! **Be Precise** How can calculating the area of the whole wall and the area of one sheet of poster board help you determine the total number of sheets of poster board needed to cover the entire area of the wall?

How Can You Be Precise When Solving Math Problems?

Visual Learning Bridge

A

Piper has a fish tank and wants to cover all four sides $\frac{6}{10}$ of the way to the top with clear plastic for insulation. She measures and finds the dimensions shown. How much plastic does Piper need? Use math words and symbols to explain how to solve.

length = 12 inches

height = 15 inches

width = 24 inches

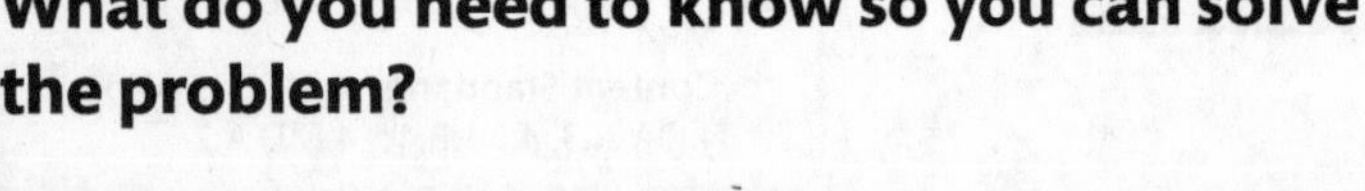

What do you need to know so you can solve the problem?

I need to find how much plastic is needed for the fish tank. I need to be precise in my calculations and explanation.

Here's my thinking.

B

How can I be precise in solving this problem?

I can

- correctly use the information given.
- calculate accurately.
- decide if my answer is clear and appropriate.
- use the correct units.

C

The height of the plastic is $\frac{6}{10}$ times 15 inches.

$\frac{6}{10} \times 15 = \frac{90}{10}$ or 9 The plastic is 9 inches high.

Front and back: $A = 9 \times 24$
$A = 216$ square inches

Each side: $A = 9 \times 12$
$A = 108$ square inches

Add: $216 + 216 + 108 + 108 = 648$ square inches

Piper needs 648 square inches of plastic.

Convince Me! **Be Precise** How did you use math words and numbers to make your explanation clear?

Name ____________________

Practice Tools Assessment

Guided Practice

Be Precise

Jeremy uses $\frac{2}{3}$ yard of tape for each box he packs for shipping. How many inches of tape does Jeremy need to pack 3 boxes?

When you are precise, you calculate accurately.

1. How can you use the information given to solve the problem?

2. How many inches of tape does Jeremy need to pack 3 boxes? Explain.

3. Explain why you used the units you did in your answer.

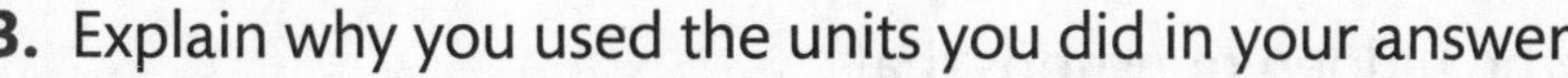

Independent Practice

Be Precise

Mrs. Reed collects shells. Each shell in her collection weighs about 4 ounces. Her collection weighs about 12 pounds in all. About how many shells are in Mrs. Reed's collection? Use Exercises 4–6 to solve.

4. How can you use the information given to solve the problem?

5. What is the total weight of Mrs. Reed's shell collection, in ounces?

6. How many shells are in Mrs. Reed's shell collection?

Problem Solving

Performance Task

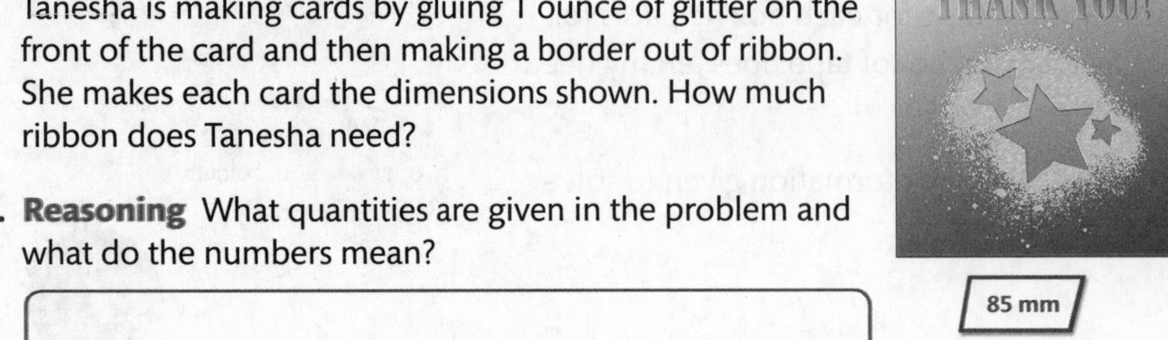

Making Thank You Cards

Tanesha is making cards by gluing 1 ounce of glitter on the front of the card and then making a border out of ribbon. She makes each card the dimensions shown. How much ribbon does Tanesha need?

7. **Reasoning** What quantities are given in the problem and what do the numbers mean?

8. **Reasoning** What do you need to find?

9. **Model with Math** What are the hidden questions that must be answered to solve the problem? Write equations to show how to solve the hidden questions.

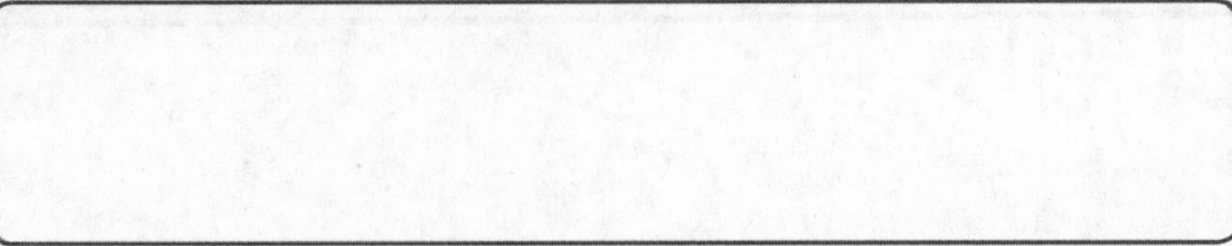

When you are precise, you specify and use units of measure appropriately.

10. **Be Precise** How much ribbon does Tanesha need? Use math language and symbols to explain how you solved the problem and computed accurately.

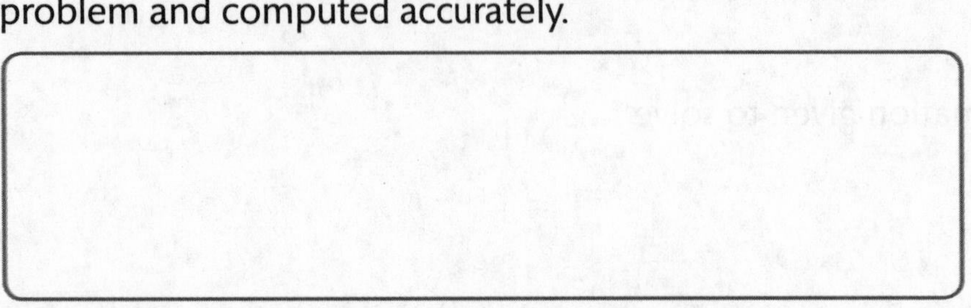

11. **Reasoning** What information was not needed in the problem?

Name ______________________________

TOPIC 13 Fluency Practice Activity

Find a Match

Work with a partner. Point to a clue.

Read the clue.

Look below the clues to find a match. Write the clue letter in the box next to the match.

Find a match for every clue.

I can ...
add and subtract multi-digit whole numbers.

Content Standard 4.NBT.B.4
Mathematical Practices MP.3, MP.6, MP.7, MP.8

Clues

A The sum is between 2,000 and 2,500.

B The difference is exactly 10,000.

C The sum is exactly 6,000.

D The difference is exactly 4,500.

E The sum is exactly 16,477.

F The sum is between 5,500 and 5,600.

G The difference is between 1,000 and 2,000.

H The difference is between 8,000 and 9,000.

☐ 10,005 + 6,472	☐ 7,513 − 5,676	☐ 35,000 − 25,000	☐ 1,234 + 4,321
☐ 1,050 + 1,200	☐ 3,778 + 2,222	☐ 10,650 − 2,150	☐ 9,000 − 4,500

TOPIC 13

Vocabulary Review

Glossary

Word List

- area
- capacity
- centimeter (cm)
- cup (c)
- formula
- gallon (gal)
- gram (g)
- kilogram (kg)
- kilometer (km)
- liter (L)
- mass
- meter (m)
- milligram (mg)
- milliliter (mL)
- millimeter (mm)
- ounce (oz)
- perimeter
- pint (pt)
- pound (lb)
- quart (qt)
- ton (T)
- weight
- fluid ounce (fl oz)

Understand Vocabulary

1. Cross out the units that are **NOT** used to measure length.

centimeter (cm) pint (pt)

pound (lb) kilogram (kg)

2. Cross out the units that are **NOT** used to measure capacity.

millimeter (mm) ounce (oz)

gallon (gal) milliliter (mL)

3. Cross out the units that are **NOT** used to measure weight.

cup (c) liter (L)

meter (m) ton (T)

4. Cross out the units that are **NOT** used to measure mass.

liter (L) kilometer (km)

milligram (mg) quart (qt)

Label each example with a term from the Word List.

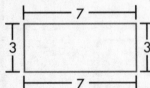

5. $2 \times 4 = 8$ square units ____________

6. $3 + 7 + 3 + 7 = 20$ units ____________

7
3 3
7

7. Area $= \ell \times w$ ____________

Use Vocabulary in Writing

8. Mike uses 24 meters of fence to enclose a rectangular garden. The length of the garden is 10 meters. What is the width? Use at least 3 terms from the Word List to explain.

Name ______________________________

TOPIC 13

Reteaching

Set A pages 481–492

Customary units can be used when measuring length, capacity, and weight.

DATA		
Length	1 foot (ft) = 12 inches (in.)	
	1 yard (yd) = 3 ft = 36 in.	
	1 mile (mi) = 1,760 yd = 5,280 ft	

DATA	
Capacity	1 cup (c) = 8 fluid ounces (fl oz)
	1 pint (pt) = 2 c = 16 fl oz
	1 quart (qt) = 2 pt = 4 c
	1 gallon (gal) = 4 qt = 8 pt

DATA	
Weight	1 pound (lb) = 16 ounces (oz)
	1 ton (T) = 2,000 lb

Convert 26 quarts to cups.

Number of quarts	×	**Cups per quart**		
26	×	4 cups	=	104 cups

Remember when converting from a larger unit to a smaller unit, multiply. Use the conversion charts to help solve.

1. 9 yards = __________ inches
2. 5 miles = __________ yards
3. 215 yards = __________ feet
4. 9 pints = __________ fluid ounces
5. 372 quarts = __________ cups
6. 1,620 gallons = __________ pints
7. 9 pounds = __________ ounces
8. 5 tons = __________ pounds
9. 12 feet = __________ inches

Set B pages 493–500

Metric units can be used to measure length, capacity, and mass.

DATA	
Length	1 centimeter (cm) = 10 millimeters (mm)
	1 meter (m) = 100 cm = 1,000 mm
	1 kilometer (km) = 1,000 m

DATA	
Capacity and Mass	1 liter (L) = 1,000 milliliters (mL)
	1 gram (g) = 1,000 milligrams (mg)
	1 kilogram (kg) = 1,000 g

Convert 30 centimeters to millimeters.

Number of cm	×	**mm per cm**		
30	×	10 mm	=	300 mm

Remember metric units can be converted using multiples of 10. Use the conversion charts to help.

1. 9 kilometers = __________ meters
2. 55 centimeters = __________ millimeters
3. 2 meters = __________ centimeters
4. 9 liters = __________ milliliters
5. 4 grams = __________ milligrams
6. 5 kilograms = __________ grams
7. 8 kilograms = __________ grams
8. 5 grams = __________ milligrams

Set C pages 501–504

The perimeter of Ted's pool is 16 yards. The pool is 3 yards wide. He has 150-square feet of plastic. Does Ted have enough plastic to cover the pool?

Use the formula for perimeter to find the length. Substitute the numbers you know.

$$\text{Perimeter} = (2 \times \ell) + (2 \times w)$$
$$16 = (2 \times \ell) + (2 \times 3)$$
$$\ell = 5$$

The length of the pool is 5 yards.

3 yards wide × 3 = 9 feet wide

5 yards long × 3 = 15 feet long

Find the area of the pool.

$$A = 15 \times 9$$
$$A = 135$$

The area of the pool is 135 square feet. 135 < 150, so Ted has enough plastic to cover the pool.

Remember to label your answer with the appropriate unit.

1. Find n.
   $P = 108$ inches

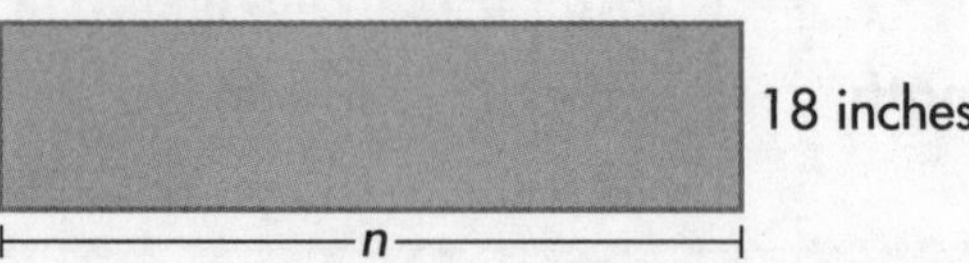

2. Find the area.

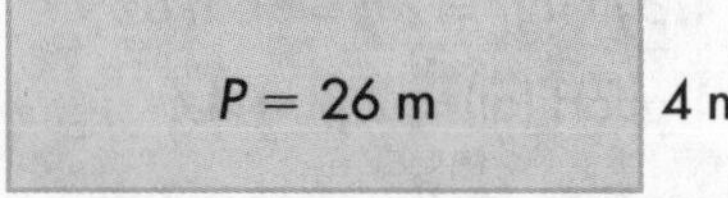

3. Find the perimeter of the square.

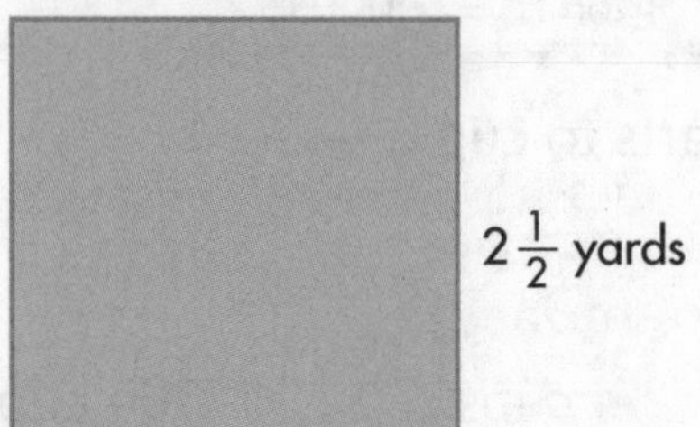

Set D pages 505–508

Think about these questions to help you **be precise.**

Thinking Habits

- Am I using numbers, units, and symbols appropriately?
- Am I using the correct definitions?
- Am I calculating accurately?
- Is my answer clear?

Remember to give an explanation that is clear and appropriate.

A puppy pen is 4 feet wide and 5 feet long.

1. Is 21 square feet of fabric large enough to make a mat for the pen? Explain.

2. Puppy fencing comes in sizes that are 12 feet, 24 feet, and 30 feet in length. Which length would be the best for the pen? How much, if any, will have to be left over? Explain.

Name ________________________________

TOPIC 13

Assessment Practice

1. A window is 5 feet long. What is the length of the window in inches?

2. Mrs. Warren bought 6 liters of lemonade for a party. How many milliliters of lemonade did she buy?

Ⓐ 9,000 milliliters

Ⓑ 6,000 milliliters

Ⓒ 3,000 milliliters

Ⓓ 1,200 milliliters

3. Select the equivalent measurement for each measurement on the left.

	72 fl oz	144 in.	108 in.	8,000 lb
9 ft	☐	☐	☐	☐
9 cups	☐	☐	☐	☐
4 tons	☐	☐	☐	☐
4 yd	☐	☐	☐	☐

4. A picnic table is 9 feet long and 3 feet wide. Write and solve an equation to find the area of the rectangular surface of the table.

5. The Girl's Club is making muffins. Mindy's recipe calls for 3 cups of buttermilk. Josie's recipe calls for 20 fluid ounces of buttermilk. Georgia's recipe calls for 1 pint of buttermilk. Whose recipe calls for the most buttermilk? Explain.

6. Andrea ran 4 kilometers over the weekend. How many meters did Andrea run?

7. Choose numbers from the box to complete the table. Some numbers will not be used.

Pounds	Ounces
$1\frac{1}{2}$	
2	
$2\frac{1}{2}$	
3	
$3\frac{1}{2}$	

8	12
16	24
32	40
45	48
56	160

8. Select each correct equation.

- ☐ 1 L = 100 mL
- ☐ 1 kg = 1,000 g
- ☐ 4 yd = 14 ft
- ☐ 15 cm = 150 mm
- ☐ 1 gal = 13 cups

9. Morgan rode her bike 2 kilometers from her house to her friend's house. From her friend's house, she rode 600 meters in all going to and from the library. Then she rode back home. How many meters did Morgan bike in all?

10. Which statement is true about the bedrooms in the drawings below?

Steve's room: 9 ft by 8 ft

Erin's room: 10 ft by 7 ft

Ⓐ Erin's room has a greater area than Steve's room.

Ⓑ Steve's room has a greater perimeter than Erin's room.

Ⓒ They both have the same perimeter.

Ⓓ None of the above

11. Tim has 3 meters of yarn. How many centimeters of yarn does Tim have?

12. Mrs. Li's classroom is 34 feet wide and 42 feet long.

Objects in Classroom	Area of Objects (square feet)
Mrs. Li's Desk	8
Fish Tank	6
Math Center	100
Reading Center	120

A. What is the area of the classroom?

B. How much area is taken up by the objects in the classroom? How much area is left for the students' desks? Write and solve equations to find the area.

13. Select the equivalent measurement for each measurement on the left.

	3,000 mL	3,000 g	3,000 mm	3,000 mg
3 g	☐	☐	☐	☐
3 m	☐	☐	☐	☐
3 L	☐	☐	☐	☐
3 kg	☐	☐	☐	☐

Name ______________________________

Watermelons

Kasia grows watermelons.

1. Kasia plants her watermelons in rows. Kasia's watermelon field has a perimeter of $71\frac{1}{3}$ yards and is $14\frac{2}{3}$ yards wide. Each row is $\frac{2}{3}$ yard wide and the rows will be planted 2 yards apart.

Watermelon Field

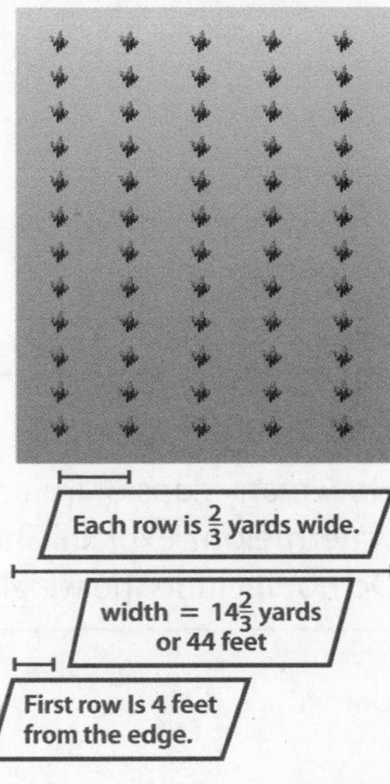
Each row is $\frac{2}{3}$ yards wide.
width = $14\frac{2}{3}$ yards or 44 feet
First row Is 4 feet from the edge.

Part A

What is the length of Kasia's field? Explain.

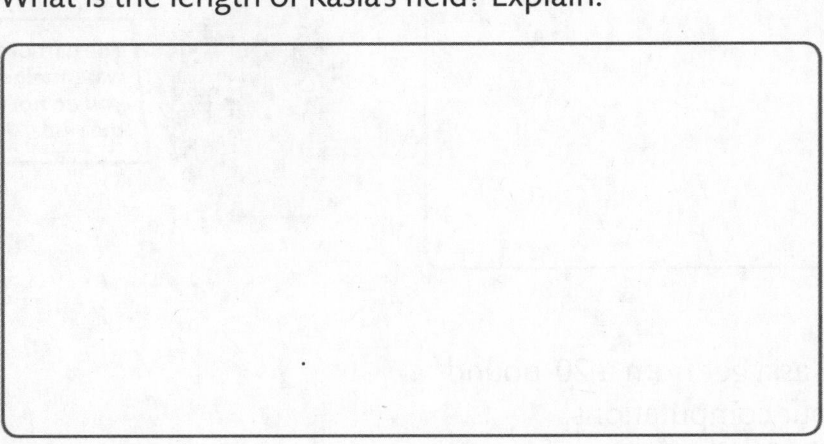

Part B

What is the area of Kasia's field? Complete the table to convert the length to feet. Be sure to use the correct units on your answer. Explain.

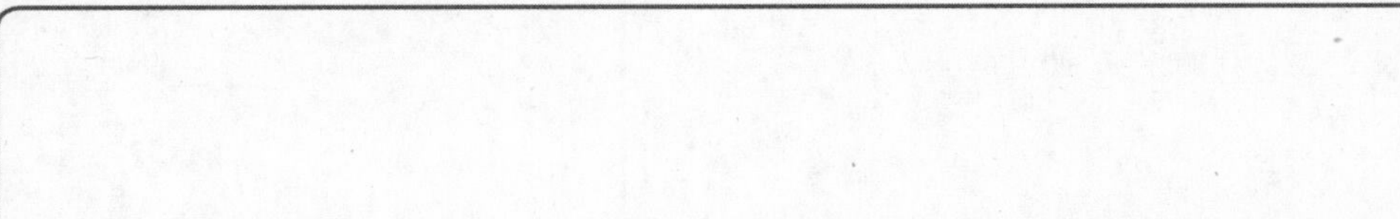

Yards	Feet
1	3
10	
20	
21	

Part C

How many rows can Kasia plant? Explain.

2. Use the information in the **Watermelon** table.

Part A

If there are twenty-eight 8-ounce servings in a 20-pound watermelon, how many pounds does the rind weigh? Explain.

Watermelon

DATA
20-pound watermelon
28 8-ounce servings
1 pound = $\frac{3}{4}$ quart of fruit

The part of the watermelon that you do not eat is the rind.

Part B

How many cups of fruit does Kasia get from a 20-pound watermelon? Explain. Show your computations. Do not include the weight of the rind.

3. Use the information from the **Watermelon and Nutrition** picture to answer the question.

How many more milligrams of fiber than potassium are in a serving of watermelon? Explain.

Watermelon and Nutrition

Each serving has 1 gram of fiber and 270 mg of potassium.

Algebra: Generate and Analyze Patterns

Essential Questions: How can you use a rule to continue a pattern? How can you use a table to extend a pattern? How can you use a repeating pattern to predict a shape?

Scientists can use an instrument called an oscilloscope to see sounds as waves.

Higher sounds have shorter wavelengths.

I can see what you are saying on the oscilloscope. Here is a project about patterns and waves.

ënVision® STEM Project: Patterns and Waves

Do Research Use the Internet or other sources to learn about 2 industries where oscilloscopes can be used. Name the industry and what can be observed using the oscilloscope.

Journal: Write a Report Include what you found. Also in your report:

- Oscilloscopes are used to observe patterns in waves. Suppose a scientist created a pattern with three levels of sounds: *quiet, loud, medium*. If the scientist repeats the pattern of sounds, what would be the 41st sound in the pattern? Explain.

Name ______________________

Review What You Know

Vocabulary

Choose the best term from the box. Write it on the blank.

- even number
- odd number
- inverse operations
- variable

1. A(n) ______________ can be divided into groups of 2 without a remainder.

2. A symbol or letter that stands for a number is called a(n) ______________.

3. Operations that undo each other are called ______________.

Addition and Subtraction Patterns

Add or subtract to find the missing number in each pattern.

4. 3, 6, 9, 12, ____, 18

5. 4, 8, 12, ____, 20, 24

6. 8, 7, 6, ____, 4, 3

7. 30, 25, 20, 15, ____, 5

8. 1, 5, 9, ____, 17, 21

9. 12, 10, 8, 6, ____, 2

Multiplication and Division Patterns

Multiply or divide to find the missing number in each pattern.

10. 1, 3, 9, 27, ____, 243

11. 64, 32, 16, ____, 4, 2

12. 1, 5, 25, ____, 625

13. 1, 2, 4, 8, ____, 32

14. 1, 4, 16, ____, 256

15. 729, 243, 81, 27, 9, ____

Problem Solving

16. Look for Relationships James places 1 counter in the first box. He places 2 counters in the second box, 4 counters in the third box, 8 counters in the fourth box, and continues the pattern until he gets to the tenth box. How many counters did James place in the tenth box?

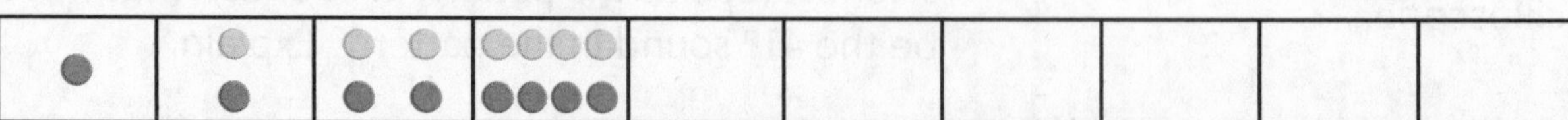

Name ____________________

PROJECT
14A

How have roller coasters changed through the years?

Project: Make a Model Roller-Coaster Car

How can you use currency from different countries?

Project: Make Your Own Currency

How can patterns be used in sidewalks?

Project: Design Your Own Sidewalk

PROJECT
14D

How many stadiums in the United States have retractable roofs?

Project: Make a Seating Diagram

Name ______________________________

Lesson 14-1
Number Sequences

I can ...
use a rule to create and extend a number pattern and identify features of the number pattern not described by the rule.

Content Standards 4.OA.C.5 Also 4.NBT.B.4, 4.OA.B.4
Mathematical Practices MP.2, MP.7, MP.8

Solve & Share

Look at the rules and starting numbers below. What are the next 6 numbers in each pattern? Tell how you decided. Describe features of the patterns. ***Solve these problems any way you choose.***

After you apply a rule, look at the resulting numbers to find features of the pattern.

Starting Number	Rule	Next 6 Numbers
18	Add 3	
17	Add 2	
40	Subtract 4	

Look Back! Look for Relationships Create two patterns that use the same rule but start with different numbers. Identify a feature of each pattern. For example, identify whether the numbers are all even, all odd, or alternate between even and odd.

How Can You Use a Rule to Continue a Pattern?

Visual Learning Bridge

A

The house numbers on a street follow the rule "Add 4." If the pattern continues, what are the next three house numbers? Describe a feature of the pattern.

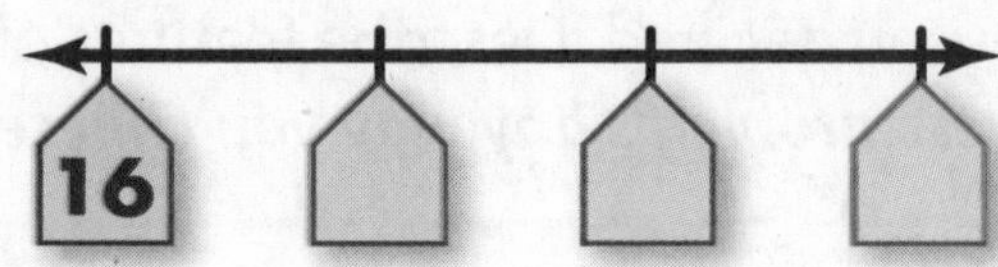

You can use a number line to help make sense of the problem and find the next three house numbers.

B

Use a number line to continue the pattern.

A rule is a mathematical phrase that tells how numbers or shapes in a pattern are related. The rule for the house numbers is "Add 4."

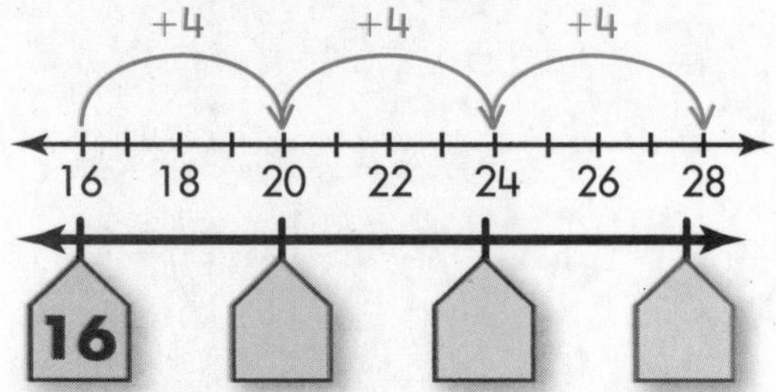

The next three house numbers are 20, 24, and 28.

C

Describe features of the pattern.

Some patterns have features that are not given in the rule.

16, 20, 24, 28

One of the features of this pattern is all of the house numbers are even numbers.

Another feature is all of the house numbers are multiples of 4.

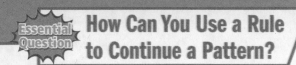

Convince Me! **Generalize** Can you use the rule "Add 4" to create a different pattern with all odd numbers? Explain.

Name ____

Another Example!

On another street, the house numbers follow the rule "Subtract 5." What are the next three house numbers after 825? Describe a feature of the pattern.

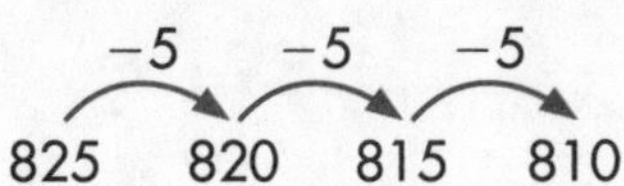

Some patterns have rules using addition, while others have rules using subtraction.

The next three house numbers are 820, 815, and 810. All of the house numbers are multiples of 5.

Guided Practice

Do You Understand?

1. Rudy's rule is "Add 2." He started with 4 and wrote the numbers below. Which number does **NOT** belong to Rudy's pattern? Explain.

4, 6, 8, 9, 10, 12

Do You Know How?

Continue the pattern. Describe a feature of the pattern.

2. Subtract 6

48, 42, 36, 30, 24, ____, ____, ____

Independent Practice

For **3–6**, continue each pattern. Describe a feature of each pattern.

3. Subtract 3: 63, 60, 57, ____, ____

4. Add 7: 444, 451, 458, ____, ____

5. Add 25: 85, 110, 135, ____, ____

6. Subtract 4: 75, 71, 67, ____, ____

For **7–12**, use the rule to generate each pattern.

7. Rule: Subtract 10

90, ____, ____

8. Rule: Add 51

16, ____, ____

9. Rule: Add 5

96, ____, ____

10. Rule: Add 107

43, ____, ____

11. Rule: Subtract 15

120, ____, ____

12. Rule: Subtract 19

99, ____, ____

Problem Solving

13. **Reasoning** Orlando delivers mail. He sees one mailbox that does not have a number. If the numbers are in a pattern, what is the missing number?

14. A bus tour runs 9 times a day, 6 days a week. The bus can carry 30 passengers. Find the greatest number of passengers who can ride the tour bus each week.

15. The year 2017 was the year of the Rooster on the Chinese calendar. The next year of the Rooster will be 2029. The rule is "Add 12." What are the next five years of the Rooster?

16. Describe a feature of the year of the Rooster pattern.

The pattern of animals repeats every 12 years.

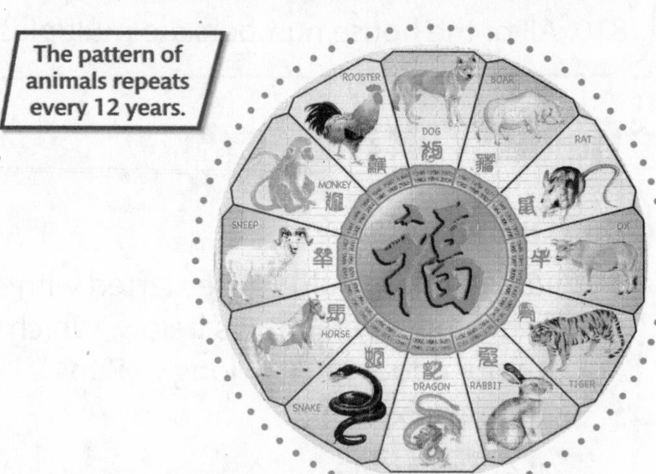

17. **Vocabulary** Define *rule*. Create a number pattern using the rule "Subtract 7."

18. **Higher Order Thinking** Some patterns use both addition and subtraction in their rules. The rule is "Add 3, Subtract 2." Find the next three numbers in the pattern.

1, 4, 2, 5, 3, 6, 4, 7, ____, ____, ____

Assessment Practice

19. Rima used "Subtract 3" as the rule to make a pattern. She started with 60, and wrote the next six numbers in her pattern. Which number does **NOT** belong in Rima's pattern?

Ⓐ 57
Ⓑ 54
Ⓒ 45
Ⓓ 26

Which number is NOT a multiple of 3?

20. Ivan counted all the beans in a jar. If he counted the beans in groups of 7, which list shows the numbers Ivan could have named?

Ⓐ 77, 84, 91, 99
Ⓑ 301, 308, 324, 331
Ⓒ 574, 581, 588, 595
Ⓓ 14, 24, 34, 44

Name ______________________________________

Activity

Lesson 14-2
Patterns: Number Rules

I can ...
use a rule to extend a number pattern, identify features of the number pattern, and use the number pattern to solve a problem.

Content Standards 4.OA.C.5 Also 4.OA.B.4, 4.NBT.B.5, 4.NBT.B.6
Mathematical Practices MP.2, MP.4

Solve & Share

There are 6 juice boxes in 1 pack, 12 in 2 packs, and 18 in 3 packs. How many juice boxes are in 4 packs? in 5 packs? in 6 packs? Use the rule to complete the table. Describe features of the pattern. Then find how many juice boxes are in 10 packs and 100 packs.

Rule: Multiply by 6

Number of Packs	Number of Juice Boxes
1	6
2	12
3	18
4	
5	
6	

You can use what you learned about multiplication to extend a pattern to find the number of juice boxes in any number of packs.

Look Back! Reasoning Create a table showing the relationship between the number of bicycles and the number of bicycle wheels. Start with 1 bicycle. Complete 5 rows of the table using the rule "Multiply by 2." Describe features of the pattern.

Essential Question What Is the Pattern?

A

There are 3 leaflets on 1 cloverleaf.
There are 6 leaflets on 2 cloverleaves.
There are 9 leaflets on 3 cloverleaves.
How many leaflets are on 4 cloverleaves?
How many cloverleaves will have 12 leaflets?

You can use a table to create, extend, and identify features of a pattern.

A cloverleaf has 3 leaflets.

B **How many leaflets are on 4 cloverleaves?**

Rule: Multiply by 3

Number of Cloverleaves	Number of Leaflets
1	3
2	6
3	9
4 $\times 3$	12

There are 12 leaflets on 4 cloverleaves. The number of leaflets is a multiple of the number of cloverleaves.

C **How many cloverleaves for 12 leaflets?**

Rule: Divide by 3

Number of Leaflets	Number of Cloverleaves
3	1
6	2
9	3
12 $\div 3$	4

There are 4 cloverleaves for 12 leaflets. The number of cloverleaves is a factor of the number of leaflets.

Convince Me! **Model with Math** If you know the number of leaflets, ℓ, what expression can you use to find the number of cloverleaves, c? If you know the number of cloverleaves, what expression can you use to find the number of leaflets?

Name ____________________

Guided Practice

Do You Understand?

1. The rule for this table is "Multiply by 4." What number does not belong?

My Marbles	John's Marbles
1	4
2	8
3	12
4	15

Do You Know How?

Complete the table. Describe a feature of the pattern.

2. Rule: Divide by 4

Total Number of Wheels	8	12	16	20
Number of Cars	2	3	4	

Independent Practice

For **3–6**, use the rule to complete each table. Describe a feature of each pattern.

You can multiply or divide to find the patterns in these tables.

3. Rule: Multiply by 8

Number of Spiders	1	2	3	4	5
Number of Legs	8		24	32	

4. Rule: Divide by 5

Number of Fingers	Number of Hands
5	1
10	2
15	
20	

5. Rule: Multiply by 16

Number of Books	1	2	3	4
Weight of Books in Ounces	16	32		

6. Rule: Divide by 2

Number of Shoes	100	234	500	730
Number of Pairs	50	117		

Problem Solving

7. The table shows how much money Joe makes painting. How much money will Joe make when he paints for 6 hours?

Rule: Multiply by 45

Hours Painting	Amount Earned
3	$135
4	$180
5	$225
6	

8. The table shows the total number of pounds of potatoes for different numbers of bags. How many bags does it take to hold 96 pounds of potatoes?

Rule: Divide by 8

Number of Pounds	Number of Bags
72	9
80	10
88	11
96	

9. Number Sense What is the greatest number you can make using each of the digits 1, 7, 0, and 6 once?

10. Algebra A penguin can swim 11 miles per hour. At this speed, how far can it swim in 13 hours? Use *s* as a variable. Write and solve an equation.

For **11–12**, the rule is "Multiply by 3."

11. Reasoning Using the rule, how many batteries do 8 flashlights need? 10 flashlights?

12. Higher Order Thinking How many more batteries do 20 flashlights need than 15 flashlights? Explain.

DATA

Batteries for Flashlights	
Number of Flashlights	Number of Batteries
1	3
2	6
3	9

Assessment Practice

13. There are 6 rolls in each package. Use the rule "Divide by 6" to show the relationship between the number of rolls and the number of packages. Use each digit from the box once to complete the table.

Number of Rolls	522	528	534	540	546	552
Number of Packages	☐☐	88	89	☐☐	9☐	9☐

0	1
2	7
8	9

Name ________________________________ Activity

Lesson 14-3
Patterns: Repeating Shapes

Solve & Share

The rule for the repeating pattern below is "Square, Triangle." What will be the 37th shape in the pattern? Explain. ***Solve this problem any way you choose.***

1st 2nd 3rd 4th 5th 6th ... 37th ?

I can ...

use a rule to predict a number or shape in a pattern.

Content Standards 4.OA.C.5 Also 4.OA.A.3, 4.NBT.B.6
Mathematical Practices MP.3, MP.6, MP.7

You can construct arguments to convince a classmate your answer is correct.

Look Back! When the pattern has 37 shapes, how many are triangles?

How Can You Use a Repeating Pattern to Predict a Shape?

Visual Learning Bridge

A

Rashad is making a repeating pattern for the rule "Triangle, Square, Trapezoid." What will be the 49th shape in the pattern?

A repeating pattern is made up of shapes or numbers that form a part that repeats.

1st
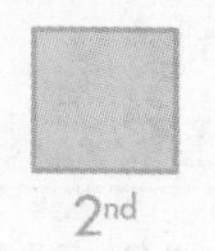
2nd
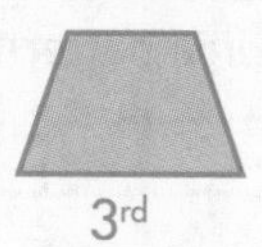
3rd
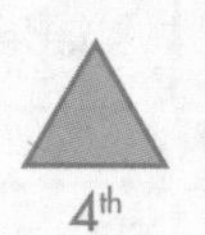
4th
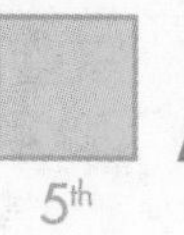
5th
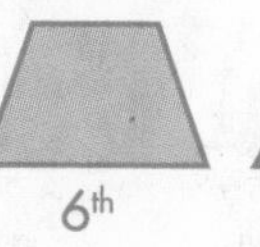
6th
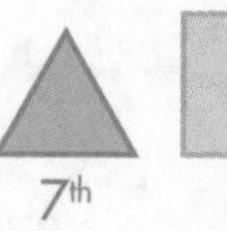
7th
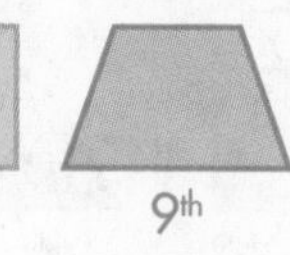
8th
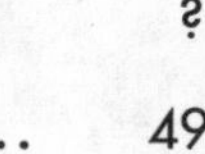
9th ... ? 49th

Look for Features of the Repeating Pattern

The trapezoid is the 3rd, 6th, and 9th shape in the pattern. The positions of the trapezoids are multiples of 3.

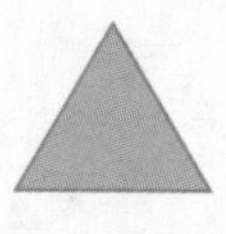

The triangle is the 1st, 4th, and 7th shape in the pattern. The positions of the triangles are 1 more than a multiple of 3.

The square is the 2nd, 5th, and 8th shape in the pattern. The positions of the squares are 1 less than a multiple of 3.

C

Use the Repeating Pattern to Solve

When you divide 49 by 3, the quotient is 16 R1. The pattern repeats 16 times. The 1st shape in the repeating pattern, a triangle, then appears.

$$3\overline{)49}\quad 16\text{R}1$$

You divide by 3 because there are 3 items in the repeating pattern.

49 is one more than a multiple of 3.

The 49th shape is a triangle.

Convince Me! **Be Precise** Suppose the rule is "Square, Triangle, Square, Trapezoid" in a repeating pattern. What is the 26th shape in the pattern? Describe features of the repeating pattern. Be precise in your description.

Name ______________________________

Another Example!

Write the next three numbers in the repeating pattern. Then name the 100th number in the pattern.

Rule: 1, 3, 5, 7

1, 3, 5, 7, 1, 3, 5, 7, 1, 3, 5, 7, 1, 3, 5 ...

There are 4 items in the repeating pattern. To find the 100th number, divide by 4. The pattern repeats 25 times. The 100th number is 7.

$$\begin{array}{r} 25 \\ 4\overline{)100} \\ -100 \\ \hline 0 \end{array}$$

A repeating pattern can be made up of shapes or numbers.

Guided Practice

Do You Understand?

1. In the "Triangle, Square, Trapezoid" example on the previous page, what will be the 48th shape? the 50th shape? Explain.

Do You Know How?

2. What is the 20th shape? The rule is "Triangle, Circle, Circle."

 ...

3. Write the next three numbers. The rule is "9, 2, 7, 6."

9, 2, 7, 6, 9, 2, 7, 6, ____, ____, ____

Independent Practice

For **4–7**, draw or write the next three items to continue each repeating pattern.

4. The rule is "Square, Triangle, Square."

 ___ ___ ___ ...

5. The rule is "Up, Down, Left, Right."

 ___ ___ ___ ...

6. The rule is "1, 1, 2."

1, 1, 2, 1, 1, 2, ____, ____, ____ ...

7. The rule is "5, 7, 4, 8."

5, 7, 4, 8, 5, 7, 4, 8, 5, 7, ____, ____, ____ ...

For **8–9**, determine the given shape or number in each repeating pattern.

8. The rule is "Tree, Apple, Apple." What is the 19th shape?

...

9. The rule is "1, 2." What is the 42nd number?

1, 2, 1, 2, 1, 2, ...

Problem Solving

10. Create a repeating pattern using the rule "Triangle, Square, Square."

11. **enVision® STEM** Margot measured the distance for 6 wavelengths of visible light as 2,400 nanometers. What is the distance for 1 wavelength?

12. **Look for Relationships** Hilda is making a repeating pattern with the shapes below. The rule is "Heart, Square, Triangle." If Hilda continues the pattern, what will be the 11th shape?

13. **Look for Relationships** Josie puts beads on a string in a repeating pattern. The rule is "Blue, Green, Yellow, Orange." There are 88 beads on her string. How many times did Josie repeat her pattern?

14. How many more years passed between the first steam locomotive and the gasoline-powered automobile than between the gasoline-powered automobile and the first diesel locomotive?

DATA

Year	Invention
1804	Steam Locomotive
1885	Gasoline-powered Automobile
1912	Diesel Locomotive

15. Louisa used the rule "Blue, Green, Green, Green" to make a bracelet with a repeating pattern. She used 18 green beads. How many beads did Louisa use to make the bracelet? How many beads were **NOT** green?

16. **Higher Order Thinking** Marcus is using shapes to make a repeating pattern. He has twice as many circles as squares. Make a repeating pattern that follows this rule.

Assessment Practice

17. Which rules give a repeating pattern that has a square as the 15th shape? Select all that apply.

- ☐ Square, Circle
- ☐ Circle, Square, Triangle
- ☐ Square, Circle, Triangle
- ☐ Circle, Triangle, Square
- ☐ Trapezoid, Circle, Square

18. Which rules give a repeating pattern that has a 7 as the 15th number? Select all that apply.

- ☐ 1, 7
- ☐ 1, 7, 9
- ☐ 1, 9, 7
- ☐ 1, 7, 7
- ☐ 7, 1, 9

Name ______________________________

Activity

Solve & Share

Evan's baby brother is stacking blocks. Using the rule "Add 1 block to the number of blocks in the previous stack," how many blocks will be in the 6th stack? Explain. Justify your answer.

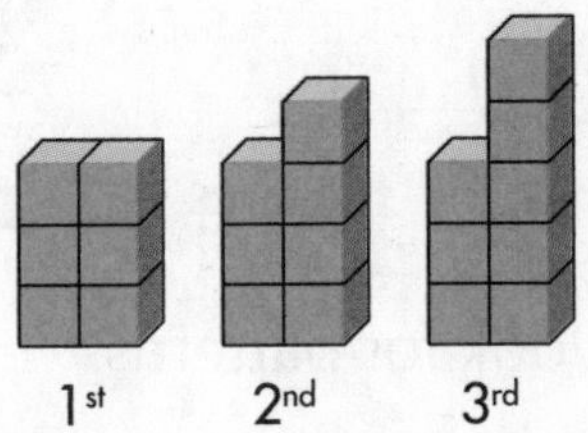

Problem Solving

Lesson 14-4

Look For and Use Structure

I can ...
use patterns to help solve problems.

Mathematical Practices MP.7 Also MP.1, MP.2
Content Standard 4.OA.C.5

Thinking Habits

- What patterns can I see and describe?
- How can I use the patterns to solve the problem?
- Can I see expressions and objects in different ways?

Look Back! Look For Relationships How many blocks are in the 10th stack? Explain.

How Can I Look For and Make Use of Structure?

Visual Learning Bridge

A

Alisa made three walls with cubes. She recorded her pattern. If she continues the pattern, how many cubes will be in a 10-layer wall? a 100-layer wall?

Rule: Each layer has 4 cubes.

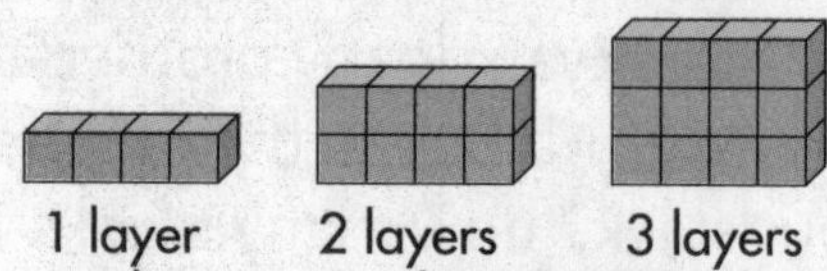
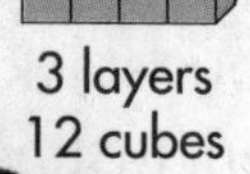

1 layer 4 cubes | 2 layers 8 cubes | 3 layers 12 cubes

What do you need to do to find the number of cubes in a 10-layer and 100-layer wall?

I need to continue the pattern using the rule and analyze the pattern to find features not stated in the rule itself.

B

How can I make use of structure to solve this problem?

I can

- look for and describe patterns in three-dimensional shapes.
- use the rule that describes how objects or values in a pattern are related.
- use features of the pattern not stated in the rule to generate or extend the pattern.

C

Make a table and look for patterns.

Number of Layers	1	2	3	4	5
Number of Cubes	4	8	12	16	20

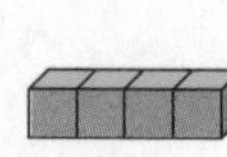
1 layer 4 cubes

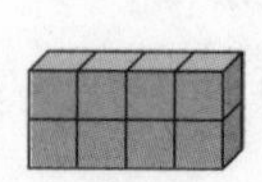
2 layers 8 cubes

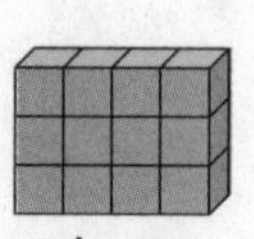
3 layers 12 cubes

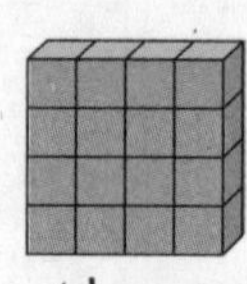
4 layers 16 cubes

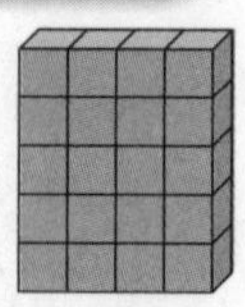
5 layers 20 cubes

There are 4 cubes in each layer. Multiply the number of layers by 4 to calculate the number of cubes.

A 10-layer wall contains $10 \times 4 = 40$ cubes.

A 100-layer wall contains $100 \times 4 = 400$ cubes.

Convince Me! Look for Relationships How could you use multiples to describe Alisa's pattern?

Name ____________________

Practice Tools Assessment

Guided Practice

Use Structure

Leah arranged triangular tiles in a pattern like the one shown. She used the rule "Multiply the number of rows by itself to get the number of small triangles." How many small triangles would be in the pattern if there were 10 rows?

1 row
$1 \times 1 = 1$

2 rows
$2 \times 2 = 4$

3 rows
$3 \times 3 = 9$

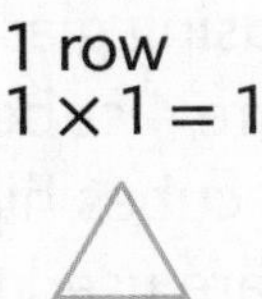
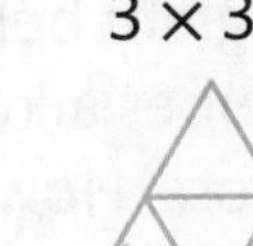

1. Complete the table to help describe the pattern.

Number of Rows	1	2	3	4	5
Number of Small Triangles	1	4	9		

When you look for relationships, you use features of the pattern not stated in the rule to extend the pattern.

2. Describe the pattern another way.

3. How many triangles would be in 10 rows?

Independent Practice

Look for Relationships

Alan built the towers shown using the rule "Each story has 2 blocks." How many blocks will a 10-story tower have? Use Exercises 4–6 to answer the question.

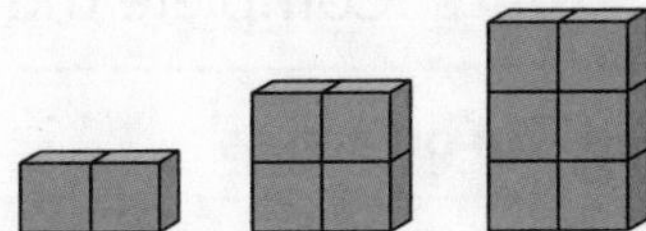

4. Complete the table to help describe the pattern.

Number of Stories	1	2	3	4	5
Number of Blocks	2	4	6		

5. What is another way to describe the pattern that is not described by the rule?

6. How many blocks are in a 10-story tower? Explain.

Problem Solving

Performance Task

Glass Stairs

An art gallery staircase is built using glass cubes. The diagram below shows 4 steps are 4 cubes high and 4 cubes across. Five steps are 5 cubes high and 5 cubes across. How many glass cubes are used to make 7 steps? Use Exercises 7–10 to answer the question.

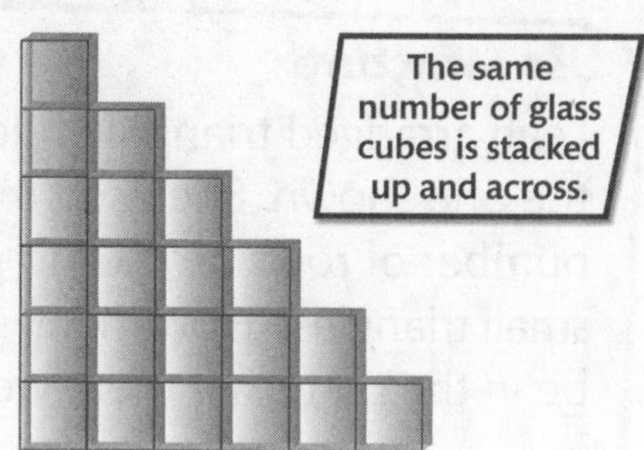

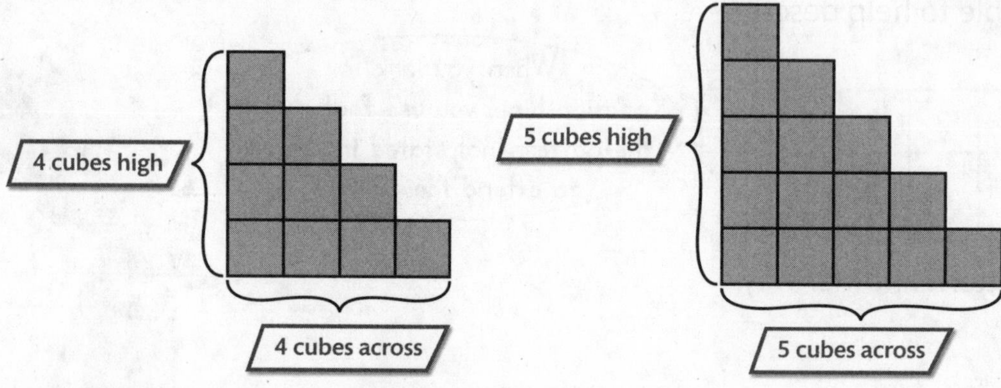

The same number of glass cubes is stacked up and across.

7. Make Sense and Persevere What do you know, and what do you need to find?

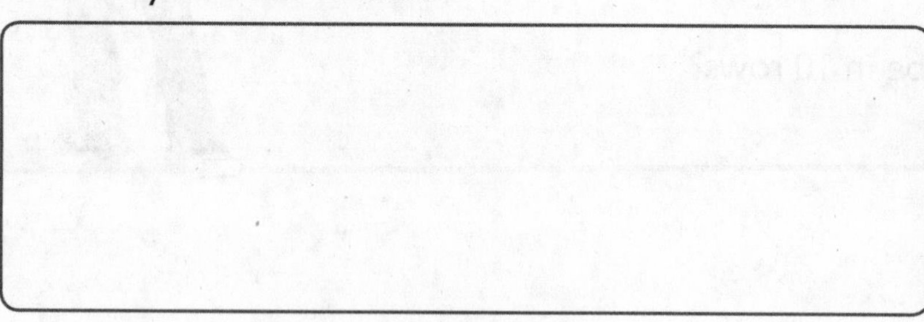

8. Reasoning Complete the table.

Cubes Up or Across	2	3	4	5	6
Total Cubes Needed	3	6			

9. Look For Relationships What pattern can you determine from the table?

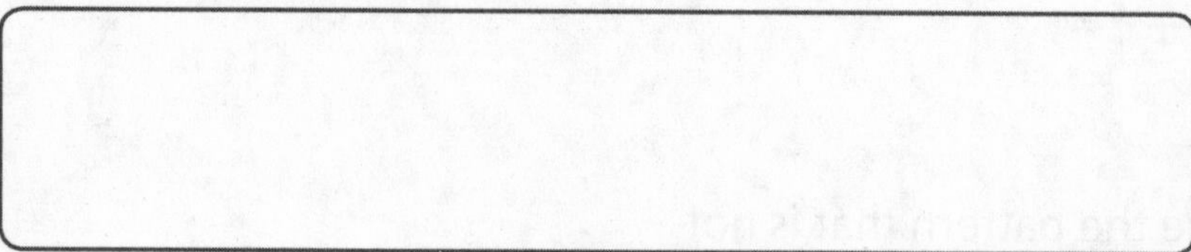

10. Reasoning How many cubes are needed for 7 steps? Write and solve an equation.

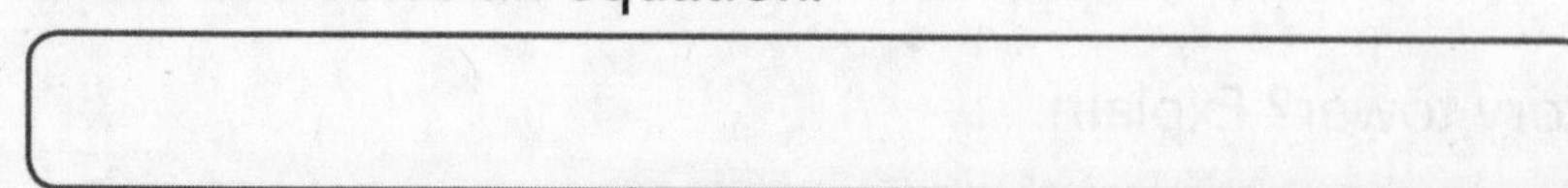

When you look for relationships, you use the rule that describes how objects or values in a pattern are related.

Name ____________________

TOPIC 14 Fluency Practice Activity

Find a partner. Get paper and a pencil. Each partner chooses a different color: light blue or dark blue.

Partner 1 and Partner 2 each point to a black number at the same time. Each partner adds the two numbers.

If the answer is on your color, you get a tally mark. Work until one partner has twelve tally marks.

I can ...
add multi-digit whole numbers.

Content Standard 4.NBT.B.4
Mathematical Practices MP.3, MP.6, MP.7, MP.8

Partner 1

5,150
10,101
11,000
23,231
40,400

49,495	14,245	47,250	30,081
32,326	17,850	40,900	12,000
8,650	11,500	16,951	42,399
26,731	12,100	23,731	7,149
13,601	10,601	19,196	43,900
14,500	20,095	5,650	12,999

Partner 2

500
1,999
3,500
6,850
9,095

Tally Marks for Partner 1	Tally Marks for Partner 2

Vocabulary Review

Glossary

Word List
- equation
- even number
- factor
- multiple
- odd number
- repeating pattern
- rule
- unknown

Understand Vocabulary

1. Circle the term that best describes 28.

even odd equation unknown

2. Circle the term that best completes this sentence:
4 is a ________ of 16.

even odd factor multiple

3. Circle the term that best describes 17.

even odd equation unknown

4. Circle the term that best completes this sentence:
9 is a ________ of 3.

even odd factor multiple

5. Draw a line from each term to its example.

equation	Multiply by 3
repeating pattern	n in $14 \div 2 = n$
rule	▲■▲■
unknown	$4 + 7 = 11$

Use Vocabulary in Writing

6. Use at least 3 terms from the Word List to describe the pattern.
50, 48, 46, 44, 42 …

Name ____________________

Reteaching

Set A pages 521–524

You can use the rule "Subtract 3" to continue the pattern.

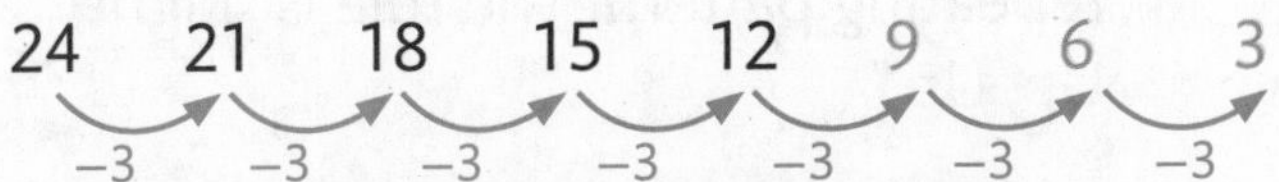

The next three numbers in the pattern are 9, 6, and 3.

A feature of the pattern is all the numbers are multiples of 3.

Another feature is all the numbers in the pattern alternate even, odd.

Remember to check that the numbers in your pattern follow the rule.

Use the rule to continue each pattern. Describe a feature of the pattern.

1. Rule: Add 20
771, 791, 811, ____, ____, ____

2. Rule: Subtract 12
122, 110, 98, ____, ____, ____

Set B pages 525–528

The regular price is twice the sale price. You can use the rule "Divide by 2" to continue the pattern.

DATA

Regular Price	Sale Price
$44	$22
$42	$21
$40	$20
$38	$19
$36	$18
$34	$17

The regular price is a multiple of the sale price, and the sale price is a factor of the regular price.

Remember to look for features of the pattern not described by the rule.

Use the rule to continue each pattern. Describe a feature of the pattern.

1. Rule: Multiply by 18

Trucks	3	5	7	9
Wheels	54	90	126	

2. Rule: Divide by 9

Earned	$81	$207	$540	$900
Saved	$9	$23	$60	

3. Rule: Multiply by 24

Days	5	10	15	20
Hours	120	240	360	

Set C pages 529–532

You can use the rule "Circle, Triangle, Square" to continue the repeating pattern.

You can use the rule to find the 25th shape in the pattern.

25 ÷ 3 = 8 R1.

The pattern will repeat 8 times, then the 1st shape will appear.

The circle is the 25th shape in the pattern.

Remember to use the rule to continue the pattern.

1. **a.** Draw the next three shapes in the repeating pattern. The rule is "Right, Up, Up."

b. Draw the 50th shape in the pattern.

2. **a.** Write the next three numbers in the repeating pattern. The rule is "3, 5, 7, 9."

3, 5, 7, 9, 3, 5, 7, ____, ____, ____

b. What will be the 100th number in the pattern?

Set D pages 533–536

Think about these questions to help you **Look For and Use Structure**.

Thinking Habits

- What patterns can I see and describe?
- How can I use the patterns to solve the problem?
- Can I see expressions and objects in different ways?

Remember to use the rule that describes how objects or values in a pattern are related.

Sam creates a pattern using the rule "Each story has 3 blocks."

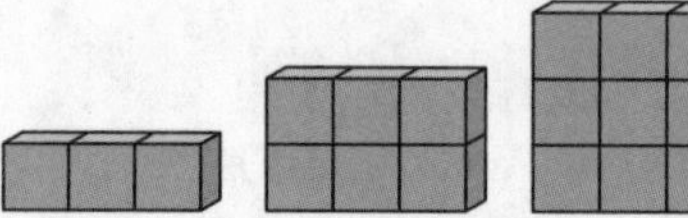

1. Draw the next shape in Sam's pattern.

2. Use the rule to continue Sam's pattern.

Stories	1	2	3	4
Blocks	3	6	9	

3. How many blocks are in the 10th shape in Sam's pattern?

Name ______________________________

1. Football players come out of the tunnel, and their jerseys have the number pattern shown below. They follow the rule "Add 4."

A. What number belongs on the front of the blank jersey? Explain.

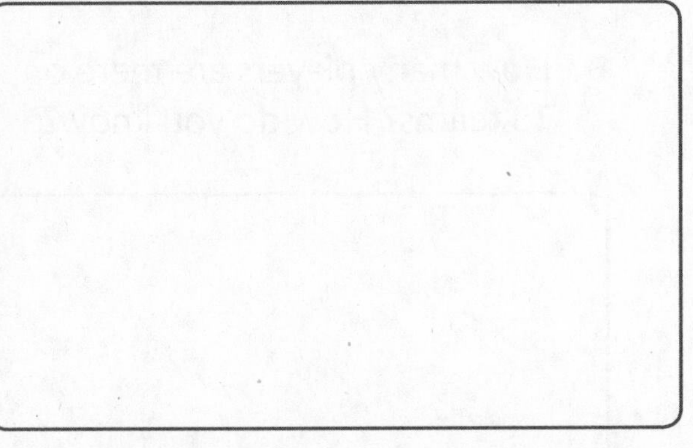

B. Describe two features of the pattern.

2. One dozen eggs is 12 eggs. Two dozen eggs is 24 eggs. Match the number of dozens to the number of eggs. The rule is "Multiply by 12."

	168 eggs	60 eggs	96 eggs	120 eggs
8 dozen	❑	❑	❑	❑
10 dozen	❑	❑	❑	❑
14 dozen	❑	❑	❑	❑
5 dozen	❑	❑	❑	❑

3. Use the rule "Multiply by 6" to continue the pattern. Then describe a feature of the pattern.

Number of Grasshoppers	3	5	7	9
Number of Legs	18	30	42	

4. Use the rule "Divide by 3" to continue the pattern. Then write 4 terms of a different pattern that follows the same rule.

729, 243, 81, ____, ____

5. Nicole arranges her shopping purchases by price. Each item costs \$6 more than the last. The first item costs \$13. The last costs \$61. Her brother John says that the price of each item is an odd number. Is John correct? Find the cost of each item to explain.

6. The rule for the repeating pattern is "5, 7, 2, 8." Write the next three numbers in the pattern. Then tell what will be the 25th number in the pattern. Explain.

5, 7, 2, 8, 5, 7, 2, 8, 5, ____, ____, ____

7. Jackson wrote different patterns for the rule "Subtract 5." Select all of the patterns that he could have written. Then write 4 terms of a different pattern that follows the same rule.

- ☐ 27, 22, 17, 12, 7
- ☐ 5, 10, 15, 20, 25
- ☐ 55, 50, 35, 30, 25
- ☐ 100, 95, 90, 85, 80
- ☐ 75, 65, 55, 45, 35

8. The rule is "Subtract 7." What are the next 3 numbers in the pattern? Describe two features of the pattern.

70, 63, 56, 49, 42, 35

9. The table shows the different number of teams formed by different numbers of players. The rule is "Divide by 8."

Players	24	32	40	72
Teams	3	4	t	9

A. How many teams can be formed with 40 players?

____ teams

B. How many players are there on 13 teams? How do you know?

10. A. Select all the true statements for the repeating pattern. The rule is "Circle, Heart, Triangle."

     ...

- ☐ The next shape is the circle.
- ☐ The circle only repeats twice.
- ☐ The 10th shape is the heart.
- ☐ The 12th shape is the triangle.
- ☐ The circle is the 1st, 4th, 7th, etc. shape.

B. How many triangles are there among the first 22 shapes?

____

Name ____________________

TOPIC 14

Performance Task

Wall Hangings

Michael uses knots to make wall hangings to sell.

1. The **Michael's Basic Wall Hanging** figure shows a simple wall hanging Michael makes by repeating the shapes shown. What is the 16th shape in the repeating pattern? The rule is "Circle, Triangle, Square." Explain.

Michael's Basic Wall Hanging

2. The **Snowflake Design** figure shows a knot Michael likes to use.

Snowflake Design

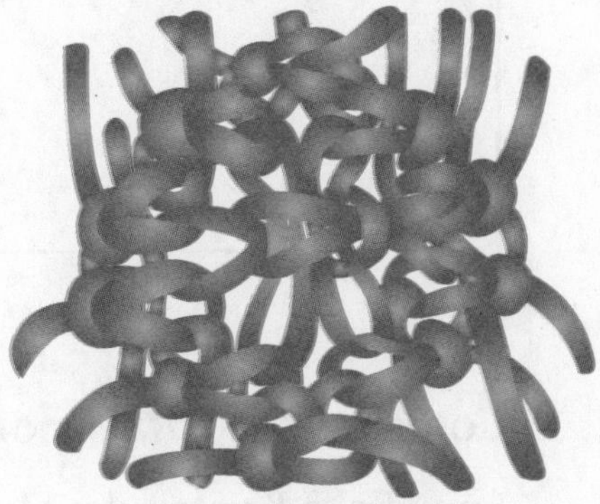

Uses 11 knots

Part A

List the number of knots that Michael uses to form 1 to 6 snowflake designs. The rule is "Add 11."

Part B

Describe a feature of the pattern you listed in Part A that is not part of the rule. Explain why it works.

3. The **Michael's Wall Hanging** figure shows the design of a wall hanging Michael makes using the **Snowflake Design**. Answer the following to find how many knots Michael ties to make a wall hanging with 28 snowflakes.

Michael's Wall Hanging

Each connector uses 3 knots.

Part A

Each column of 4 snowflakes has 4 connectors. There are also 4 connectors between columns. Complete the **Connectors** table using the rule "Add 8 connectors for each column." Describe a feature of the pattern.

Connectors

Columns	1	2	3	4	5
Connectors	4	12			

Part B

Complete the **Total Knots** table using the following rules.

Snowflake Knots rule: Multiply the number of snowflakes by 11.

Connector Knots rule: Multiply the number of connectors from the **Connectors** table by 3.

Total Knots rule: Add the number of snowflake knots and the number of connector knots.

Total Knots

Columns	Snowflakes	Snowflake Knots	Connector Knots	Total Knots
1	4	44	12	56
2	8			
3	12			
4	16			
5	20			

TOPIC 15

Geometric Measurement: Understand Concepts of Angles and Angle Measurement

Essential Questions: What are some common geometric terms? How can you measure angles?

Digital Resources

Interactive Student Edition · Activity · Visual Learning · Video · Practice · Assessment · Games · Tools · Glossary

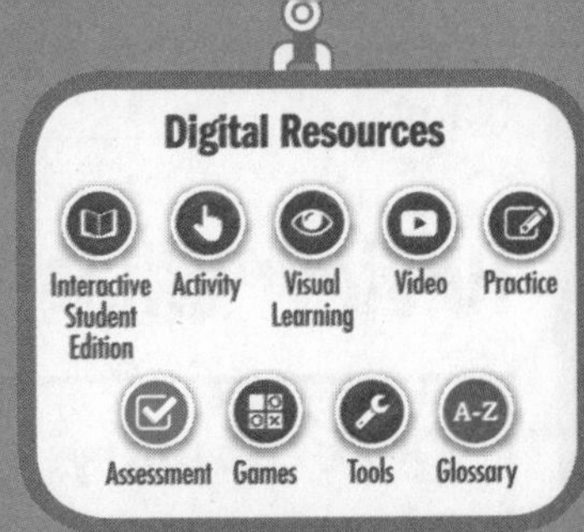

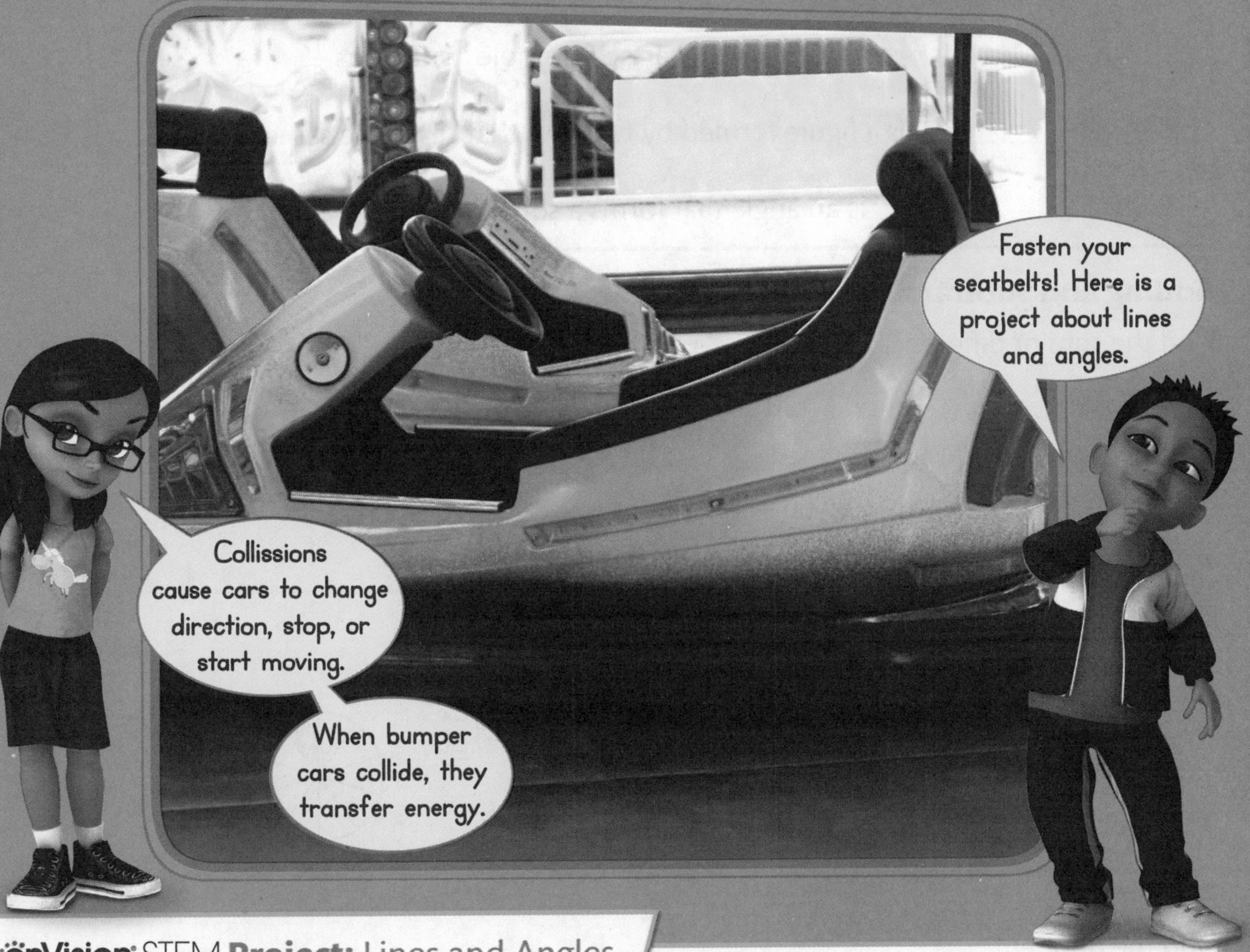

Fasten your seatbelts! Here is a project about lines and angles.
Collissions cause cars to change direction, stop, or start moving.
When bumper cars collide, they transfer energy.

enVision STEM Project: Lines and Angles

Do Research Use the Internet or other sources to research the area of the world's largest bumper car floor. Find where it is located and when it was built.

Journal: Write a Report Include what you found. Also in your report:

- Draw a diagram of a bumper car collision. Use an angle to show how a car might change direction after it collides with something. Measure and label the angle you drew.
- Describe your angle using some of the vocabulary terms in this topic.

Name ______________________________

Review What You Know

Vocabulary

Choose the best term from the box. Write it on the blank.

- angle
- right angle
- line
- sixth

1. A(n) __________ is one of 6 equal parts of a whole, written as $\frac{1}{6}$.

2. A(n) __________ is a figure formed by two rays that share the same endpoint.

3. A(n) __________ is an angle that forms a square corner.

Adding and Subtracting

Find the sum or difference.

4. 45 + 90 **5.** 120 − 45 **6.** 30 + 150

7. 180 − 135 **8.** 60 + 120 **9.** 90 − 45

Parts of a Whole

Tell the fraction that represents the shaded part of the whole.

10. 

11. 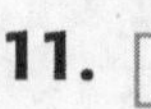 

12. 

Dividing

Find the quotient.

13. 360 ÷ 6 **14.** 180 ÷ 9 **15.** 360 ÷ 4

Problem Solving

16. Make Sense and Persevere Gary has $4. Mary has twice as many dollars as Gary. Larry has 4 fewer dollars than Mary. How much money do Gary, Mary, and Larry have in all?

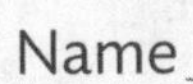

Name ______________________

Pick a Project

PROJECT 15A

Can you find angles in stringed instruments?

Project: Make a Stringed Instrument

PROJECT 15B

How are angles important in origami?

Project: Present an Origami Animal

PROJECT 15C

How are angles formed by airplane paths?

Project: Trace a Flight Plan

3-ACT MATH PREVIEW

Math Modeling

Game of Angles

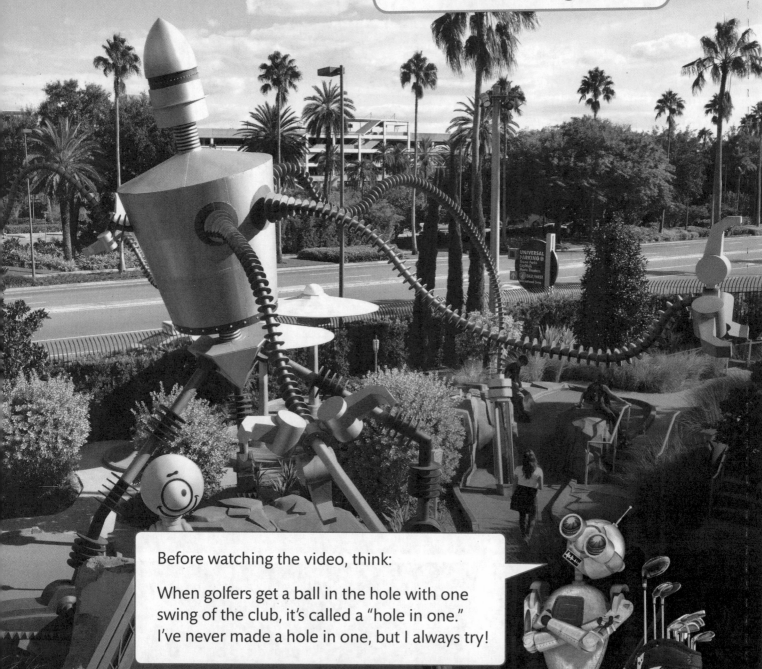

Before watching the video, think:

When golfers get a ball in the hole with one swing of the club, it's called a "hole in one." I've never made a hole in one, but I always try!

I can ...

model with math to solve a problem that involves measuring angles and computing with angle measures.

Mathematical Practices MP.4 Also MP.1, MP.6

Content Standards 4.MD.C.6 Also 4.MD.C.5, 4.G.A.1

Name ______________________________ Activity

Solve & Share

Lesson 15-1
Lines, Rays, and Angles

I can ...
recognize and draw lines, rays, and different types of angles.

Content Standards 4.G.A.1 Also 4.MD.C.5a
Mathematical Practices MP.2, MP.6, MP.7

A right angle forms a square corner, like the one shown below. Find examples of right angles in your classroom. Draw two angles that are open less than the right angle. ***Solve this problem any way you choose.***

The closer the sides of an angle, the smaller the angle measure. *Show your work in the space below!*

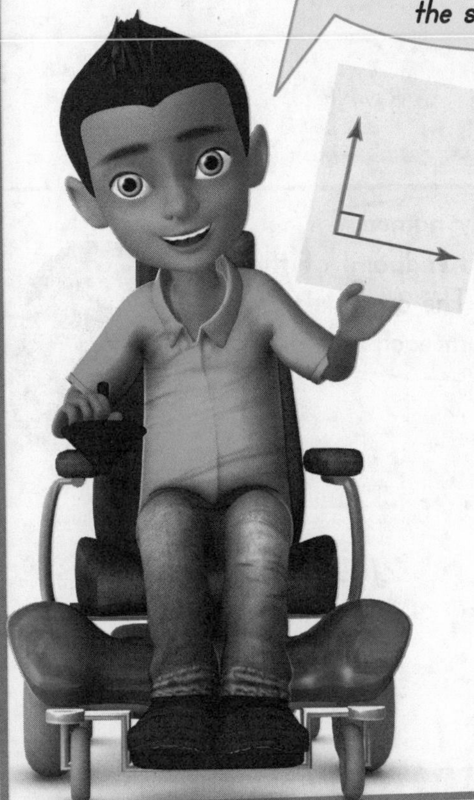

Look Back! Reasoning Draw an angle that is open more than a right angle.

What Are Some Common Geometric Terms?

Visual Learning Bridge

A

Point, line, line segment, ray, right angle, acute angle, obtuse angle, and straight angle are common geometric terms.

Lines and parts of lines are named for their points. A ray is named with its endpoint first.

Geometric Term	Example	Label	What You Say
A point is an exact location in space.	Z	Point Z	Point Z
A line is a straight path of points that goes on and on in opposite directions.	A B	$\overleftrightarrow{AB}$	Line AB
A line segment is a part of a line with two endpoints.	G R	$\overline{GR}$	Line Segment GR
A ray is a part of a line that has one endpoint and continues on forever in one direction.	N P	$\overrightarrow{NP}$	Ray NP

B

An angle is formed by two rays that have the same endpoint.

Angles are usually named with 3 letters. The shared endpoint of the rays is the center letter. The other letters represent points from each ray.

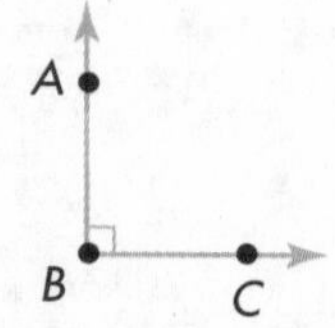

$\angle ABC$ is a right angle. A right angle forms a square corner.

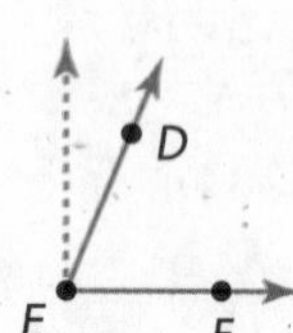

$\angle DEF$ is an acute angle. An acute angle is open less than a right angle.

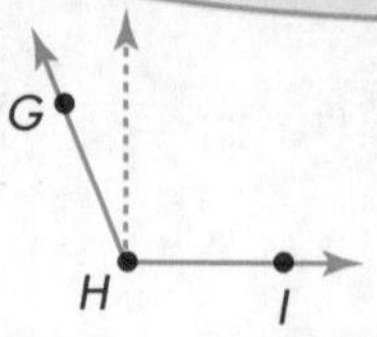

$\angle GHI$ is an obtuse angle. An obtuse angle is open more than a right angle but less than a straight angle.

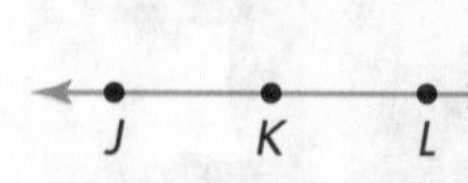

$\angle JKL$ is a straight angle. A straight angle forms a straight line.

Convince Me! **Look for Relationships** Complete each figure to show the given angle.

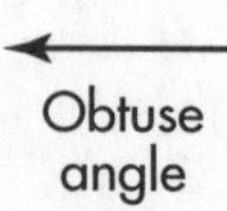

Obtuse angle

Straight angle

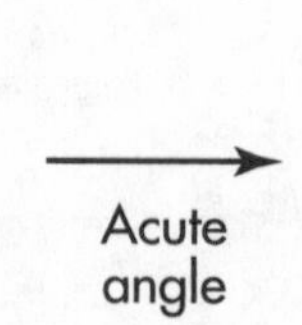

Acute angle

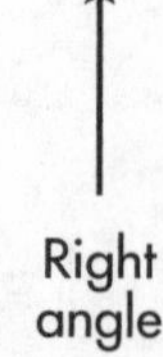

Right angle

Name ___________________________

Practice Tools Assessment

Guided Practice

Do You Understand?

1. What geometric term describes a part of a line that has one endpoint? Draw an example.

2. What geometric term describes a part of a line that has two endpoints? Draw an example.

3. What geometric term describes an angle that forms a square corner? Draw an example.

Do You Know How?

For **4–7**, use geometric terms to describe what is shown.

4. P X

5.

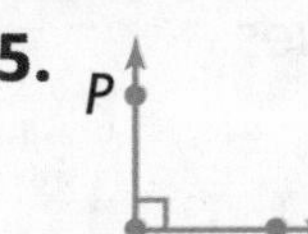

6. B Y

7.

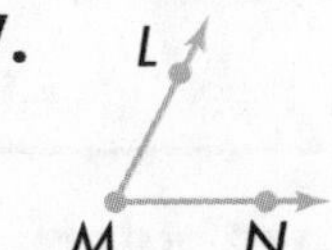

Independent Practice

For **8–11**, use geometric terms to describe what is shown.

8. H O S

9. B D

10. X Y

11. P S T

For **12–15**, draw the geometric figure for each term.

12. Line segment

13. Point

14. Ray

15. Line

Problem Solving

For **16–18**, use the map of Nevada. Write the geometric term that best fits each description. Draw an example.

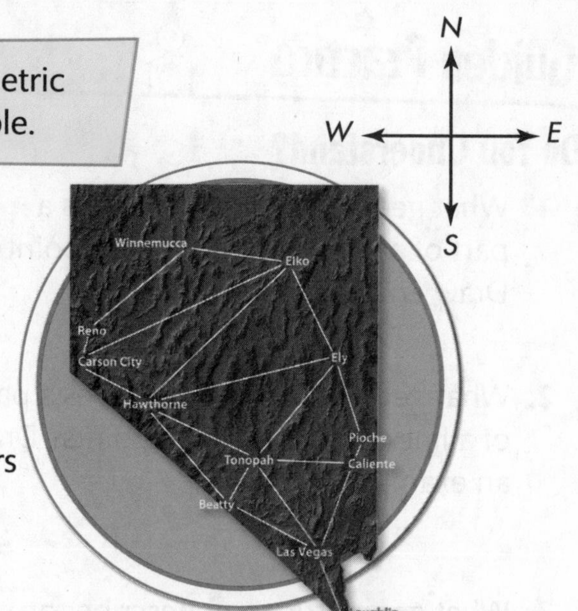

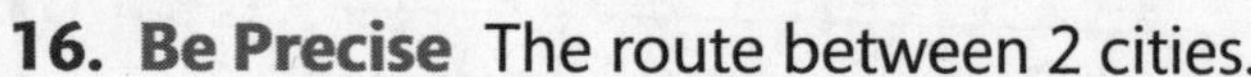

16. Be Precise The route between 2 cities.

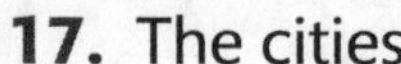

17. The cities

18. The corner formed by the north and west borders

19. Ⓐ-Ⓩ **Vocabulary** Write a definition for *right angle*. Draw a right angle. Give 3 examples of right angles in the classroom.

20. Higher Order Thinking Nina says she can make a right angle with an acute angle and an obtuse angle that have a common ray. Is Nina correct? Draw a picture and explain.

Assessment Practice

21. Which geometric term describes ∠*HJK*?

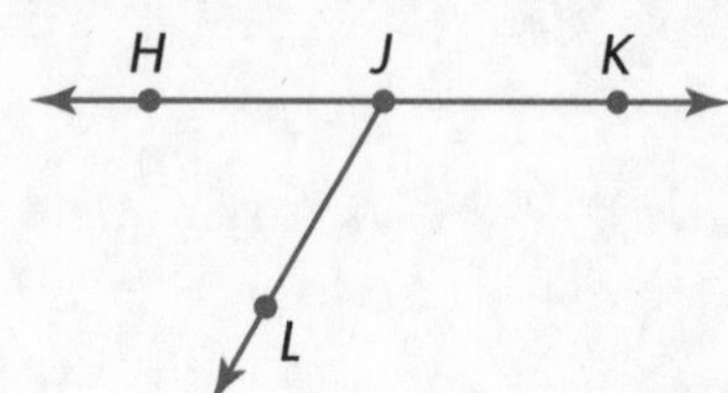

Ⓐ Acute angle
Ⓑ Obtuse angle
Ⓒ Right angle
Ⓓ Straight angle

22. Lisa drew 2 rays that share an endpoint. Which of the following is Lisa's drawing?

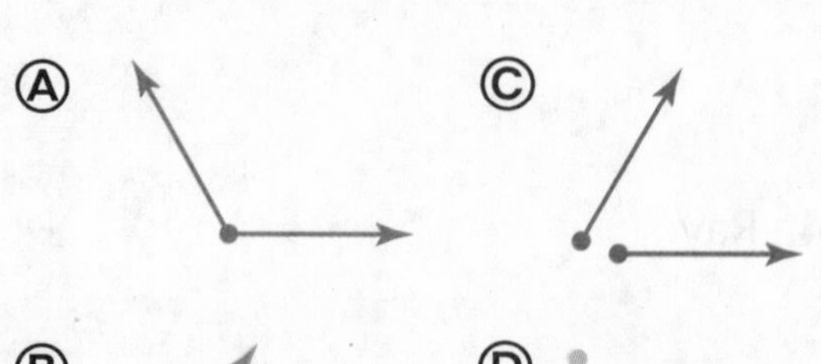

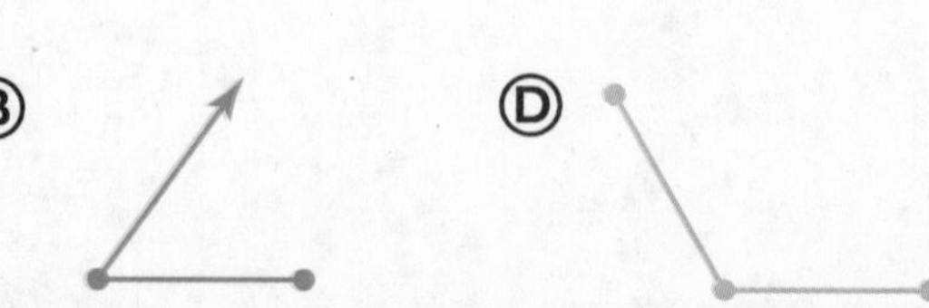

Name ______________________

Lesson 15-2
Understand Angles and Unit Angles

I can ...
use what I know about fractions to measure angles.

Content Standards 4.MD.C.5a Also 4.NF.A.1, 4.NF.B.3b
Mathematical Practices MP.1, MP.3

Solve & Share

If a clock shows it is 3 o'clock, how could you describe the smaller angle made by the two hands of the clock? ***Solve this problem any way you choose.***

You can make sense of the problem by using what you know about acute, right, obtuse, and straight angles. *Show your work in the space below!*

Look Back! At 3 o'clock, what two fractions do the hands divide the clock into?

What Is the Unit Used to Measure Angles?

A

An angle is measured with units called degrees. An angle that turns through $\frac{1}{360}$ of a circle is called a unit angle. How can you determine the angle measure of a right angle and the angles that turn through $\frac{1}{6}$ and $\frac{2}{6}$ of a circle?

You measure length in inches, area in square centimeters, and capacity in ounces. You measure an angle in degrees, °. A full circle has an angle measure of 360°.

$1° = \frac{1}{360}$ of a circle

B Divide to find the angle measure of a right angle.

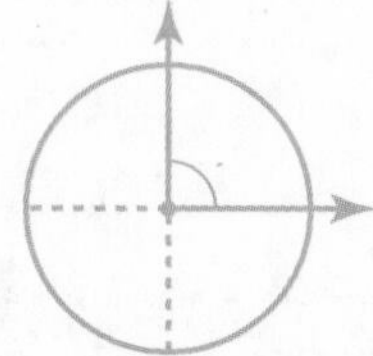

Right angles divide a circle into 4 equal parts.

$360° \div 4 = 90°$

The angle measure of a right angle is 90°.

C Divide to find the measure of an angle that turns through $\frac{1}{6}$ of a circle.

$\frac{1}{6}$ of a circle is one part of the circle that is divided into 6 equal parts.

$360° \div 6 = 60°$

The angle measure is 60°.

D Add to find the measure of an angle that turns through $\frac{2}{6}$ of a circle.

$\frac{1}{6} = 60°$ $\frac{2}{6} = ?$

Remember $\frac{2}{6} = \frac{1}{6} + \frac{1}{6}$.

Add to calculate the measure of $\frac{2}{6}$ of a circle.

$60° + 60° = 120°$

The angle measure of $\frac{2}{6}$ of a circle is 120°.

Convince Me! **Critique Reasoning** Susan thinks the measure of angle *B* is greater than the measure of angle *A*. Do you agree? Explain.

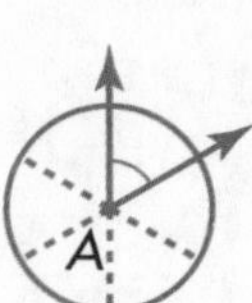

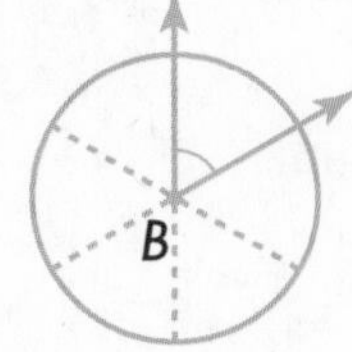

Name ____

Another Example!

Find the fraction of a circle that an angle with a measure of 45° turns through.

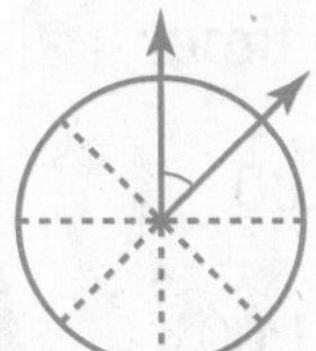

A 45° angle turns through $\frac{45}{360}$ of a circle.

$45° \times 8 = 360°$, so 45° is $\frac{1}{8}$ of 360°.

One 45° angle is $\frac{1}{8}$ of a circle.

$45° = \frac{1}{8}$ of a 360° circle

Guided Practice

Do You Understand?

1. What fraction of the circle does a 120° angle turn through?

2. Mike cuts a pie into 4 equal pieces. What is the angle measure of each piece? Write and solve an equation.

Do You Know How?

3. A circle is divided into 9 equal parts. What is the angle measure of one of those parts?

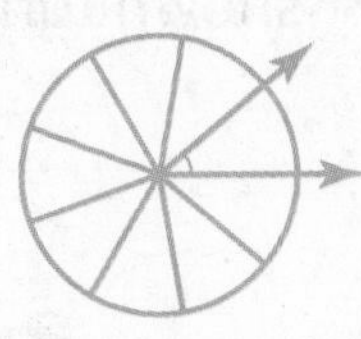

4. An angle turns through $\frac{2}{8}$ of the circle. What is the measure of this angle?

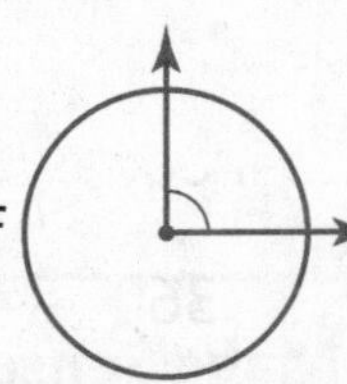

Independent Practice

For **5–8**, find the measure of each angle.

5. The angle turns through $\frac{1}{5}$ of the circle.

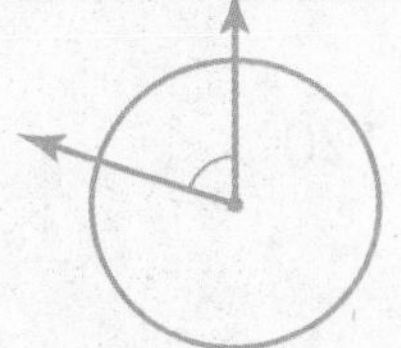

6. The angle turns through $\frac{3}{8}$ of the circle.

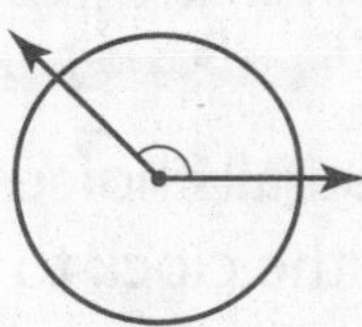

7. The angle turns through $\frac{2}{5}$ of the circle.

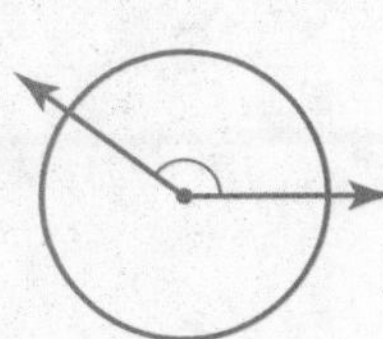

8. The angle turns through $\frac{2}{6}$ of the circle.

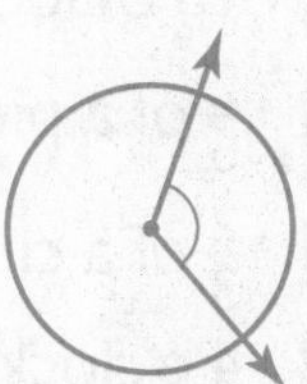

Problem Solving

9. Use the clock to find the measure of the smaller angle formed by the hands at each time.

a. 3:00

b. 11:00

c. 2:00

10. Algebra Jacey wrote an equation to find an angle measure. What do the variables *a* and *b* represent in Jacey's equation?
$360° \div a = b$

11. enVision® STEM A mirror can be used to reflect a beam of light at an angle. What fraction of a circle would the angle shown turn through?

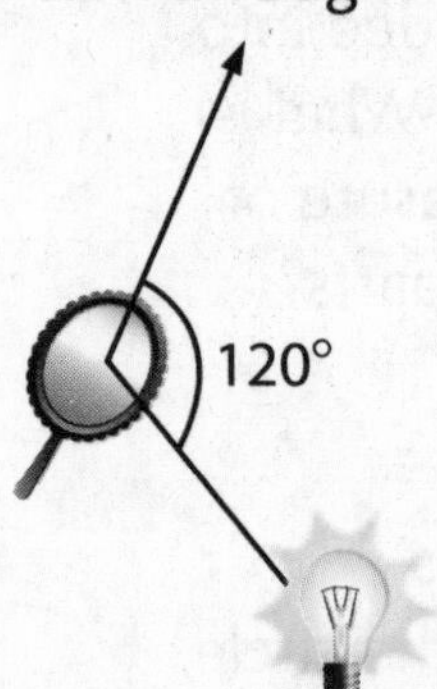

12. Malik paid \$32.37 for three books. One book cost \$16.59. The second book cost \$4.27. How much did the third book cost? Use bills and coins to solve.

\$32.37

\$16.59	\$4.27	*b*

13. Make Sense and Persevere A pie was cut into equal parts. Four pieces of the pie were eaten. The 5 pieces that remained created an angle that measured 200°. What was the angle measure of one piece of pie?

14. Higher Order Thinking Jake cut a round gelatin dessert into 8 equal pieces. Five of the pieces were eaten. What is the angle measure of the dessert that was left?

Assessment Practice

15. Select all choices that show an angle measure of 120°. Use the clock to help.

- ☐ 10 o'clock
- ☐ $\frac{2}{6}$ of a pie
- ☐ $\frac{2}{3}$ of a circle
- ☐ 4 o'clock
- ☐ 8 o'clock

Name ______________________________________

Lesson 15-3
Measure with Unit Angles

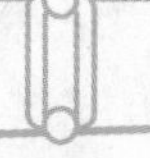

I can ...
use angles I know to measure angles I do not know.

Content Standards 4.MD.C.5b Also 4.MD.C.5a
Mathematical Practices MP.1, MP.5, MP.8

Solve & Share The smaller angles on the tan pattern block shown each measure 30°. How can you use the angles on the pattern block to determine the measure of the angle below? ***Solve this problem any way you choose.***

You can make sense and persevere in solving the problem. *Show your work in the space below!*

Look Back! Two right angles make a straight angle. How many 45° angles form a straight angle? Explain.

Essential Question

How Can You Measure Angles?

Visual Learning Bridge

A

Holly traced around a trapezoid pattern block. She wants to find the measure of the angle formed shown to the right. What can Holly use to measure the angle?

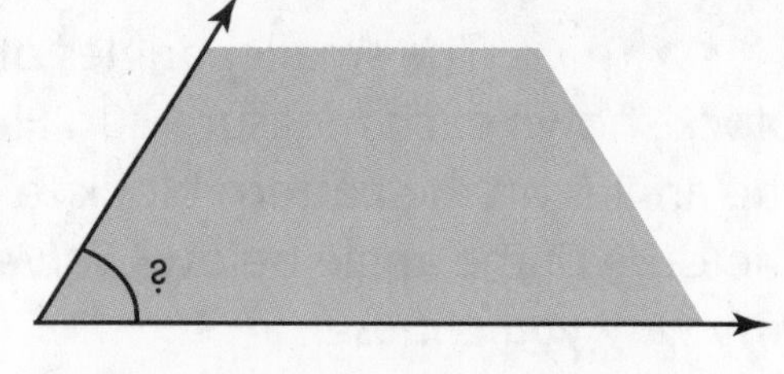

The measure of a unit angle is 1 degree. Just like adding inches + inches, you can add degrees + degrees. So $5° = 1° + 1° + 1° + 1° + 1°$ or $5 \times 1°$.

B

Use an angle you know to find the measure of another angle.

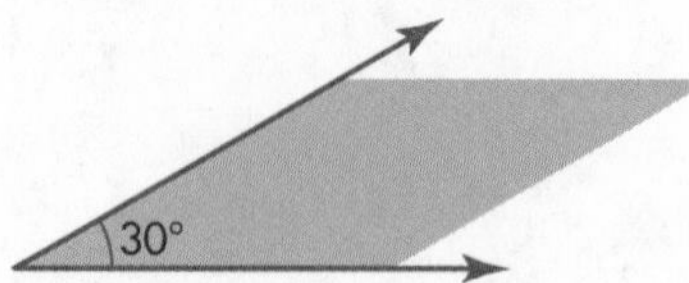

The smaller angle of the tan pattern block measures 30°.

A 30-degree angle turns through 30 one-degree angles.

C

The angle of the trapezoid pattern block is equal to 2 of the smaller angles of the tan pattern block. Each smaller angle is 30°.

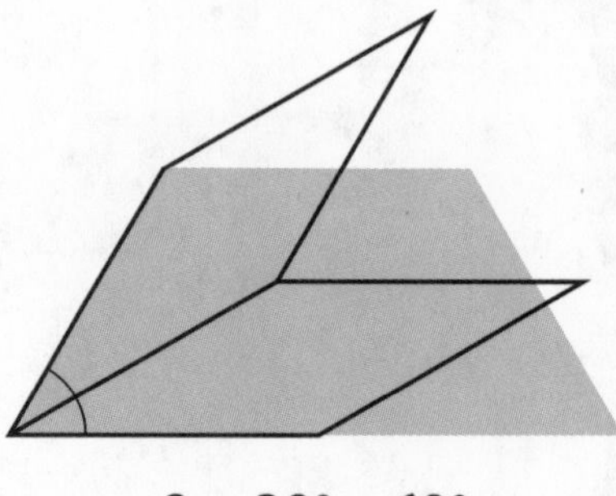

$2 \times 30° = 60°$

The measure of the trapezoid angle is 60°.

A 60-degree angle turns through 60 one-degree angles.

Convince Me! **Generalize** What do you notice about the number of one-degree angles in an angle measure?

Name

Practice Tools Assessment

Guided Practice

Do You Understand?

1. How many 30° angles are in a 180° angle? Explain.

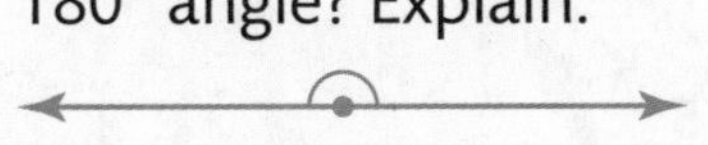

2. How many 15° angles are in a 180° angle? Use your answer to Exercise 1 to explain.

Do You Know How?

For **3–4**, use angles you know to find the measure of each angle. Explain how the angles in the square can help.

3.

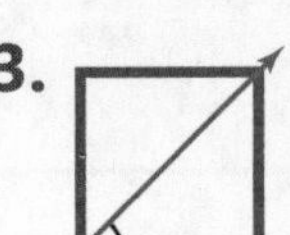

4.

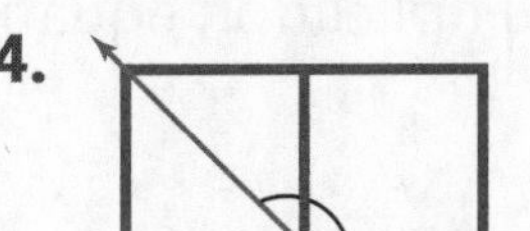

Independent Practice

For **5–13**, find the measure of each angle. Use pattern blocks to help.

5.

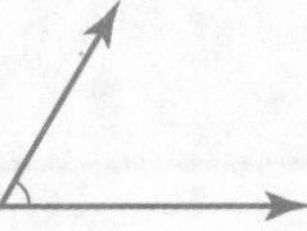

6.

7.

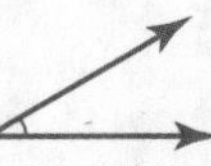

8.

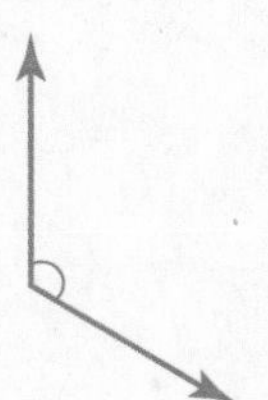

9.

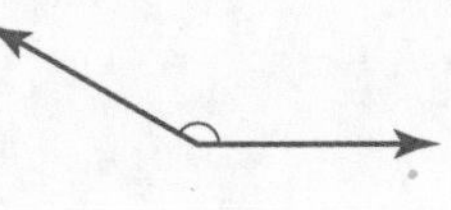

10.

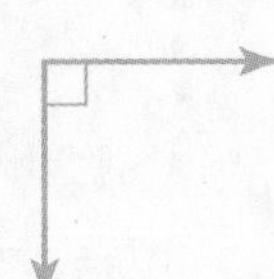

11.

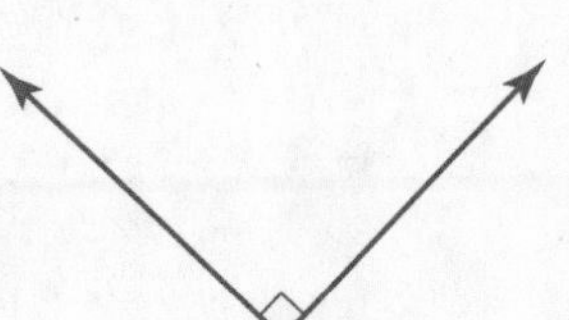

12.

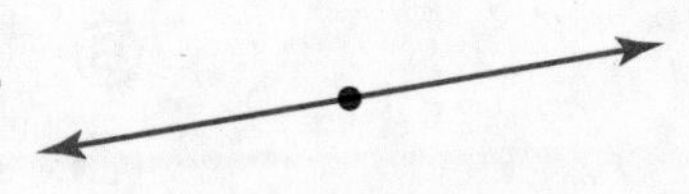

13.

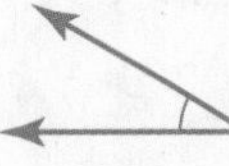

Problem Solving

14. Use Appropriate Tools What is the measure of the angle of the yellow hexagon pattern block?

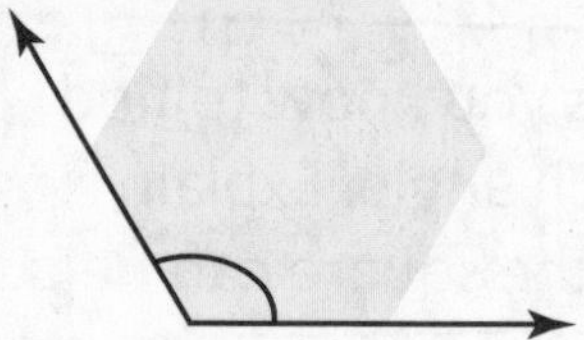

15. What is the measure of the smaller angle formed by the clock hands when it is 5:00?

16. How many 30° angles are in a circle? Write and solve a multiplication equation to explain.

17. How many unit angles make up the smaller angle formed by the hands of a clock when it is 3:00? Explain.

18. Veronica purchases a rug with a length of 16 feet and a width of 4 feet. One fourth of the rug is purple and the rest is blue. What is the area of the blue part of the rug?

19. Higher Order Thinking The hands of a clock form a 120° angle. Name two different times it could be.

Assessment Practice

20. The clock reads 9:00. What is the angle measure?

Ⓐ 90°
Ⓑ 180°
Ⓒ 270°
Ⓓ 360°

21. How many 60° angles are in 360° angle?

Ⓐ 3
Ⓑ 6
Ⓒ 10
Ⓓ 12

Name ______________________________ Activity

Lesson 15-4

Measure and Draw Angles

I can ...

use a protractor to measure and draw angles.

Content Standards 4.MD.C.6 Also 4.MD.C.5b
Mathematical Practices MP.3, MP.5, MP.6

Solve & Share

Find the measure of ∠ABC. ***Solve this problem any way you choose.***

A protractor can help you measure and draw angles. The angle measures are positioned around the curved edge in a double number line. Which number line should be read to make sense in this problem?

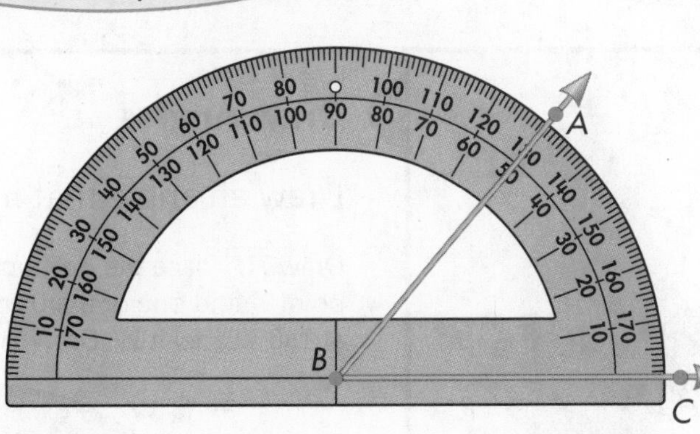

Look Back! Use Appropriate Tools Use the protractor to draw an angle that measures 110°.

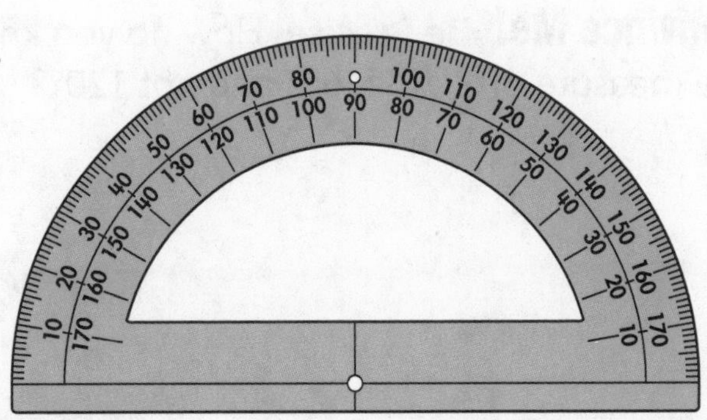

Essential Question

How Do You Use a Protractor?

Visual Learning Bridge

A

A protractor is a tool that is used to measure and draw angles. A partially folded crane is shown at the right. Measure ∠PQR.

The angle, ∠PQR, can also be written as ∠RQP.

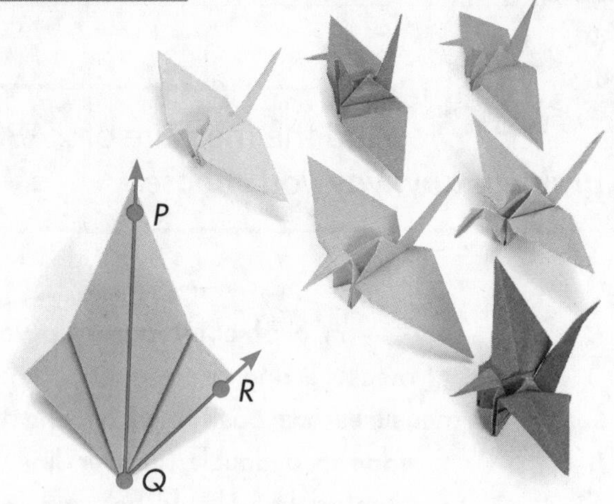

B

Measure Angles

Measure ∠PQR.

Place the protractor's center on the angle's vertex, Q. Place one of the 0° marks on $\overrightarrow{QR}$. Read the measure where $\overrightarrow{QP}$ crosses the protractor. If the angle is acute, use the lesser number. If the angle is obtuse, use the greater number.

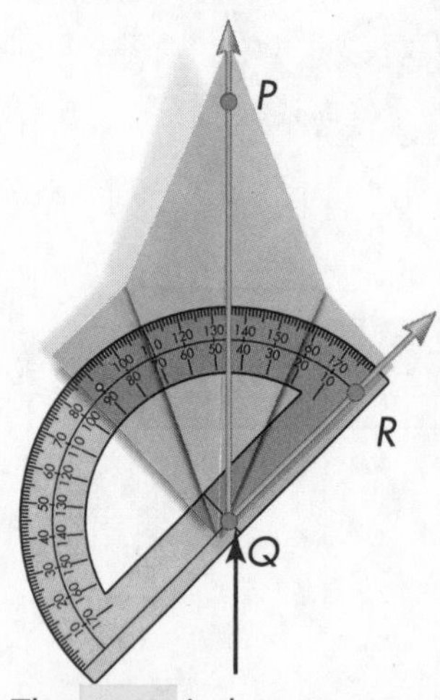

The vertex is the common endpoint of the rays that form the angle.

The measure of ∠PQR is 45°.

C

Draw Angles

Draw an angle that measures 130°.

Draw $\overrightarrow{TU}$. Place the protractor so the center is over point T, and one of the 0° marks is on $\overrightarrow{TU}$. Place a point at 130°. Label it W. Draw $\overrightarrow{TW}$.

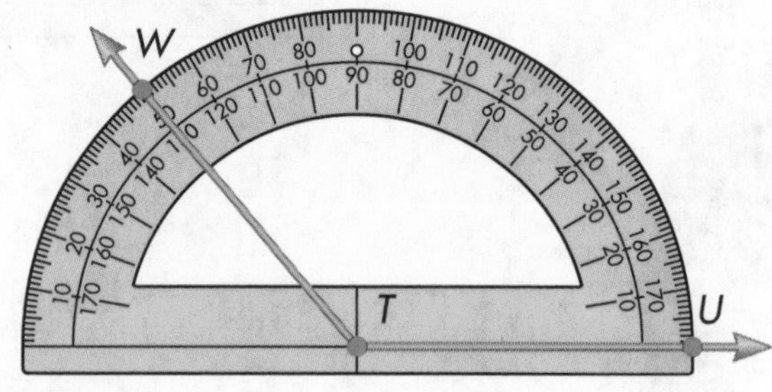

The measure of ∠WTU is 130°.

Convince Me! **Be Precise** How do you know the measure of ∠UTS is 60° and not 120°?

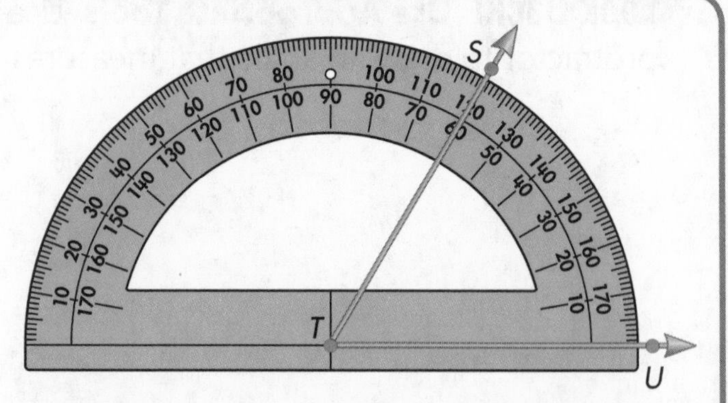

Name ______________________________

Guided Practice

Do You Understand?

1. What is the angle measure of a straight line?

2. What are the vertex and rays of ∠*ABC*? Explain.

Do You Know How?

For **3–4**, use a protractor to measure each angle.

3.

4.

For **5–6**, use a protractor to draw each angle.

5. 110°

6. 50°

Independent Practice

For **7–14**, measure each angle. Tell if each angle is acute, right, or obtuse.

Remember an acute angle is less than 90° and an obtuse angle is greater than 90° but less than 180°.

7.

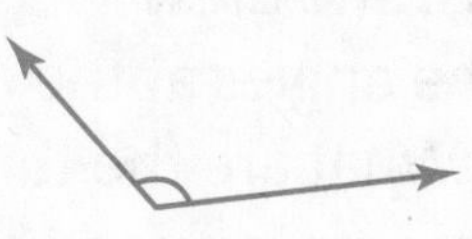

8.

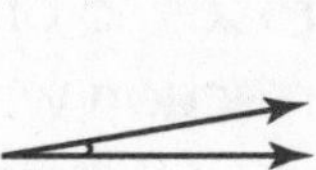

9.

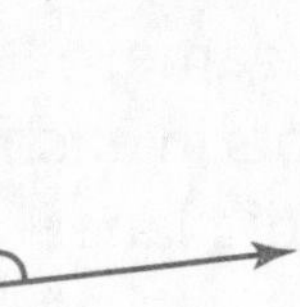

10.

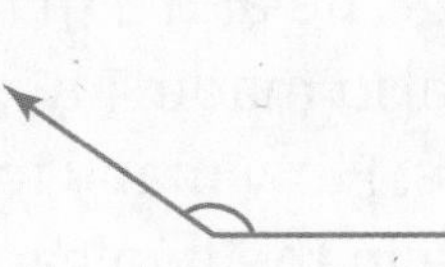

11.

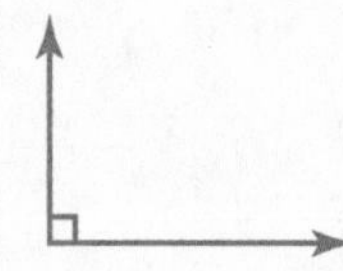

12.

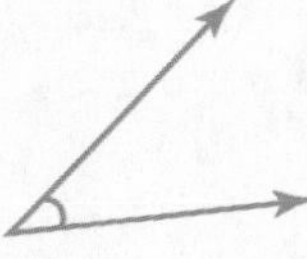

13.

14.

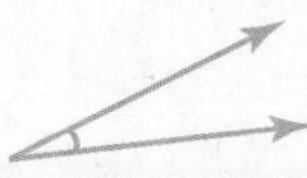

For **15–18**, use a protractor to draw an angle for each measure.

15. 140°

16. 180°

17. 65°

18. 25°

Problem Solving

19. Measure all the angles created by the intersection of Main Street and Pleasant Street. Explain how you measured.

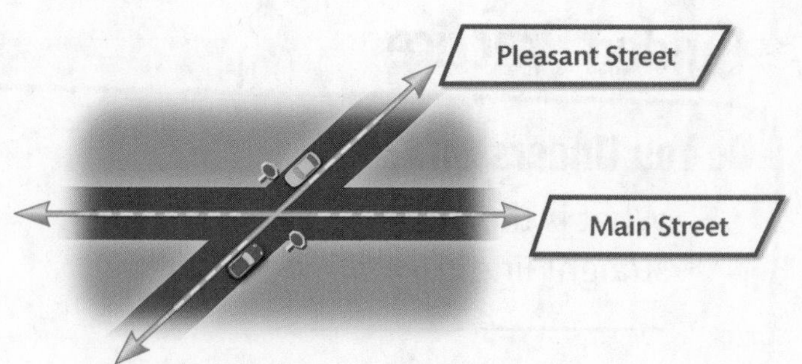

20. Use a protractor to find the measure of the angle, then use one of the angle's rays to draw a right angle. Find the measure of the the angle that is **NOT** a right angle.

21. **Critique Reasoning** Gail and 3 friends share half a pie. Each piece of pie is the same size. Gail believes each piece of pie has an angle measure of 25°. Is Gail correct? Explain.

22. Janet made 5 three-point shots in her first game and 3 in her second game. She also made 4 two-point shots in each game. How many total points did Janet score in the two games?

23. **Higher Order Thinking** Maya designed two intersecting roads. She drew the roads so one of the angles at the intersection was 35°. What are the three other angle measurements formed by the intersection?

Assessment Practice

24. Find the measure of the angle shown.

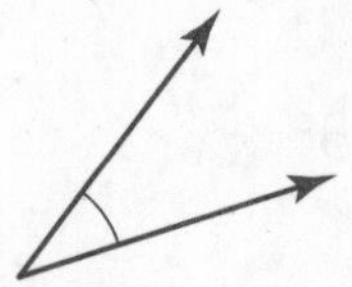

25. Find the measure of the angle shown.

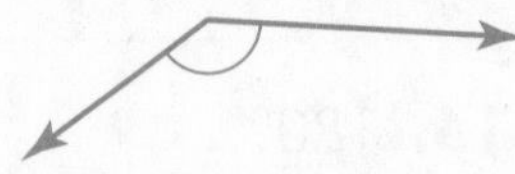

Name ______________________ Activity

Lesson 15-5
Add and Subtract Angle Measures

I can ...
use addition and subtraction to solve problems with unknown angle measures.

Content Standards 4.MD.C.7 Also 4.NBT.B.4
Mathematical Practices MP.1, MP.4, MP.7

Solve & Share

Draw $\overrightarrow{BC}$ that divides $\angle ABD$ into two smaller angles. Measure each angle. ***Solve this problem any way you choose.***

You can look for relationships with the three angles you measure. How is the sum of the measures of the two smaller angles related to the measure of the larger angle?

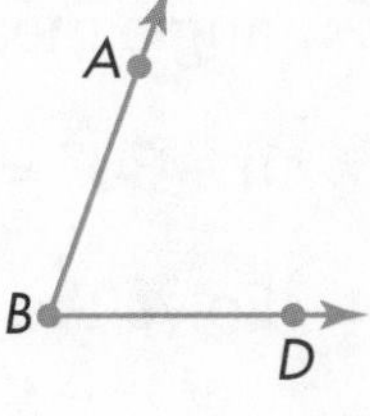

Look Back! How can you relate the measures of the two smaller angles to the measure of the larger angle above using an equation?

How Can You Add and Subtract to Find Unknown Angle Measures?

Visual Learning Bridge

A

Elinor designs wings for biplanes. First she draws a right angle, ∠ABC. Then she draws $\overrightarrow{BE}$. She finds ∠EBC measures 30°. How can Elinor find the measure of ∠ABE without using a protractor?

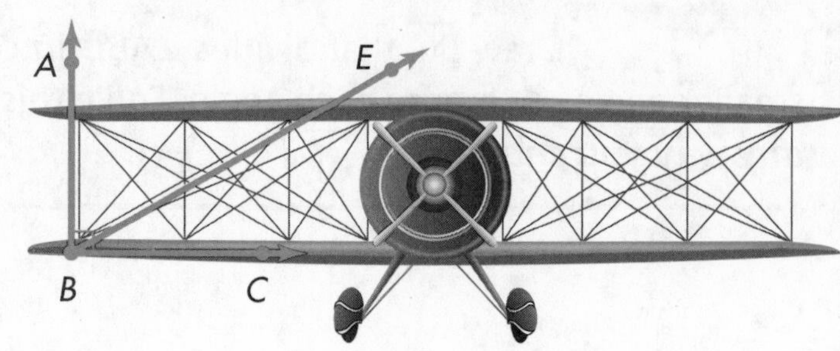

∠ABC is decomposed into two non-overlapping parts.

B

∠EBC and ∠ABE do not overlap, so the measure of right ∠ABC is equal to the sum of the measures of its parts.

The measure of ∠ABC equals the measure of ∠ABE plus the measure of ∠EBC.

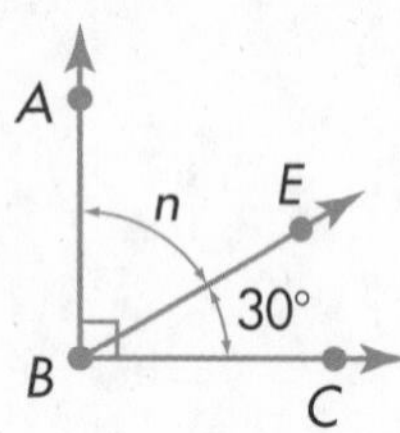

C

Write an equation to determine the missing angle measure.

$n + 30° = 90°$

Solve the equation.

$n = 90° - 30°$
$n = 60°$

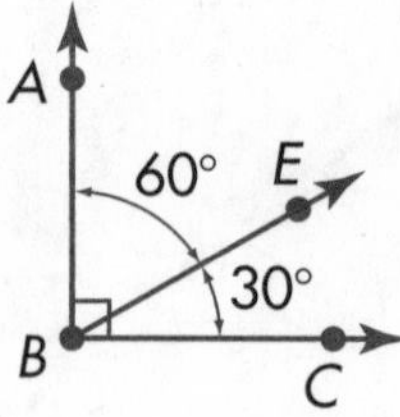

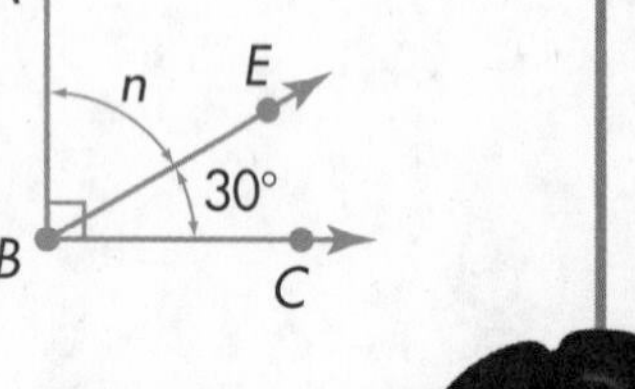

All right angles measure 90°.

The measure of ∠ABE is 60°.

Convince Me! **Make Sense and Persevere** ∠ABD is a straight angle. What is the measure of ∠ABE if the measure of ∠DBC is 115° and the measure of ∠CBE is 20°? How did you decide? Write and solve an equation.

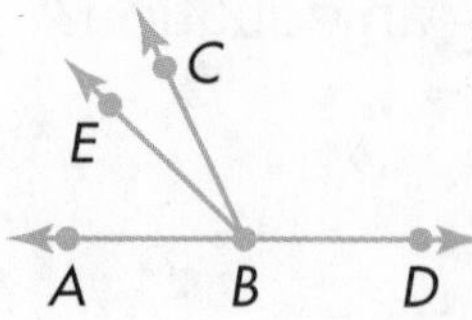

Name ______________________________

Guided Practice

Do You Understand?

1. Use the information below to draw and label a diagram.
$\angle PQR$ measures 45°.
$\angle RQS$ measures 40°.
$\angle PQR$ and $\angle RQS$ do not overlap.
Write and solve an equation to find the measure of $\angle PQS$.

Do You Know How?

For **2–3**, use the diagram to the right of each exercise. Write and solve an equation to find the missing angle measure.

2. What is the measure of $\angle EBC$ if $\angle ABE$ measures 20°?

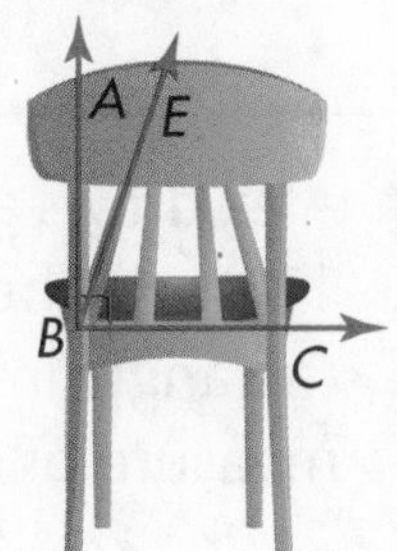

3. What is the measure of $\angle AEB$ if $\angle CEB$ measures 68°?

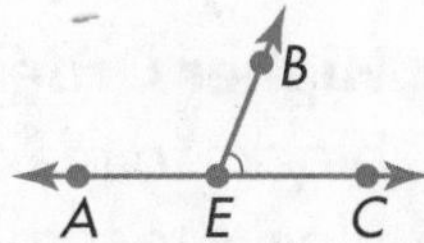

Independent Practice

For **4–7**, use the diagram to the right. Write and solve an addition or subtraction equation to find the missing angle measure.

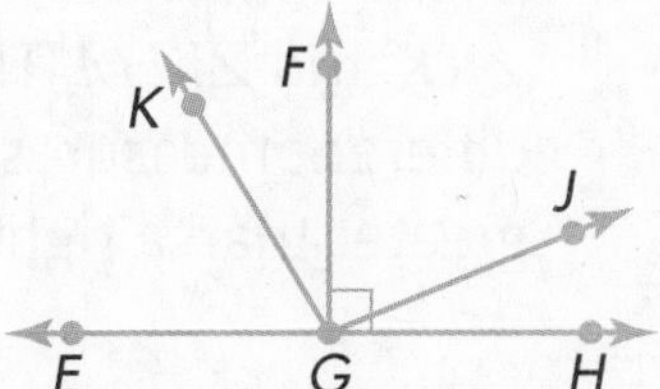

4. What is the measure of $\angle FGJ$ if $\angle JGH$ measures 22°?

5. What is the measure of $\angle KGF$ if $\angle EGK$ measures 59°?

6. Use the angle measures you know to write an equation to find the angle measure of $\angle EGH$. What kind of angle is $\angle EGH$?

7. Which two non-overlapping angles that share a ray make an obtuse angle? Use addition to explain.

Problem Solving

8. Shane says a straight angle always has 180° degrees. Is Shane correct? Explain.

9. **Model with Math** Talla earns 85¢ for cans she recycles. If she gets a nickel for each can, how many cans does Talla recycle? Draw a bar diagram to represent how to solve the problem.

10. Alex draws an angle that measures 110°. He then draws a ray that divides the angle into 2 equal parts. What is the measure of each smaller angle?

11. Six angles share a vertex. Each of the angles has the same measure. The sum of the measures of the angles is 330°. What is the measure of one angle?

12. **Higher Order Thinking** Li uses pattern blocks to make a design. He puts 5 pattern blocks together, as shown in the diagram. The measure of $\angle LJK$ is 30°. Name all the 60° angles shown that have point J as a vertex.

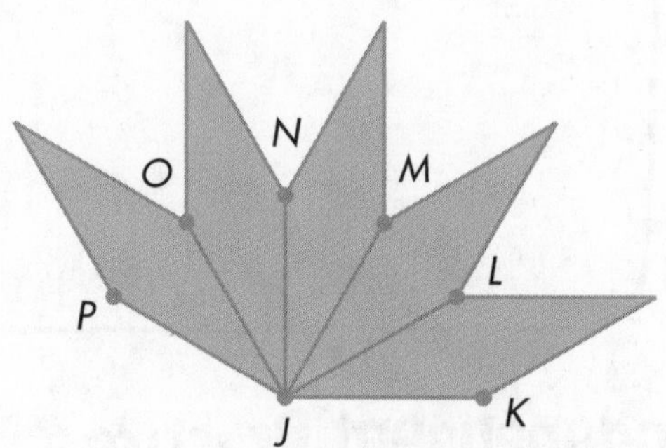

Assessment Practice

13. Carla drew two acute non-overlapping angles that share a ray and labeled them $\angle JLK$ and $\angle KLM$. The two angles have different measures. Carla says $\angle JLM$ is greater than a right angle.

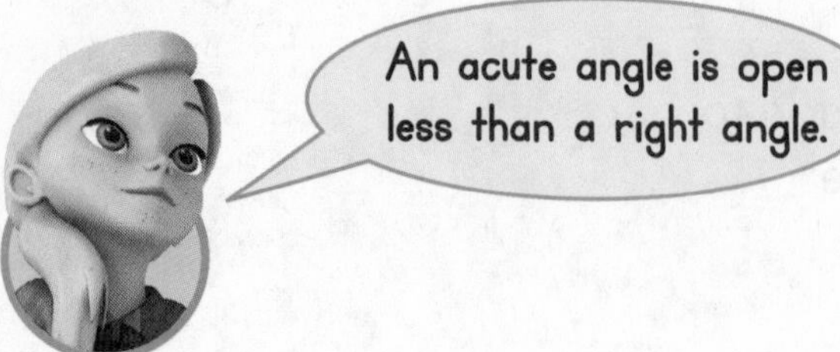

An acute angle is open
less than a right angle.

Part A

Is it possible for Carla to be correct? Write to explain.

Part B

Write an equation showing one possible sum for Carla's angles.

Name ____________________

Problem Solving

Lesson 15-6

Use Appropriate Tools

I can ...

use appropriate tools strategically to solve problems.

Mathematical Practices MP.5 Also MP.1, MP.2, MP.4
Content Standards 4.MD.C.6 Also 4.OA.A.3, 4.NF.B.3c 4.MD.C.5, 4.MD.C.7

Solve & Share

Caleb is standing next to the tallest building in a city. Determine the measure of the 3 angles with the vertex at the tallest building and rays on the music hall, the live theater, and the art museum. Tell what tool you used and explain why the measures make sense relative to each other.

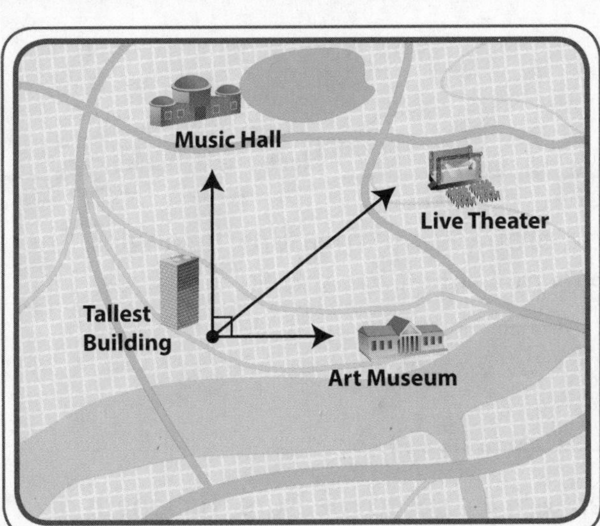

Thinking Habits

Be a good thinker!
These questions can help you.

- Which tools can I use?
- Why should I use this tool to help me solve the problem?
- Is there a different tool I could use?
- Am I using the tool appropriately?

Look Back! Use Appropriate Tools Could you use a ruler to find the angle measures? Explain.

Visual Learning

Glossary

How Can You Select and Use Appropriate Tools to Solve Problems?

Visual Learning Bridge

A

Trevor and Holly are drawing trapezoids to make a design. They need to find the measures of the angles formed by the sides of the trapezoid and the length of each side of the trapezoid. What tools are needed to find the measures of the angles and the lengths of the sides?

What do you need to do to copy the trapezoid?

I need to measure the angles, then measure the sides.

Here's my thinking.

B

Which tool can I use to help me solve this problem?

I can

- decide which tool is appropriate.
- explain why it is the best tool to use.
- use the tool correctly.

C

Use a protractor to measure the angles. The angles measure 120° and 60°.

Then, use a ruler to measure the length of each side. The lengths are $\frac{3}{4}$ inch, $\frac{3}{4}$ inch, $\frac{3}{4}$ inch, and $1\frac{1}{2}$ inches.

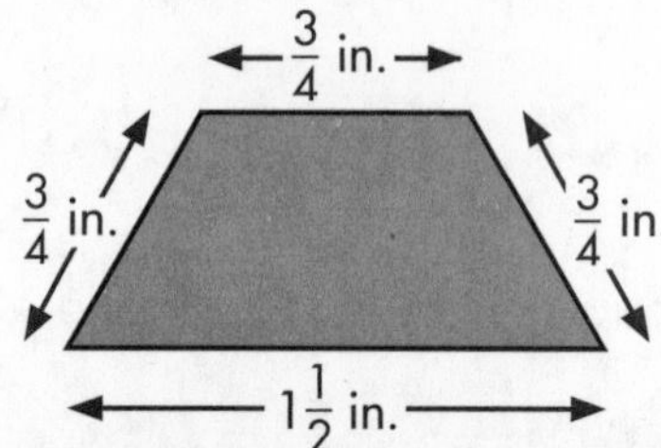

Convince Me! **Use Appropriate Tools** What other tools could be used to solve this problem? Why are a protractor and a ruler more appropriate than other tools?

Name ______________________

Guided Practice

Lee brought $1\frac{3}{5}$ pounds of apples to the picnic. Hannah brought $\frac{4}{5}$ pound of oranges. Lee said they brought $2\frac{2}{5}$ pounds of fruit in all. Lee needs to justify that $1\frac{3}{5} + \frac{4}{5} = 2\frac{2}{5}$.

When you use appropriate tools, you select the best tool to use.

1. What tool could Lee use to justify the sum?

Available Tools
Place-value blocks
Fraction strips
Rulers to $\frac{1}{8}$ inch
Grid paper
Counters

2. How can Lee use a tool to justify the sum? Draw pictures of the tool you used to explain.

Independent Practice

Use Appropriate Tools

What are the measures of the sides and angles of the parallelogram shown? Use Exercises 3–5 to help solve.

3. What tools can you use to solve this problem?

4. Explain how to use the tool you chose to find the measures of the angles. Label the figure with the measures you find.

5. Explain how to use the tool you chose to find the lengths of the sides. Label the figure with the measures you find.

Problem Solving

Performance Task

Mural

Before Nadia paints a mural, she plans what she is going to paint. She sketches the diagram shown and wants to know the measures of $\angle WVX$, $\angle WVY$, $\angle XVY$, and $\angle YVZ$.

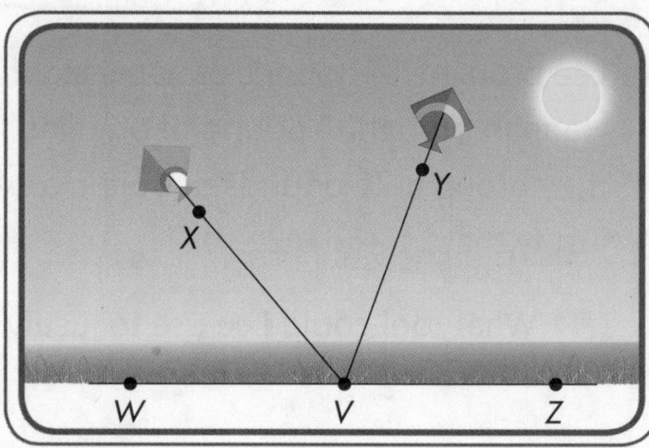

6. **Reasoning** What quantities are given in the problem and what do the numbers mean? What do you know from the diagram?

7. **Make Sense and Persevere** What do you need to find?

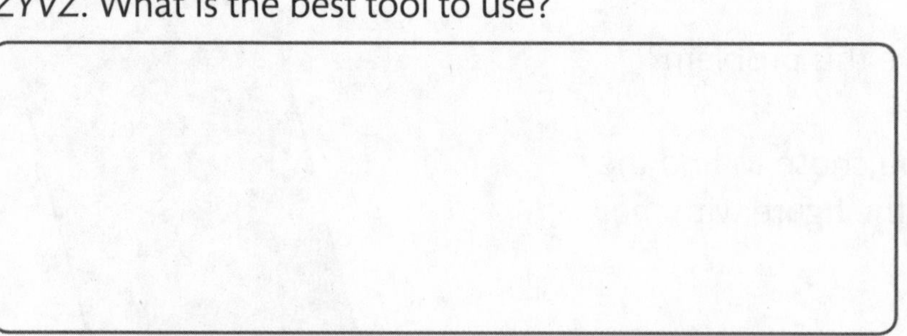

8. **Use Appropriate Tools** Measure $\angle WVX$, $\angle WVY$, and $\angle YVZ$. What is the best tool to use?

When you use appropriate tools, you decide if the results you get with the tool make sense.

9. **Model with Math** Write and solve an equation which could be used to find the measure of $\angle XVY$. What is the measure of the angle?

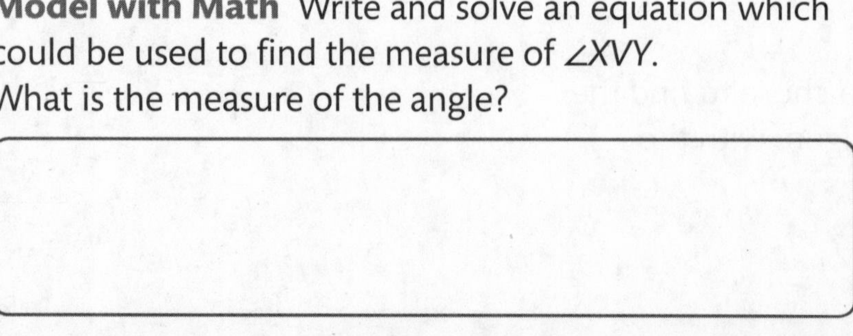

Name ____________________

Shade a path from **START** to **FINISH**. Follow sums and differences that are between 20,000 and 25,000. You can only move up, down, right, or left.

Fluency Practice Activity

I can ...
add and subtract multi-digit whole numbers.

Content Standard 4.NBT.B.4
Mathematical Practices MP.2, MP.6, MP.7

Start

66,149 − 44,297	13,000 + 13,000	11,407 + 13,493	35,900 − 12,605	30,000 − 9,825
40,350 − 20,149	18,890 + 190	13,050 + 11,150	60,000 − 33,900	41,776 − 18,950
89,000 − 68,900	12,175 + 18,125	12,910 + 12,089	67,010 − 42,009	42,082 − 19,582
56,111 − 32,523	22,009 + 991	11,725 + 11,450	75,000 − 45,350	65,508 − 42,158
99,000 − 81,750	9,125 + 9,725	18,517 + 8,588	38,000 − 19,001	37,520 − 16,215

Finish

TOPIC 15

Vocabulary Review

Word List

- acute angle
- angle measure
- degree (°)
- line
- line segment
- obtuse angle
- point
- protractor
- ray
- right angle
- straight angle
- unit angle
- vertex

Understand Vocabulary

1. Cross out the terms that do **NOT** describe an angle with a square corner.

acute angle right angle

obtuse angle straight angle

2. Cross out the terms that do **NOT** describe an angle open less than a right angle.

acute angle right angle

obtuse angle straight angle

3. Cross out the terms that do **NOT** describe an angle that forms a straight line.

acute angle right angle obtuse angle straight angle

4. Cross out the terms that do **NOT** describe an angle open more than a right angle, but less than a straight angle.

acute angle right angle obtuse angle straight angle

Label each example with a term from the Word List.

5. ________________

6. ________________

7. ________________

8. ________________

Use Vocabulary in Writing

9. Describe how to measure an angle. Use at least 3 terms from the Word List in your explanation.

Name ___

TOPIC 15

Reteaching

Set A pages 549–552

A ray has one endpoint and continues on forever in one direction.

A line segment is a part of a line with two endpoints.

An angle is formed by two rays with a common endpoint.

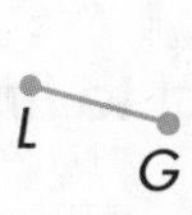

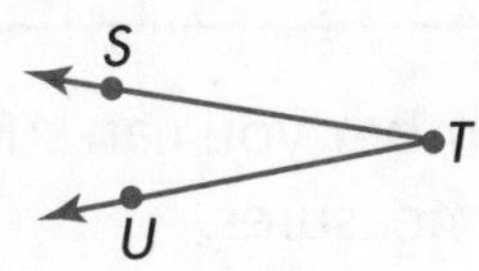

Remember that a line segment is a part of a line.

Use geometric terms to describe what is shown.

1. 

2. 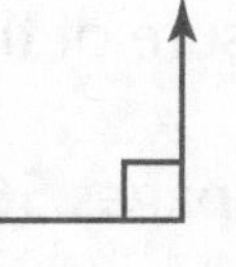

3.

4.

Set B pages 553–556

The angle below is $\frac{1}{3}$ of the circle.

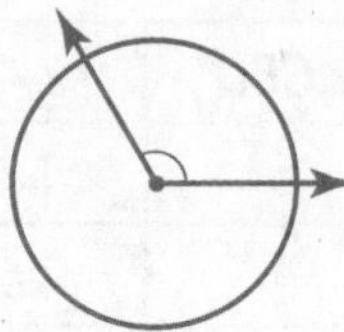

$\frac{1}{3}$ means 1 of 3 equal parts.

$360° \div 3 = 120°$

The measure of this angle is 120°.

Remember there are 360° in a circle.

A circle is cut into eighths. What is the angle measure of each piece?

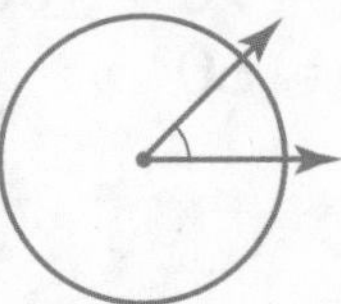

1. Use division to solve.

2. Use multiplication to solve.

Set C pages 557–560

You can use an angle you know to find the measure of other angles. The smaller angle of the tan pattern block has a measure of 30°.

Three of the 30° angles will fit into the angle.
Add: $30° + 30° + 30° = 90°$

The measure of this angle is 90°.

Remember you can use any angle that you know the measure of to find the measure of other angles.

Find the measure of each angle. Use pattern blocks.

1. 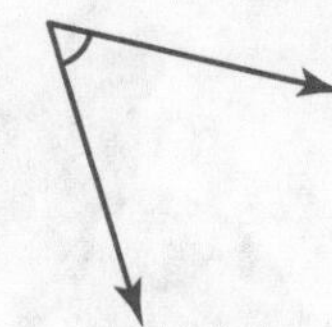

2. 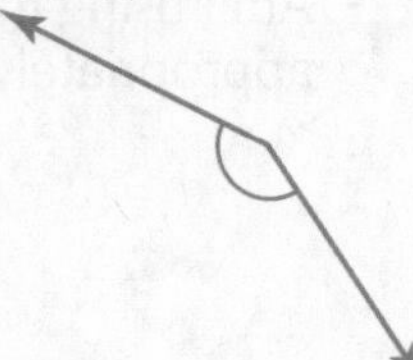

Set D pages 561–564

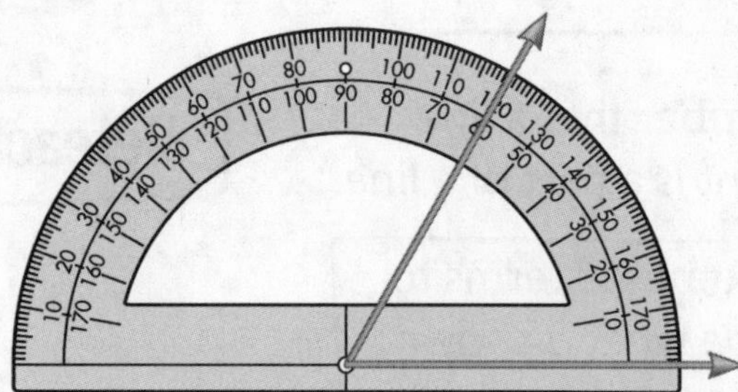

The measure of this angle is 60°.

Remember that a straight angle has a measure of 180°.

Measure the angles.

1. 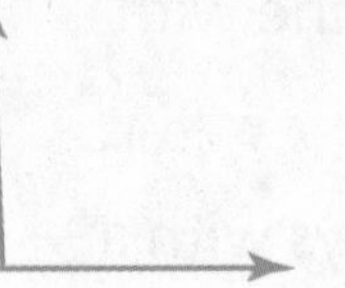

2. 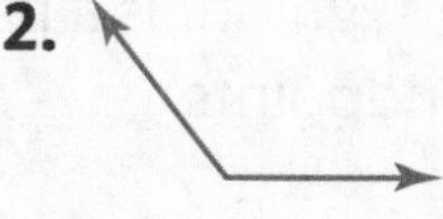

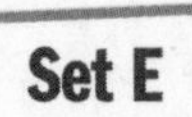

Set E pages 565–568

When an angle is decomposed into non-overlapping parts, the angle measure of the whole is the sum of the angle measures of the parts.

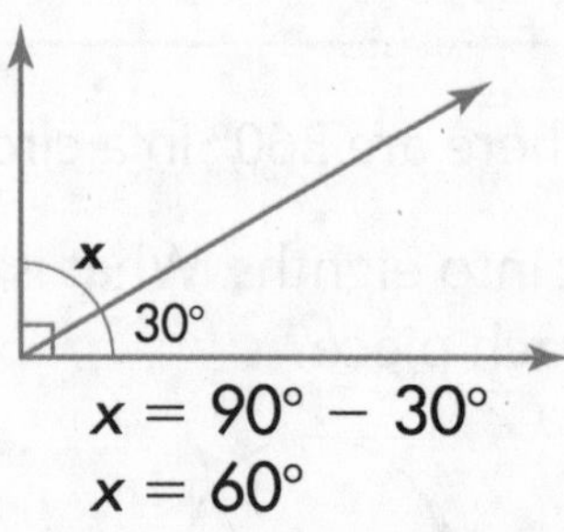

$x = 90° - 30°$
$x = 60°$

Remember you can subtract to find angle measures.

$\angle ABD$ is decomposed into two non-overlapping angles, $\angle ABC$ and $\angle CBD$. Complete the table.

Angle Measure (degrees)		
$\angle ABC$	$\angle CBD$	$\angle ABD$
100°	45°	145°
95°		155°
105°		170°
	25°	140°
122°	36°	

Set F pages 569–572

Think about these questions to help you **use appropriate tools** strategically.

Thinking Habits

- Which tools can I use?
- Why should I use this tool to help me solve the problem?
- Is there a different tool I could use?
- Am I using the tool appropriately?

Remember there may be more than one appropriate tool to use to solve a problem.

One-eighth of the pie is missing from the tin.

1. What tools can Delia use to measure the angle of the missing piece?

2. How can you calculate the measure?

Name ____________________

1. What is the measure of the angle shown below? Name a type of angle that has an angle measure greater than the angle shown.

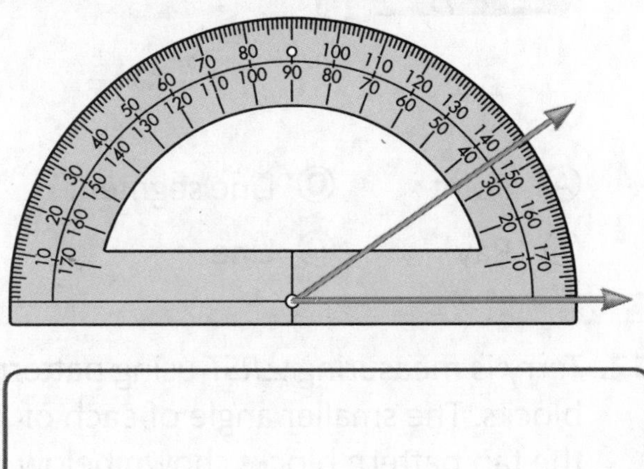

2. Megan needs to find the measures of the angles on a bridge.

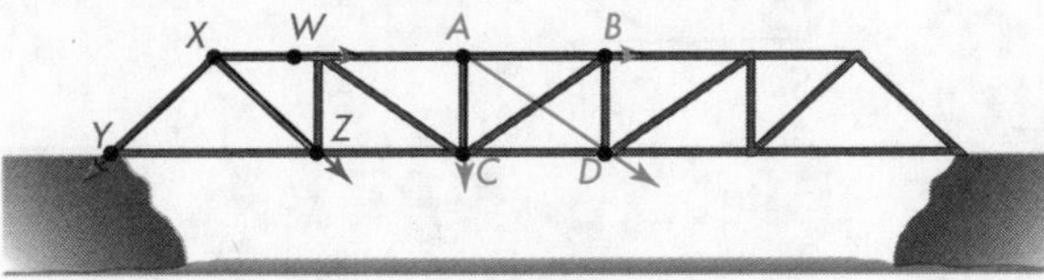

A. Find the measure of ∠*YXW* if ∠*YXZ* is 85° and ∠*ZXW* is 40°. Write and solve an addition equation.

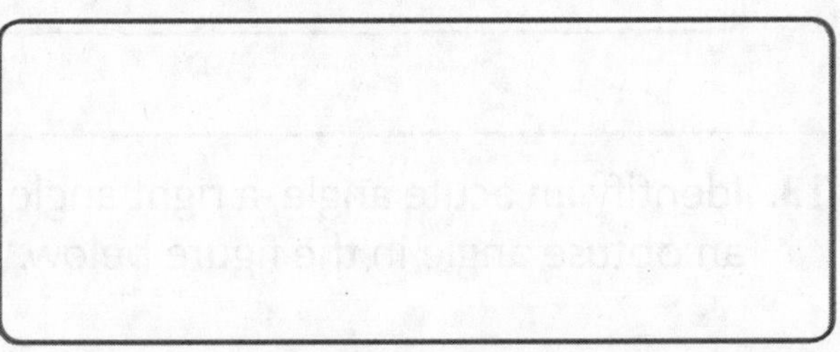

B. Find the measure of ∠*CAD* if ∠*CAB* is a right angle and ∠*DAB* is 45°. Write and solve a subtraction equation.

3. If you divide a circle into 360 equal angles, what is the angle measure of each angle?

4. Choose the correct term from the box to complete each statement.

Line Segment	Ray

A [ ] has one endpoint.

A [ ] has two endpoints.

5. Draw an example of a line $\overleftrightarrow{RS}$. Label a point *T* between points *R* and *S*. Using point *T*, draw ray $\overrightarrow{TV}$.

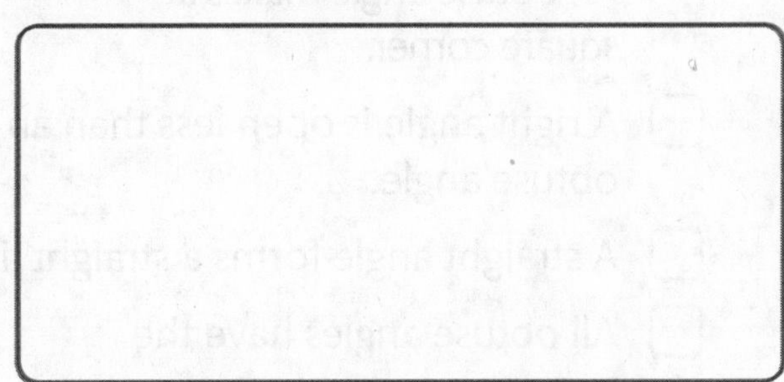

6. ∠*JKL* is a straight angle decomposed into 2 non-overlapping angles, ∠*JKM* and ∠*MKL*. If ∠*MKL* measures 104°, what type of angle is ∠*JKM*? What is the measure of ∠*JKM*?

7. $\angle ABC$ has a measure of 40° and $\angle CBD$ has a measure of 23°. The angles share a ray and form $\angle ABD$. Write and solve an equation to find the measure of $\angle ABD$.

8. Emma cuts slices from pies. Match each fraction with the equal angle measure.

	120°	180°	36°	60°
$\frac{1}{2}$ of a pie	❑	❑	❑	❑
$\frac{1}{3}$ of a pie	❑	❑	❑	❑
$\frac{1}{6}$ of a pie	❑	❑	❑	❑
$\frac{1}{10}$ of a pie	❑	❑	❑	❑

9. Select all the true statements.

- ☐ An acute angle is open less than a right angle.
- ☐ An obtuse angle makes a square corner.
- ☐ A right angle is open less than an obtuse angle.
- ☐ A straight angle forms a straight line.
- ☐ All obtuse angles have the same measure.

10. Two wooden roof beams meet at a 60° angle. Draw an angle to represent how the beams meet.

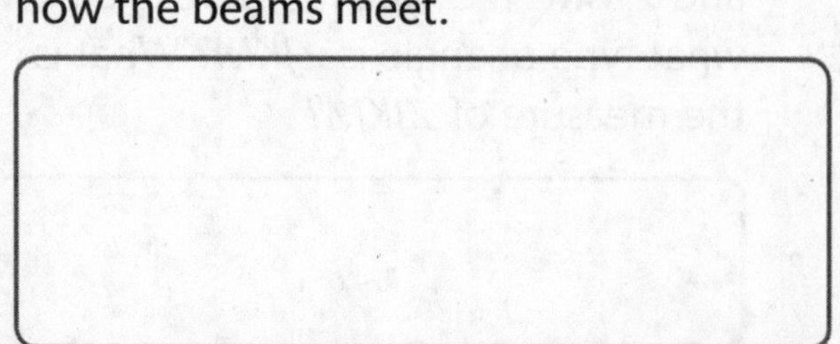

11. Which geometric term best describes the light that shines from a flashlight?

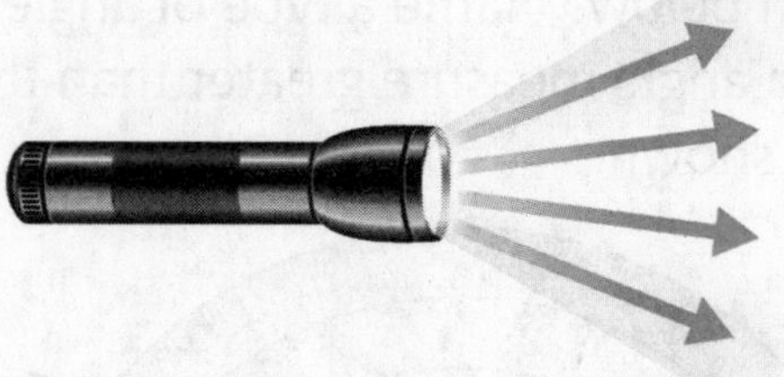

Ⓐ Point
Ⓑ Ray
Ⓒ Line segment
Ⓓ Line

12. Terry is measuring $\angle RST$ using pattern blocks. The smaller angle of each of the tan pattern blocks shown below measures 30°. What is the measure of $\angle RST$? Explain.

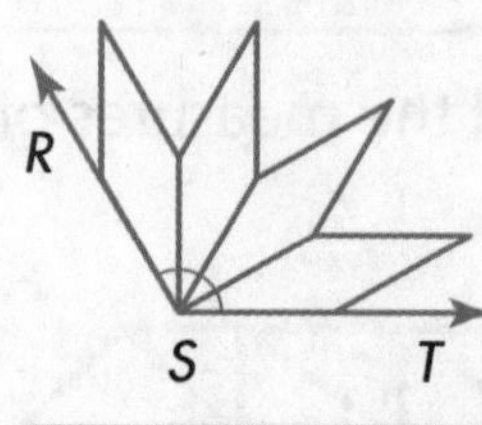

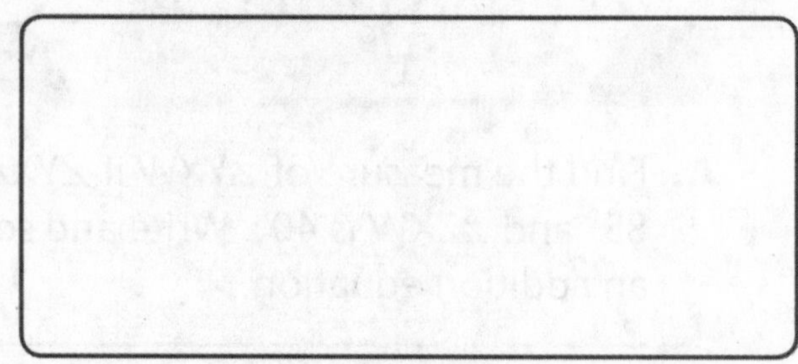

13. Identify an acute angle, a right angle, and an obtuse angle in the figure below.

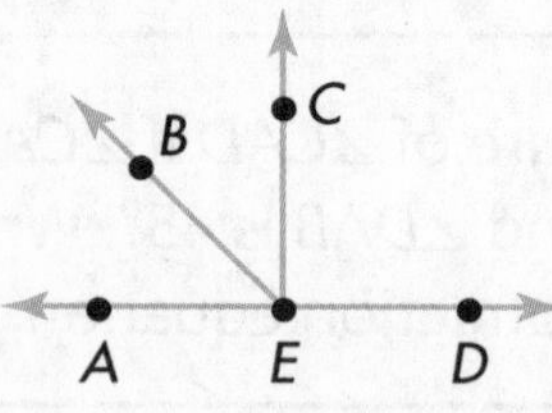

Name ______________________________

TOPIC 15

Performance Task

Ancient Roads

The ancient Romans built roads throughout their empire. Many roads were paved with stones that fit together. The spaces between the stones were filled with sand and gravel. Many of these roads still exist today, over 2,000 years after they were built.

1. As seen in the **Roman Road** figure, the stones formed angles and geometric figures.

Roman Road

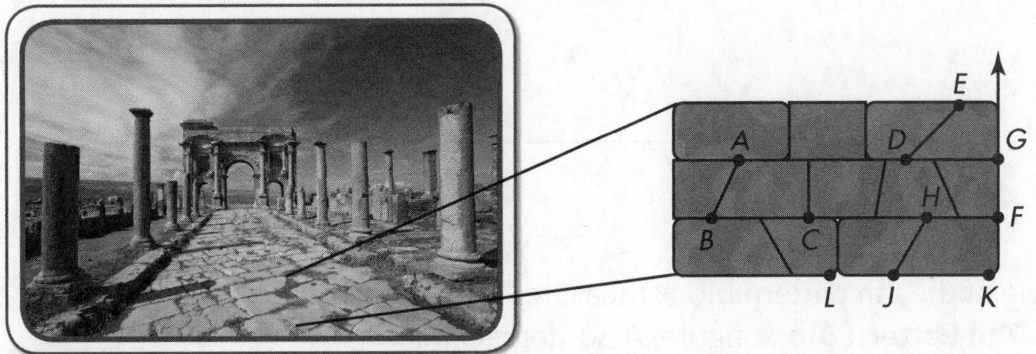

Part A

What geometric figure has one endpoint at *F* and goes on forever through point *G*?

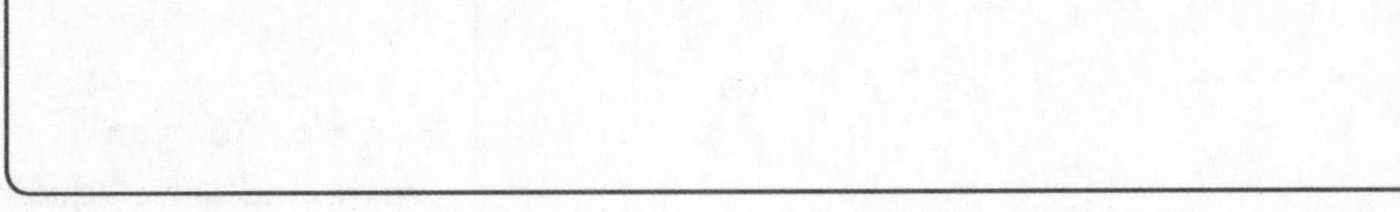

Part B

Is ∠*EDA* right, acute, or obtuse? Explain.

Part C

∠*EDG* turns through $\frac{1}{8}$ of a circle. What is its angle measure? Explain.

2. Answer the following to find the measure of $\angle HJK$ and $\angle HJL$ in the **Measuring a Roman Road** figure.

Measuring a Roman Road

H
L
J
K

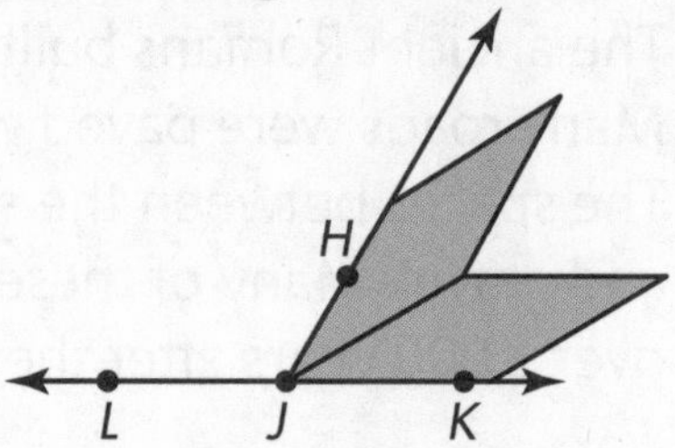

Part A

Name two tools you could use to measure the angles.

Part B

The smaller angle of the tan pattern block measures 30°, as shown in the **Tan Pattern Block** figure. A 30-degree angle is 30 one-degree angles. What is the measure of $\angle HJK$ in the **Measuring a Roman Road** figure? Explain.

Tan Pattern Block

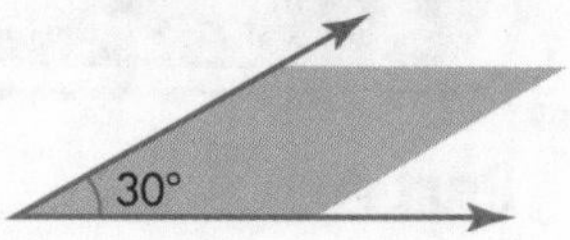

30°

You can write and solve equations to find unknown angle measures.

Part C

What is the measure of $\angle HJL$ in the **Measuring a Roman Road** figure? Write and solve an equation to find the measure of the angle.

TOPIC 16

Lines, Angles, and Shapes

Essential Questions: How can you classify triangles and quadrilaterals? What is line symmetry?

Digital Resources

Interactive Student Edition | Activity | Visual Learning | Video | Practice | Assessment | Games | Tools | Glossary

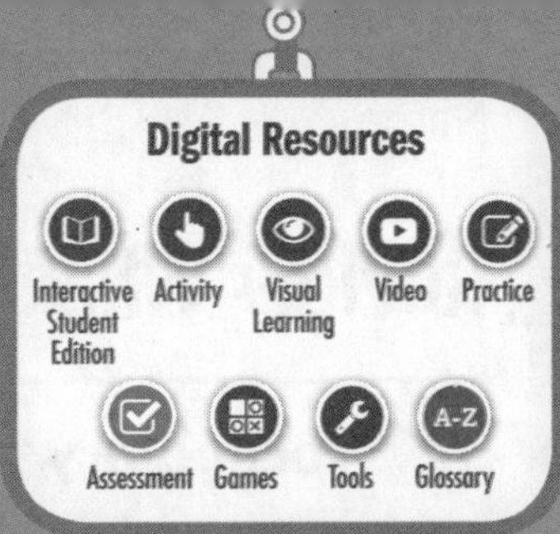

Chameleons can move their eyes one at a time!
When they do, they are able to see in two directions at once, helping them find food and stay safe.
They can see the math that is all around them! Here is a project about senses and symmetry!

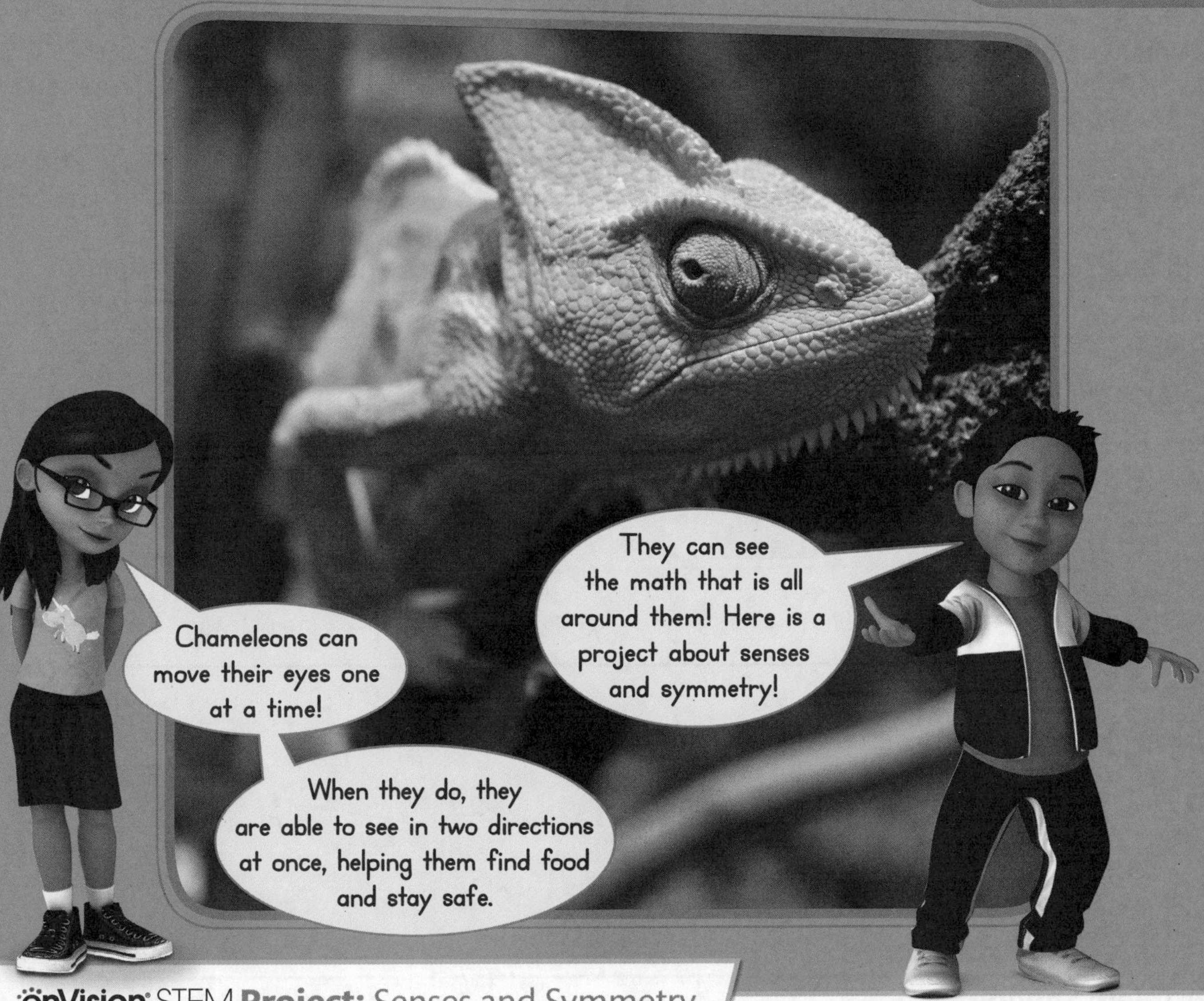

enVision® STEM Project: Senses and Symmetry

Do Research The location of an animal's eyes helps it to survive in the wild. Use the Internet or other sources to find why some animals have eyes on the sides of their head and others have eyes on the front.

Journal: Write a Report Include what you found. Also in your report:

- Most animals are the same on both sides of their body. Use a line of symmetry to help make a simple drawing of your favorite animal's face. Draw both sides of the animal's face the same. Explain how you know that both sides of your drawing are the same.

Name ______________________________

Review What You Know

Vocabulary

Choose the best term from the box. Write it on the blank.

- angle
- quadrilateral
- polygon
- triangle

1. A ____________ is a closed figure made up of straight line segments.

2. A polygon with three sides is a(n) ____________.

3. A(n) ____________ is formed by two rays with the same endpoint.

Shapes

Choose the best term to describe each shape. Use each term once.

Rectangle   Rhombus   Trapezoid

4. 

5. 

6. 

Lines

Use geometric terms to describe what is shown.

7. 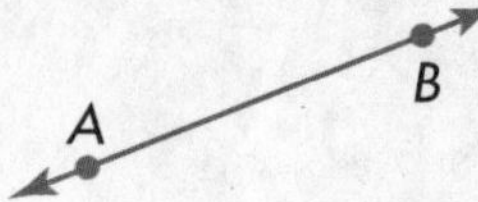

8. 

9. 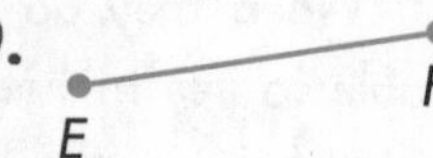

Problem Solving

10. **Generalize** Which generalization about these figures is **NOT** true?

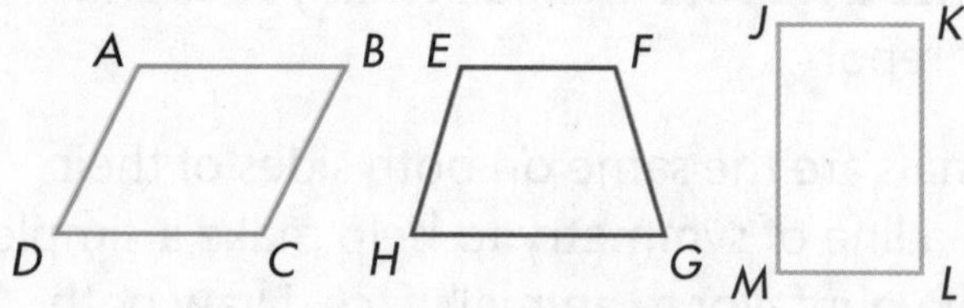

Ⓐ Each figure is a quadrilateral.

Ⓑ Each figure has two pairs of parallel sides.

Ⓒ Each figure has at least two sides of equal length.

Ⓓ Each figure has 4 angles.

Name ______________________

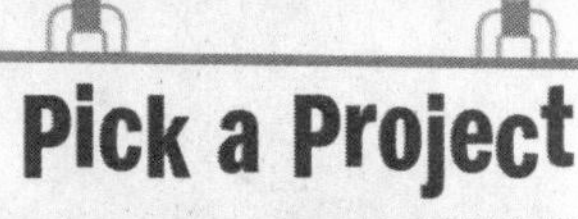

How are dictionaries useful?

Project: Create a Picture Dictionary

How can shapes be used in art at the Dali Museum?

Project: Create Cubist Art

Do snowflakes have lines of symmetry?

Project: Make Snowflakes

Can animals have symmetry?

Project: Draw a Line-Symmetric Animal

Name ______________________

Activity

Lesson 16-1
Lines

I can ...
draw and identify perpendicular, parallel, and intersecting lines.

Content Standard 4.G.A.1
Mathematical Practices MP.3, MP.6

Solve & Share

The number line below is an example of a line. A line goes on forever in a straight path in two directions. Draw the following pairs of lines: two lines that will never cross, two lines that cross at one point, two lines that cross at two points. If you cannot draw the lines, tell why.

0 1 2 3 4 5 6 7 8 9

Be precise. Think of and use math language you already know. *Show your work in the space below!*

Look Back! Terry said, "The lines shown intersect at three points." Is Terry correct? Explain.

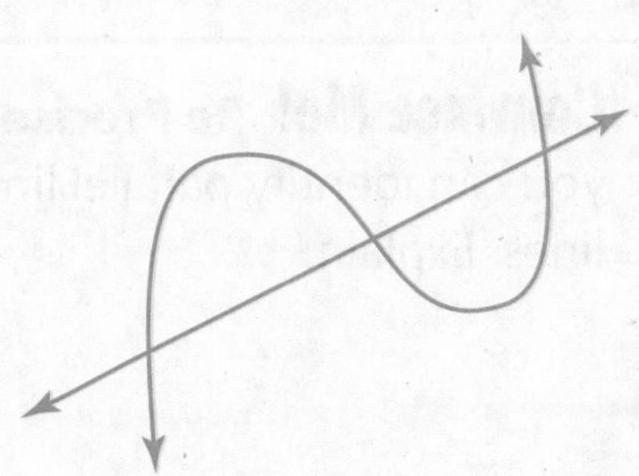

How Can You Describe Pairs of Lines?

Visual Learning Bridge

A

A line is a straight path of points that goes on and on in opposite directions. A pair of lines can be described as parallel, perpendicular, or intersecting.

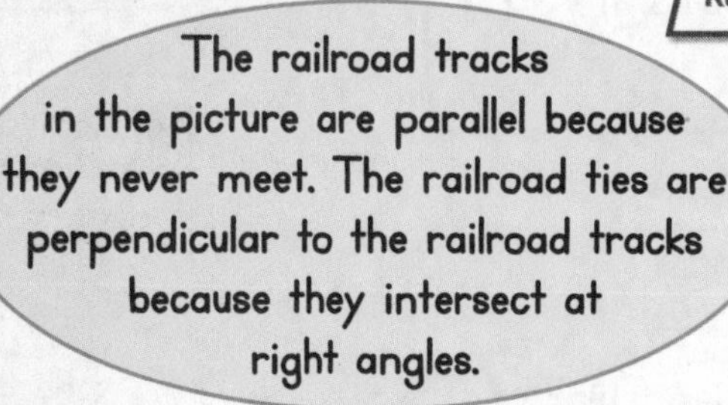

The railroad tracks in the picture are parallel because they never meet. The railroad ties are perpendicular to the railroad tracks because they intersect at right angles.

Railroad tie
Railroad track

B

Pairs of lines are given special names depending on their relationship.

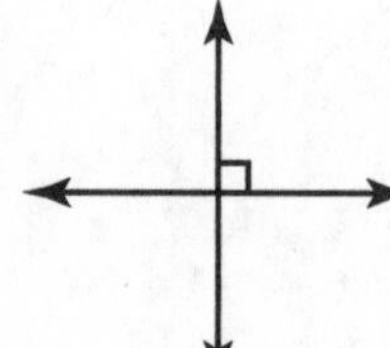

Perpendicular lines are also intersecting lines. But intersecting lines are not parallel lines.

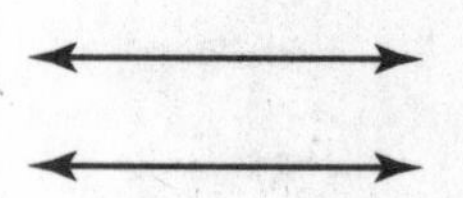

Parallel lines never intersect.

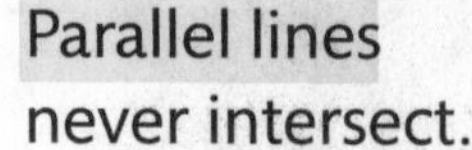

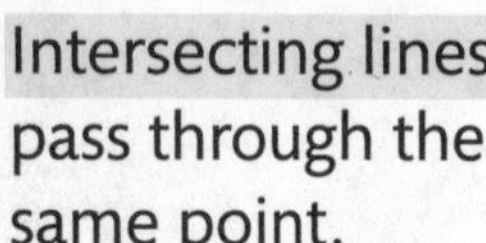

Intersecting lines pass through the same point.

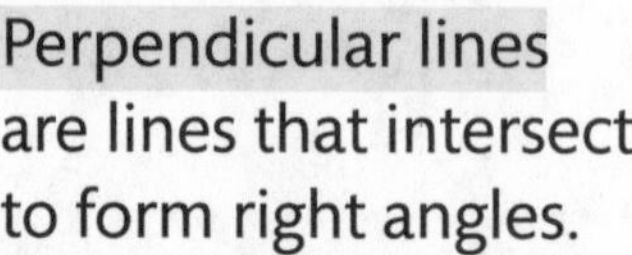

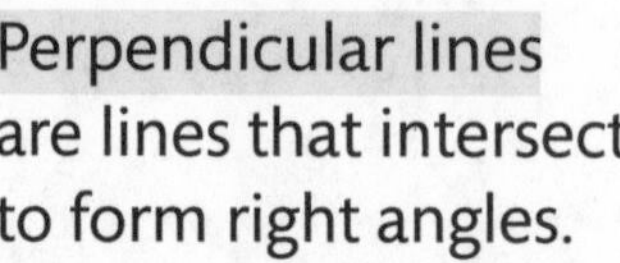

Perpendicular lines are lines that intersect to form right angles.

Convince Me! **Be Precise** Find examples in your classroom where you can identify parallel lines, intersecting lines, and perpendicular lines. Explain.

Name ______________________

Guided Practice

Do You Understand?

1. What geometric term could you use to describe the top and bottom edges of a book? Why?

2. The blades of an open pair of scissors look like what pair of lines? Why?

Do You Know How?

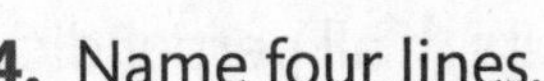

For **3–6**, use the diagram.

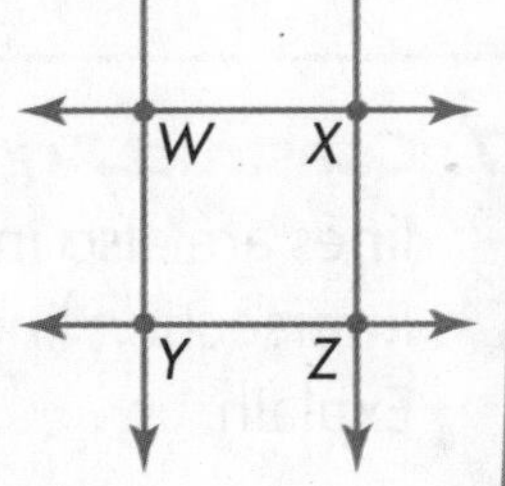

3. Name four points.

4. Name four lines.

5. Name two pairs of parallel lines.

6. Name two pairs of perpendicular lines.

Independent Practice

For **7–12**, use geometric terms to describe what is shown. Be as specific as possible.

7.

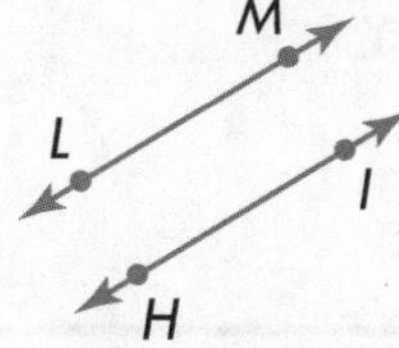

8.

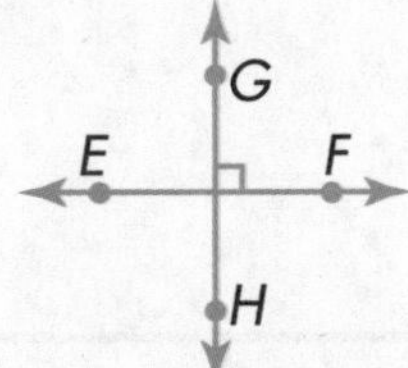

9.

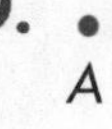

10.

11.

12.

For **13–15**, draw what is described by the geometic terms.

13. Perpendicular lines

14. Intersecting lines

15. Parallel lines

Problem Solving

16. **Critique Reasoning** Bella names this line $\overleftrightarrow{LM}$. Miguel names the line $\overleftrightarrow{LN}$. Who is correct? Explain.

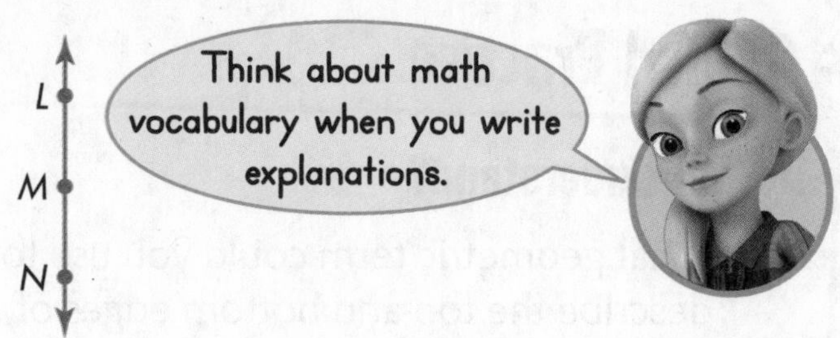

L
M
N
Think about math vocabulary when you write explanations.

17. **Construct Arguments** If all perpendicular lines are also intersecting lines, are all intersecting lines also perpendicular lines? Explain.

18. Draw three lines so two of the lines are perpendicular and the third line intersects the perpendicular lines at exactly one point. Label the lines with points.

19. **Higher Order Thinking** $\overleftrightarrow{AB}$ is parallel to $\overleftrightarrow{CD}$, and $\overleftrightarrow{CD}$ is perpendicular to $\overleftrightarrow{EF}$. If a line through B and D is perpendicular to $\overleftrightarrow{AB}$, what is the relationship between $\overleftrightarrow{BD}$ and $\overleftrightarrow{EF}$?

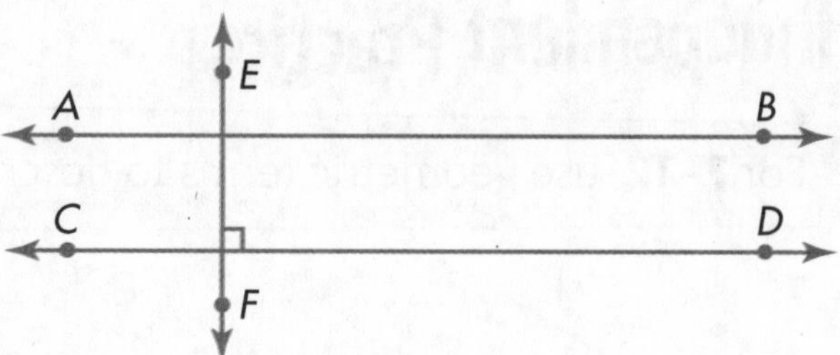

Assessment Practice

20. Which geometric term would you use to describe the power cables shown at the right?

Ⓐ Perpendicular lines

Ⓑ Parallel lines

Ⓒ Intersecting lines

Ⓓ Points

What relationship do the power cables have to each other?

Name ____________________ Activity

Lesson 16-2
Classify Triangles

Solve & Share

Sort the triangles shown below into two or more groups. Explain how you sorted them. ***Solve this problem any way you choose.***

I can ...
reason about line segments and angles to classify triangles.

Content Standards 4.G.A.2 Also 4.OA.C.5, 4.MD.C.5, 4.G.A.1
Mathematical Practices MP.2, MP.6, MP.8

A D F

C E G

B

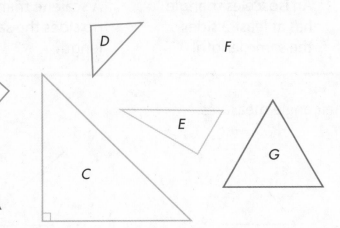

You will use what you have learned about different types of angles to analyze and categorize triangles. *Show your work in the space above!*

Look Back! Generalize What is true about all 7 triangles you sorted?

 Visual Learning  Glossary

Essential Question How Can You Classify Triangles?

Visual Learning Bridge

A Triangles can be classified by the line segments that make their sides.

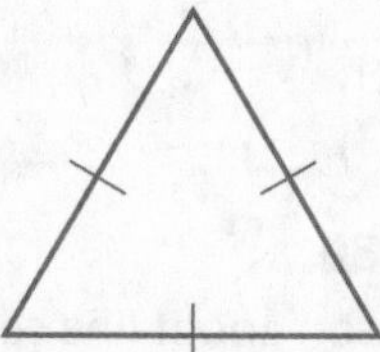

An equilateral triangle has 3 sides the same length.

An isosceles triangle has at least 2 sides the same length.

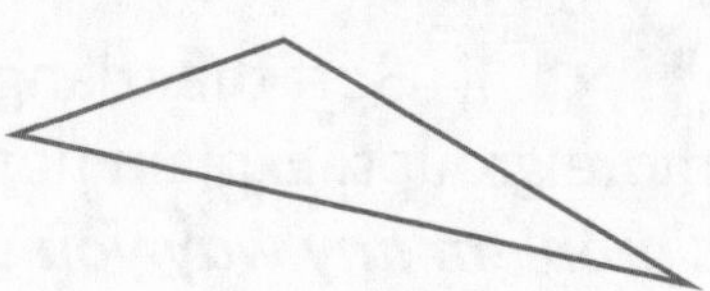

A scalene triangle has no sides the same length.

B Triangles can be classified by their angle measures.

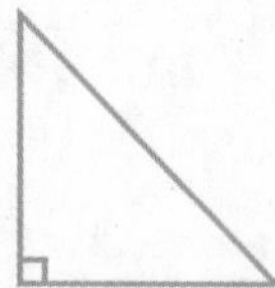

A right triangle has one right angle.

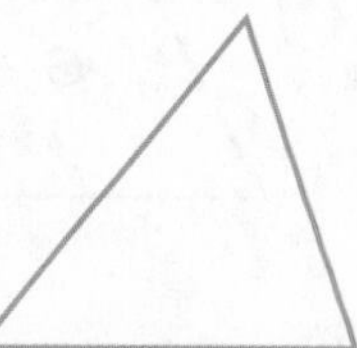

An acute triangle has three acute angles. All of its angles measure less than a right angle.

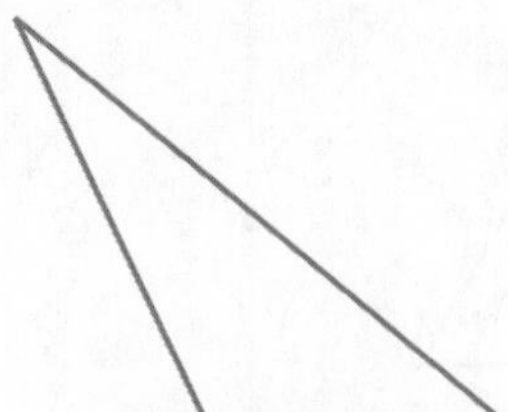

An obtuse triangle has one obtuse angle. One angle has a measure greater than a right angle.

Triangles can be classified by both their angle measures and their sides. The red triangle is an obtuse, scalene triangle.

Convince Me! **Be Precise** Can a triangle have more than one obtuse angle? Explain.

Name ____________________

Another Example!

The pattern follows the rule: right triangle, acute triangle, right triangle, acute triangle.... It also follows the rule: isosceles, scalene, scalene, isosceles, scalene.... Draw a triangle that could be next in the pattern and explain.

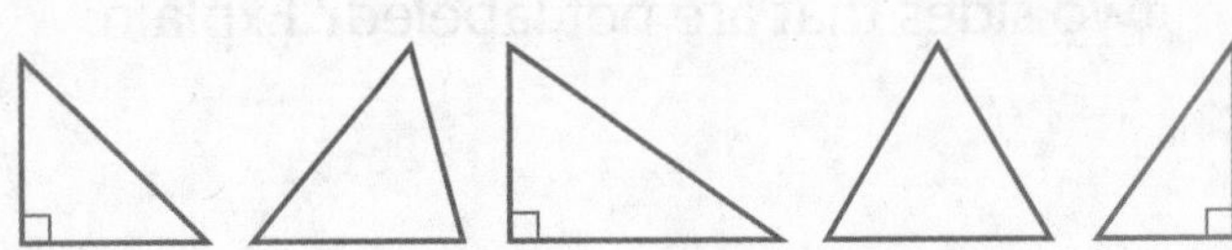

For the first rule, the next triangle is acute. For the second rule, it is scalene. So, the next triangle is an acute, scalene triangle. It can be the same as the second triangle in the pattern or it can be a different acute, scalene triangle.

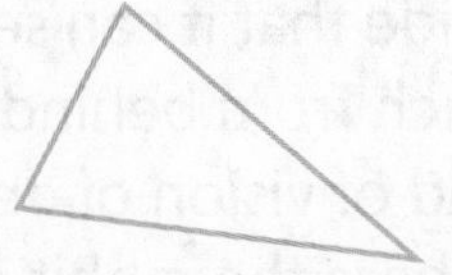

Guided Practice

Do You Understand?

1. Is it possible to have an obtuse acute triangle? Explain.

2. Can a triangle have more than one right angle? If so, draw an example.

Do You Know How?

For **3–4**, classify each triangle by its sides, and then by its angles.

3. 

4. 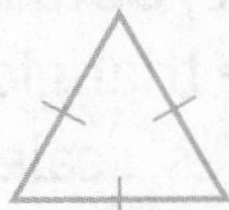

Independent Practice

For **5–10**, classify each triangle by its sides, and then by its angles.

5. 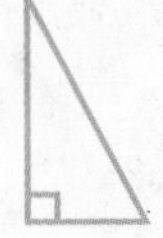

6. 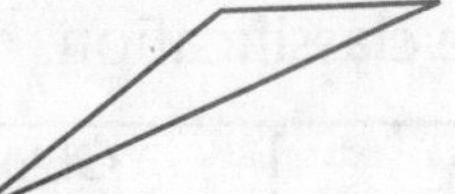

7. 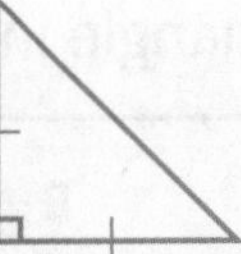

8. 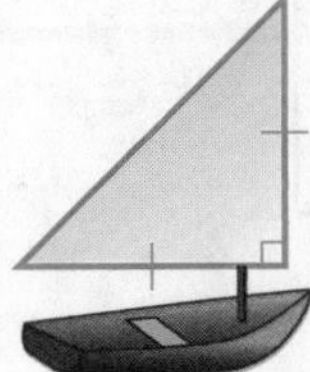

9. 

10. 

Problem Solving

11. Reasoning The backyard shown at the right is an equilateral triangle. What do you know about the lengths of the other two sides that are not labeled? Explain.

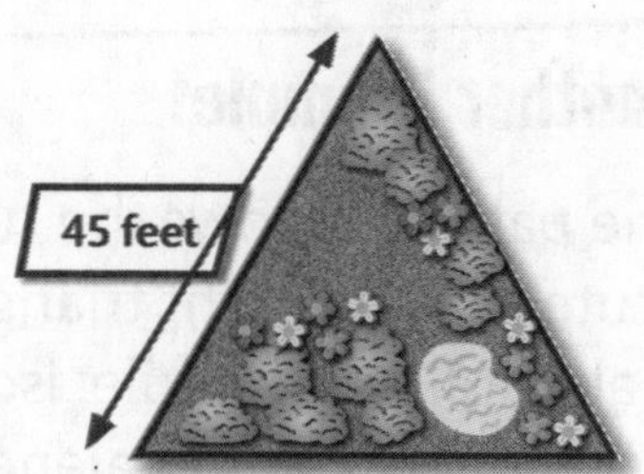

12. enVision® STEM A rabbit's field of vision is so wide that it can see predators that approach from behind. The diagram shows the field of vision of one rabbit and the field where the rabbit cannot see. Classify the triangle by its sides and its angles.

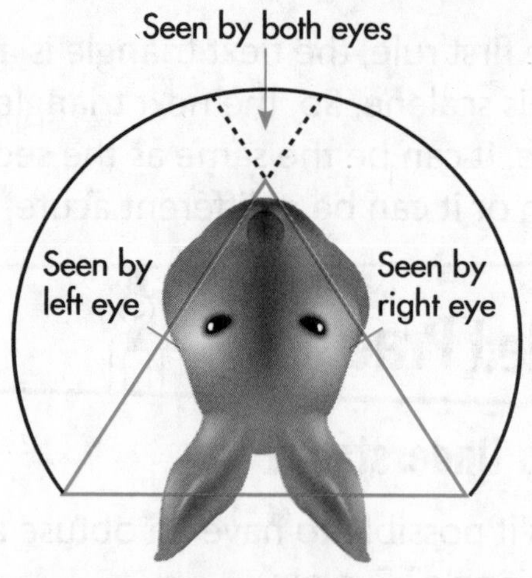

13. A pattern follows the rule: obtuse triangle, obtuse triangle, right triangle, obtuse triangle.... It also follows the rule: isosceles, scalene, isosceles, scalene... Draw a triangle that could be the fifth shape in the pattern and explain.

14. Higher Order Thinking Mitch draws a triangle with one obtuse angle. What are all the possible ways to classify the triangle by its angle measures and side lengths? Explain.

Assessment Practice

15. Draw each triangle in its correct angle classification.

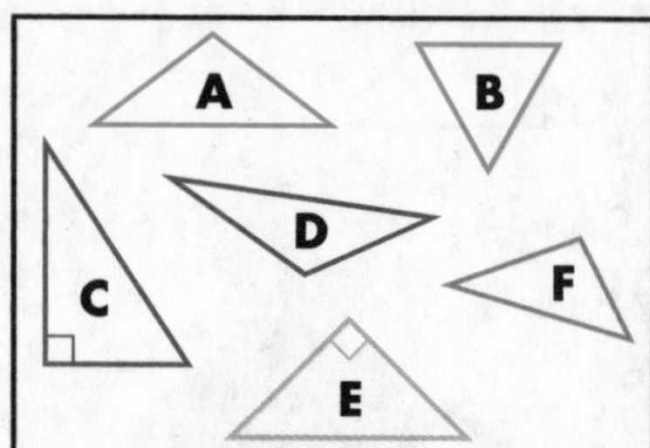

Acute	Obtuse	Right

Name ______________________

Activity

Lesson 16-3
Classify Quadrilaterals

Solve & Share

Draw three different four-sided shapes that have opposite sides parallel. Explain how your shapes are alike and how they are different. ***Solve this problem any way you choose.***

I can ...
reason about line segments and angles to classify quadrilaterals.

Content Standards 4.G.A.2 Also 4.G.A.1
Mathematical Practices MP.3, MP.7, MP.8

You can generalize and use what you know about parallel lines and angles to draw quadrilaterals. *Show your work in the space below!*

Look Back! What attributes do your shapes have in common?

How Can You Classify Quadrilaterals?

Visual Learning Bridge

A

Quadrilaterals can be classified by their angles or the line segments that make their sides. Which of the quadrilaterals shown have only one pair of parallel sides? Which have two pairs of parallel sides?

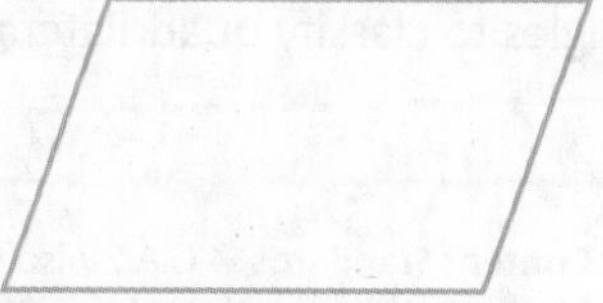

A parallelogram has 2 pairs of parallel sides.

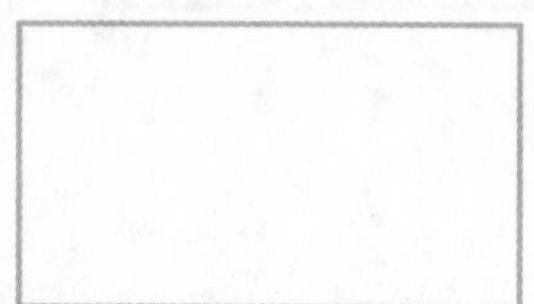

A rectangle has 4 right angles. It is also a parallelogram.

A square has 4 right angles and all sides are the same length. It is a parallelogram, a rectangle, and a rhombus.

A quadrilateral is a polygon with four sides.

B

A rhombus is a quadrilateral that has opposite sides that are parallel and all of its sides are the same length. It is also a parallelogram.

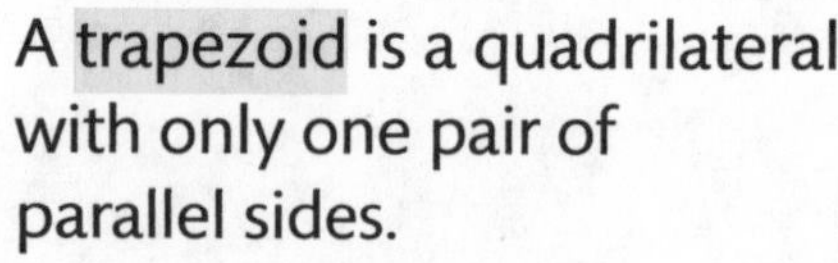

A trapezoid is a quadrilateral with only one pair of parallel sides.

Trapezoids have only one pair of parallel sides. Parallelograms, rectangles, squares, and rhombuses all have two pairs of parallel sides.

Convince Me! **Use Structure** How are a parallelogram and a rectangle the same? How are they different?

Name ____________________

Another Example!

Perpendicular sides form right angles. Can a trapezoid have perpendicular sides?

A trapezoid can have two right angles that form perpendicular sides. A trapezoid with two right angles is called a right trapezoid.

Guided Practice

Do You Understand?

1. What is true about all quadrilaterals?

2. What is the difference between a square and a rhombus?

3. Shane drew a quadrilateral with at least 2 right angles and at least 1 pair of parallel sides. Name three quadrilaterals Shane could have drawn.

Do You Know How?

For **4–7**, write all the names possible for each quadrilateral.

4. 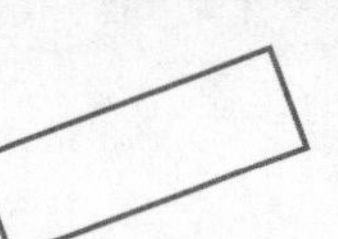

5. 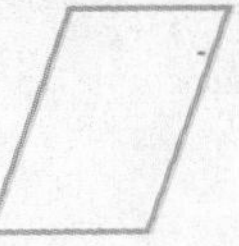

6. 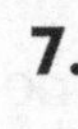

7. 

Independent Practice

For **8–11**, write all the names possible for each quadrilateral.

8. 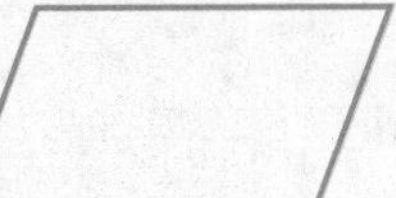

9. 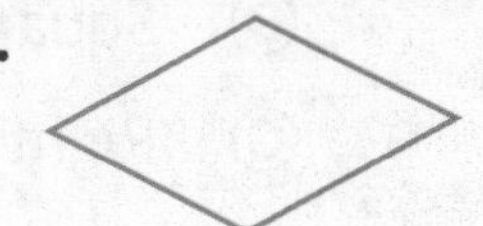

10. 

11. 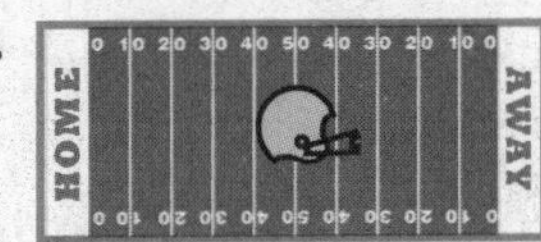

Problem Solving

12. The pattern follows the rule: quadrilateral with no parallel sides, quadrilateral with two pairs of parallel sides, quadrilateral with two pairs of parallel sides, quadrilateral with no parallel sides, quadrilateral with two pairs of parallel sides.... Draw quadrilaterals that could be the next three in the pattern.

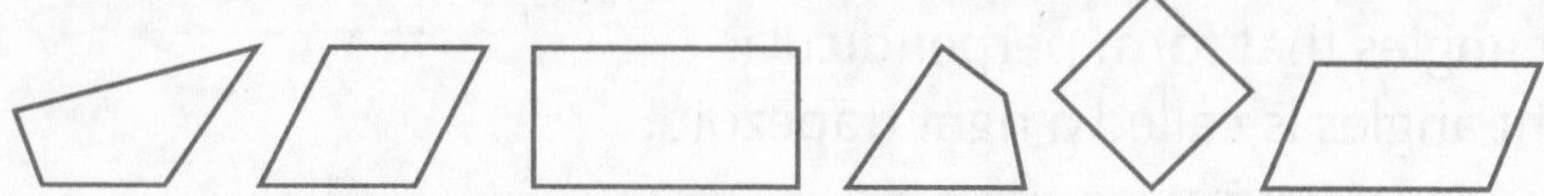

13. Critique Reasoning Tia says every square is a rectangle, and every square is a rhombus, so every rectangle must be a rhombus. Do you agree? Explain.

14. Number Sense What number comes next in the pattern? The rule is "Multiply the position number by itself." Describe a feature of the pattern.

1, 4, 9, 16, ☐

15. Higher Order Thinking Could you use the formula for finding the perimeter of a square to find the perimeter of another quadrilateral? Explain.

The formula for the perimeter of a square is $P = 4 \times s$.

Assessment Practice

16. Select all the possible names for the shape below.

- ☐ Quadrilateral
- ☐ Rhombus
- ☐ Trapezoid
- ☐ Parallelogram
- ☐ Rectangle

17. Which shape has only 1 pair of parallel sides?

Ⓐ Rhombus

Ⓑ Square

Ⓒ Right trapezoid

Ⓓ Parallelogram

Name ____________________

Activity

Lesson 16-4
Line Symmetry

I can ...
recognize and draw lines of symmetry and identify line-symmetric figures.

Content Standard 4.G.A.3
Mathematical Practices MP.2, MP.3, MP.7

Solve & Share

How many ways can you fold the square so one half fits exactly on top of the other half? How many ways can you fold the letter so one half fits exactly on top of the other half? ***Solve this problem any way you choose.***

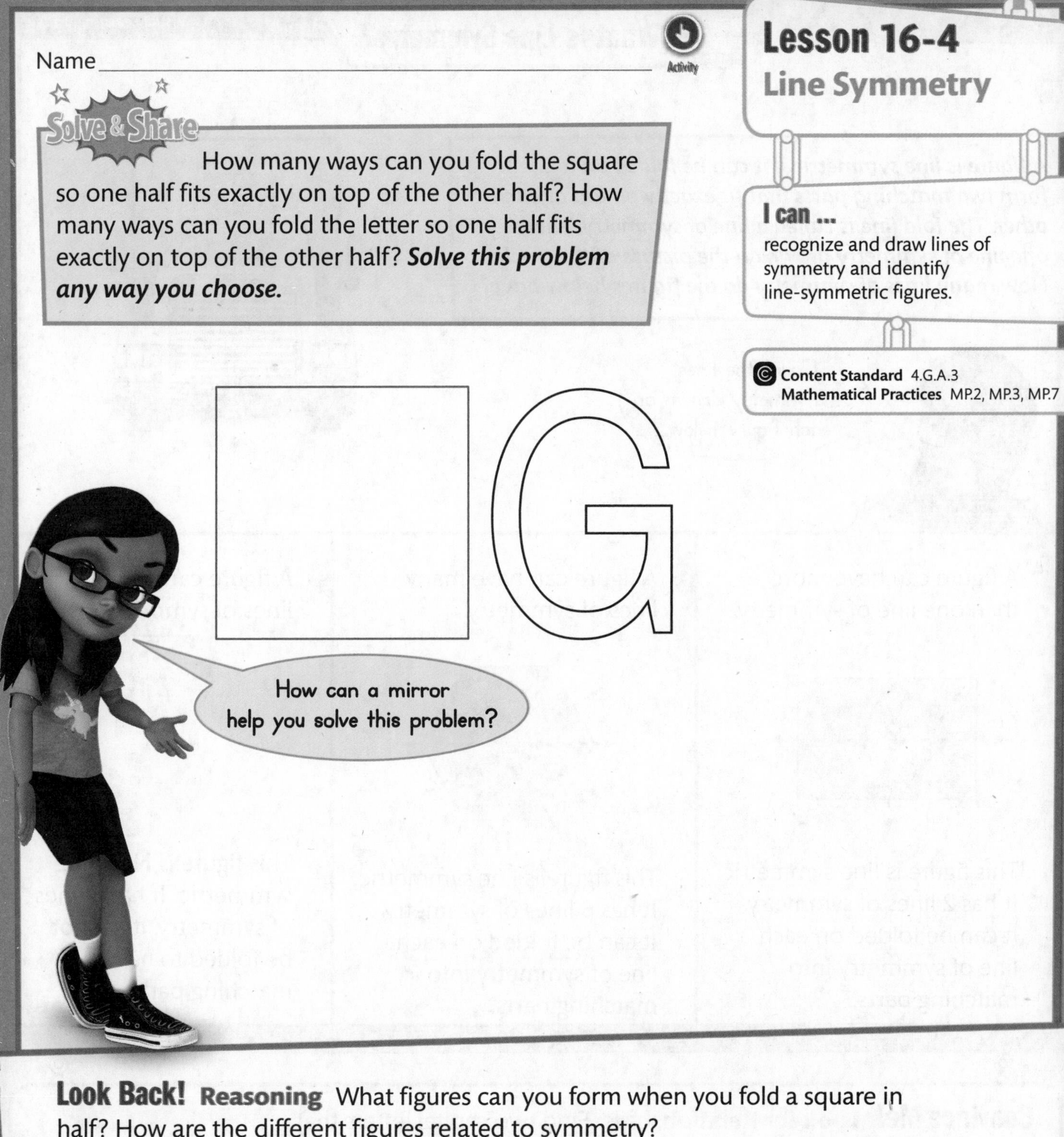

G
How can a mirror help you solve this problem?

Look Back! Reasoning What figures can you form when you fold a square in half? How are the different figures related to symmetry?

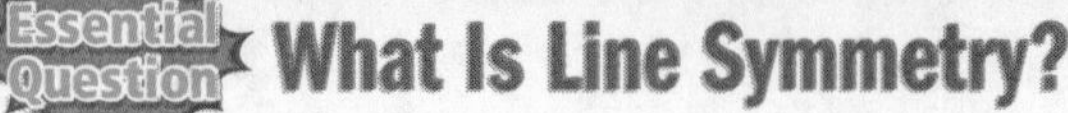

What Is Line Symmetry?

Visual Learning Bridge

A

A figure is line symmetric if it can be folded on a line to form two matching parts that fit exactly on top of each other. The fold line is called a line of symmetry. There is one line of symmetry drawn on the picture of the truck. How many lines of symmetry do the figures below have?

Count the lines of symmetry drawn on each figure below.

B A figure can have more than one line of symmetry.

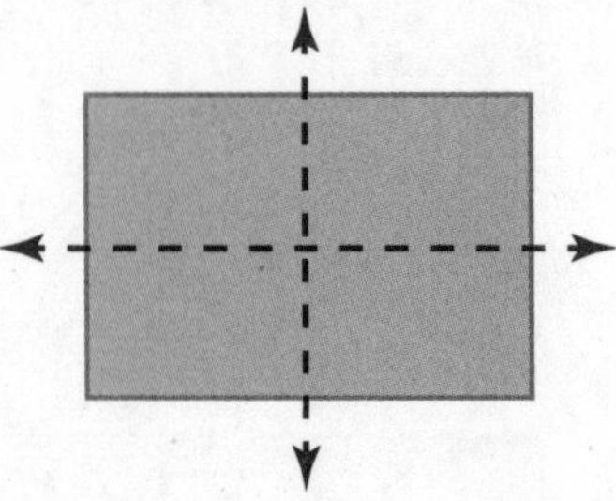

This figure is line symmetric. It has 2 lines of symmetry. It can be folded on each line of symmetry into matching parts.

C A figure can have many lines of symmetry.

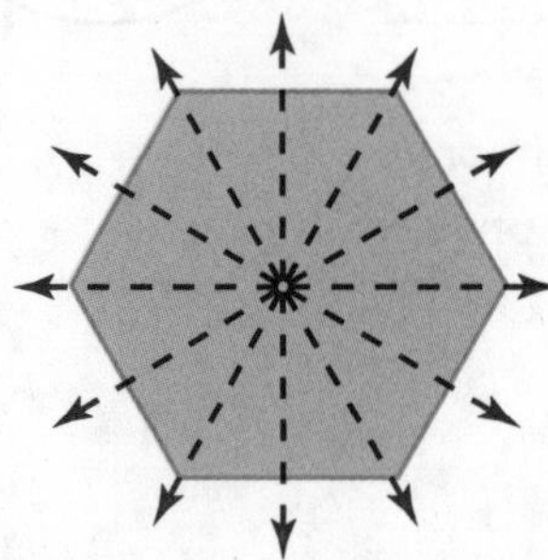

This figure is line symmetric. It has 6 lines of symmetry. It can be folded on each line of symmetry into matching parts.

D A figure can have no lines of symmetry.

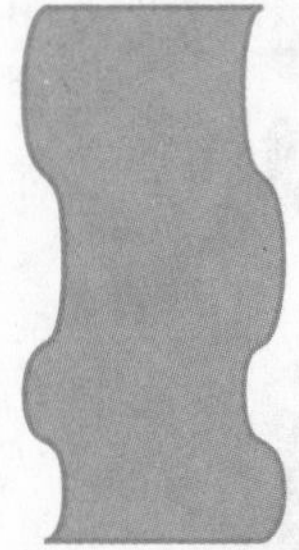

This figure is **NOT** line symmetric. It has 0 lines of symmetry. It cannot be folded to have matching parts.

Convince Me! **Look for Relationships** Find two capital letters that have exactly one line of symmetry. Find two capital letters that have exactly two lines of symmetry.

Name ________________

Guided Practice

Do You Understand?

1. How many lines of symmetry does the letter R have?

2. How many lines of symmetry does the figure below have?

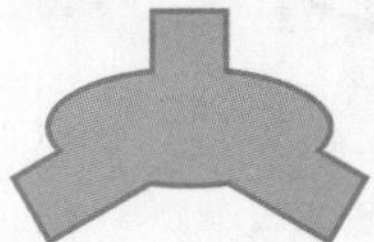

3. How many lines of symmetry can you find for a circle? Do you think you can count them?

Do You Know How?

For **4–5**, tell if each line is a line of symmetry.

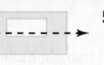

4. **5.**

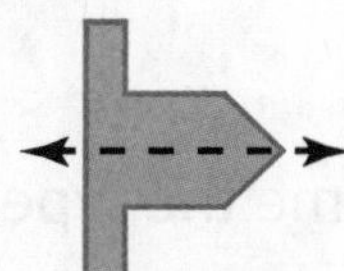

For **6–7**, tell how many lines of symmetry each figure has.

6. **7.**

Independent Practice

For **8–11**, tell if each line is a line of symmetry.

8.

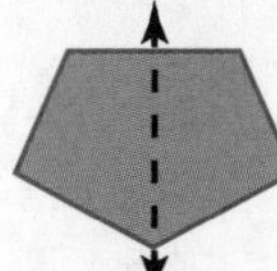

9.

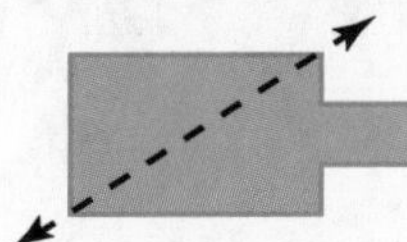

10.

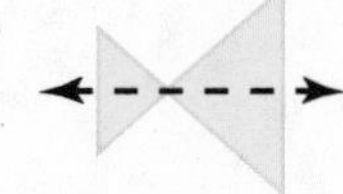

11.

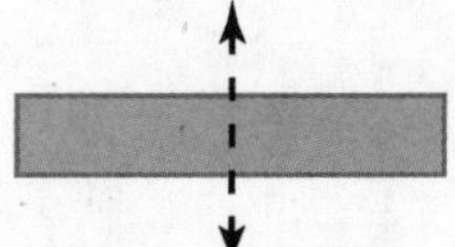

For **12–19**, decide if each figure is line symmetric. Draw and tell how many lines of symmetry each figure has.

12.

13.

14.

15.

16.

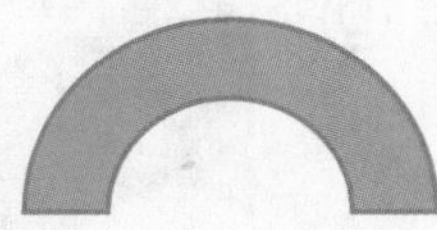

17.

18.

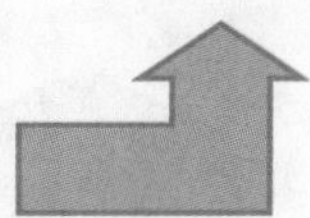

19.

Problem Solving

20. The Thomas Jefferson Memorial is located in Washington, D.C. Use the picture of the memorial at the right to decide whether the building is line symmetric. If so, describe where the line of symmetry is.

21. Name the type of triangle outlined in green on the picture of the memorial.

22. **Construct Arguments** How can you tell when a line is **NOT** a line of symmetry?

23. **Higher Order Thinking** How many lines of symmetry can a parallelogram have? Explain.

Assessment Practice

24. Which figure has six lines of symmetry? Draw lines as needed.

Ⓐ 

Ⓒ 

Ⓑ 

Ⓓ 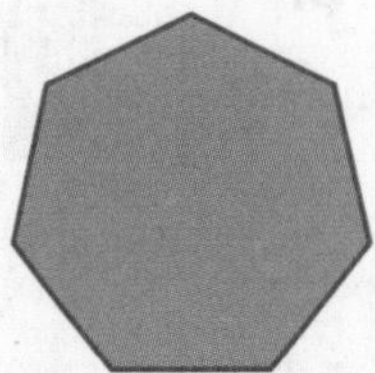 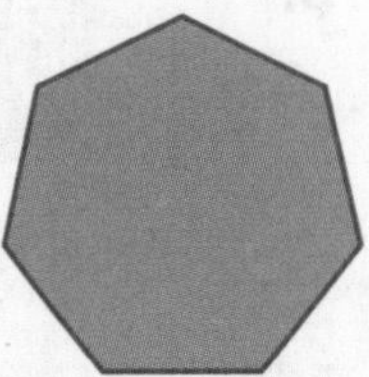

25. Which figure is **NOT** line symmetric?

Ⓐ 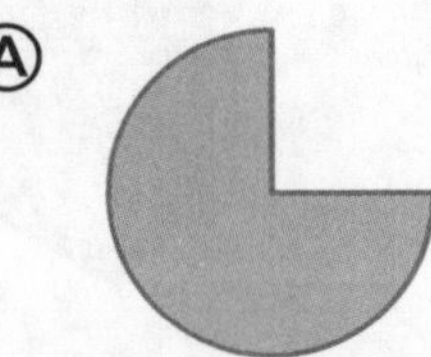

Ⓒ  

Ⓑ 

Ⓓ 

Name ______________________________ Activity

Lesson 16-5
Draw Shapes with Line Symmetry

Solve & Share

Craig and Julia are designing kites. A kite will fly well if the kite has line symmetry. Does Craig's or Julia's kite have line symmetry? Explain. Then, design your own kites. Design one kite with 2 lines of symmetry and another kite with 3 lines of symmetry. ***Solve this problem any way you choose.***

I can ...
draw a figure that has line symmetry.

Content Standard 4.G.A.3
Mathematical Practices MP.1, MP.3, MP.4

Craig's Design
Julia's Design
You can construct arguments. What math vocabulary can you use to explain why Craig's or Julia's kite designs will fly well?

Look Back! Can both Craig's and Julia's kites be folded into matching parts? If one of the kites is not line symmetric, can it be changed so that it is? Explain.

How Can You Draw Figures with Line Symmetry?

Visual Learning Bridge

A

Sarah wants to design a line-symmetric tabletop. She sketched half of the tabletop. What are two ways Sarah can complete her design?

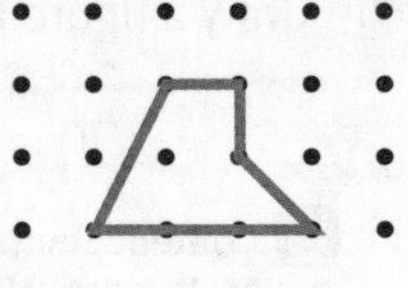

The tabletop is line symmetric if the design can be folded along a line of symmetry into matching parts.

B

One Way

Draw a line of symmetry.

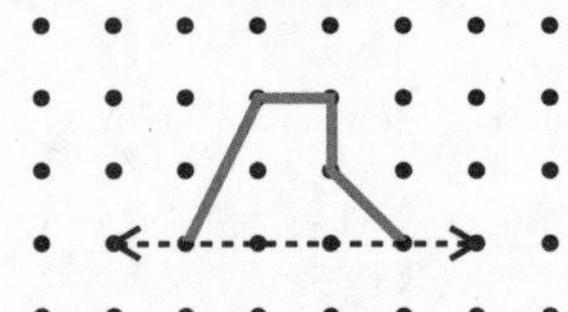

Complete Sarah's design on the opposite side of the line of symmetry.

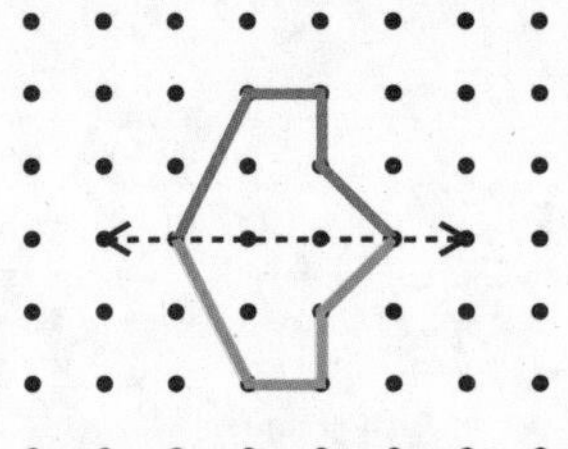

The design for the tabletop is now line symmetric.

C

Another Way

Draw a different line of symmetry.

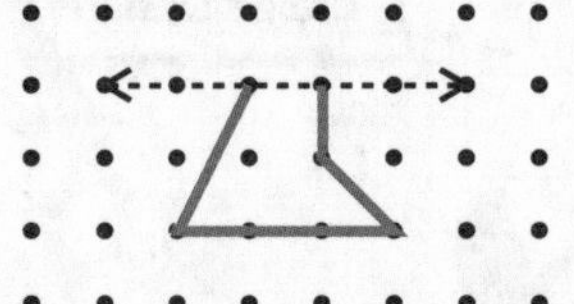

Complete Sarah's design on the opposite side of the line of symmetry.

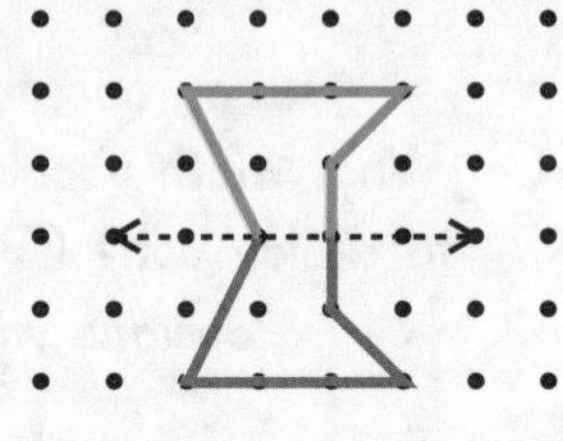

The design for the tabletop is now line symmetric.

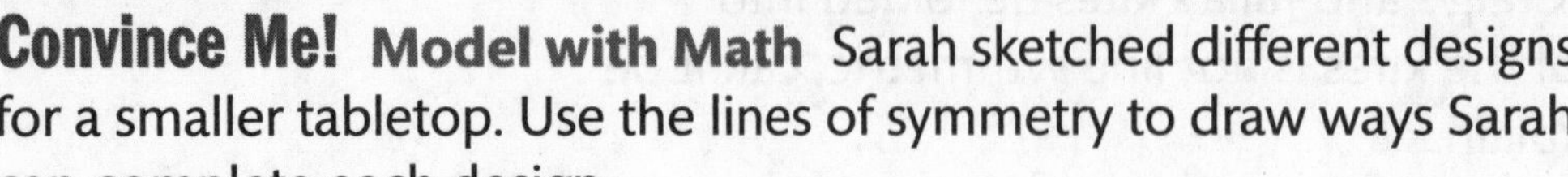

Convince Me! Model with Math Sarah sketched different designs for a smaller tabletop. Use the lines of symmetry to draw ways Sarah can complete each design.

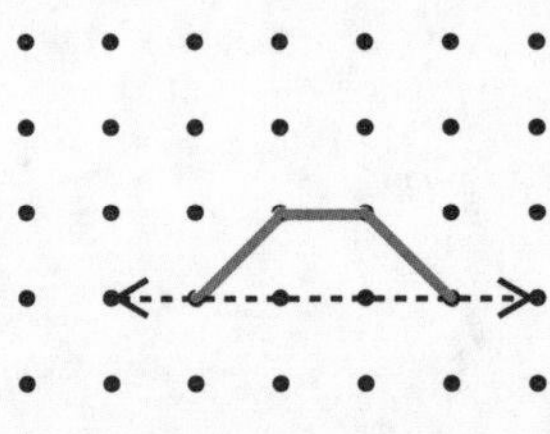

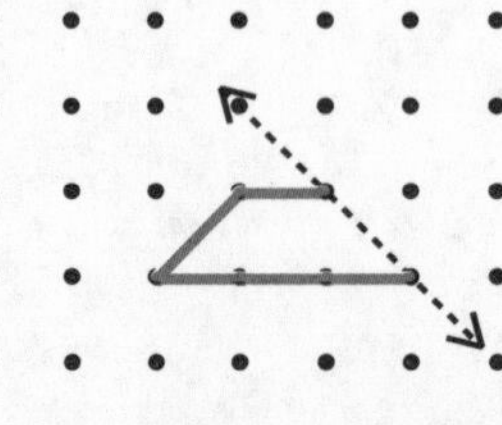

Name

Practice Tools Assessment

Guided Practice

Do You Understand?

1. Chandler tried to complete Sarah's design from the previous page. Describe the error Chandler made.

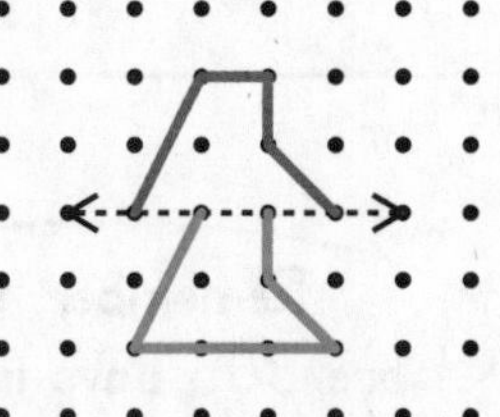

2. How can folding a piece of paper help to determine if a line in a figure is a line of symmetry?

Do You Know How?

For **3–4**, use the line of symmetry to draw a line-symmetric figure.

3.

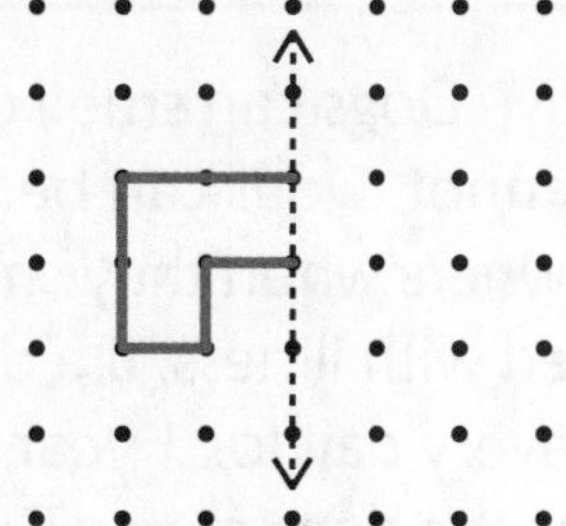

4.

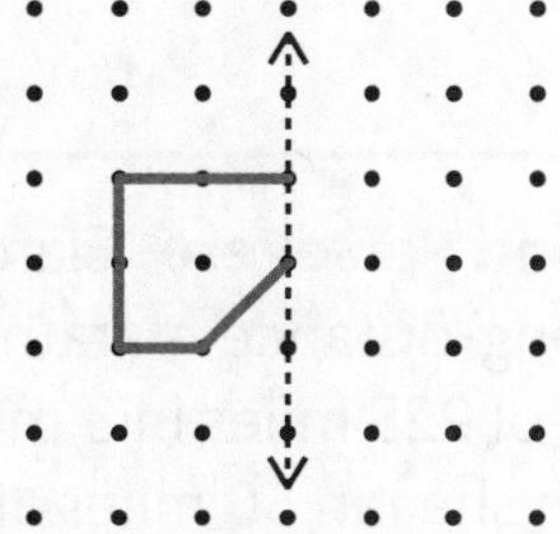

Independent Practice

For **5–10**, use the line of symmetry to draw a line-symmetric figure.

5.

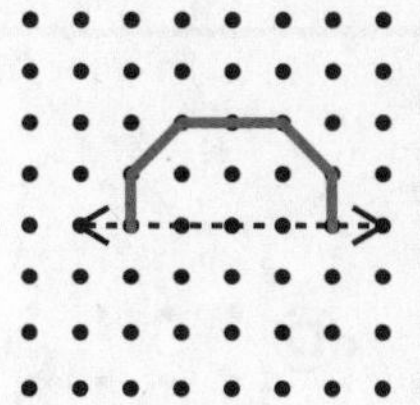

6.

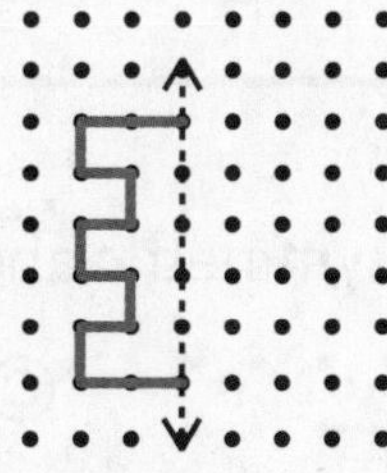

7.

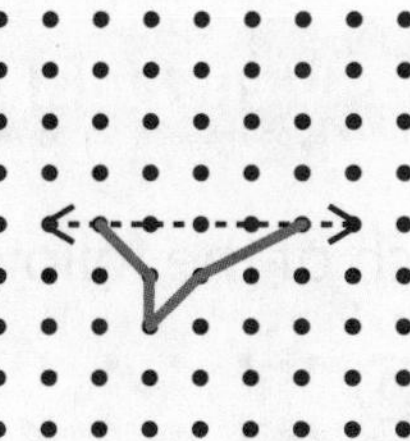

8.

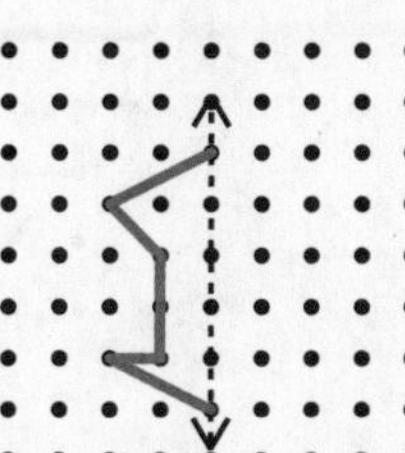

9.

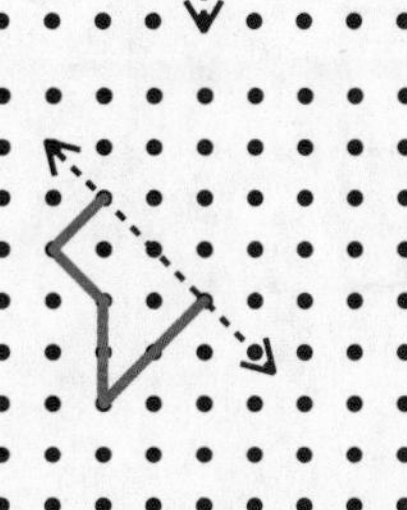

10.

Problem Solving

11. Draw a figure that has no lines of symmetry.

12. Vanessa drew a figure that has an infinite number of lines of symmetry. What figure could Vanessa have drawn?

13. **enVision® STEM** Dogs can smell odors that humans cannot. Dogs can be trained to alert their owners when they smell odors associated with illness. If a dog trains 2 hours every day for 1 year, how many hours has the dog trained?

Remember, there are 365 days in a year.

14. **Make Sense and Persevere** Clare trained for a long-distance marathon. She ran a total of 225 miles in 3 months. The first month she ran 50 miles. If she ran 25 more miles each month, how many miles did she run in her third month of training?

15. **Higher Order Thinking** Can you draw a line that divides a figure in half but is **NOT** a line of symmetry? Use the figures below to explain.

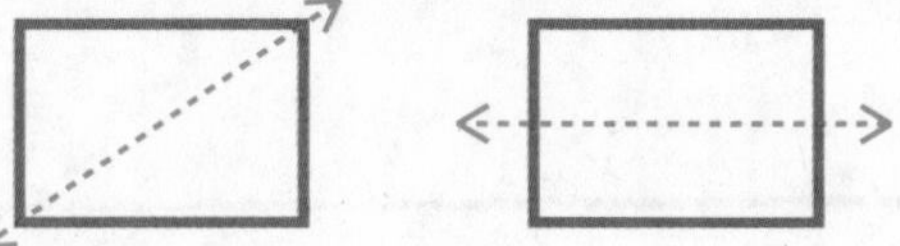

Assessment Practice

16. Which of the following figures is line symmetric about the dashed line?

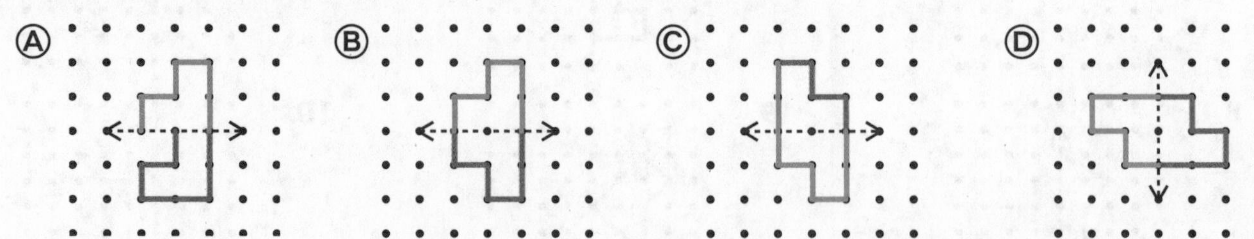
Ⓐ
Ⓑ
Ⓒ
Ⓓ

Name ______________________________

Activity

Problem Solving

Lesson 16-6

Critique Reasoning

I can ...

critique the reasoning of others by using what I know about two-dimensional shapes.

Mathematical Practices MP.3 Also MP.2, MP.6

Content Standards 4.G.A.2 Also 4.MD.A.3, 4.G.A.1

Solve & Share

Nathan gave the answer shown to the following question. True or False? All right triangles have two sides the same length. How do you respond to Nathan's reasoning?

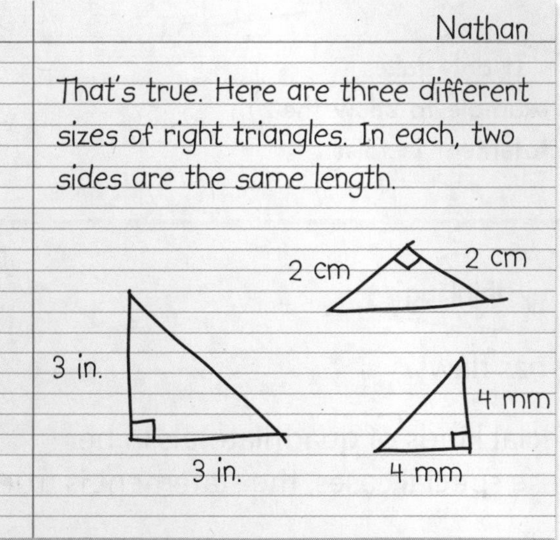

Nathan
That's true. Here are three different sizes of right triangles. In each, two sides are the same length.
2 cm
2 cm
3 in.
3 in.
4 mm
4 mm

Thinking Habits

Be a good thinker! These questions can help you.

- What questions can I ask to understand other people's thinking?
- Are there mistakes in other people's thinking?
- Can I improve other people's thinking?

Look Back! Critique Reasoning Nathan answered another question. True or false: A triangle can have two right angles. Nathan says this is not possible. Do you agree or disagree? Explain.

How Can You Critique the Reasoning of Others?

Visual Learning Bridge

A

Abby gave the answer shown to the following question.

True or False? Every quadrilateral has at least one right angle.

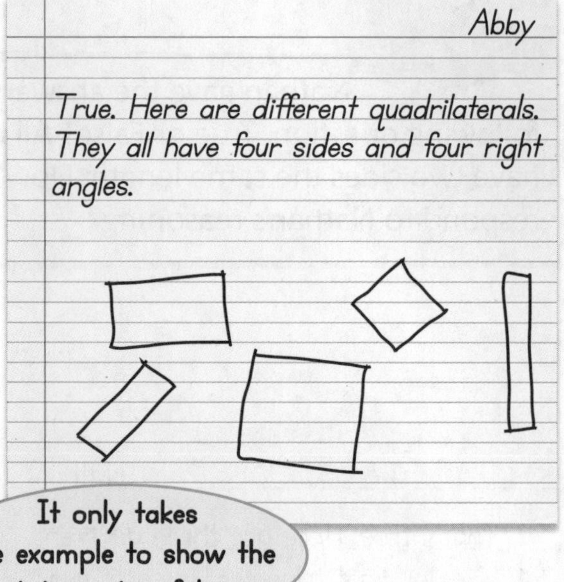

Abby
True. Here are different quadrilaterals. They all have four sides and four right angles.

What is Abby's reasoning to support her statement?

Abby drew quadrilaterals that have right angles.

It only takes one example to show the statement is false.

Here's my thinking.

B

How can I critique the reasoning of others?

I can

- ask questions about Abby's reasoning.
- look for flaws in her reasoning.
- decide whether all cases have been considered.

C

Abby's reasoning has flaws.

She used only special kinds of quadrilaterals in her argument. For these special cases, the statement is true.

Here is a quadrilateral that has no right angles. It shows the statement is not true about ***every*** quadrilateral.

The statement is false.

Convince Me! **Be Precise** Would Abby's reasoning be correct if the question was changed to: True or False? Some quadrilaterals have at least one right angle. Explain.

Name

Guided Practice

Critique Reasoning

Anthony said all multiples of 4 end in 2, 4, or 8. He gave 4, 8, 12, 24, and 28 as examples.

1. What is Anthony's argument? How does he support it?

2. Describe at least one thing you could do to critique Anthony's reasoning.

3. Does Anthony's reasoning make sense? Explain.

Independent Practice

Critique Reasoning

Marista said the polygons shown all have the same number of angles as they have sides.

4. Describe at least one thing you could do to critique Marista's reasoning.

5. Does Marista's reasoning make sense? Explain.

When you critique reasoning, you decide whether or not another student's conclusion is logical.

6. Can you think of any examples that prove all polygons don't have the same number of sides as angles? Explain.

Problem Solving

Performance Task

Dog Pen
Caleb is designing a dog pen for the animal shelter. He has 16 feet of fence, including the gate. His designs and explanation are shown. Critique Caleb's reasoning.

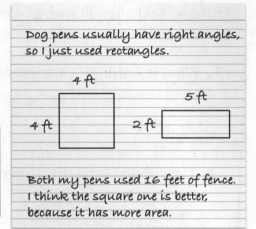

Dog pens usually have right angles, so I just used rectangles.

4 ft
4 ft
5 ft
2 ft

Both my pens used 16 feet of fence. I think the square one is better, because it has more area.

7. **Reasoning** What quantities are given in the problem and what do the numbers mean?

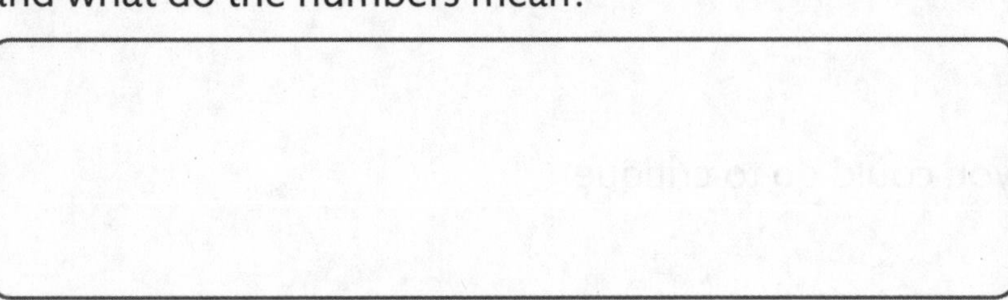

8. **Critique Reasoning** What can you do to critique Caleb's thinking?

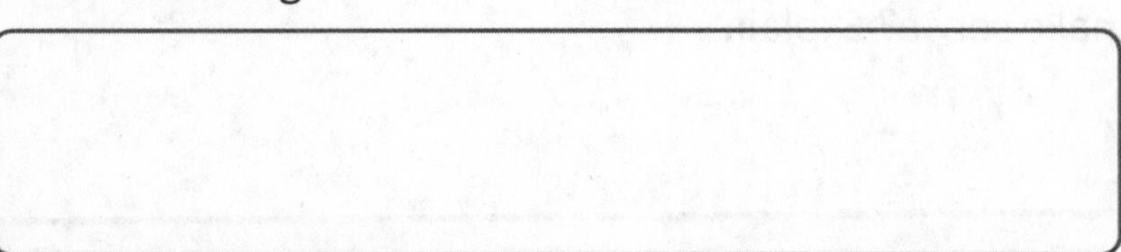

9. **Be Precise** Did Caleb correctly calculate the perimeter of each fence? Explain.

When you critique reasoning, you ask questions to help understand someone's thinking.

10. **Critique Reasoning** Does Caleb's reasoning make sense? Explain.

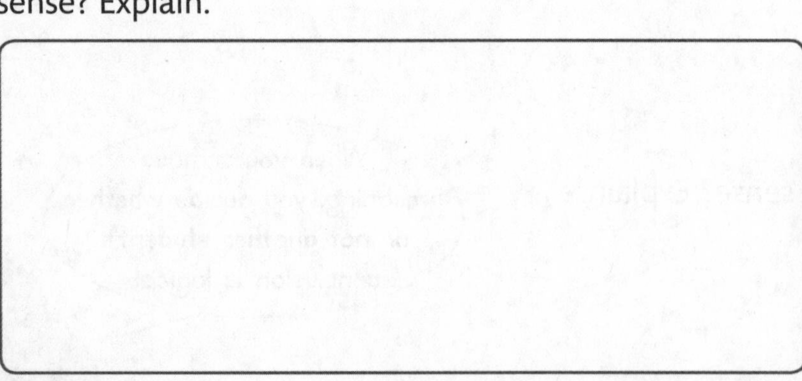

11. **Be Precise** Explain how you know what units to use in your explanation.

Name ____________________

Fluency Practice Activity

TOPIC 16

Find a Match

Work with a partner. Point to a clue. Read the clue.

Look below the clues to find a match. Write the clue letter in the box next to the match.

Find a match for every clue.

I can ...
add multi-digit whole numbers.

Content Standard 4.NBT.B.4
Mathematical Practices MP.3, MP.6, MP.7, MP.8

Clues

A The sum is between 650 and 750.

B The sum is between 1,470 and 1,480.

C The sum is exactly 1,550.

D The sum is between 1,350 and 1,450.

E The sum is exactly 790.

F The sum is exactly 1,068.

G The sum is between 1,100 and 1,225.

H The sum is exactly 1,300.

☐ 510 + 240 + 550	☐ 225 + 350 + 125	☐ 400 + 850 + 150	☐ 50 + 390 + 1,110
☐ 125 + 125 + 225 + 315	☐ 475 + 475 + 175	☐ 500 + 425 + 325 + 225	☐ 500 + 250 + 250 + 68

Word List

- acute triangle
- equilateral triangle
- intersecting lines
- isosceles triangle
- line of symmetry
- line symmetric
- obtuse triangle
- parallel lines
- parallelogram
- perpendicular lines
- rectangle
- rhombus
- right triangle
- scalene triangle
- square
- trapezoid

Understand Vocabulary

Write T for *true* and F for *false*.

1. _____ An acute triangle is a triangle with one acute angle.

2. _____ An isosceles triangle has at least two equal sides.

3. _____ A figure is line symmetric if it has at least one line of symmetry.

4. _____ Perpendicular lines form obtuse angles where they intersect.

5. _____ A trapezoid has two pairs of parallel sides.

Write *always*, *sometimes*, or *never*.

6. An equilateral triangle ______________ has three equal sides.

7. Parallel lines ______________ intersect.

8. A scalene triangle ______________ has equal sides.

9. A rectangle is ______________ a square.

10. A rhombus ______________ has opposite sides that are parallel.

Use Vocabulary in Writing

11. Rebecca drew a figure. Describe Rebecca's figure. Use at least 3 terms from the Word List in your description.

Name ______________________________

TOPIC 16

Reteaching

Set A pages 585–588

Pairs of lines are given special names: parallel, intersecting, or perpendicular.

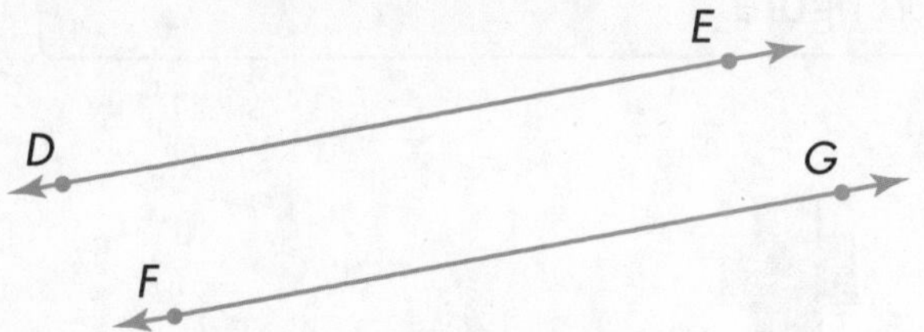

$\overleftrightarrow{DE}$ and $\overleftrightarrow{FG}$ are parallel lines.

Remember to use geometric terms when describing what is shown.

1.

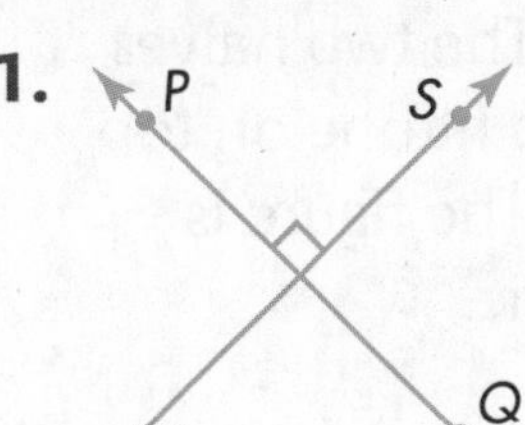

2.

Set B pages 589–592

Triangles can be classified by their sides and angles.

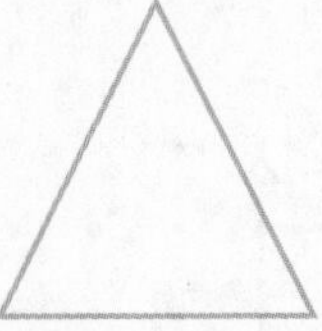

Two sides are the same length, and each angle measures less than a right angle. It is an isosceles, acute triangle.

Remember to classify each triangle by its sides and then by its angles.

1.

2.

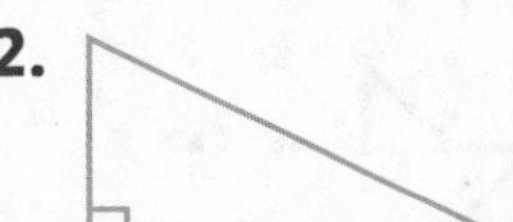

Set C pages 593–596

Name the quadrilateral.

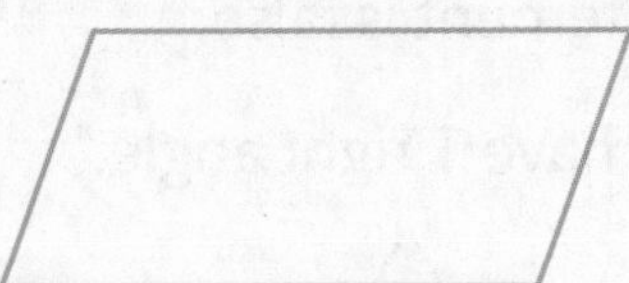

Opposite sides are parallel. There are no right angles. All sides are not the same length. It is a parallelogram, but not a rectangle, rhombus, or square.

Remember that a quadrilateral can be a rectangle, square, trapezoid, parallelogram, or rhombus.

Write all the names possible for each quadrilateral.

1.

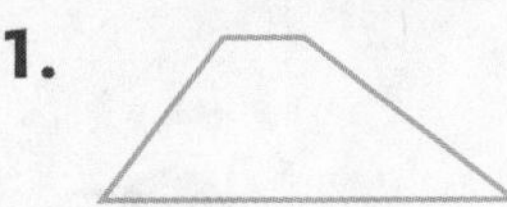

2.

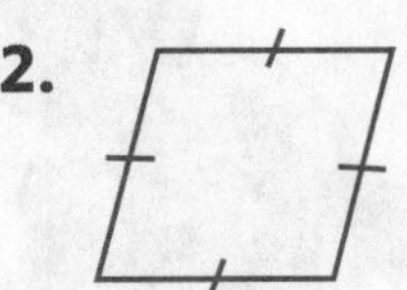

Set D pages 597–600

How many lines of symmetry does the figure have?

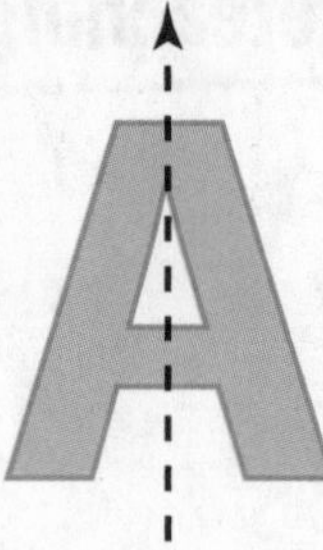

Fold the figure along the dashed line. The two halves are equal and fit one on top of the other. The figure is line symmetric.

It cannot be folded on another line, so it has 1 line of symmetry.

Remember that figures can have many lines of symmetry.

Draw and tell how many lines of symmetry for each figure.

1. 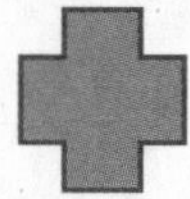

2. 

Set E pages 601–604

Complete a design with line symmetry.

Draw a line of symmetry for the shape.

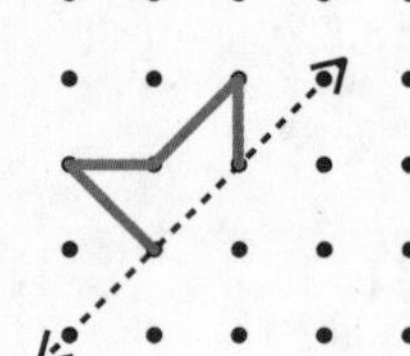

Complete the design on the opposite side of the line of symmetry.

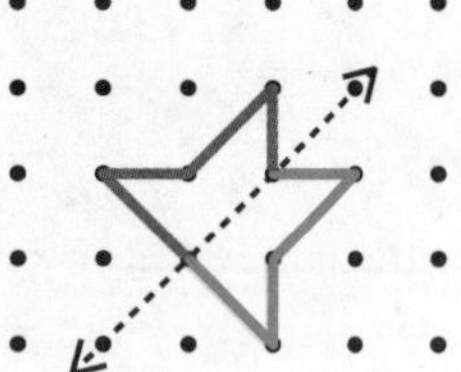

Remember, for a figure to be line symmetric, it must have a line of symmetry.

Complete the designs.

1. 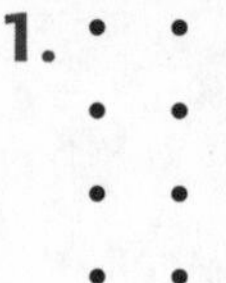

2. 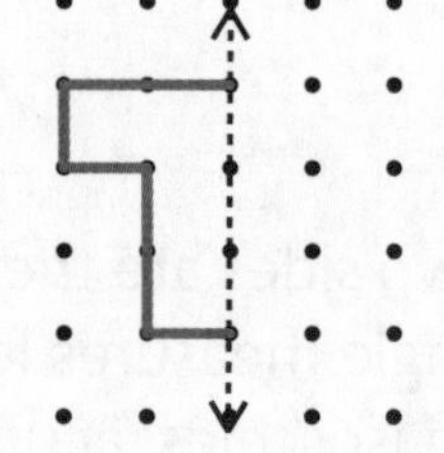

Set F pages 605–608

Think about these questions to help you **critique the reasoning** of others.

Thinking Habits

Be a good thinker! These questions can help you.

- What questions can I ask to understand other people's thinking?
- Are there mistakes in other people's thinking?
- Can I improve other people's thinking?

Remember that it only takes one counter-example to show the statement is false.

Derek says, "All triangles have 1 right angle."

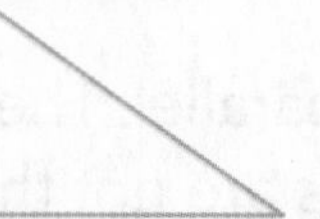
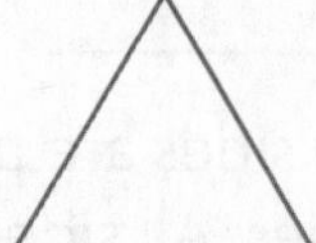

1. Use the figures above to critique Derek's statement.

2. What kinds of triangles **NEVER** have right angles?

Name 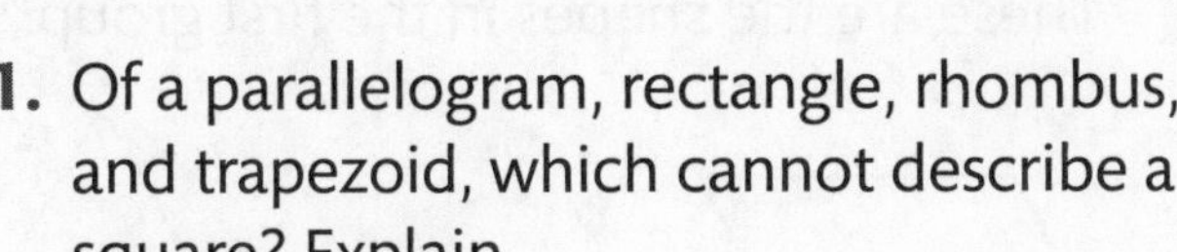

1. Of a parallelogram, rectangle, rhombus, and trapezoid, which cannot describe a square? Explain.

2. How many acute angles are there in an equilateral triangle?

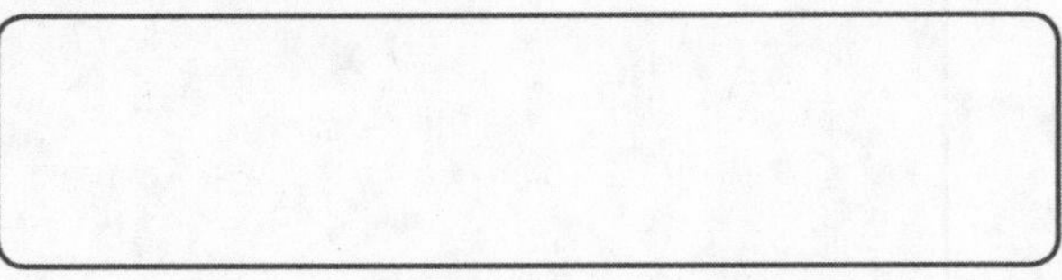

3. Gavin drew different-colored lines. Draw a line that is parallel to $\overleftrightarrow{SR}$.

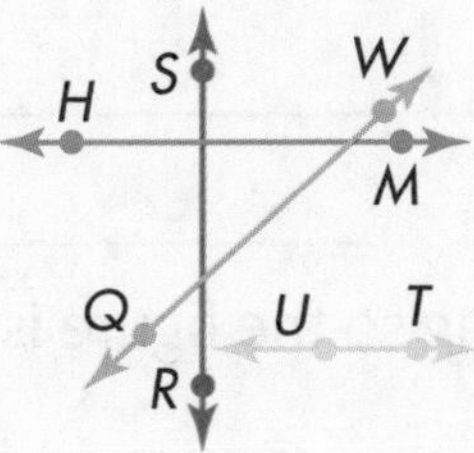

4. Marci described the light from the sun as a line that starts at the sun and continues on forever. Which geometric term best describes Marci's description of the sun's light?

5. Four of Mrs. Cromwell's students decorated a bulletin board with the shapes shown below. Order the students' shapes in order from fewest lines of symmetry to most lines of symmetry.

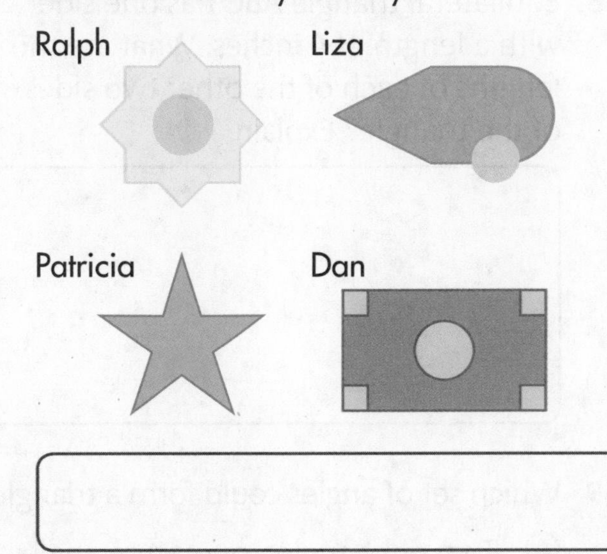

6. Are all intersecting lines perpendicular? Draw a picture to help explain your answer.

7. A four-sided figure with two pairs of parallel sides cannot be what type of quadrilateral? Explain.

8. Equilateral triangle *ABC* has one side with a length of 4 inches. What are the lengths of each of the other two sides of the triangle? Explain.

9. Which set of angles could form a triangle?

Ⓐ Two right angles, one acute angle

Ⓑ One obtuse angle, one right angle, one acute angle

Ⓒ Two obtuse angles, one acute angle

Ⓓ One right angle, two acute angles

10. A figure has one angle formed from a pair of perpendicular lines, one pair of parallel sides, and no sides with equal lengths. What geometric term can be used to name this figure?

11. Dina's teacher asks her to describe the top and bottom edges of her ruler using a geometric term. What term could Dina use?

12. Shapes are divided into two groups. These are the shapes in the first group.

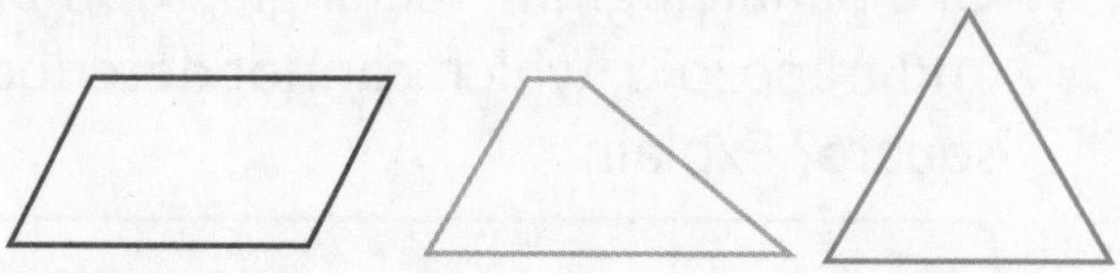

The following shapes do not belong in the group above. These are the shapes in the second group.

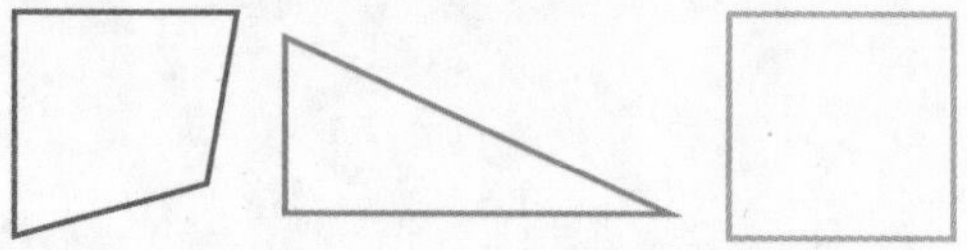

What generalization can be made about the shapes in the first group?

13. Complete the drawing so the figure is line symmetric.

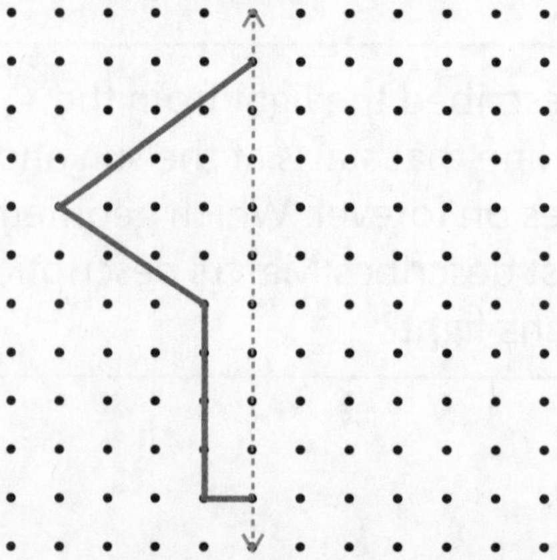

Name ______________________________

Ottoman Art

The Ottoman Empire lasted from 1299 until 1922. Much of the art from this period contained geometric shapes.

1. Use the **Ottoman Empire** figure to answer the following.

Part A

Name a pair of parallel lines and explain why the lines are parallel.

Ottoman Empire

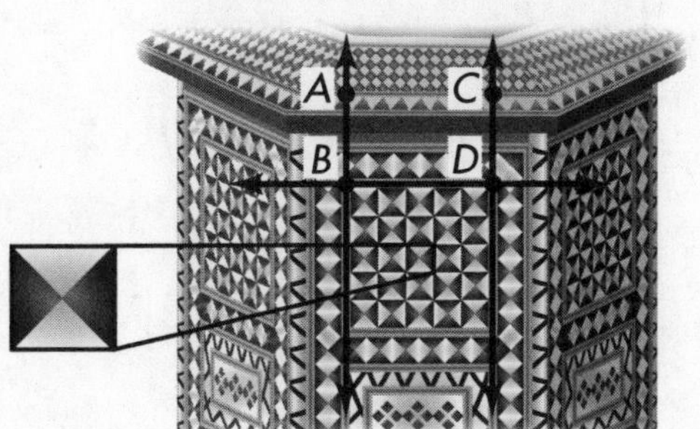

Part B

The enlarged part of the figure shows 4 triangles that are all the same type. Classify these triangles by their sides and by their angles. Explain.

Part C

Olivia said the 4 triangles were inside a square. When asked other possible names for the square, she said it was a quadrilateral, a parallelogram, and a rectangle. Critique Olivia's reasoning.

2. The basic shape used in the **Ottoman Scarf** is a quadrilateral. Answer the following about this shape.

Ottoman Scarf

W
X
Z
Y

Part A

What are all the names you can use for this quadrilateral? Explain.

Part B

Corbin drew a triangle by connecting the points *W*, *X*, and *Y*. He said the triangle is acute because it has acute angles. Critique Corbin's reasoning.

Part C

Draw all lines of symmetry on the **Decorative Plate**. How many lines of symmetry does the plate have? Explain.

Decorative Plate

Photographs

Every effort has been made to secure permission and provide appropriate credit for photographic material. The publisher deeply regrets any omission and pledges to correct errors called to its attention in subsequent editions.

Unless otherwise acknowledged, all photographs are the property of Savvas Learning Company LLC.

Photo locators denoted as follows: Top (T), Center (C), Bottom (B), Left (L), Right (R), Background (Bkgd)

1 MarclSchauer/Shutterstock; **3** (T) Cowardlion/Shutterstock, (C) Dabarti CGI/Shutterstock, (B) Birgit Tyrrell/Alamy Stock Photo; **4** (Bkgrd) Monkey Business Images/Shutterstock; Ajt/Shutterstock, **24** Petr84/Fotolia. **33** forkART Photography/Fotolia; **35** (T) Sean Pavone/Shutterstock, **35** (B) North Wind Picture Archives/Alamy Stock Photo; **36** (T) Naeblys/Alamy Stock Photo; **36** (B) Beata Bar/Shutterstock; **38** Richard Cavalleri/Shutterstock; **50** Alexey Usachev/Fotolia; **54** Pavel L Photo and Video/Shutterstock; **60** Digital Vision/Thinkstock; **66** WaterFrame_mus/Alamy Stock Photo. **77** John Hoffman/Shutterstock; **79** (T) Vm2002/Shutterstock, (C) DenGuy/E+/Getty Images, (B) Viju Jose/Shutterstock; **80** (Bkgrd) Ivonne Wierink/Shutterstock; AlexLMX/Shutterstock, **98** Stevanzz/Fotolia; **112** Andrew Breeden/Fotolia. **125** Majeczka/Shutterstock; **127** (T) RosalreneBetancourt 5/Alamy Stock Photo, (B) Rolf Nussbaumer Photography/Bill Draker/Rolfnp/Alamy Stock Photo; **128** (T) John Green/Cal Sport Media/Alamy Stock Photo, (B) Christophe Petit Tesson/Epa/REX/Shutterstock; **148** Steve Byland/Shutterstock; **152** 2011/Photos To Go. **165** Mark McClare/Shutterstock; **166** CristinaMuraca/Shutterstock; **167** (T) Stephen Vincent/Alamy Stock Photo, (C) Colors and shapes of underwater world/Moment/Getty Images, (B) Tierfotoagentur/A. Mirsberger/Alamy Stock Photo; **168** (Bkgrd) Konstantin Gushcha/Shutterstock, Andrey Armyagov/Shutterstock. **221** ShutterStock; **223** (T) Itsik Marom/Alamy Stock Photo, (B) David Fleetham/Alamy Stock Photo; **224** (T) Brian Lasenby/Shutterstock, (B) Willyam Bradberry/Shutterstock; **236** (L) JackF/Fotolia; (R) Smileus/Shutterstock. **257** ShutterStock; **259** (T) Danita Delimont/Alamy Stock Photo, (C) Keith Birmingham/Pasadena Star-News/San Gabriel Valley Tribune/ZUMA Wire/Alamy Live News/Alamy Stock Photo, (B) Nikola Obradovic/Shutterstock; **260** (Bkgrd) Simon Belcher/Alamy Stock Photo; Ivonne Wierink/Shutterstock, **268** Comstock Images/Jupiter Images; **270** Womue/Fotolia. **289** Kletr/Shutterstock; **291** (T) Robert Stainforth/Alamy Stock Photo, (B) T.W. van Urk/Shutterstock; **292** (T) Oksana Mizina/Shutterstock, (B) Elnur/Shutterstock; **296** Hamik/Fotolia. **329** Adrio Communications Ltd/Shutterstock; **331** (T) Goodluz/Shutterstock, (C) Everett Collection Inc/Alamy Stock Photo, (B) Xuanhuongho/Shutterstock; **332** (Bkgrd) Rattiya Thongdumhyu/Shutterstock; AlenKadr/Shutterstock, **336** Oleksii Sagitov/Shutterstock; **364** Werner Dreblow/Fotolia. **381** Pk7comcastnet/Fotolia; **383** (T) 123RF, (B) Monkey Business Images/Shutterstock; **384** (T) Hxdyl/Shutterstock, (B) Realy Easy Star/Caterina Soprana/Alamy Stock Photo; **394** JLV Image Works/Fotolia. **413** NASA; **415** (T) Oliveromg/Shutterstock, (C) Radius Images/Alamy Stock Photo, (B) Tuasiwatn/Shutterstock; **416** (Bkgrd) Tom Wang/Shutterstock, (T) Yuliya Evstratenko/Shutterstock, (B) KK Tan/Shutterstock. **441** Bork/Shutterstock; **443** (T) Lynn Y/Shutterstock, (B) Evren Kalin Bacak/Shutterstock; **444** (T) Narin Nonthamand/Shutterstock, (B) Richard Brown/Alamy Stock Photo; **448** Hemera Technologies/ThinkStock; **461** StockPhotosArt/Fotolia; **475** (L) Proedding/Fotolia, (CL) Donfink/Fotolia (CR) Tim elliott/Fotolia, (R) Petergyure/Fotolia; **476** Redwood/Fotolia. **477** Katrina Brown/Fotolia; **479** (T) Mark Winfrey/Shutterstock, (C) Borisov Studio/Shutterstock, (B) Fototaras/Shutterstock; **480** (Bkgrd) John Dorado/Shutterstock, (T) Poznyakov/Shutterstock, (B) Billion Photos/Shutterstock; **489** (L) Glass and Nature/Shutterstock, (C) Fesus Robert/Shutterstock, (R) Kseniya Abramova/123RF; **492** Duncan Noakes/Fotolia; 500 Sergio Martínez/Fotolia; **513** (T) Margouillat photo/Shutterstock, (B) LittleMiss/Shutterstock; **516** (T) Margouillat photo/Shutterstock, (B) Little Miss/Shutterstock. **517** luchschen/Shutterstock; **519** (T) David McGill71/Shutterstock, (B) Catarena/123RF; **520** (T) Homo Cosmicos/Shutterstock, (B) Matthew Wilkinson/Alamy Stock Photo; **524** Chinatown/Alamy Stock Photo; **526** Photo24/Stockbyte/Getty Images. **545** James Kingman/Shutterstock; **547** (T) Oleksiy Avtomonov/Shutterstock, (C) Jules_Kitano/Shutterstock, (B) Petruk Viktor/Shutterstock; **548** (Bkgrd) Peter Etchells/Shutterstock, Sarapon/Shutterstock; **579** WitR/Shutterstock. **581** Dja65/Shutterstock; **583** (T) Mukul Gupchup/Ephotocorp/Alamy Stock Photo, (B) Sean Pavone/Shutterstock; **584** (T) Mariia Tagirova/Shutterstock, (B) Edwin Godinho/Shutterstock; **586** Arina P Habich/Shutterstock; **600** Gary Blakeley/Fotolia; **616** (T) Thampapon/Shutterstock, (B) Orhan Cam/Shutterstock